MORE STATISTICAL AND METHODOLOGICAL MYTHS AND URBAN LEGENDS

This book provides an up-to-date review of commonly undertaken methodological and statistical practices that are based partially in sound scientific rationale and partially in unfounded lore. Some examples of these "methodological urban legends" are characterized by manuscript critiques such as: (a) "your self-report measures suffer from common method bias"; (b) "your item-to-subject ratios are too low"; (c) "you can't generalize these findings to the real world"; or (d) "your effect sizes are too low."

What do these critiques mean, and what is their historical basis? *More Statistical and Methodological Myths and Urban Legends* catalogs several of these quirky practices and outlines proper research techniques. Topics covered include sample size requirements, missing data bias in correlation matrices, negative wording in survey research, and much more.

Charles E. Lance is Principal, Organizational Research & Development and former Professor of Industrial/Organizational Psychology at the University of Georgia, USA.

Robert Vandenberg is the Robert O. Arnold Professor of Business in the Department of Management, Terry College of Business at the University of Georgia, USA.

MORE STATISTICAL AND METHODOLOGICAL MYTHS AND URBAN LEGENDS

*Edited by Charles E. Lance
and Robert J. Vandenberg*

NEW YORK AND LONDON

First published 2015
by Routledge
711 Third Avenue, New York, NY 10017

and by Routledge
27 Church Road, Hove, East Sussex BN3 2FA

Routledge is an imprint of the Taylor & Francis Group, an informa business

© 2015 Taylor & Francis

The right of the editors to be identified as the authors of the editorial material, and of the authors for their individual chapters, has been asserted in accordance with sections 77 and 78 of the Copyright, Designs and Patents Act 1988.

All rights reserved. No part of this book may be reprinted or reproduced or utilised in any form or by any electronic, mechanical, or other means, now known or hereafter invented, including photocopying and recording, or in any information storage or retrieval system, without permission in writing from the publishers.

Trademark notice: Product or corporate names may be trademarks or registered trademarks, and are used only for identification and explanation without intent to infringe.

Library of Congress Cataloging-in-Publication Data
A catalog record for this title has been requested.

ISBN: 978-0-415-83898-6 (hbk)
ISBN: 978-0-415-83899-3 (pbk)
ISBN: 978-0-203-77585-1 (ebk)

Typeset in Bembo
by Apex CoVantage, LLC

CONTENTS

List of Contributors	*ix*
Introduction *Charles E. Lance and Robert J. Vandenberg*	1

PART I
General Issues 7

1 Is Ours a Hard Science (and Do We Care)? *Ronald S. Landis and José M. Cortina*	9
2 Publication Bias: Understanding the Myths Concerning Threats to the Advancement of Science *George C. Banks, Sven Kepes and Michael A. McDaniel*	36

PART II
Design Issues 65

3 Red-Headed No More: Tipping Points in Qualitative Research in Management *Anne D. Smith, Laura T. Madden and Donde Ashmos Plowman*	67

vi Contents

4 Two Waves of Measurement Do Not a Longitudinal
Study Make 85
Robert E. Ployhart and William I. MacKenzie Jr.

5 The Problem of Generational Change: Why
Cross-Sectional Designs Are Inadequate for
Investigating Generational Differences 100
*Brittany Gentile, Lauren A. Wood, Jean M. Twenge,
Brian J. Hoffman and W. Keith Campbell*

6 Negatively Worded Items Negatively Impact
Survey Research 112
Dev K. Dalal and Nathan T. Carter

7 Missing Data Bias: Exactly How Bad Is Pairwise Deletion? 133
Daniel A. Newman and Jonathan M. Cottrell

8 Size Matters . . . Just Not in the Way that You Think:
Myths Surrounding Sample Size Requirements for
Statistical Analyses 162
Scott Tonidandel, Eleanor B. Williams and James M. LeBreton

PART III
Analytical Issues **185**

9 *Weight* a Minute . . . What You See in a Weighted
Composite Is Probably Not What You Get! 187
Frederick L. Oswald, Dan J. Putka and Jisoo Ock

10 Debunking Myths and Urban Legends about
How to Identify Influential Outliers 206
Herman Aguinis and Harry Joo

11 Pulling the Sobel Test Up By Its Bootstraps 224
Joel Koopman, Michael Howe and John R. Hollenbeck

PART IV
Inferential Issues **245**

12 "The" Reliability of Job Performance Ratings Equals 0.52 247
Dan J. Putka and Brian J. Hoffman

Contents vii

13 Use of "Independent" Measures Does Not Solve the
Shared Method Bias Problem 276
Charles E. Lance and Allison B. Siminovsky

14 The Not-So-Direct Cross-Level Direct Effect 292
Alexander C. LoPilato and Robert J. Vandenberg

15 Aggregation Aggravation: The Fallacy of the
Wrong Level Revisited 311
David J. Woehr, Andrew C. Loignon and Paul Schmidt

16 The Practical Importance of Measurement Invariance 327
Neal Schmitt and Abdifatah A. Ali

Index *347*

CONTRIBUTORS

Herman Aguinis, Indiana University
Abdifatah A. Ali, Michigan State University
George C. Banks, Longwood University
W. Keith Campbell, University of Georgia
Nathan T. Carter, University of Georgia
José M. Cortina, George Mason University
Jonathan M. Cottrell, University of Illinois, Urbana–Champaign
Dev K. Dalal, University of Connecticut
Brittany Gentile, University of Georgia
Brian J. Hoffman, University of Georgia
John R. Hollenbeck, Michigan State University
Michael Howe, University of Alabama
Harry Joo, Indiana University
Sven Kepes, Virginia Commonwealth University
Joel Koopman, University of Cincinnati
Charles E. Lance, Organization Research and Development
Ronald S. Landis, Illinois Institute of Technology
James M. LeBreton, Pennsylvania State University
Andrew C. Loignon, University of North Carolina, Charlotte
Alexander C. LoPilato, University of Georgia
William I. MacKeznie Jr., University of Alabama–Huntsville
Laura T. Madden, East Carolina University
Michael A. McDaniel, Virginia Commonwealth University
Daniel A. Newman, University of Illinois, Urbana–Champaign
Jisoo Ock, Rice University

x Contributors

Frederick L. Oswald, Rice University
Donde Ashmos Plowman, University of Nebraska, Lincoln
Robert E. Ployhart, University of South Carolina
Dan J. Putka, Human Resources Research Organization
Paul Schmidt, University of North Carolina, Charlotte
Neal Schmitt, Michigan State University
Allison B. Siminovsky, University of Georgia
Anne D. Smith, University of Tennessee
Scott Tonidandel, Davidson College
Jean M. Twenge, San Diego State University
Robert J. Vandenberg, University of Georgia
Eleanor B. Williams, Davidson College
David J. Woehr, University of North Carolina, Charlotte
Lauren A. Wood, University of Georgia

INTRODUCTION

Charles E. Lance and Robert J. Vandenberg

Welcome back! After a dozen-year or so odyssey through approximately 40 topics, we are now proud to present our second edited volume containing *More Statistical and Methodological Myths and Urban Legends* (SMMULs). About a decade ago, Vandenberg (2004, 2006) introduced the idea of SMMULs to the organizational and behavioral science communities, defined later by Lance (2011) as:

> . . . rules of thumb, maxims, truisms, and guidelines for research conduct, that is, "received doctrines" (Barrett, 1972, p. 1), that are taught in under-graduate and graduate classes, enforced by gatekeepers (e.g., grant panels, reviewers, editors, dissertation committee members), discussed among col-leagues, and otherwise passed along among pliers of the trade far and wide and from generation to generation.
>
> *(pp. 280–281)*

This book has been about a year and a half in the making, but it has a longer backstory. What follows is a brief recap of what brings us to this new collec-tion of SMMULs and a general overview of what it is that we offer you in this volume.

In the beginning, and over the years, Vandenberg became increasingly disen-chanted with how seemingly arbitrary standards and rules of thumb were being levied against authors of journal article submissions, theses, dissertations, grant proposals, and so forth, and informal discussions with colleagues at conferences and otherwise confirmed that he was not alone in his discontent with this state of affairs (see Vandenberg, 2006). This angst was the major motivating force for the first-ever symposium on SMMULs that Vandenberg (2004) showcased at one of the best-ever attended All-Academy (of Management) sessions in New Orleans.[1]

2 Charles E. Lance and Robert J. Vandenberg

As a follow-up to this symposium, Vandenberg (2006) traced the history of the development of the SMMUL idea through the years of discussions with friends and colleagues and facilitated the publication of three of the 2004 Academy symposium papers in a Feature Topic in *Organizational Research Methods* in 2006. These three papers were the top three cited *ORM* papers in 2006, and as of this writing (April 2014), these three papers—Spector (2006) on method variance, Lance, Butts, and Michels (2006) on statistical cutoff criteria, and James, Mulaik, and Brett (2006) on mediation—were the 2nd, 9th, and 15th most often cited articles, respectively, in *ORM*'s history. Researchers have been paying attention!

Then, beginning in 2007, we began organizing SMMUL sessions for presentation at the meeting of the Society for Industrial and Organizational Psychology (SIOP), a tradition that has continued for eight years running. In 2014, we showcased our ninth collection of SMMULs in Honolulu, HI. These symposia have always been well attended, often by overflowing crowds, and have always been among the most popular SIOP sessions.

And so it was natural that we collected these SIOP papers and commissioned a few others to comprise our first edited book on SMMULs (Lance & Vandenberg, 2009a), the development of which is documented in our introduction (Lance & Vandenberg, 2009b). We asked chapter authors to follow a loose but common outline: (a) identify and document the legend that is addressed by the chapter, (b) determine the kernel of truth that apparently fueled the legend initially, (c) document also the myths and lore concerning the legend that have accumulated over the course of its development, and (d) sort out truth from fiction, making recommendations to researchers who will face the issue at hand. Most authors followed this outline (more or less). To a tee, all chapters made valuable and well-received contributions to our edited volume.

Since its publication, we have gotten a number of indications that our first Urban Legends book was quite well received. Of course, we solicited testimonials for the book that are published on the book's back cover that attest to the wisdom of the innovative chapters contained therein (thanks, Neal, Dave, and Tom, for the kind words!). We're also aware of two unsolicited reviews of our first book. Malcolm Ree (2009) referred to our book as "thought provoking . . . the arguments are convincing and the arguments, including those with which you might disagree, provide sufficient documentations for your further consideration . . . doctoral students should have a copy of Lance and Vandenberg before they set words to paper in their dissertation proposals" (p. 879, thanks, Malcolm!). Also, Stephen Truhon (2009) says that "owning a copy of this book is essential for any researcher interested in issues regarding statistics and methods." Some more kind words indeed. We're also aware of several doctoral methods seminars whose syllabi have incorporated chapters of our book into the curriculum and one seminar for which our book is the primary text. In 2012, Chang-Ya Hu led a team that translated our book into Mandarin Chinese (see Figure 0.1).

Introduction **3**

FIGURE 0.1

Also on an international note, Lance has presented invited seminars based on our work at the National Taiwan University of Science and Technology in 2007, Nanyang Technological University (Singapore, 2010), McGill University (Montreal, 2010), and Dublin City University in 2013, and Vandenberg has presented seminars at the University of Alabama (2011) and University of South Australia (2013)

4 Charles E. Lance and Robert J. Vandenberg

and conducted a webcast for the Center of Research Methods and Analysis (CARMA, 2013). Lance also presented a keynote address sponsored by the Center for Creative Leadership to the North Carolina Society for Industrial and Organizational Psychology in 2013. And, as a final testimonial, Lance has had five copies of our book "borrowed" from his office at the University of Georgia.[2]

So, a sequel seemed to be a natural follow-up to our first book, but Vandenberg had a better idea. He invited Lance to edit a second Feature Topic in *ORM* consisting of five stimulating papers on controversial SMMULs concerning meta-analysis, significance testing, formative measurement, control variables, and structural equation model fit written by some of the most prominent researchers in the area (Aguinis, Pierce, Bosco, Dalton, & Dalton, 2011; Cortina & Landis, 2011; Edwards, 2011; Spector & Brannick, 2011; Williams & O'Boyle, 2011). The Spector and Brannick, Edwards, and Aguinis and colleagues papers were the most, second, and fourth most often cited *ORM* papers in 2011, and although it is still early, these papers are continuing to be frequently cited and may well end up joining their 2006 counterparts as citation classics.

But many important SMMULs remained, several of which we and/or our colleagues had presented previously at scientific conferences (notably SIOP) or had as "in progress" works, and it is these papers that we are now proud to present in our second SMMULs book. The chapters in our first book clustered around "statistical issues" and "methodological issues," consistent with the book's title. And while the broad outline for the present book's chapters is the same as for the first volume (state the legend, identify the kernel of truth, trace the accompanying lore or myth, separate fact from fiction, and make recommendations for researchers) the clusters of issues that the chapters address are a bit different. The first two chapters address rather general issues of the integrity of (a) our research paradigms in the social and organizational sciences relative to those in areas traditionally thought of as the "harder" sciences and (b) the cumulative knowledge base that is now amassing in the social and organizational sciences. The second cluster of chapters addresses a number of important issues concerning the design of social and organizational research studies. Many of the issues addressed in these chapters concern choices a researcher can make prior to data collection and analysis and thus reflect some of the most important commitments a researcher must make along the way to investigating the question at hand. The third cluster of chapters concerns how we analyze and otherwise treat the data we do collect. Researchers always have choices here, and whether we choose to weight some parts of the data differentially (Chapter 9), how we treat unusual, influential, or outlying data points (Chapter 10), or analyze the data toward testing for mediation effects (Chapter 11), how we treat the data can well influence what we learn from them. The fourth and final cluster of chapters addresses various aspects of the question "Ok, now that we have the data, how do we make the best sense of them?" Data do not speak to us directly; rather, we must interpret data in the light of prevailing theory and perhaps numerous analytic alternatives, and these are the concerns addressed in this cluster of chapters.

We hope you enjoy reading this book's chapters. And even if you cannot go so far as to say that you "enjoyed" reading them (like you might say after finishing your favorite author's latest novel!), we hope you find them stimulating, thought provoking, and perhaps even provocative. As the editors of these chapters, we can both attest to the fact that we learned quite a lot along the way while working with the authors on drafts of their chapters. And so to the authors of this book's chapters, we offer a hearty "thank you!" Thanks for agreeing to be part of our effort, thanks for providing your high-quality submissions, thanks for responding to our editorial suggestions and, not the least of all, thanks for being on time (or in some cases, close at least). We look forward to working with you again in the future, and remember—there are no alligators lurking in New York's sewers!

Notes

1 There was standing room only in a ballroom-sized meeting room. The way Vandenberg tells the story, he stopped counting at 400 attendees (Lance & Vandenberg, 2009b)!
2 As yet, these copies have not been returned, but it is hoped that they are being put to good use.

References

Aguinis, H., Pierce, C. A., Bosco, F. A., Dalton, D. R., & Dalton, C. M. (2011). Debunking myths and urban legends about meta-analysis. *Organizational Research Methods, 14,* 306–331.

Barrett, G. V. (1972). Research models of the future for industrial and organizational psychology. *Personnel Psychology, 25,* 1–17.

Cortina, J. M., & Landis, R. S. (2011). The Earth is not round ($p < .00$). *Organizational Research Methods, 14,* 332–349.

Edwards, J. R. (2011). The fallacy of formative measurement. *Organizational Research Methods, 14,* 370–388.

James, L. R., Mulaik, S. A., & Brett, J. M. (2006). A tale of two methods. *Organizational Research Methods, 9,* 233–244.

Lance, C. E. (2011). More statistical and methodological myths and urban legends. *Organizational Research Methods, 14,* 279–286.

Lance, C. E., Butts, M. M., & Michels, L. C. (2006). The sources of four commonly reported cutoff criteria: What did they really say? *Organizational Research Methods, 9,* 202–220.

Lance, C. E., & Vandenberg, R. J. (2009a). *Statistical and methodological myths and urban legends: Doctrine, verity and fable in the organizational and social sciences.* New York, NY: Routledge.

Lance, C. E., & Vandenberg, R. J. (2009b). Introduction. In C. E. Lance & R. J. Vandenberg (Eds.), *Statistical and methodological myths and urban legends: Doctrine, verity and fable in the organizational and social sciences* (pp. 1–4). New York, NY: Routledge.

Ree, M. (2009). Review of statistical and methodological myths and urban legends: Doctrine, verity, and fable in the social and organizational sciences. *Personnel Psychology, 62,* 878–880.

Spector, P. E. (2006). Method variance in organizational research: Truth or urban legend? *Organizational Research Methods, 9,* 221–232.

Spector, P. E., & Brannick, M. (2011). Methodological urban legends: The misuse of statistical control variables. *Organizational Research Methods, 14,* 287–305.

Truhon, S. A. (2009). Rules of thumb in the eye. *PsycCRITIQUES, 54.* Retrieved April 14, 2009 from http://dx.doi.org/10.1037/a0015195

Vandenberg, R. J. (2004, August). *Statistical and methodological myths and urban legends: Where pray tell did they get this idea?* Symposium chaired at the meeting of the Academy of Management, New Orleans, LA.

Vandenberg, R. J. (2006). Statistical and methodological myths and urban legends: Where pray tell did they get this idea? *Organizational Research Methods, 9,* 194–201.

Williams, L. J., & O'Boyle, E., Jr. (2011). The myth of global fit indices and alternatives for assessing latent variable relations. *Organizational Research Methods, 14,* 350–369.

PART I
General Issues

1

IS OURS A HARD SCIENCE (AND DO WE CARE)?

Ronald S. Landis and José M. Cortina

Perhaps no other distinction in science engenders as much emotion as that between the so-called "hard" and "soft" sciences. From early in one's academic training, this distinction is drawn clearly and with much accompanying inference. Scientists and laypersons alike are familiar with this distinction and would probably concur that the hard sciences (e.g., chemistry, physics) study phenomena with a degree of objectivity and certainty that the soft sciences (e.g., psychology, sociology) do not. Ask undergraduate or graduate students in any scientific discipline and they will be quick to indicate on which side of the fence they fall. If the hard sciences are revered, respected, and honored, the soft sciences are often looked upon with skepticism, doubt, and derision.

These differences might not be such a big deal if they were confined to backroom discussions in the halls of academia. Unfortunately, the negative perceptions of the soft sciences have implications for policy decisions and research funding. One need look no further than National Science Foundation (NSF) funding allocations to see that this is so. In March 2013, the United States Senate approved a measure that included an amendment to restrict NSF funding of political science research (Nelson, 2013). This followed on the heels of a similar vote in spring 2012 by the United States House of Representatives (Lane, 2012). Passionate responses to these votes have come from both sides of the issue and have been noted in several respected media outlets. For example, Lane (2012) noted that "the NSF shouldn't fund *any* social science research." On the other side, Wilson (2012) pointed out the significant gains associated with research in the social sciences. Wilson importantly notes that such gains are most likely to accrue from "soft" science research that is methodologically rigorous. In short, the roots of this distinction run deep and appear to be ingrained in not only our scientific, but also our societal consciousness.

10 Ronald S. Landis and José M. Cortina

The purposes of this chapter are to use the hard/soft distinction and debate to (a) identify an unavoidable kernel of truth behind our collective categorization as a soft science, (b) discuss the ways in which this categorization is unwarranted, (c) identify a second kernel of truth that we have brought upon ourselves, and (d) recommend practices that can improve the quality of our science and promote greater confidence in our results. We start with a review of the hard/soft distinction with particular attention to an important case involving the National Academy of Sciences. We use this case as a foundation upon which to identify the core characteristics that appear to delimit hard and soft sciences. We then offer interpretations of how these characteristics apply to industrial and organizational (I/O) psychology and why we are typically viewed as a soft science.

Huntington, Lang, and the National Academy of Sciences

A high-profile example of the differentiation between hard and soft science is the case of Samuel Huntington's candidacy for admission to the National Academy of Sciences (NAS). Huntington's nomination met strong opposition from an NAS member, Serge Lang. In short, Lang, a mathematician, questioned the scientific merit and contributions of Huntington, a political scientist (Diamond, 1987). At the core of Lang's criticism was the explicit (or implicit) belief that the hard sciences are superior to the soft sciences.

Huntington's credentials for election appeared to be beyond question. He served as president of the American Political Science Association, held a named professorship at Harvard, authored several widely read books, received a "best book" award (for the social and behavioral sciences) from the Association of American Publishers, and was deemed worthy of NAS membership by current members (i.e., those nominating Huntington) who themselves were eminent scholars in their respective fields. On the other side of the issue, Lang had just been elected to the academy the prior year. To be fair, some of the rationale and rhetoric behind the ensuing debates regarding Huntington's candidacy have been characterized as socio-political differences between the two scientists. These reasons, to the extent they are true, fall outside the current discussion.

The heart of the issue appears to be that Lang perceived the work of Huntington to be "soft." As Diamond (1987, p. 35) noted, hard sciences are often considered more deserving of our respect due to their use of "firm evidence" provided through "controlled experiments and highly accurate measurements." Of course, Diamond (1987) was quick to point out that science is something more general. In his words, "It means the enterprise of explaining and predicting—gaining knowledge of—natural phenomena, by continually testing one's theories against empirical evidence." It would be difficult to argue against the observation that we in the organizational sciences use less precise measures and exercise less experimental control than is usually the case in the physical sciences. Organizational scientists claim that this is an unavoidable byproduct of the study of human beings with their stubborn idiosyncrasy and damnable free will. Still, our measures and designs are messy, and therein, perhaps, lay a kernel of truth.

Whether we believe Huntington should or should not have gained entry into the NAS, this story clearly illustrates that the hard/soft distinction can have rather significant personal and professional ramifications. As social scientists, many of us may find ourselves sympathetic to Huntington. Indeed, as this example illustrates, the characterization of our field by others as soft is a matter of concern for us as individuals and as a field. Lest the Lang example be written off as an interesting historical anecdote without relevance to contemporary discussions regarding science, we remind the reader of similar incidents that have occurred in the past couple of years in the halls of Congress. The distinction between hard and soft sciences is alive and well. In the next section, we explore the distinction between the hard and soft sciences in greater detail.

Hard versus Soft Sciences

The distinction between hard and soft sciences is familiar to scientists and laypersons alike. To be clear, hard sciences are those usually described as physical or natural sciences such as physics, chemistry, astronomy, and biology. Soft sciences are those such as psychology, sociology, anthropology, and political science and are often labeled social sciences. Though this distinction might also be drawn in terms of physical and social sciences, these terms do not appear to carry the baggage of the former, as they are more descriptive in nature. When terms such as "hard" and "soft" are used instead, however, categorization is compounded with a judgment of quality and rigor. Indeed, hard sciences are inferred as being characterized by greater experimental rigor, replicability, and quality. The word "soft" in soft sciences is intended as a pejoration and as shorthand for the lack of the aforementioned characteristics (or at least for substantial weakness on these dimensions). Indeed, proponents of the hard/soft division often cast the soft sciences as lacking the rigor of their hard-science counterparts. Opponents of the division, on the other hand, point to the fact that hard sciences often do not strictly adhere to rigorous methods and that each of the hard sciences once was characterized as lacking sufficient rigor.

Howard (1993) makes several key points regarding the hard/soft distinction and the extent to which psychology is, can be, or should strive to be considered a hard science. Howard notes that the goal of hard sciences is to perfectly predict the behavior of the objects of interest (e.g., motion of planets). Such a view of science is predicated on the belief that a given theory is preferable to others in a particular area of study if that theory allows for more accurate prediction of the focal object's behavior. As Howard (1993, p. 43) points out, "If the 'more is better' rule of thumb were true for psychological research, the question of whether psychology is as 'hard' a discipline as physics could easily be answered with a resounding no."

Meehl (1978) criticized psychology's reliance on group mean difference statistics and pointed to the lack of strong theory as one key reason for the lack of precise prediction. He noted that statistical significance tests do not appear in physics textbooks. Instead, he noted that physicists have sufficiently strong theories that allow for precise predictions of patterns of results. The researcher can then simply eyeball the outcomes and discern the extent to which results are in sufficient concordance with those predicted by his/her strong theory. Cohen (1977, p. 78) echoed this sentiment when he suggested "that the behavioral sciences are not as far advanced as the physical sciences."

There can be little doubt that psychological research has been plagued by nondirectional hypotheses. Suggesting (and testing) that two groups simply differ from one another is certainly less elegant and satisfying than predicting, for example, the precise point of a given planet minutes, hours, days, or even years in the future. Although we have largely abandoned nondirectional hypotheses for directional hypotheses, we have been reluctant to take the next step toward interval hypotheses and are very far from point hypotheses (Cortina & Chen, 2005). Again, if prediction is the only criterion by which we characterize scientific disciplines on the hard/soft continuum, then psychology is almost certainly soft (Howard, 1993).

Simonton (2004) offered a quantitative assessment of the status of psychology relative to the disciplines of physics, chemistry, biology, and sociology. Placing fourth in the hierarchy (just behind biology and noticeably ahead of sociology), the categorization of psychology as a soft science appears to be warranted. Such self-reflection on the status of psychology, and indeed any discipline, relative to others has a long history.

Lilienfeld (2012) recently commented on the extent to which others view psychological research as largely unscientific. Even though most of his examples were drawn from clinical psychology, the fundamental points he makes are nonetheless relevant for research and researchers in the organizational sciences. For more than 150 years, psychology has clearly been viewed as a soft science, if even a science at all (Coon, 1992). These perceptions are consistent among scientists and laypersons alike (Lilienfeld, 2012). Of the myriad statistics reported by Lilienfeld, perhaps most sobering is that only 11% of individuals surveyed indicated that psychology is the profession best suited for improving organizational productivity as compared to 37% who indicated that business persons were most appropriate for this role. Speculating as to why psychology has such a soft reputation, Lilienfeld suggested six potential criticisms. These include the idea that psychology is merely common sense, that psychology does not use scientific methods, that psychology cannot yield meaningful generalizations because every individual is unique, that our results are not replicable, that our science cannot make precise predictions, and that psychology is overall not useful to society.

Though Lilienfeld (2012) offers cogent rebuttals to each of the criticisms, they nonetheless fuel the continued perception of the softness of our field. This is troubling given evidence that psychological research produces results that are just as strong as if not stronger than results from medical research (Lipsey & Wilson, 1993). For example, Lipsey and Wilson report notably large effects for various employee training programs on several important outcomes (d = .42 to .67). In comparison, effect sizes from medical treatments are noticeably smaller (e.g., drug therapy for hypertension and quality of life (d = .11 to .28). To be fair, other examples reported in Lipsey and Wilson can be used to argue that medical research produces larger effect sizes than psychological research. That, however, only illustrates the point that to call one of these areas of research hard and another soft would appear wildly arbitrary in the face of such similarities.

Like most other categorizations of humans, differentiation between hard and soft sciences produces in-groups and out-groups. The in-group is to be revered, respected, and aspired to while the out-group is not. By way of analogy, one can imagine the hard sciences as being an elite fraternity and the soft sciences as being the backup fraternity. For example, the protagonists in *Animal House* begin by visiting the elite Omega Theta Pi fraternity in the hopes of being asked to join. As psychologists, we appear to want to join the elite science fraternity. Alas, the protagonists in the movie are not deemed worthy by those in Omega house and instead must settle for the less-than-prestigious Delta house. Psychology appears to suffer from a similar fate (without the toga parties, of course).

There would certainly be advantages to being recognized as a serious (i.e., hard) science. Rather than merely attempting to gain entry into the hard sciences club, however, we should instead devote our time and energies toward refining our science. Instead of focusing on and minimizing those aspects of our work that distinguish us from the natural sciences, we should instead focus on those elements that make us a science. We study human behavior in complex situations that unfold over time. This in and of itself doesn't make us less scientific. Insofar as we deserve to be labeled as soft, it is because of the ways that we choose to study such behavior.

Another contributing factor to the perception of our field as soft is a general lack of knowledge on the part of the public as to what we do. Television shows, movies, and novels are replete with examples of hard scientists solving important and often times life-and-death problems. Unfortunately, pop culture also offers many high-profile examples of crackpot, fast-food charlatan-psychologists (both real and fictional) offering up their McSessions a few minutes at a time (e.g., Dr. Phil, Dr. Laura, Frasier Crane). Of particular importance to the current chapter, these high-profile examples paint all of psychology and perhaps all of the social sciences with the same broad brush and contribute to the impression that we are soft, atheoretical, and methodologically weak.

One of the features that makes studying human behavior different (and fundamentally more difficult) from the study of, say, planetary behavior is that humans have the capacity to exert free will and actively determine their behavior in a given context. To expect or demand that our theories and/or results allow for perfect prediction of individual behavior is not realistic. Perfect prediction would require

14 Ronald S. Landis and José M. Cortina

the assumption that all causes of individual behavior can be identified (Cohen, 1977; Howard, 1993). Yet, if our physical science colleagues demand 100% variance explained, then perhaps we should strive for nothing less. Or should we?

We have both scientific and anecdotal data that corroborate the notion that humans do have free will and can actively alter their behavior. Perhaps we are little more than electrons moving about a nucleus, but the available data suggest otherwise. Certainly, our science would be held in higher esteem if such patterns were found, but the world, or at least the part of it that we study, would instantly become a much less interesting place.

The hard/soft distinction plays at least two roles. First, it influences how others view what we do and the value that they place on it. Second, it influences how we view ourselves. We submit that the second of these functions is under our own control. If we view ourselves as second-class scientists, we almost certainly will be just that. To some degree, this is an instance of self-handicapping at its worst. We can simply take our medicine and sit in the corner of science while the "real" work is accomplished by others. On the other hand, we can choose to acknowledge that even though others may view us as soft, we can push and grow our scientific discipline through greater rigor (both theoretical and methodological) and promote our results.

Problems of Conceptualization and Operationalization

Fundamentally, Diamond (1987) argued that at least part of the criticism of soft sciences stems from the operationalization of key constructs. Lang's objections were based on the belief that Huntington's work was inferior as illustrated by his use of the phrase "pseudo mathematics" and his direct critique of the measurement of constructs such as social frustration. Ultimately, these reactions reflect a fundamental challenge to the notion that social scientists can ever truly measure anything.

For example, if we are asked to measure a physical attribute of an individual such as height, we may disagree on the appropriate metric (e.g., meters or feet), but we will likely have little disagreement once we select an instrument. Why? Height is an observable characteristic that does not require inference. Imagine, however, that we are tasked with measuring an attribute such as an individual's level of cooperativeness. We first must agree that cooperativeness (as an individual characteristic) exists and precisely what constitutes this construct. Lang's criticisms of soft science would appear to be targeted directly at this step of our inquiry. Do our fundamental phenomena of interest truly exist if we cannot directly see, feel, touch, taste, or hear them? Our position is that these types of phenomena most certainly exist. Such characteristics are not quite so apparent as those studied by those in the natural sciences, but there are many examples of entities and phenomena that were unmeasurable but for which we developed tools that now allow measurement (e.g., gravitons, the rotation of planetary orbits). So, to suggest that some sciences are inferior simply because they study phenomena that are not directly observable seems to be not only unnecessarily limiting but also hypocritical.

We in the organization sciences clearly attempt to measure things that are more elusive than height. We can agree that individuals have height, that height is a meaningful individual difference, and that we can define it as something like the distance from the soles of one's feet to the top of one's head. How we define cooperativeness is likely to engender greater disagreement, and some may even question whether cooperativeness is truly a meaningful construct as distinct from, say, agreeableness, prosocial personality, and so forth. So, if we wish to study cooperativeness, we must be careful to sufficiently define the construct in a way that is clear, internally consistent, and distinct from other constructs. Regardless of the care with which we define our construct, there are likely to be differences among studies with regard to definitions simply because the thing being defined is a construct. Does this mean that we should, for this reason, refuse to study cooperativeness, or that it does not exist?

To complicate this situation further, consider the measurement of cooperativeness. Even if two scientists agree on a definition of the construct, they will not necessarily agree on how best to measure it. One scientist may choose to rely on self-report Likert scales, while the other may use observational data. Because there is no way to prove that one of these methods is, in an absolute sense, better, both are likely to exist in research on cooperativeness. Is the fact that there is not complete consensus on measurement, or that perfect measurement is not possible, reason to abandon the measurement of cooperativeness? Volumes have been written on psychometrics, and a discussion of the topic is well beyond the scope of this chapter. Instead, we simply point out that conceptualization and measurement are critical components of our science. Although there are many ways in which the natural sciences are more difficult than ours, the fact that we must define and measure unobservable constructs adds an element of difficulty to our sciences that doesn't exist in others. Does this really make us softer? If so, then we will, at least for the foreseeable future, be relegated to the soft side of the ledger.

Acknowledging these realities about the phenomena that we study does not mean that we should have a "second-class" view of ourselves. Indeed, hard and soft seem like labels that confuse a more critical distinction: good versus bad science. Who among us would prefer a "hard" science of trivial matters involving measures that are concrete but unrelated to the phenomena of interest? We submit that "doing science" is as, if not more, important than identifying some areas of study as somehow intrinsically more important or interesting than others.

Imagine living 500 years ago and wondering why hurricanes hit coastal areas. What are some of the possible explanations? God, sea monsters, other people control weather, or perhaps the earth naturally distributing heat around the globe. Science gives us a mechanism for answering the question: falsifiability.[1]

As science progressed, we went from predicting hurricanes hours ahead of time to days ahead of time to multiple days ahead of time because science gave us a means for testing competing theories as to what drives these systems. We still cannot perfectly predict where hurricanes will form or exactly how they will strengthen or even move. The point is that science gave us the tools to do a better job than we could do without applying scientific principles and methods.

The methods that organizational researchers use are akin to those of our hard-science counterparts. Namely, we attempt to offer testable hypotheses based on sound theory that are then tested using well-described and reproducible methods. Just because we cannot assert that a given person will behave in a particular way in a particular context does not mean that our application of science was any less rigorous than that of someone who can assert that an object will fall at the speed of gravity.

Hedges (1987, p. 443) stated that social scientists "know intuitively that there is something 'softer' and less cumulative about our research results than about those of the physical sciences." Although Hedges (1987) was more interested in the cumulation of research (i.e., meta-analysis) than with rigor per se, his evidence indicated some parallels between results found in the physical and social sciences. These similarities do not definitively condemn the hard/soft distinction but do indicate that the distinction should not necessarily make us feel inferior. In fact, Hedges (1987) suggests that the manner in which physical science researchers handle the lack of consistency observed in their research could serve as a model for social scientists. In particular, Hedges (1987) suggested that in the hard sciences "theories are *not* sought" every time an experiment yields inconsistent results. Rather, methodological explanations are typically identified. Theories, in this way, serve as a strong foundation and are not discarded or dramatically revised in the face of inconsistent results. Perhaps if our theories were treated through this lens of stability, our science would be taken more seriously. Alternatively, perhaps our theories are so flimsy that they should be revised in light of a single disconfirmation (a point to which we will later return).

Challenging Perceptions of Being Soft

In many ways, the organizational sciences are as rigorous, complex, and objective as they have ever been. We have made great progress in measurement, research design, and data analysis, often leading the charge into the future. In this section, we provide examples of ways in which our field has developed methodologically.

Measurement

Of the various methodological categories, none can be considered more central to and defined by the organizational sciences than measurement. Although there may be fields whose graduate students receive more training in the administration of measures, none are likely to deliver more training in the development and evaluation of measures than ours. We offer the following examples as supporting evidence.

Cognitive Ability

Perhaps of the greatest contribution by psychology to society has been work on the measurement of cognitive ability. From Binet's pioneering work in this area at the turn of the 20th century through contemporary applications such as computer adaptive versions of popular standardized admissions tests like the Graduate Record Examination (GRE), test design, development, and administration have had dramatic (cf. Herrnstein & Murray, 1994; Lemann, 1999) influences on society, education, industry, and the military. Though often controversial, the evidence in support of psychological testing is strong and compelling (Meyer et al., 2001).

Structured Employment Interviews

As observed many times before, the employment interview is a technique or mechanism rather than a construct. Our field has developed the concept of structure in interviews and has shown how important this structure is. A highly structured interview is one whose items and scoring are standardized across interviewees. Huffcutt and Arthur (1994) showed that whereas unstructured interviews are relatively uncorrelated with performance (and difficult to defend in court), structured interviews are among the best predictors of performance, explaining one third of the variance in performance. Additionally, Cortina, Goldstein, Payne, Davison, and Gilliland (2000) showed that structured interview scores explain considerable performance variance beyond cognitive ability and conscientiousness. This is especially encouraging given that interviews display less adverse impact than do many other predictors of performance (Ployhart & Holtz, 2008).

Situational Judgment Tests (SJTs)

SJTs ask respondents to read a description of (or watch) a situation, usually interpersonal, and to choose the response that is most likely to resolve the issue described in the situation. Response options are scored via expert judgments. SJTs, like structured interviews, are time consuming to develop, but they display excellent criterion-related validity and lower adverse impact than many selection tools (Lievens, Peeters, & Schollaert, 2008; Whetzel, McDaniel, & Nguyen, 2008).

Alternatives/Refinements to Self-Reports of Personality

It is universally acknowledged that personality is important to nearly every aspect of organizational functioning. Indeed, for many entry-level jobs, it is difficult to identify important predictors of performance that aren't driven by personality

(Cortina & Luchman, 2012). Though there are various conceptualizations of the structure of personality, the Five Factor Model (FFM) has wide acceptance and endorsement by researchers (e.g., McCrae & Costa, 1987). In fact, the FFM serves as the foundation for several widely used measures of personality including the NEO-PI-R and the International Personality Item Pool (IPIP). And yet, researchers and practitioners alike have relied almost exclusively on self-report measures of personality in spite of the well-known problems of intentional distortion and self deception.

In the last 20 years, however, our field has explored alternatives to self-report that do not rely so heavily on the candor and self-insight of the respondent. For example, Larry James and colleagues have developed conditional reasoning techniques to measure personality. These "implicit" measures are intended to elicit personality rather than ask about it (James, 1998). Various studies have shown that respondents taking implicit measures are unaware that they measure personality. More importantly, implicit measures predict performance better than do self-report measures without increasing adverse impact (see Uhlmann et al., 2012, for a review of implicit measures). Although implicit measures are notoriously difficult to develop, Motowidlo, Hooper, & Jackson (2006) described an application of SJTs that results in an implicit measure of personality that may reduce these noted difficulties.

Research Design

We have also made great progress in the design of our studies and note the following examples.

Experience Sampling

Until recently, most of the phenomena that we studied were assumed to be static. One result of this assumption was that many of our most important constructs were conceptualized solely from a between-person perspective. For example, it was assumed that a good organizational citizen today would be a good organizational citizen tomorrow. Experience sampling allows us to observe within-person fluctuations in activity, and this has opened our eyes to new conceptualizations of core concepts (Dimotakis, Ilies, & Judge, 2013).

Regarding citizenship, consider the experience sampling study by Ilies, Scott, and Judge (2006). In this study, the authors showed that intraindividual variability in citizenship can be explained by positive affect and satisfaction. In other words, a person is more likely to engage in citizenship when he or she is experiencing positive affect and satisfaction than when he or she is not. Furthermore, these intraindividual relationships are moderated by a stable trait (i.e., agreeableness) such that these intraindividual relationships are stronger for those who are predisposed to be agreeable. This is not to say that there are not mean differences in citizenship (or job attitudes). Rather, experience sampling modeling (ESM) has allowed us to see that there are factors that fluctuate within a person that explain within-person variance in citizenship, and if an organization desires consistently high citizenship, then it should ensure that those factors remain at a level that is conducive to citizenship.

As another example, Jones and colleagues (2013) used an experience sampling approach to study the changes in strategies that pregnant women use to conceal or reveal their pregnancies to coworkers over the course of pregnancy. By sampling over the course of multiple months and multiple interactions, Jones was able to reveal not only that there was considerable within-person variability in strategies but that the within-person trends tended to be nonlinear, with different strategies waxing in importance at different stages of the pregnancy.

Field Experiments

The organizational sciences have always called for more field research because of the level of fidelity that these settings offer. At the same time, we appreciate the support for causal inferences offered by experiments. Field experiments are, nevertheless, rare because organizations are typically unwilling to allow control groups and because the very nature of some variables makes them difficult to manipulate (King, Hebl, Botsford Morgan, & Ahmad, 2013). How, for example, would one experimentally study the effects of applicant gender or pregnancy?

Hebl, King, Glick, Singeltary, and Kazama (2007) conducted a field experiment of the effects of applicant pregnancy on interactions with store managers, and to our knowledge, they did so without impregnating anyone! These authors developed pregnancy prostheses that were worn (experimental group) or not worn (control group) by confederates who posed as people seeking either jobs or retail assistance. In this way, real-world interactions could be studied while holding characteristics other than pregnancy constant.

King, Shapiro, Hebl, Singletary, and Turner (2006) did something similar in a study of obesity stigma. These authors developed an obesity prosthesis that allowed them to manipulate obesity in addition to factors such as whether the obese person appeared to be working on reducing their obesity. The latter construct was manipulated by having confederates carry either a diet soda or a Dairy Queen Blizzard. The Hebl and colleagues and King and colleagues studies represent highly creative approaches to research design that conquer problems that had been considered intractable, perhaps even impregnable (you knew it was coming).

Data Analysis

We have also made great strides in data analytic techniques. Consider the following examples.

Complex Causal Models

As the complexity of our conceptual models has increased, so have the requirements that we place upon our data. As a result, our data analytic techniques have had to advance rapidly. For example, a model that has become quite popular is the moderated mediation model. Holland, Shore, and Cortina (2014) found 68 different papers from two years of *Journal of Applied Psychology* (JAP) and *Academy of Management Journal* (AMJ) that tested moderated mediation models. Edwards and Lambert (2007) offered in-depth guidance regarding the testing of a variety of moderated mediation models, of which there are many. This continues a tradition of advancements in testing such models that goes back at least as far as James and Brett (1984).

The organizational sciences have also contributed greatly to the development of structural equation modeling (SEM). There are too many aspects of SEM to which we have contributed to go into detail, but they include item parceling (Hall, Snell, & Foust, 1999; Landis, Beal, & Tesluk, 2000), outliers (Rensvold & Cheung, 1999), model fit (Cheung & Rensvold, 2001; Nye & Drasgow, 2011; Williams & O'Boyle, 2011), mediation models (Cheung & Lau, 2008; James, Mulaik, & Brett, 2006), moderation models (Cortina, Chen, & Dunlap, 2001), latent growth models (Cheung, 2007), construct equivalence (Bou & Satorra, 2010; Cheung, 2008; Vandenberg & Lance, 2000), congruence (Cheung, 2009; Edwards, 2009), and method variance (Williams, Hartman, & Cavazotte, 2010), just to name a few.

Multilevel/Nested Models

The organizational sciences have also contributed enormously to the analysis of nested data. The work of Bliese and Ployhart (2002) is considered seminal in the area of growth modeling. Similarly, Bliese and Hanges (2004) is required reading for those who want to understand the consequences of ignoring nesting. Chen, Bliese, and Mathieu (2005) is a foundational work regarding homology. We have also expanded the frontiers of multilevel modeling with work on time-invariant covariates (Cheung, 2007), growth mixture modeling (Wang & Bodner, 2007), mediation (Zhang, Zyphur, & Preacher, 2009), multilevel item response theory (IRT) (Tay, Diener, Drasgow, & Vermunt, 2011), analysis of dyadic data (Gooty & Yammarino, 2011), dynamic growth modeling (Ployhart & Kim, 2013), and spurious relationships (Braun, Kuljanin, & DeShon, 2013).

We Reap What We Sow

The previous review represents the good news and provides evidence that psychology is rigorous in many ways. The bad news is that, for all of the advancements to which our methodological experts have contributed, our research still contains myriad basic errors that simply shouldn't occur in a field that wants to be considered rigorous. We see this as an enormous problem that is only getting worse.

Our Theories Are a Hot Mess

We Don't Test Our Theories

Although this volume has a research methods focus, Edwards (2010) and others have explained that theory building is just another, complementary method for answering research questions. Or at least it should be. Our top journals, and many of the others, require papers to make "theoretical contributions." This means that the focus of a paper must be on hypotheses that have never been offered before. Replication is fine but incidental. The hook for a paper must be that which is unique to it. Indeed, the authors of this chapter have served as action editors for more than 500 manuscripts, of which perhaps 50 were accepted for publication. We can remember only a couple that did not contain new theory and whose contribution lay in providing a categorically superior test for existing theory.

On its surface, this seems admirable. We want not only an empirical answer to our research questions but also a theoretical one. The problem is this: Our theories never really get tested. If one opens the nearest copy of *JAP* or *AMJ*, one notices that the theory in a given paper is tested empirically in that paper (Kacmar & Whitfield, 2000). Because future papers on that topic, however, must develop and test their own theories, there is no margin in testing previous ones. While it is true that linkages proposed in previous papers get tested in subsequent papers, these tests are incidental and are therefore often tested poorly. Only the original proposer of the linkage goes to the trouble of testing it well. Of course, there are notable exceptions to this (e.g., Azjen's Theory of Planned Behavior, Schneider's Attraction-Selection-Attrition theory), but these are the exceptions that prove the rule.

The situation is even worse for theories proposed in purely theoretical papers. Of course, the papers published in *Academy of Management Review* (*AMR*) are not empirical, so they contain no tests of the linkages proposed. But do the many empirical studies that cite *AMR* papers (*AMR* has the highest impact factor of any business-related journal) do so because they are testing the theories proposed in those *AMR* papers? Kacmar and Whitfield (2000) and more recently Edwards, Berry, and Kay (2013) have shown that this is most certainly not the case. Specifically, the empirical papers that cite review papers do so because they need the credibility gained from citing top-tier papers and because they cover similar topics, not because they are testing the theories in those papers.

So, the theories in our empirical journals are tested once and the theories in our review journals are not tested at all. If our theories aren't tested, if instead they represent untested speculation resting upon previous untested speculation, then it is difficult to refer to the ultimate result as "theoretical development." Instead, we have a rather keen irony:

22 Ronald S. Landis and José M. Cortina

By requiring theoretical development, we guarantee that it doesn't happen.

Why would this be? Perhaps a clue lies in the advice given in correspondence with submitters to *AMR*. It is recommended that submitters become well acquainted with Sutton and Staw (1995), which itself draws heavily from sources such as Kaplan (1964) and Weick (1989). Sutton and Staw (1995) explain that neither references nor catalogs/definitions of variables nor path diagrams nor hypotheses represent theory. References reflect knowledge of previous research, catalogs reflect knowledge of relevant variables, and hypotheses and path diagrams represent clarity with regard to the connections among variables. Sutton and Staw (1995) explain repeatedly that although these are necessary for theory, they are insufficient in the absence of the logic that leads to the hypotheses. We agree. Papers that reflect ignorance of previous work, of relevant variables, or of arguments connecting them cannot possibly advance theory. It seems to us, however, that it is very rare for papers published in good journals to omit the logic that connects the variables in their models. Add to this the fact that our current practices seem to result in theories that are untestable, or at least untested, and we have a thorny problem. The journal review process screens out papers that omit relevant literature, omit relevant variables, and lack clarity regarding the relationships among them, but according to Sutton and Staw (1995), these are the things that *aren't* theory. What is it that is getting screened in, and why are the things that get screened in ever revisited, let alone tested?

Perhaps part of the problem is summarized in this statement from Sutton and Staw (1995): "it is easier to identify features of manuscripts that are not theory than it is to specify exactly what good theory is" (p. 378). Indeed, Sutton and Staw (1995) provide very little specific guidance regarding what good theory is. But consider this less-appreciated suggestion from Sutton and Staw (1995): "Strong theory usually stems from a single or small set of research ideas" (p. 377). Review papers and introduction sections that stem from single ideas are generally rejected as being too narrow. Indeed, both authors of the present chapter have, in their capacities as reviewers and editors, levied this exact criticism on countless occasions.

Far from insisting that models be self-contained and parsimonious, the gatekeepers of our field require that authors tackle relatively broad questions. Broad questions require large models, and large models require many variables, many transmitting mechanisms, and many explanations for the linkages among them. This, perhaps, requires the "disciplined imagination" referred to by Weick (1989) and referenced by Sutton and Staw (1995). One could argue that "disciplined imagination" is a euphemism for "fiction," and fictional claims are notoriously difficult to test.

Another source of the problem is the relatively recent obsession with "overarching theoretical frameworks." Sutton and Staw (1995) call for justification of linkages, but this is no longer sufficient. An additional requirement for theoretical papers is that they rest upon an overarching framework that ties all of the linkages together. It is difficult to determine whence this particular requirement came, as it is not mentioned in either the older (e.g., Sutton & Staw, 1995) or the newer (e.g., Kilduff, 2006, 2007; LePine & King, 2010) guidance on publishing in *AMR*. Nevertheless, it has come up in every submission of which we are aware in the last 5 to 10 years. The reason given for this de facto additional requirement is that it makes the model easier to test. Given that our models don't actually get tested, perhaps we could agree as a field to do away with this particular hurdle.

In any case, our field has a widespread problem on the theory side, and it may very well be that we have intentionally brought this upon ourselves. Perhaps Van Maanen (1989) was right when he suggested that we scrap new theory for a while and try to observe what actually happens in organizations. What a crazy thought.

Need for Complexity—2; Capacity for Complexity—1

Thus the score stands. It seems that our desire for more-complex theories has outpaced our capacity for developing them. Each new method seems to bring with it implied conceptual complexities with which researchers have not had to cope in the past. We offer here two of many possible examples. First, consider multilevel models. It is not uncommon for researchers to study the effects of level 1 (e.g., the individual level) and level 2 (e.g., the group level) predictors on level 1 outcomes. Thus, one might propose a main effect for the level 1 predictor, a main effect for the level 2 predictor, and an interaction.

We are all familiar with the notion that, for situations in which people are nested within groups, at least two levels of equation are required: level 1 equations in which outcomes (y) that vary within group are regressed onto predictors that vary within group and level 2 equations in which level 1 coefficients are regressed onto group-level characteristics. Initial level 1 analyses create separate equations linking y to the level 1 predictor (assuming there is only one). The level 2 slope equation then tells us the degree to which group characteristics are related to the magnitude/direction of level 1 relationships (i.e., a cross-level interaction such that the level 2 predictor moderates the level 1 relationship).

The level 2 intercept equation, although seemingly simpler because it involves only an additive model, creates conceptual problems. As LoPilato and Vandenberg have pointed out (Chapter 14, this volume), significant weights in level 2 intercept equations are usually interpreted as evidence of cross-level main effects, that is, y_{ij} (the y value of person i in group j) is influenced by the value of group j on the level 2 predictor. Unfortunately, this is impossible, as the group-level predictor is constant within group. Instead, the weight for the level 2 intercept equation provides evidence for the relationship between the level 2 predictor and $\bar{y}_j$, the mean of y for group j. In other words, this weight links one group characteristic to another and does not, therefore, represent a

24 Ronald S. Landis and José M. Cortina

cross-level effect. In yet other words, it isn't possible for an individual's value of y to be influenced by a characteristic of a group to which that individual belongs!

As another example, consider once again moderated mediation models. At first blush, it would seem that combining mediation, which is well understood, with moderation, which is also well understood, shouldn't present much of a problem. And yet . . .

Consider the model (see Figure 1.1) from Seo, Goldfarb, and Barrett (2010). The cognitive processes box with the dotted line represents an unmeasured mediator of the relationship between decision frame and risk taking. Affect is posited to partially transmit the effect of decision frame onto risk taking. But if the mediator is unmeasured, then what is the operational model? That is, how would we connect decision frame and affect to risk taking? Seo and colleagues (2010) suggest that if the dotted box goes away, then it is replaced by a direct arrow from affect to the line connecting frame to risk as per Figure 1.2 (i.e., an interaction). The case that Seo and colleagues make, however, is one in which affect, like frame, affects cognitive processes, which in turn affect risk taking. The affect-as-moderator interpretation seems to be an artifact of the strange way in which the original figure is represented, that is, with a line from one variable that goes through a box and a line from a different arrow that goes through one boundary for that box in order to intersect with the other line. But what if we make a seemingly superficial change to the original diagram as per Figure 1.3? Now if we remove the mediator, with what are we left? We are left with an additive, two-predictor model as in Figure 1.4. As Holland and colleagues (2014) point out, it is unlikely that anyone would confuse this additive model with a multiplicative one if the original diagram had looked like Figure 1.3.

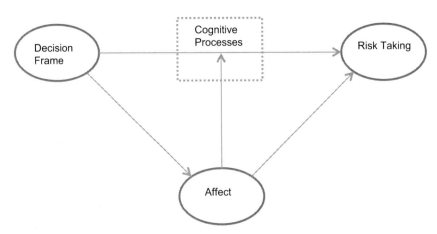

FIGURE 1.1 Cognitive and Affective Processes Underlying the Framing Effect

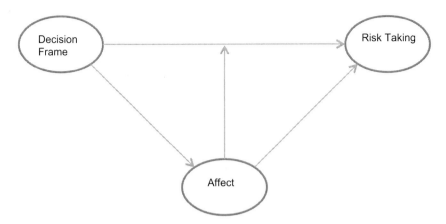

FIGURE 1.2

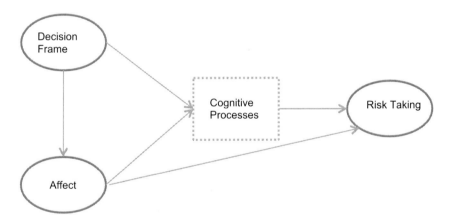

FIGURE 1.3

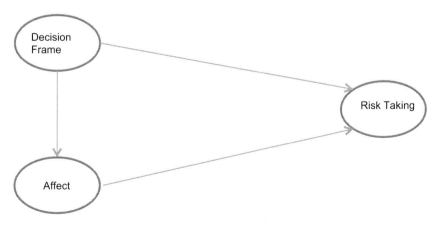

FIGURE 1.4

Never Mind Complexity, How about Specificity?

As Edwards (2010), Edwards and Berry (2010), and many others have pointed out, our propositions are, at best, directional. That is, our hypothesis regarding the connection between X and Y would state either that Y increases as X increases or that Y decreases as X increases. Our theoretical "contributions" come from adding variables such that as X increases, both Y1 and Y2 increase, or that as X increases, M increases, and as M increases, Y increases, or that as partialled XM increases, Y increases. What we don't do is contribute to theory by hypothesizing something more specific than the sign of the relationship.

This has led to what Leavitt, Mitchell, and Peterson (2010) refer to as our dense theoretical landscape. Rather than refining our theories by specifying effect magnitude among existing variables or by stipulating the conditions under which the theory does not hold, we add variables. In particular, we add variables and connect them to existing theories with new directional hypotheses.

It is true that new variables can be used to stipulate boundary conditions. A moderator variable, W, can be introduced such that at certain levels of W, the relationship between X and Y that had been part of the original model no longer holds. This would be an example of what Cortina and Folger (1998) referred to as an embedded null effect, that is, a null effect embedded within an interaction. The difficulty here lies in getting beyond the bias against null effects that has been described by many authors (e.g., Frick, 1995; Greenwald, 1993).

The embedded null also involves stipulation of effect magnitude, which we are loath to do. But why would this be? One very real possibility is that we avoid magnitude hypotheses because they are more difficult to support empirically (Edwards, 2010; Gray & Cooper, 2010). In other words, we avoid the question because we won't like the answer. Does anyone really believe that that is a good way to develop theory?

We Prefer to Infer

We call ourselves psychologists, and yet we eschew any approach to understanding organizational phenomena that actually involves the brain. Brain science might actually help us to get to a point where we can measure the things that we care about with something like the precision with which planetary trajectories can be measured. And yet, it sometimes seems that we prefer to infer.

There have been papers published in our field that explain the benefits of what might be called neuromanagement—or, as Becker and Cropanzano (2010) call it, organizational neuroscience (e.g., Adis & Thompson, 2013; Becker, Cropanzano, & Sanfey, 2011; Volk & Koehler, 2012). The possibilities are endless, and yet our field remains almost entirely skeptical. Some of our skepticism may be warranted, but why would we be so reluctant to pursue research on what we know to be the source of all of the phenomena in which we are interested?

We offer this bit of anecdotal yet shocking evidence of the reluctance of our field to consider brain research. One of the authors of this chapter recently had a review paper on the physiology of sleepiness and its effects on workplace outcomes rejected. That part isn't the least bit shocking, particularly to the author in question, for whom such letters are entirely commonplace. What is shocking is the primary reason for the rejection. Consider this quote from the action letter: "Your manuscript focuses primarily on the physical, biological and psychological consequences of sleep deprivation. It is only tangentially related to management or organizational theory." In other words, the editor, apparently channeling Dilbert, didn't see what the brain had to do with management.

Surely Our Design and Analysis Are Beyond Reproach

As we mentioned earlier, our field has made great strides in the content of our Methods sections. Unfortunately, it seems that our knowledge and skills can't keep pace with our design and analysis needs and desires.

We Say Yes When We Mean No

How often have we seen the Discussion sections of observational studies calling for more experiments? Lab studies calling for more field research? Cross-sectional studies calling for more longitudinal research? Individual-level studies calling for more group-level research? And yet, what happens when reviewers review papers that respond to these calls?

Every research design has its advantages and disadvantages. Lab studies have more control but less fidelity. Longitudinal studies allow one to examine processes unfolding over time but contain the possibility of carryover effects. Group research allows one to capture the interactive nature of the workplace but places inordinate demands on the subject pool. This is not to say that it isn't possible to improve fidelity in lab settings (see Dietz, Bedwell, Oglesby, Salas, & Keeton, 2013) or to minimize carryover effects or to create adequately powered group studies. Rather, we merely wish to point out that if we want the advantages of certain types of design, then we have to be willing to accept their disadvantages as well. Instead, it seems that we often demand the advantages of alternative designs while simultaneously holding them to standards that they cannot meet.

Consider once again the Hebl and colleagues (2007) pregnancy stigma paper mentioned earlier. This field experiment manipulated pregnancy of the confederate by utilizing a pregnancy prosthesis. The details of the interaction between the confederate and a store employee were noted by the confederate, recorded by the confederate, and observed by a second confederate. The results of the study were fascinating. The effect of pregnancy on the interaction depended upon whether the reason for the conversation was interest in employment or retail help. Pregnant

28 Ronald S. Landis and José M. Cortina

women interested in employment were treated coldly. Pregnant women looking for help were drowned in bonhomie.

One of the authors of the present chapter was the action editor for this paper, and he loved it. A multisource field experiment on a sensitive topic with interesting results! He was therefore surprised to see that both reviewers hated the paper. One of their primary complaints was that confederates were not blind to condition. In other words, confederates were aware that they were wearing pregnancy prostheses! Oddly, the authors of the paper were *unable to conceal this fact* (emphasis added for sarcasm) from the confederates, and the reviewers considered this to be a deal breaker.

In the opinion of the action editor, the reviewers were applying to this field experiment the same criteria that they would apply to a low-fidelity, paper people study. And if those are the criteria to be applied, then the result is that researchers don't conduct field experiments in this area because the criteria cannot be met.

There are many, many other examples. Those who conduct research on groups and teams have been held to the same sample size requirements as individual-level studies. Those who explore alternatives to self-report personality measurement because of the flaws inherent in self-report have had their alternative measures criticized because they do not correlate strongly enough with self-report measures. Every method has its strengths and weaknesses. If we want to take advantage of the strengths, then we must put up with the weaknesses.

We Are Stuck in Our Analytic Ways

Although there are ways in which our data analysis techniques have improved, we seem entrenched in the approaches that we (think we) know and stubbornly resistant to novel approaches. We are in the habit of ignoring certain aspects of methodology and emphasizing others without any clear reason for the choice.

Consider approaches such as catastrophe modeling and spline regression. Both deal with discontinuous or at least nonmonotonic change, which has been shown to be ubiquitous in temporal models of performance (e.g., Keil & Cortina, 2001). And yet, we continue to think, and therefore model and study, in monotonic terms (Guastello, 2013).

Consider qualitative methods. Those of us trained in quantitative methods have a hard time getting our heads around qualitative research. It would be difficult to argue against the notion that there is a lot more going on in human interactions than can be captured by the typical set of measures in a quantitative study. Indeed, we would suggest that recent interest in "big data" is driven by the possibility of getting at complexities and subtleties to which we haven't had access in the past. This possibility is what drives qualitative research. The authors of the present chapter admit that we would have a difficult time describing some of the approaches detailed in Denzin and Lincoln's (1998) "Strategies of Qualitative Inquiry" as science. Nevertheless, we would challenge anyone who has read Klein, Ziegert,

Knight, and Xiao (2006) to make the case that nothing of value was discovered in that paper, or that the same amount of wisdom could have been uncovered by a conventional, quantitative approach.

Consider model fit indices. It is almost impossible to publish a paper that includes SEM if the common model fit indices do reach conventional levels. Even if all of the paths that were defended in the Introduction section are substantial in magnitude and statistically significant, reviewers generally consider CFI < .90 or RMSEA > .10 to be deal breakers. And yet, it seems that very few people understand what these fit indices tell us. In fact, this must be true, because if it were not, reviewers would pay these fit indices very little mind! Our fit indices are interpreted as if they told us whether we were correct to include the paths that we included. In other words, they are interpreted as if they told us whether the data support the arguments in the Introduction. Instead, they tell us whether we were correct to exclude the paths that we excluded, a topic that usually takes up not a single word in the Introduction! Some common fit indices contain a small penalty for lack of parsimony (e.g., AGFI), but all of the common ones are driven by omitted paths. Any SEM text explains this simple fact, and yet we as a field continue to use these indices as if they told us what we want them to tell us rather than what they actually do tell us.

While we are on the subject of SEM, consider the degrees-of-freedom values that are attached to fit indices. The habit in our field is to pay these no mind, which is a shame given how often they reveal that the models that we are told are being tested are different from the models actually being tested. Consider a simple CFA model with two correlated latent variables, each with three indicators. This model contains 21 "knowns" (6 observed variances and 15 unique covariances), 13 "unknowns" (6 loadings, 6 error variances, and one latent correlation), and therefore 8 degrees of freedom. But what if the authors report chi-squared or any of its derivatives based on 7 degrees of freedom? The answer is that you now have no way of knowing what model was tested! It is a good bet, however, that the model that was actually tested contains a path that the authors didn't mention, likely a correlation between residual terms, which is almost never justifiable in a cross-sectional model (Landis, Edwards, & Cortina, 2009). We don't yet know how often this occurs, but a first approximation based on an ongoing study is that at least one third of SEM papers published in our top journals contain such a discrepancy!

As another example, consider that fully mediated models are not uncommon in our field, especially those embedded within larger path models. And how do we test for full mediation? We don't. In an ongoing review of moderated mediation papers, Holland and colleagues (2014) found that not a single moderated mediation paper published in *JAP* or *AMJ* in 2010 or 2011 that hypothesized full mediation conducted a formal test of it. Not one. In the same study, it was found that, whereas our field generally recognizes the value of direct paths (i.e., partial mediation) in additive models, we almost always forget to consider them in multiplicative models. Why should it be that additive effects are transmitted by multiple factors but multiplicative effects are transmitted only by single factors? It shouldn't.

Conclusions and Recommendations

The purpose of the present chapter is to encourage researchers in our field to recognize the perception that our science is viewed as soft as a call to arms. We cannot and should not ignore how important audiences (including the public at large, government agencies and personnel, and scientists in other disciplines) view our science. We must take a more active role in shaping these perceptions by better communicating what we do well, refining our theories, testing our theories, adopting stronger research designs, employing more sophisticated data analyses, and being more thoughtful about how we disseminate our research (i.e., publication policies and processes). There are various things that we as researchers can do to improve the image and reality of our field.

- If we want to have a seat at the funding table and greater respect in the scientific and lay communities, we must be stronger scientists and better communicators.
- We mustn't be reluctant to learn from other disciplines. While it is true that our physiological colleagues could learn a lot about measurement and validation from us, we would learn about biology from them.
- Methodological expertise is never permanent. The procedures that are at the cutting edge today are comically flawed tomorrow. We must continue to acquire new methodological skills through resources such as CARMA, and yes, even the interwebs.

On the other hand, researchers are understandably loath to pursue research strategies that are not rewarded by the gatekeepers who decide what does and doesn't get published.

- Our publication process is driven by expectations.
    - If gatekeepers were to publish tests of existing theories, we would conduct them.
    - If gatekeepers rewarded more refined theoretical statements, we will develop them.
    - If gatekeepers were more inclined to publish papers with difficult but messy designs, we would use those designs.
    - If gatekeepers encouraged alternative measurement strategies, we would apply them.
    - If gatekeepers insisted on the most up-to-date analytic tests, we would conduct them.
    - If gatekeepers insist on appropriate application of analytic tests, we would apply them properly.

Whether our field is viewed by others as a hard or soft science is, ultimately, beyond our direct control. Nevertheless, we can and must be more active in increasing and promoting the quality of our research, the rigor by which we pursue our questions, and the clarity through which we communicate our results.

Note

1 The purpose of this chapter is not to get into a discussion of the relative benefits of adopting a particular scientific philosophy (e.g., Fisherian v. Bayesian). We use the term "falsifiability" here to mean that application of the scientific method involves an accumulation of evidence.

References

Adis, C. S., & Thompson, J. C. (2013). A brief primer on neuroimaging methods for industrial/organizational psychology. In J. Cortina & R. Landis (Eds.), *Modern research methods for the study of behavior in organizations* (pp. 405–442). New York, NY: Routledge.

Becker, W. J., & Cropanzano, R. (2010). Organizational neuroscience: The promise and prospects of an emerging discipline. *Journal of Organizational Behavior, 31*, 1055–1059.

Becker, W. J., Cropanzano, R., & Sanfey, A. G. (2011). Organizational neuroscience: Taking organizational theory inside the neural black box. *Journal of Management, 37*, 933–961.

Bliese, P., & Hanges, P. (2004). Being both too liberal and too conservative: The perils of treating grouped data as though they were independent. *Organizational Research Methods, 7*, 400–417.

Bliese, P. D., & Ployhart, R. E. (2002). Growth modeling using random coefficient models: Model building, testing and illustrations. *Organizational Research Methods, 5*, 362–387.

Bou, J. C., & Satorra, A. (2010). A multigroup structural equation approach: A demonstration by testing variation of firm profitability across EU samples. *Organizational Research Methods, 13*, 738–766.

Braun, M. T., Kuljanin, G., & DeShon, R. P. (2013). Spurious relationships in growth curve modeling: The effects of stochastic trends on regression-based models. In J. Cortina & R. Landis (Eds.), *Modern research methods for the study of behavior in organizations* (pp. 161–198). New York, NY: Routledge.

Chen, G. Bliese, P. D. Mathieu, J. E. (2005). Conceptual framework and statistical procedures for delineating and testing multilevel theories of homology. *Organizational Research Methods, 8*, 375–409.

Cheung, G. W. (2008). Testing equivalence in the structure, means, and variances of higher-order constructs with structural equation modeling. *Organizational Research Methods, 11*, 593–613.

Cheung, G. W. (2009). A multiple-perspective approach to data analysis in congruence research. *Organizational Research Methods, 12*, 63–68.

Cheung, G. W., & Lau, R. S. (2008). Testing mediation and suppression effects of latent variables bootstrapping with structural equation models. *Organizational Research Methods, 11*, 296–325.

Cheung, G. W., & Rensvold, R. B. (2001). The effects of model parsimony and sampling error on the fit of structural equation models. *Organizational Research Methods, 4*, 236–264.

32 Ronald S. Landis and José M. Cortina

Cheung, M.W.L. (2007). Comparison of methods of handling missing time-invariant covariates in latent growth models under the assumption of missing completely at random. *Organizational Research Methods, 10,* 609–634.

Cohen, J. (1977). *Statistical power analysis for the behavioral sciences.* San Diego, CA: Academic Press.

Coon, D. J. (1992). Testing the limits of sense and science: American experimental psychologists combat spiritualism. *American Psychologist, 47,* 143–151.

Cortina, J. M., & Chen, G. (2005, April). *Supporting inferences from the observational design.* Paper presented at the 20th annual meeting of the Society for Industrial and Organizational Psychology, Los Angeles, CA.

Cortina, J. M., Chen, G., & Dunlap, W. P. (2001). Testing interaction effects in LISREL: Examination and illustration of available procedures. *Organizational Research Methods, 4,* 324–360.

Cortina, J. M., & Folger, R. G. (1998). When is it acceptable to accept a null hypothesis: No way, Jose? *Organizational Research Methods, 1,* 334–350.

Cortina, J. M., Goldstein, N. B., Payne, S. C., Davison, H. K., & Gilliland, S. W. (2000). The incremental validity of interview scores over and above cognitive ability and conscientiousness scores. *Personnel Psychology, 53,* 325–351.

Cortina, J. M., & Luchman, J. (2012). Personnel selection and employee performance. In S. Highhouse (Ed.), *Industrial and organizational psychology* (Vol. 12 of the *Handbook of psychology*; pp. 143–183). New York, NY: Wiley.

Denzin, N., & Lincoln, Y. (1998). *Strategies of qualitative inquiry.* Thousand Oaks, CA: Sage.

Diamond, J. (1987). *Soft sciences are often harder than hard sciences.* Retrieved online February 2, 2014, from http://bama.ua.edu/~sprentic/607%20Diamond%201987.htm

Dietz, A. S., Bedwell, W. L., Oglesby, J. M., Salas, E., & Keeton, K. E. (2013). Synthetic task environments for improving performance at work: Principles and the road ahead. In J. Cortina & R. Landis (Eds.), *Modern research methods for the study of behavior in organizations* (pp. 349–380). New York, NY: Routledge.

Dimotakis, N., Ilies, R., & Judge, T. A. (2013). Experience sampling methodology. In J. Cortina & R. Landis (Eds.), *Modern research methods for the study of behavior in organizations* (pp. 319–348). New York, NY: Routledge.

Edwards, J. R. (2009). Latent variable modeling in congruence research: Current problems and future directions. *Organizational Research Methods, 12,* 34–62.

Edwards, J. R. (2010). Reconsidering theoretical progress in organizational and management research. *Organizational Research Methods, 13,* 615–619.

Edwards, J. R., & Berry, J. W. (2010). The presence of something or the absence of nothing: Increasing theoretical precision in management research. *Organizational Research Methods, 13,* 668–689.

Edwards, J. R., Berry, J. W., & Kay, V. S. (2013). *Bridging the great divide between theoretical and empirical management research.* Working paper, Kenan-Flagler Business School, University of North Carolina.

Edwards, J. R., & Lambert, L. S. (2007). Methods for integrating moderation and mediation: A general analytical framework using moderated path analysis. *Psychological Methods, 12,* 1–22.

Frick, R. W. (1995). Accepting the null hypothesis. *Memory & Cognition, 23,* 132–138.

Gooty, J., & Yammarino, F. J. (2011). Dyads in organizational research: Conceptual issues and multilevel analyses. *Organizational Research Methods, 14,* 456–483.

Gray, P. H., & Cooper, W. H. (2010). Pursuing failure. *Organizational Research Methods, 13,* 620–643.

Greenwald, A. G. (1993). Consequences of prejudice against the null hypothesis. In G. Keren & C. Lewis (Eds.), *A handbook of data analysis in the behavioral sciences* (pp. 419–460). Hillsdale, NJ: Erlbaum.

Guastello, S. J. (2013). Catastrophe theory and its applications in industrial/organizational psychology. In J. Cortina & R. Landis (Eds.), *Modern research methods for the study of behavior in organizations* (pp. 29–62). New York, NY: Routledge.

Hall, R. J., Snell, A. F., & Foust, M. S. (1999). Item parceling strategies in SEM: Investigating the subtle effects of unmodeled secondary constructs. *Organizational Research Methods, 2*, 233–256.

Hebl, M. R., King, E. B., Glick, P., Singletary, S. L., & Kazama, S. (2007). Hostile and benevolent reactions toward pregnant women: Complementary interpersonal punishments and rewards that maintain traditional roles. *Journal of Applied Psychology, 92*, 1499–1511.

Hedges, L. V. (1987). How hard is hard science, how soft is soft science? The empirical cumulativeness of research. *American Psychologist, 42*, 443–455.

Herrnstein, R. J., & Murray, C. (1994). *The bell curve: Intelligence and class structure in American life.* New York, NY: Free Press.

Holland, S., Shore, D., & Cortina, J. M. (2014). *Moderated mediation: What are we doing and what should we be doing?* Working paper, Department of Psychology, George Mason University.

Howard, G. S. (1993). When psychology looks like a "soft" science, it's for good reason! *Journal of Theoretical and Philosophical Psychology, 13,* 42–47.

Huffcutt, A., & Arthur, W., Jr. (1994). Hunter and Hunter (1984) revisited: Interview validity for entry-level jobs. *Journal of Applied Psychology, 79,* 184–190.

Ilies, R., Scott, B. A., & Judge, T. A. (2006). The interactive effects of personal traits and experienced states on intraindividual patterns of citizenship behavior. *Academy of Management Journal, 49,* 561–575.

International Personality Item Pool: A scientific collaboratory for the development of advanced measures of personality traits and other individual differences (http://ipip.ori.org/). Internet website.

James, L. R. (1998). Measurement of personality via conditional reasoning. *Organizational Research Methods, 1,* 131–163.

James, L. R., & Brett, J. (1984). Mediators, moderators, and tests for mediation. *Journal of Applied Psychology, 69,* 307–321.

James, L. R., Mulaik, S. A., & Brett, J. M. (2006). A tale of two methods. *Organizational Research Methods, 9,* 233–244.

Jones, K. P., King, E. B., Gilrane, V. L., McCausland, T. C., Cortina, J. M., & Grimm, K. J. (2013). The baby bump: Managing a dynamic stigma over time. *Journal of Management.* Advance online publication.

Kacmar, K., & Whitfield, J. (2000) An additional rating method for journal articles in the field of management. *Organizational Research Methods, 3,* 392–406.

Kaplan, A. (1964). *The conduct of inquiry.* New York, NY: Thomas Y. Cromwell, Inc.

Keil, C. T., & Cortina, J. M. (2001). Degradation of validity over time: Test and extension of Ackerman's model. *Psychological Bulletin, 127,* 673–697.

Kilduff, M. (2006). Editor's comments: Publishing theory. *Academy of Management Review, 31,* 252–255.

Kilduff, M. (2007). Editor's comments: The top ten reasons why your paper might not be sent out for review. *Academy of Management Review, 32,* 700–702.

King, E. B., Hebl, M. R., Botsford Morgan, W., & Ahmad, A. S. (2013). Field experiments on sensitive organizational topics. *Organizational Research Methods, 16,* 501–521.

King, E. B., Shapiro, J. L., Hebl, M. R., Singletary, S. L., & Turner, S. (2006). The stigma of obesity in customer service: Remediation strategies and bottom-line consequences of interpersonal discrimination, *Journal of Applied Psychology, 91*, 579–593.

Klein, K. J., Ziegert, J. C., Knight, A. P., & Xiao, Y. (2006). Dynamic delegation: Shared, hierarchical, and deindividualized leadership in extreme action teams. *Administrative Science Quarterly, 51*, 590–621.

Landis, R. S., Beal, D. J., & Tesluk, P. E. (2000). A comparison of approaches to forming composite measures in structural equation models. *Organizational Research Methods, 3*, 186–207.

Landis, R. S., Edwards, B. D., & Cortina, J. M. (2009). On the practice of allowing correlated residuals among indicators in structural equation models. In C. E. Lance & R. J. Vandenberg (Eds.), *Statistical and methodological myths and urban legends* (pp. 193–215). New York, NY: Routledge.

Lane, C. (2012, June 6). Congress should cut funding for political science research. *Washington Post*. Retrieved on May 31, 2013, from www.washingtonpost.com/opinions/congress-should-cut-funding-for-political-science-research/2012/06/04/gJQAuAJMEV_story.html

Leavitt, K., Mitchell, R. R., & Peterson, J. (2010). Theory pruning: Strategies to reduce our dense theoretical landscape. *Organizational Research Methods, 13*, 644–667.

Lemann, N. (1999). *The big test: The secret history of the American meritocracy.* New York, NY: Farrar, Straus, & Giroux.

LePine, J. A., & King, A. W. (2010). Editors' comments: Developing novel theoretical insight from reviews of existing theory and research. *Academy of Management Review, 35*(4), 506–509.

Lievens, F., Peeters, H., & Schollaert, E. (2008). Situational judgment tests: A review of recent research. *Personnel Review, 37*, 426–441.

Lilienfeld, S. O. (2012). Public skepticism of psychology: Why many people perceive the study of human behavior as unscientific. *American Psychologist, 67*, 111–129.

Lipsey, M. W., & Wilson, D. B. (1993). The efficacy of psychological, educational, and behavioral treatment: Confirmation from meta-analysis. *American Psychologist, 48*, 1181–1209.

McCrae, R. R., & Costa, P. T., Jr. (1987). Validation of the five-factor model of personality across instruments and observers. *Journal of Personality and Social Psychology, 52*, 81–90.

Meehl, P. E. (1978). Theoretical risks and tabular asterisks: Sir Karl, Sir Ronald, and the slow progress of soft psychology. *Journal of Consulting and Clinical Psychology, 45*, 806–834.

Meyer, G. J., Finn, S. E., Eyde, L. D., Kay, G. G., Moreland, K. L., Dies, R. R., Eisman, E. J., Kubiszyn, T. W., & Reed, G. M. (2001). Psychological testing and psychological assessment: A review of evidence and issues. *American Psychologist, 56*, 128–165.

Motowidlo, S. J., Hooper, A. C., & Jackson, H. L. (2006). Implicit policies about relations between personality traits and behavioral effectiveness in situational judgment items. *Journal of Applied Psychology, 91*, 749–761.

Nelson, L. A. (2013, March 21). Money for military, not poli sci. *Inside Higher* Ed. Retrieved on January 2, 2014, from www.insidehighered.com/news/2013/03/21/senate-votes-defund-political-science-research-save-tuition-assistance-budget-bill

Nye, C. D., & Drasgow, F. (2011). Assessing goodness of fit: Simple rules of thumb simply do not work. *Organizational Research Methods, 14*, 548–570.

Ployhart, R. E., & Holtz, B. C. (2008). The diversity–validity dilemma: Strategies for reducing racioethnic and sex subgroup differences and adverse impact in selection. *Personnel Psychology, 61*, 153–172.

Ployhart, R. E., & Kim, Y. (2013). Dynamic longitudinal growth modeling. In J. Cortina & R. Landis (Eds.), *Modern research methods for the study of behavior in organizations* (pp. 63–98). New York, NY: Routledge.

Rensvold, R. B., & Cheung, G. W. (1999). Identification of influential cases in structural equation models using the jackknife method. *Organizational Research Methods, 2*, 293–308.

Seo, M.-G., Goldfarb, B., & Barrett, L. F. (2010). Affect and the framing effect within individuals across time: Risk taking in a dynamic investment game. *Academy of Management Journal, 53*, 411–431.

Simonton, D. K. (2004). Psychology's status as a scientific discipline: Its empirical placement within an implicit hierarchy of the sciences. *Review of General Psychology, 8*, 59–67. doi:10.1037/1089-2680.8.1.59

Sutton, R. I., & Staw, B. M. (1995). What theory is not. *Administrative Science Quarterly, 40*, 371–384.

Tay, L., Diener, E., Drasgow, F., & Vermunt, J. K. (2011). Multilevel mixed-measurement IRT analysis: An explication and application to self-reported emotions around the world. *Organizational Research Methods, 14*, 177–207.

Uhlmann, E. L., Leavitt, K., Menges, J. I., Koopman, J., Howe, M., & Johnson, R. E. (2012). Getting explicit about the implicit: A taxonomy of implicit measures and guide for their use in organizational research. *Organizational Research Methods, 15,* 553–601.

Vandenberg, R. J., & Lance, C. E. (2000). A review and synthesis of the measurement invariance literature: Suggestions, practices, and recommendations for organizational research. *Organizational Research Methods, 3*, 4–69.

Van Maanen, J. (1989). Some notes on the importance of writing in organization studies. *Harvard Business School Research Colloquium*, 27–33. Boston: Harvard Business School.

Volk, S., & Koehler, T. (2012). Brains and games: Applying neuroeconomics to organizational research. *Organizational Research Methods, 15*, 522–552.

Wang, M., & Bodner, T. E. (2007). Growth mixture modeling: Identifying and predicting unobserved subpopulations with longitudinal data. *Organizational Research Methods, 10*, 635–656.

Weick, K. E. (1989). Theory construction as disciplined imagination. *Academy of Management Review, 14*, 516–531.

Whetzel, D. L., McDaniel, M. A., & Nguyen, N. T. (2008). Subgroup differences in situational judgment test performance: A meta-analysis. *Human Performance, 21*, 291–309.

Williams, L. J., Hartman, N., & Cavazotte, F. (2010). Method variance and marker variables: A review and comprehensive CFA marker technique. *Organizational Research Methods, 13*, 477–514.

Williams, L. J., & O'Boyle, E. (2011). The myth of global fit indices and alternatives for assessing latent variable relations. *Organizational Research Methods, 14*, 350–369.

Wilson, T. D. (2012, July 12). Stop bullying the "soft" sciences. *Los Angeles Times*. Retrieved on May 31, 2013, from http://articles.latimes.com/2012/jul/12/opinion/la-oe-wilson-social-sciences-20120712

Zhang, Z., Zyphur, M. J., & Preacher, K. J. (2009). Testing multilevel mediation using hierarchical linear models: Problems and solutions. *Organizational Research Methods, 12*, 695–719.

2

PUBLICATION BIAS

Understanding the Myths Concerning Threats to the Advancement of Science

George C. Banks, Sven Kepes and Michael A. McDaniel

Concerns have been raised regarding the extent to which the scientific literature is free from bias (Banks & O'Boyle, 2013; Ioannidis & Doucouliagos, 2013; Kepes & McDaniel, 2013; Schmidt & Hunter, in press). In particular, researchers across scientific fields have been investigating the potential of publication bias as a threat to the advancement of science and evidence-based practice. Publication bias exists to the extent the literature that is publically available is not representative of completed studies on a particular relation of interest (Kepes, Banks, McDaniel, & Whetzel, 2012; Rothstein, Sutton, & Borenstein, 2005). In the organizational sciences, publication bias has most often been investigated by examining the potential for systematic differences between samples that appear in the published or readily accessible literature and those that do not (i.e., sample-level publication bias). In other fields, outcome-level publication bias (i.e., outcome-reporting bias), that is, the selective reporting of results, such as dropping unsupported hypotheses and related results from a manuscript (Kepes & McDaniel, 2013), has also been investigated (McGauran et al., 2010). Consistent with most disciplines, we use the term "publication bias" with reference to both sample-level and outcome-level publication bias.

Publication bias can result in distorted, typically inflated effect size estimates (Kepes et al., 2012; Schmidt & Oh, 2013) as well as theory proliferation (Leavitt, Mitchell, & Peterson, 2010). Both effects harm the advancement of science as well as evidence-based practice (Banks & McDaniel, 2011; Briner & Rousseau, 2011). There is evidence of sample-level publication bias across scientific areas, including medicine (Kicinski, 2013; Sterne et al., 2011; Sutton, 2009), psychology (Ferguson & Brannick, 2012; Kepes & McDaniel, 2013), education (Banks, Kepes, & Banks, 2012), economics (Ioannidis & Doucouliagos, 2013), and in the organizational sciences (Kepes et al., 2012; Kepes, Banks, & Oh, 2014; O'Boyle, Rutherford, &

Banks, in press; Vevea, Clements, & Hedges, 1993). Additionally, evidence of outcome-level publication bias has been documented in medicine (Chan & Altman, 2005; Dwan et al., 2008), sociology and political science (Gerber & Malhotra, 2008a, 2008b), psychology (Simonsohn, Nelson, & Simmons, 2014), and the organizational sciences (McDaniel, Rothstein, & Whetzel, 2006; O'Boyle, Banks, & Gonzalez-Mule, in press). A review of published scientific literature has indicated that the percentage of statistically significant results has increased by more than 22% from 1990 to 2007 (Fanelli, 2012). We suggest that it is likely that publication bias contributed to this increase in published statistically significant results and, in turn, that such results increase the likelihood of future publication bias.

Despite the growing body of publication bias research, several myths exist regarding publication bias. These myths relate to the operational definitions, causes, and approaches to detect and prevent this bias. This chapter reviews some of the myths, discusses the kernel of truth related to each myth, and then offers recommendations for future research.

Myth # 1: Publication Bias Is Concerned with the Availability of All Possible Effect Sizes in All Areas of a Scientific Field

In the typical case of publication bias, studies with small sample sizes and small magnitude effects are suppressed[1] from the published literature because the results are often not statistically significant. This suppression makes these studies difficult to locate when reviewing a literature (Hopewell, Clarke, & Mallett, 2005; Rothstein & Hopewell, 2009). Rothstein and colleagues (2005) defined publication bias as the extent to which "the research that appears in the published literature is systematically unrepresentative of the population of completed studies" (p. 1). To our knowledge, all publication bias studies prior to 2012 focused on relations between specific variables (e.g., an employment test and job performance, the Mozart effect on spatial ability). No one had attempted to declare that entire research literatures (e.g., organizational sciences) were free of or afflicted by publication bias.

In an attempt to investigate publication bias, Dalton, Aguinis, Dalton, Bosco and Pierce (2012) examined correlation matrices of published and unpublished studies and compared the statistical significance of the results in these two types of sources. Having found no difference, the authors stated, "we find that, contrary to the established belief, the file drawer problem is of little, if any, consequence for meta-analytically derived theoretical conclusions and applications in OBHRM [organizational behavior and human resource management], I-O psychology, and related fields" (p. 225). However, we observe a misconception in Dalton and colleagues' (2012) belief regarding what publication bias concerns and suggest that this limitation stems in part from the definition presented by Rothstein and colleagues (2005). Dalton and colleagues (2012) focused on the availability of all possible effect sizes in the management and I-O psychology literatures rather than effect sizes of focal relations. We observe that the Rothstein and colleagues (2005) definition did not

38 George C. Banks et al.

explicitly specify the need to focus on focal relations. Consequently, we suggest that Dalton and colleagues (2012) misunderstood the publication bias literature and created confusion regarding how publication bias is operationally defined and assessed. Specifically, they created a myth that publication bias is concerned with the availability of all possible effect sizes in a scientific field rather than specific focal relations.

Kernel of Truth

The kernel of truth to this myth is that publication bias is often concerned with the availability of effect sizes based on their statistical significance. Yet publication bias is concerned with the availability of effect sizes on specific relations of interest (Banks & O'Boyle, 2013; Kepes & McDaniel, 2013). In fact, Dalton and colleagues (2012) acknowledged this limitation in their work and stated,

> we have not, however, established this phenomenon at the focal level. Our data do not provide an insight into whether such comparisons would maintain for studies—published and non-published—particularly focused on, for example, the 'Big Five' personality traits or employee withdrawal behaviors (e.g., absenteeism, transfers, and turnover).
>
> *(p. 244)*

Due to this limitation, they were unable, for example, to differentiate the variables from the correlation matrices that were dependent, independent, control, or moderator variables. This is important to consider because publication bias is more likely to emerge when some of the *hypothesized* relations are not found to be statistically significant (Kepes, McDaniel, Banks, Hurtz, & Donovan, 2011; Kepes, McDaniel, Brannick, & Banks, 2013). In sum, we assert that inferences cannot be made about the extent to which publication bias is or is not a problem based on the evidence provided by Dalton and colleagues (2012).

We note that meta-analytic reviews in the organizational sciences may not exclusively focus on relations that were explicitly of interest in the primary study. For example, Hunter and Schmidt (2004) explained that

> many meta-analyses focus on questions that were not central to the primary studies from which data are taken. For example, sex differences (in traits, abilities, attitudes, etc.) are rarely the central focus of a study; instead, they tend to be reported on an incidental basis, as supplementary analysis. Hence, these results tend not to be subject to publication bias because they are close to irrelevant to the central hypotheses.
>
> *(p. 497)*

As a result, there may be instances when publication bias is less likely to occur because the relations of interest for a meta-analysis were not the sole or major focus of the primary studies. Nonetheless, there is no existing evidence that indicates the frequency with which meta-analyses address questions that were not central to primary studies. Conversely, it is reasonable to assert that most meta-analyses are conducted on variables that were central to the hypotheses of primary research studies (Kepes et al., 2012).

Sorting Truth from Fiction

Publication bias involves the systematic suppression of effect sizes that are of interest to the research community. Consequently, the original definition of publication bias by Rothstein and colleagues (2005) may be refined to avoid confusion. Publication bias can be described as the extent to which research available to a reviewer is systematically unrepresentative of the population of completed studies on a specific relation of interest. Thus, investigations into the existence of publication bias studies should be focused on focal relations.

For example, Gerber and Malhotra (2008a, 2008b) examined the potential for an abundance of p-values just below the .05 threshold necessary to achieve statistical significance by the traditional standard. To accomplish this, these researchers coded p-values that were associated with hypothesized relations. Thus, they did not look at the statistical significance of variables that were not hypothesized to be correlated. The authors concluded that publication bias likely exists in the most methodologically rigorous journals within sociology and political science.

As another example, for 142 studies, O'Boyle, Banks, and Gonzalez-Mule (in press) investigated the chrysalis effect, which describes how dissertations undergo a metamorphosis from unpublished manuscripts to published journal articles. The authors focused specifically on hypothesized relations, and their results showed that the ratio of supported to unsupported hypotheses more than doubled (.82 to 1.00 versus 1.94 to 1.00) in the transition from a dissertation to journal article. This finding provided explicit and compelling evidence of outcome-level publication bias. Similarly, Bosco, Field, and Pierce (2012) found that mean correlations were noticeably larger when variable pairs were hypothesized to relate rather than not expected to relate. Combined, these studies demonstrate that publication bias clearly exists in the organizational science literatures, although it may not be present in all topics in the literature (Bosco et al., 2012; Gerber & Malhotra, 2008a, 2008b).

In meta-analytic reviews, sensitivity analyses should be used to estimate the extent of publication bias on relations of interest. A sensitivity analysis assesses the degree to which changes in analyses or included data influence results and conclusions (Greenhouse & Iyengar, 2009); publication bias analyses are best viewed as sensitivity analyses. To the degree that results and conclusions are not affected by publication bias, one can describe the results as robust. In the social sciences, publication bias findings have ranged from minimal or no bias (Banks et al., 2014; Chiaburu, Peng, Oh, Banks, & Lomeli, 2013; Harrison et al., in press; Kepes et al., 2012; Kepes et al., 2014) to more moderate and extreme cases of potential bias (e.g., Ferguson & Brannick, 2012; McDaniel, McKay, & Rothstein, 2006; McDaniel, Rothstein, & Whetzel, 2006; O'Boyle, Rutherford, & Banks, in press; Whetzel, 2006). For example, research that examined the relation between leader-member exchange (LMX) and team-member exchange (TMX) has shown little to no evidence of publication bias (Banks et al., 2014). Conversely, work in the field of entrepreneurship showed a strong likelihood of publication bias when examining the innovation-firm performance relationship (O'Boyle, Rutherford, & Banks, in press). Similarly, investigations into the possibility of publication bias in the natural sciences have always (to our knowledge) focused on specific relations of interest rather than the availability of all possible effect sizes (e.g., Blackwell, Thompson, & Refuerzo, 2009; Curfman, Morrissey, & Drazen, 2006; Song et al., 2010; Turner, Matthews, Linardatos, Tell, & Rosenthal, 2008).

In sum, the detection, evaluation, and prevention of publication bias should focus on relations of interest. The extent to which publication bias is a problem likely varies across research topics with large bias in some areas, moderate bias in others, and minimal or no bias in the remaining areas (Dickersin, 2005; Rothstein et al., 2005; Schmidt & Hunter, 2014). Hence the conclusion by Dalton and colleagues (2012) that "our results indicate that the methodological practice of estimating the extent to which results are not vulnerable to the file drawer problem may be eliminated" (p. 243) is clearly wrong. Sensitivity analyses to evaluate the presence and magnitude of publication bias are warranted (American Psychological Association, 2008, 2010; Borenstein, Hedges, Higgins, & Rothstein, 2009; Kepes et al., 2013; O'Boyle, Rutherford, & Banks, in press; Schmidt & Hunter, 2014). If the possibility of publication bias is investigated in a specific research topic, and no publication bias is found, we can have greater confidence in the robustness of the results. Such findings can only increase our confidence in the robustness of meta-analytic results and the trustworthiness of our cumulative scientific knowledge (Kepes et al., 2014; Kepes & McDaniel, 2013; McDaniel, Rothstein, & Whetzel, 2006).

Myth #2: The Editorial Review Process Is the Primary Cause of Publication Bias

There is also a myth related to the potential causes of publication bias. Specifically, there is a common misconception that editors and reviewers are the primary cause of publication bias. However, in the context of the medical literature, Dickersin (2005) wrote, "despite the consistent findings that only a small fraction of studies are not published because they are turned down by journals, investigators have persisted in naming bias at the editorial level as the main reason why negative or null results are not published" (p. 21; see also Chalmers & Dickersin, 2013). Hence, authors may be the primary cause of publication bias.

Kernel of Truth

There is a kernel of truth to this myth, as it is likely that editors and reviewers may have predispositions to reject manuscripts that contain mixed or statistically nonsignificant results. Evidence suggests that reviewers in the social sciences may be biased by positive results in that they are more likely to recommend that a manuscript with statistically significant findings be published compared to the same manuscript without statistically significant findings (e.g., Epstein, 1990; Mahoney, 1977). Anecdotal evidence also suggests that rejection letters often state that papers are being rejected because the hypotheses were not supported. Recently, Emerson and colleagues (2010) found similar results and illustrated that reviewers were more likely to be critical of research methods and to find purposefully planted errors within a manuscript when the results were negative. Thus, the body of evidence indicates that editors and reviewers do play a role in the existence of publication bias.

Additionally, investigations indicate the existence of a type of bias referred to as *outlet bias*. This bias can be described "as occurring when the place of publication is associated with the direction or strength of the study findings" (Song et al., 2010, p. 3). It appears that studies submitted to higher-quality journals may be more likely to be accepted if they contain a high percentage of supported hypotheses (i.e., statistically significant results). Findings from the natural sciences, such as studies in ecology and medicine, suggest that primary studies with predominantly statistically significant results are more likely to be published in higher-impact journals (Easterbrook, Gopalan, Berlin, & Matthews, 1991; Etter & Stapleton, 2009; Murtaugh, 2002).

However, there is also evidence in the medical literature that editors and reviewers may not be responsible for much of the publication bias. One study considered 745 manuscripts submitted to the *Journal of the American Medical Association* (Olson et al., 2002). The investigators concluded that there was no meaningful difference in the likelihood of publication between those studies with positive findings compared to those with negative results. Although there is some evidence that both editors and reviewers contribute to the existence of publication bias, it appears that authors are the primary cause of publication bias (Chalmers & Dickersin, 2013; Dickersin, 2005).

Sorting Truth from Fiction

Research indicates that authors are more likely to submit their studies to a journal if the findings are statistically significant (Kepes & McDaniel, 2013; Schmidt & Hunter, 2014). Clearly, authors have a greater opportunity to engage in practices that result in publication bias prior to the peer-review process (Chalmers & Dickersin, 2013). Banks and McDaniel (2011) detailed nine reasons that authors or organizations may not want to submit a study to the peer-review process (see also Kepes et al., 2014). For instance, the findings of one's study might not be statistically significant or the results may be contrary to theory or past findings. Authors may not submit such a

42 George C. Banks et al.

study and instead submit other studies that they believe have a greater chance of acceptance in a journal (i.e., studies with statistically significant results).

When authors are focused on submitting studies with results they believe have the best chance of being published (i.e., studies with significant results; Hartshorne & Schachner, 2012; Sterling & Rosenbaum, 1995), the authors cause publication bias by not submitting manuscripts with statistically nonsignificant results. Additionally, because organizational researchers typically test multiple hypotheses using multiple variables, authors may only report those with statistically significant findings (Kepes & McDaniel, 2013; O'Boyle, Banks, & Gonzalez-Mule, in press). For example, McDaniel, Rothstein, and Whetzel (2006) found that an employment test vendor, with a test product that yields multiple scale scores, reported the validity for some scales for a given sample but not for other scales for the same sample. This reporting practice is consistent with an inference of outcome-level publication bias designed to suppress small-magnitude results.

Evidence from psychological research also indicated that authors are likely to be the primary cause of publication bias (e.g., Greenwald, 1975). Cooper, DeNeve, and Charlton (1997) examined author behavior concerning 117 completed studies. Of these studies, approximately 62% had statistically significant results and 50% of these were submitted for peer review to conferences compared to just 7% of the studies with statistically nonsignificant findings. In terms of submissions for publication, those with statistically significant results were submitted 74% of the time compared to just 4% for studies with statistically nonsignificant findings. Consequently, it is clear that authors often engage in practices that result in publication bias.

In summary, evidence suggests that editors and reviewers are one cause of publication bias (Emerson et al., 2010; Epstein, 1990; Mahoney, 1977). However, authors are likely to be the primary cause of this bias (Chalmers & Dickersin, 2013; Cooper et al., 1997; Dickersin, 2005; Greenwald, 1975) because they have control over their data and decide whether a manuscript based on that data is submitted to a journal (Banks & McDaniel, 2011). If reviewers elect to reject a study because the results are not statistically significant, authors can resubmit their study to another journal or attempt to find other means to disseminate their results. Authors likely make the accurate assumption (Kepes & McDaniel, 2013) that editors and reviewers have a preference for positive results because such results are newsworthy (Dickersin, 2005). Thus, papers with mostly statistically nonsignificant results may never be disseminated, yielding publication bias and an overestimation of effect magnitude in our published literature.

Myth #3: The Failsafe N and Subgroup Comparisons Are the Best Publication Bias Detection Techniques

Until now, we have explored myths stemming from the definition of publication bias and the potential causes of this bias. We now consider myths related to how publication bias may be detected and prevented. There are numerous tests that can be used to detect the potential presence and influence of publication bias. However, evidence suggests that from 2005 to 2010, only 31% of meta-analytic reviews in the organizational sciences tested for the possibility of publication bias (Banks, Kepes, & McDaniel, 2012; Kepes et al., 2012). Furthermore, when such tests were performed, the failsafe N and the subgroup comparison by data source (e.g., published vs. unpublished) were the two most popular techniques. However, neither of these methods allows for an adequate assessment of publication bias (Becker, 1994, 2005; Evans, 1996). In brief, the majority of meta-analytic reviews in the organizational sciences do not consider the threat of publication bias and, when considered, authors use methods that are arguably the least effective at evaluating the presence of this bias and do not assess the magnitude of the bias.

Given the widespread use of the failsafe N and subgroup comparisons by data source, there appears to be a belief that these methods are adequate techniques to assess the potential threat of publication bias. There are some kernels of truth behind this belief. After a brief review of these truths, we will present a summary of the current state of the literature that includes a discussion of recommended techniques for evaluating the presence of publication bias in meta-analytic reviews.

Kernel of Truth

The failsafe N was first introduced by Rosenthal (1979) as a means to examine the possibility of publication bias. The failsafe N procedure purports to estimate the number of statistically nonsignificant effect sizes that would be needed to make a statistically significant meta-analytic mean effect size statistically nonsignificant. Hence, the kernel of truth is that the failsafe N was the first offered technique to detect the presence of publication bias. The method was offered to address the concern that the conclusion of a meta-analytic review could change if a large number of missing, statistically nonsignificant results were obtained and added to the review. Thus, Rosenthal proposed the following question: If a statistically significant meta-analytic result was obtained, how many more effect sizes would be needed to reduce it to a point of statistical nonsignificance (i.e., nullify the result)? If the number of additional effect sizes was small, one might have cause for concern. If the number was large, one could be more confident that the meta-analytic mean effect size magnitude was not meaningfully influenced by publication bias.

McDaniel and colleagues (2006) provided an example of the limited utility of the failsafe N using a scenario in which an employer must choose between two different employment selection tests (Tests A and B), each measuring the same construct. For Test A, the mean validity is .25 compared to a mean validity of .20 for Test B. McDaniel and colleagues (2006) explained that, all else being equal (cost, ease of administration, etc.), the employer might select to use Test A if one assumes no publication bias. However, as noted by McDaniel and colleagues, "Knowing that it takes 80 file drawer studies to nullify the validity of Test A and

44 George C. Banks et al.

100 file drawer studies to nullify the validity of Test B does not help to determine the validity of the tests in the absence of publication bias" (2006, p. 930). As such, the failsafe N provides no useful information concerning the validity of the two tests and does not inform the decision concerning which test to use.

Several reviews have described the substantial limitations of the failsafe N (Becker, 1994, 2005; Evans, 1996). Here, we draw largely on Becker (2005). The first limitation is that the failsafe N is based on the improbable assumption that all missing effect sizes are zero in magnitude. Second, the failsafe N focuses on the statistical significance of meta-analytic estimates and ignores the magnitude of the effect size, which is of greater importance. Third, different approaches yield widely varying estimates of the failsafe N. Fourth, no statistical criteria are available to assist in interpretation. Fifth, the failsafe N does not incorporate sample size information. To address limitations of the failsafe N, modifications have been offered (Orwin, 1983), but these modifications do not improve the effectiveness of the technique substantially (Becker, 2005; Higgins & Green, 2011). In sum, Becker (2005, p. 111) suggested that "the failsafe N should be abandoned in favor of other more informative analyses." Despite all the evidence against the use of failsafe N, editors and reviewers in organizational science journals often recommend its use.

Similarly, the subgroup comparison has been used as a means to evaluate the presence of publication bias. For instance, Schmidt and colleagues (1985) compared published and unpublished samples to determine if published samples reported more statistically significant results than those samples that were unpublished. Similarly, Lipsey and Wilson (1993) and McKay and McDaniel (2006) reported mean effect size estimates by data source. Thus, the kernel of truth concerning the use of the subgroup comparison is that one can sometimes find mean effect size differences between published and unpublished samples. The limitation of a subgroup comparison is that it only provides an estimate of the difference between *identified published* and *identified unpublished* samples. Thus, the analysis is based on the assumption that all samples with relevant effect sizes, published and unpublished, have been identified and included in the meta-analysis. This is improbable in the social sciences (Hopewell et al., 2005; Kepes et al., 2012) and particularly improbable for unpublished samples (Ferguson & Brannick, 2012). Finally, publication bias can be in the same direction or in opposite directions in effect size distributions subset by data source (Kepes et al., 2014).

Sorting Truth from Fiction

The truth is that the failsafe N should never be used for publication bias analyses, and the comparison by data source is a suboptimal test of publication bias. We do not discourage the use of data source comparisons (e.g., published vs. unpublished), but the analyses should be supplemented with methods that permit clearer inferences about the extent and magnitude of publication bias (e.g., Banks et al., 2014; Kepes et al., 2012). More advanced methods, used in combination to triangulate the

Publication Bias **45**

results, are recommended (Kepes et al., 2012; Kepes et al., 2014). These methods include contour-enhanced funnel plots (Palmer, Peters, Sutton, & Moreno, 2008; Peters, Sutton, Jones, Abrams, & Rushton, 2008; Sterne et al., 2011), trim and fill (Duval, 2005; Duval & Tweedie, 2000a, b), cumulative meta-analysis (Borenstein et al., 2009; McDaniel, 2009), and selection models (Hedges & Vevea, 2005; Vevea & Woods, 2005). We describe each in the following sections.

Funnel Plots

A funnel plot is used to illustrate graphically the magnitude of an effect size plotted along an X axis relative to precision (inverse of a sample's standard error) presented along a Y axis (see Figure 2.1). In homogenous distributions of effect sizes (i.e., distributions in which effect size variation is solely due to random sampling error), effect sizes from large samples have less random sampling error (i.e., greater precision) on average and tend to cluster at the top of the funnel plot around the estimated mean. Conversely, smaller samples with greater random sampling error (i.e., less precision) tend to vary more widely. In the absence of heterogeneous variance (e.g., variance due to moderators), the distribution of samples in the funnel plot will be symmetrical (see Figure 2.1a; Sterne, Gavaghan, & Egger, 2005). In the event that publication bias has suppressed small-magnitude effects, small samples with results that are statistically nonsignificant will be absent, resulting in an asymmetric distribution (see Figure 2.1b).

Funnel plot asymmetry due to heterogeneity (i.e., variance not due to random sampling error) is possible and may distort conclusions concerning publication bias. Any form of heterogeneity can cause problems when drawing inferences concerning publication bias analyses, but a heterogeneity cause (e.g., moderator) that covaries with sample size is particularly problematic. For example, small-sample studies may use more reliable measures (e.g., biological markers of strain associated with work stress) yielding larger-magnitude effects, but large-sample studies may rely on self-report measures, yielding smaller-magnitude effects. In this scenario, effect size will likely be correlated with sample size, resulting in funnel plot asymmetry that may be mistaken for publication bias. Thus, it is recommended that publication bias tests be used within more homogeneous subgroups or that techniques such as meta-regression be used (Kepes et al., 2012).

Although the suppression of small-magnitude effects is likely to be the most common scenario in data affected by publication bias, asymmetry may be due to suppression of large-magnitude effects. In these circumstances, effect size suppression may occur when large-magnitude effects are socially uncomfortable to report, such as with age, race, or sex differences (McDaniel, McKay, & Rothstein, 2006; Tate & McDaniel, 2008). To help differentiate asymmetry due to heterogeneity from asymmetry due to publication bias, one can use contour-enhanced funnel plots. These plots incorporate contour lines that correspond to commonly used values of statistical significance (i.e., $p < .05$ and $p < .10$), which aids in

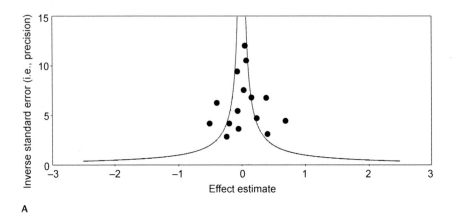

A

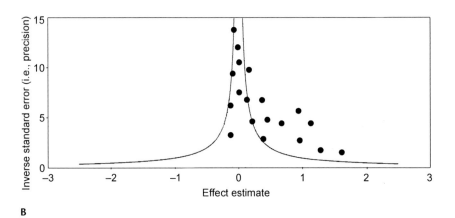

B

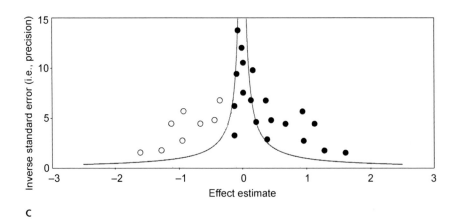

C

FIGURE 2.1 Exemplar funnel plots

distinguishing publication bias from other causes of funnel plot asymmetry (Kepes et al., 2012; Peters et al., 2008; Sterne et al., 2011).

Trim and Fill

The trim and fill technique evaluates the symmetry of funnel plot distributions and seeks to estimate the magnitude of the mean effect if the assumed suppressed studies were present. When the funnel plot distribution is asymmetric (e.g., small-sample, small-magnitude effect sizes are missing from a distribution), the trim and fill procedure "trims" effect sizes from the nonskewed side in the funnel plot in an iterative approach until a symmetrical distribution is achieved. A new mean based on this trimmed distribution is calculated. Next, trimmed effect sizes are returned to the distribution and a set of imputed effect sizes is added to the distribution to achieve symmetry (see Figure 2.1c) around the new mean. At the conclusion of this process, one has the mean of the original effect size distribution and the mean of a distribution containing both the original effect sizes and the imputed effected sizes (sometimes called the trim and fill adjusted distribution). To the extent that the two means are different, one can infer the degree or magnitude of the publication bias.

Kepes and colleagues (2012) developed decision rules that can be adopted to judge the importance of the magnitude of the difference in means (McDaniel, Rothstein, & Whetzel, 2006; Rothstein et al., 2005). For example, small or no differences between the original meta-analytic estimates and the adjusted estimates may be interpreted as minimal to no evidence for publication bias. Specifically, one might declare that less than a .05 absolute change and less than a 20% relative change in the mean estimates suggest that publication bias is at most minimal. One might interpret moderate publication bias if there is at least a .05 absolute change and more than a 20% relative change but less than 40% in the meta-analytic estimate. Finally, if there is a large-magnitude difference between the original meta-analytic estimate and the adjusted estimate, one might conclude that an extreme case of publication bias exists. One might interpret that there is a large degree of publication bias if there is at least a .05 absolute change and at least a 40% relative change in the meta-analytic estimate. These or other decision rules could be used for specific research efforts (see Kepes et al., 2012; Kepes et al., 2014).

Some cautions are necessary concerning trim and fill analyses. Given the effect size imputation, it is unwise to interpret the mean of the trim and fill adjusted distribution as the "true" estimate of the mean effect. Rather, one compares the difference between the two means as a sensitivity test to judge the likelihood of bias stemming from effect size suppression. Trim and fill also assumes that the effect sizes are homogeneous (e.g., no moderators are present), and the method is not robust to violations of this assumption (Terrin, Schmid, Lau, & Olkin, 2003). Trim and fill would best be used on subdistributions in which moderators are largely controlled. One could also consider a meta-regression procedure (Weinhandl & Duval, 2012) that controls for variance due to moderators and then applies trim and fill to the residuals.

48 George C. Banks et al.

Also, trim and fill can be combined with the contour-enhanced funnel plot. If the imputed effect sizes are not statistically significant, one can infer publication bias due to suppression of statistically nonsignificant effect sizes. If the imputed studies are statistically significant, one should look for a small sample effect (Kepes et al., 2012; Kepes et al., 2014; Peters et al., 2008).

Selection Models

Selection models (Hedges & Vevea, 2005; Vevea & Woods, 2005) are another technique to detect publication bias and have a different set of assumptions than methods that rely on funnel plot symmetry. Selection models allow one to examine how meta-analytic results may be affected by selection processes that are influenced by study characteristics, typically statistical significance. When a meta-analysis does not consider the possibility that publication bias is present, one is making the assumption that one has 100% of all extant effect sizes in the meta-analysis and, thus, that no bias is present. Selection models, as typically applied, assume that the probability of a sample being observed (i.e., included in the meta-analysis) depends to some extent on the statistical significance of the effect size. Selection models then reweight effect sizes based on their statistical significance.

In the organizational sciences, a priori selection models are typically used (Hedges & Vevea, 2005; Kepes et al., 2012; Vevea & Woods, 2005). As an example, when operating under the assumption of moderate publication bias, an effect size with a p-value in the range of .000 to .005 can be assigned a 100% probability of being included in a meta-analysis (a weight of 1.0). Conversely, an effect size with a p-value that falls within the range of .500 to .650 might only have a 60% probability of being observed and hence would be assigned a weight of .60 (for a complete list of proposed weights under moderate and severe assumptions of publication bias, see Table 5 in Vevea & Woods, 2005). After assigning weights to effect sizes based on their statistical significance, an adjusted meta-analytic effect size estimate is calculated. As with the trim and fill analysis, the difference between the original adjusted mean estimates allows inferences regarding the potential effects of publication bias on the original mean estimate. Thus, the same decision rules can be applied to judge the degree of publication bias (see Kepes et al., 2012). Vevea and Wood (2005) reported that selection models are relatively robust to effect size heterogeneity.

Cumulative Meta-analysis

Cumulative meta-analysis is a technique that requires one to sort a set of effect sizes based on a characteristic of interest. A set of meta-analyses is then calculated in an iterative process whereby effect sizes are added one at a time to the analysis, each time calculating a new mean estimate. When used as a publication bias analysis, one sorts effect sizes by precision as illustrated in Figure 2.2. Thus, the most precise

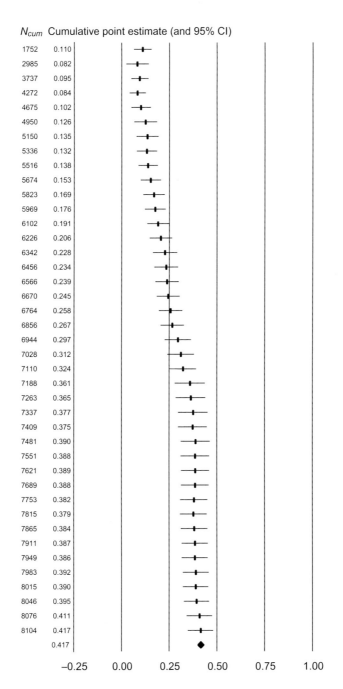

FIGURE 2.2 Exemplar cumulative meta-analysis

50 George C. Banks et al.

sample is added first, followed by the second most precise sample and so forth. The mean effect size estimates calculated at each step can be illustrated in a forest plot. Evidence of "drift" in a forest plot is consistent with an inference of publication bias. In the typical case of publication bias in which small-sample, small-magnitude effect sizes have been suppressed, the plot of cumulative mean estimates drifts to the right (the mean effect size gets larger as less-precise effects are iteratively added to the distribution). Decision rules are needed to determine the severity of the drift (Kepes et al., 2012). For example, one might compare the five most precise samples to the final cumulative mean estimate or the cumulative mean estimate of the most- and least-precise samples (e.g., the 25% most- and least-precise samples; Kepes et al., 2012) and examine the magnitude of the difference. Alternatively, one can compare the cumulative means at fixed intervals (e.g., every 10th mean) or at fixed intervals of cumulative sample size (e.g., compare the means at cumulative samples based on 5,000 observations versus 10,000 observations).

Other Methods

Other publication bias methods are available, including Egger's test of the intercept (Egger, Smith, Schneider, & Minder, 1997) and Begg and Mazumdar's (1994) rank correlation test. Yet, because of their low statistical power and related statistical concerns, Kepes and colleagues (2012) did not recommended their use for every examination of publication bias.

Triangulation

As with all statistical techniques, the methods to detect and adjust for publication bias are only as good as their underlying assumptions. If assumptions are inaccurate, any method may reach erroneous results (Ioannidis, 2008). Nonetheless, if one does not use sensitivity analyses to test for the potential of publication bias, one runs the risk of making the false assumption that publication bias is not an issue and this assumption is not tested in any form (Vevea & Woods, 2005). Consequently, we recommend that researchers test for publication bias in all meta-analyses using multiple publication bias detection techniques that rely on different assumptions.

The use of multiple publication bias methods is a form of triangulation (Kepes et al., 2012; Kepes et al., 2014). Triangulation can be defined as the use of "multiple reference points to locate an object's exact position" (Jick, 1979, p. 602). In management research, triangulation characterizes the use of multiple study designs, settings, samples, and methods to investigate a particular phenomenon (Sackett & Larson, 1990). The use of multiple publication bias methods triangulates conclusions concerning publication bias in that one obtains multiple publication bias results using methods that do not necessarily share the same assumptions (Ferguson & Brannick, 2012; Kepes et al., 2012; Kepes et al., 2014). For example, some methods use asymmetry to inform inferences of publication bias, while other methods use the magnitude of mean differences or drift in cumulative meta-analysis to inform inferences.

Future research should attempt to better understand the influence of artifactual variance (e.g., measurement error, range restriction) as well as outliers on the robustness of the various publication bias techniques. Relatedly, more research is needed to address the effect of heterogeneity in publication bias analyses. In addition, more work is needed to examine the effects of outcome-level publication bias on meta-analytic estimates (Biemann, 2013; Hahn, Williamson, Hutton, Garner, & Flynn, 2000; Kirkham, Riley, & Williams, 2011; Williamson & Gamble, 2007). However, the best approach to mitigate publication bias is to engage in practices to prevent publication bias from occurring in the first place. We conclude this chapter by discussing a myth related to the prevention of publication bias.

Myth #4: Publication Bias May Not Be of Concern in the Social Sciences because It Is Prevented by Reporting Correlation Matrices, Testing Multiple Hypotheses, and Conducting Systematic Searches in Meta-analytic Reviews

Despite the fact that empirical evidence for the presence of publication bias has been found in virtually all scientific fields where it has been investigated, it has been suggested that publication bias may not be as much of a concern in the organizational sciences (Dalton et al., 2012; Hunter & Schmidt, 2004). Based on the publication bias research conducted to date, Schmidt has changed his position on publication bias and now considers it a topic that should be addressed (Schmidt & Hunter, 2014). The assertion that publication bias is not a concern in the organizational sciences is in part drawn from the observation that studies published in organizational science journals typically report correlation matrices and test multiple hypotheses. The argument is also based on assertions that the results are less likely to depend on the statistical significance of an individual outcome and that unpublished studies can be identified through systematic searches. Thus, it is assumed that statistically nonsignificant effect sizes are still available in the publically available literature and, as a result, a myth has emerged that publication bias may not be of concern in the social sciences.

Kernel of Truth

The kernel of truth is that some practices can reduce the potential for publication bias. Correlation matrices allow researchers to report multiple relations, and, in particular, relations that may not have been the main focus of a primary study. However, many, perhaps most, meta-analyses draw data from studies where the research question addressed in the meta-analysis is a central part of "interesting" hypotheses in primary studies (Kepes et al., 2012), such as job satisfaction, personality traits, transformational leadership, leader-member exchange (LMX), and predictors of individual- and firm-level performance. Thus, assertions that meta-analyses concern relations between variables tangential to the main focus of the primary studies are often likely incorrect (Kepes et al., 2012).

Additionally, in the organizational sciences, researchers typically test multiple hypotheses, unlike, for instance, in medical research. This practice makes it less likely that authors are dependent upon the success of any one hypothesis. Hence, researchers may not have their paper rejected because of a lack of support for any one particular hypothesis. When testing multiple hypotheses, at least some hypotheses may be supported by chance. As a result, it may be uncommon that a researcher does not have any statistically significant findings to report. Testing of multiple hypotheses may make it easier for some null results to be published, but it may not completely eliminate publication bias. For example, O'Boyle and colleagues (in press) found that recent doctoral graduates showed a strong preference for eliminating unsupported hypotheses from their dissertation studies and a strong preference for adding supported hypotheses post hoc before submitting their dissertation study for publication. These researchers also appeared to engage in practices such as adding and deleting data as well as adding and removing variables in order to turn unsupported hypotheses into supported ones. Additionally, researchers sometimes collect data using multiple operationalizations of the same variables and may only report the variables and relations that were statistically significant. These examples illustrate outcome-level publication bias. When unsupported hypotheses are dropped and others are added post hoc with a preference for statistically significant results, biased correlation matrices get published (Biemann, 2013). Consequently, neither the use of correlation matrices nor the practice of testing multiple hypotheses is likely to prevent publication bias, although they may reduce it to some degree.

Additionally, it is asserted that a thorough systematic search can be used to identify unpublished studies that should be included in a meta-analytic review. By identifying and including effect sizes from unpublished studies, it has been suggested that meta-analytic reviews can overcome the threat of publication bias (Hopewell et al., 2005; Hunter & Schmidt, 2004; Rothstein & Hopewell, 2009). Thus, identifying unpublished samples (i.e., their effect sizes) and including them in a meta-analytic review can be considered a best practice that should be encouraged (Rothstein, 2012). However, it is difficult to conclude that even the most thorough systematic searches will identify all unpublished samples or a representative sample of them. For example, Ferguson and Brannick (2012) observed that unpublished samples in meta-analyses are often from the authors that conducted the meta-analysis. Although it is appropriate to include such unpublished samples, it is not credible to suggest that a meta-analytic study contains all unpublished samples or that the identified and included samples are representative of all unpublished samples. Also, even when relevant unpublished samples can be identified, the authors of such samples may be unable or unwilling to share the studies (e.g., Banks, Batchelor, & McDaniel, 2010; Banks et al., 2014; McDaniel & Kepes, in press).

Sorting out Truth from Fiction

A systematic search is unlikely to identify *all* samples with relevant effect sizes (Hopewell et al., 2005), nor do the reporting of correlation matrices and testing of multiple hypotheses eliminate the suppression of entire samples or even individual outcomes (Sutton & Pigott, 2005). Correlation matrices, testing multiple hypotheses, and systematic searches of the literature are means to reduce the potential presence of publication bias. However, such steps cannot completely prevent this bias from being a concern in the organizational sciences. In the last section of this chapter, we briefly describe steps that can be implemented to prevent such publication bias from occurring.

Recommendations for Preventing Publication Bias

Honor Codes

Honor codes are a potential means to reduce outcome-level publication bias (i.e., outcome-reporting bias). If journals were to implement an honor code, they would ask authors submitting a paper for review to sign a statement acknowledging that they did not engage in any questionable research practices (QRPs; e.g., O'Boyle, Banks, & Gonzalez-Mule, in press). In the event that authors did engage in QRPs, they would have the opportunity to acknowledge the QRP and disclose the practice and the logic behind it. QRPs include adding and dropping hypotheses from a study with a preference for those with statistically significant results. QRPs also include adding data (to increase statistical power) and dropping data (e.g., removing outliers), altering data, and adding and dropping variables, as well as hypothesizing after the results are known (Kerr, 1998). QRPs could range from more benign in nature, such as not reporting all dependent variables collected in a study, to clear ethical violations, such as falsifying data. The use of the term "QRP" is meant to suggest that although such practices may be questionable, they may not be unethical because their use may sometimes be appropriate but at other times inappropriate, depending on the specific practice and context (e.g., the deletion of outliers). However, it is clear that QRPs can result in outcome-level publication bias (O'Boyle et al., in press).

Researchers could also be asked to disclose other variables collected or investigated, as it is often common in observational studies in the social sciences to collect as much data as possible. The Journal Article Reporting Standards (JARS) of the American Psychological Association (2008) recommend such a disclosure. Honor codes can serve to prevent researchers from engaging in QRPs out of ignorance and would give journals the ability to more easily retract an article or print an

54 George C. Banks et al.

erratum should evidence emerge that authors engaged in QRPs that led to publication bias. Unfortunately, such cases do occur in the field of management, as illustrated by the recent retractions issued by some of our top journals, including the *Academy of Management Journal, Journal of Management Studies, Journal of Business Venturing, Organization Science*, and *Strategic Management Journal* for the work completed by Ulrich Lichtenthaler. The practice of implementing such codes of conduct has proven to be effective for the reduction of some questionable practices (Ariely, 2012; Mazar, Amir, & Ariely, 2008).

Supplemental Information on the Internet

Providing supplemental information would allow for the dissemination of additional materials about one's study design, the study population, and any analyses and results not included in the submitted or published article. It is possible that reviewers and editors recommend the removal of such information because they do not find this information to be necessary or informative or because of space constraints. Online supplemental information would provide authors and journals with the opportunity to make this information widely available at little or no cost. As noted by Kepes and McDaniel (2013), if the Internet has room for millions of cat videos, it has room for such supplemental information. This should serve to reduce concerns due to publication bias (Wertil, Schob, Brunner, & Steurer, 2013).

Data Sharing

Journals should consider requesting that authors submit their raw data along with their manuscript (Kepes & McDaniel, 2013). This practice would increase editors' and reviewers' confidence in the analysis, as they would be able to analyze the data themselves should they have any questions. Additionally, journals could make the data available on their websites at the time of publication or after a grace period (e.g., 3 years). Thus, other researchers would have the opportunity to replicate the results and include the data in a meta-analytic review more easily (Kepes & McDaniel, 2013).

Two-stage Review Process

Kepes and colleagues (Kepes, Bennett, & McDaniel, 2014; Kepes & McDaniel, 2013) also suggested the implementation of a two-stage review process to minimize the use of QRPs. Editors and reviewers are biased toward the publication of articles with statistically significant results (e.g., Epstein, 1990; Mahoney, 1977) and are less critical of a study's methods when most results are positive (Emerson et al., 2010). Thus, blinding them to a study's Results and Discussion sections during an initial stage of the review process could minimize the introduction of these and related biases in the editorial review process. In the first stage, reviewers could be presented with the

Introduction and Methods sections, including a detailed description of the analysis approach, and the editor would receive comments and ratings free from any bias that might be created due to the support or lack of support from the results. Based on the comments from the reviewers, the author(s) would revise the paper and resubmit it. This submission could include the Results and Discussion sections. Then the reviewers would only have to check if the authors actually followed their previously submitted and reviewed methods and analysis plan and provided an appropriate discussion of results.

Incentives for B- and C-tier Journals

Universities should consider providing incentives for publications in B- and C-tier journals. It is not uncommon for universities, particularly for top research universities, to provide incentives only for A-tier journal publications. This incentive system may discourage authors from working on manuscripts that have been rejected from the best journals and may perpetuate publication bias (Kepes & McDaniel, 2013). Hence, publication bias could be mitigated if researchers were still provided with at least some sort of incentive for disseminating their studies in outlets other than A-tier journals.

Journal Submission and Communications

Another suggestion is the release of original journal submissions as well as communications among action editors, reviewers, and authors (Kepes & McDaniel, 2013; O'Boyle, Banks, & Gonzalez-Mule, in press). Editors, reviewers, and authors could be made aware in advance that their communications will be publically available. This might discourage researchers from engaging in QRPs once the review process has begun, and it might discourage editors and reviewers from encouraging the engagement in QRPs (e.g., presenting post hoc hypotheses as a priori).

Replications and Prospective Meta-analysis

Another recommendation for reducing issues related to publication bias is to encourage more replication studies. Journals should consider dedicating space solely for exact and conceptual replication studies. Only limited journal space would be required to publish replication studies because a literature review and theoretical framework would not need to be described (Kepes & McDaniel, 2013; O'Boyle, Banks, & Gonzalez-Mule, in press).

Additionally, prospective meta-analyses can be implemented as means to encourage simultaneous replication studies (Berlin & Ghersi, 2005). Prospective meta-analyses involve a group of researchers who collaborate to collect multiple samples in an investigation of the same research questions. Such an approach

56 George C. Banks et al.

would allow for the standardization of research designs (e.g., measures) and the a priori inclusion of moderating variables that should be considered across the different research teams and samples. It would thus allow researchers to simultaneously replicate findings. Additionally, a prospective meta-analysis allows for the triangulation of results because of the use of multiple measures and design approaches. Finally, because prospective meta-analyses are planned prior to data collection, results tend to be reported regardless of whether they are statistically significant. Hence, this approach should serve to reduce publication bias.

Study and Protocol Registration

Numerous calls have been made for the registration of studies prior to completion as well as the creation of research registries for studies that have been completed but have not been published (Banks, Kepes, & Banks, 2012; Banks, Kepes, & McDaniel, 2012; Banks & McDaniel, 2011; Bennett & Miao, 2013; Ferguson & Brannick, 2012; Kepes et al., 2012; Kepes et al., 2014; Kepes & McDaniel, 2013). Additionally, incomplete research registries have plagued the medical field, where they have already begun to be implemented (Chan, 2008). However, following the mandatory registration requirement for medical trials (De Angelis et al., 2004), there was a substantial increase in the number of registrations. Furthermore, the registration data were more complete. Thus, the registration requirement resulted in less data suppression and more publically available data (Zarin, Tse, & Ide, 2005; Zarin, Tse, Williams, Califf, & Ide, 2011), which should yield more accurate mean effect size estimates in meta-analytic reviews. Therefore, anything short of mandatory participation in registries may still lead to a biased meta-analytic samples in which there are systematic differences between those researchers that willingly participate in the registries and those that do not (Strech, 2011).

Conclusion

Publication bias can present a serious threat to the advancement of science. Publication bias has been documented in several investigations in the organizational sciences. As conscientious researchers, we should evaluate the extent to which this bias exists within individual literature areas and take proactive steps to prevent it from occurring. The recommendations discussed throughout this chapter are summarized in Table 2.1.

In this chapter, we reviewed myths related to publication bias. Specifically, we clarified that publication bias is concerned with systematic differences between the literature that is available to a reviewer and the population of completed studies on a particular relation of interest. We also discussed that although reviewers and editors may contribute to publication bias, authors are likely the primary cause. Next, we described evidence showing that the majority of meta-analytic studies in the organizational sciences do not assess the potential presence of

TABLE 2.1 Recommendations

Recommendation	Description

Myth #1: Publication bias is concerned with the availability of all possible effect sizes in all areas of a scientific field.

| • Focus on specific relations of interest | – Investigations into the existence and prevalence of publication bias should focus on specific relations of interest. |

Myth #2: The editorial review process is the primary cause of publication bias.

| • Disseminate results | – Authors should make efforts to disseminate their results regardless of the outcomes of their analyses. |

Myth #3: There is a perception that the failsafe N and subgroup comparison are the best publication bias detection techniques.

• Triangulate the mean effect size	– Meta-analytic researchers should address potential publication bias by using multiple advanced techniques (e.g., trim and fill, selection models, cumulative meta-analysis) in order to triangulate the meta-analytic mean effect size estimate.
• Test within subgroups	– Publication bias tests should be employed within homogeneous subgroups when feasible to decrease the possibility that heterogeneity distorts conclusions.
• Consider the influence of heterogeneity	– Future research should consider the influence of heterogeneity due to artifactual variance (e.g., measurement error), outliers, and moderators on the accuracy of publication bias tests.

Myth #4: Publication bias may not be of concern in the social sciences because it is prevented by reporting correlation matrices, testing multiple hypotheses, and conducting systematic searches in meta-analytic reviews.

• Honor code	– Honor codes should be employed by journals to enhance the probability that submitting authors did not engage in any questionable research practices that might lead to outcome-level publication bias.
• Supplemental information online	– Supplemental information should be provided online by journals so that authors may provide additional information about their study design and the population of their study, as well as to report additional outcomes.
• Data sharing	– Journals should require that authors submit their raw data and syntax along with their submitted studies in order to increase transparency and to allow for replications. Journals could make the data available on their websites after a grace period (e.g., 3 years).
• Two-stage review process	– A two-stage review process should be implemented in which reviewers are only allowed to see the Results and Discussion sections of a study after they have reviewed the Introduction and Methods sections of the study.
• Incentives for B- and C-tier journals	– Universities should offer incentives for researchers to publish in B- and C-tier journals to keep them from abandoning studies when it appears no longer likely that they will be published in an A-tier journal.

(Continued)

58 George C. Banks et al.

TABLE 2.1 (Continued)

Recommendation	Description
• Journal submission and communications	— Journals should release original manuscript submissions as well as the communications among action editors, reviewers, and authors in order to provide greater transparency meant to reduce questionable research practices that might occur in the review process.
• Replications and prospective meta-analyses	— Journals should dedicate space solely for replication studies. Additionally, prospective meta-analyses should be implemented as means to encourage simultaneous replication studies.
• Study and protocol registration	— Registries should be created that allow for protocol registration prior to conducting a study so as to discourage questionable research practices and outcome-level publication bias that could occur after a study was conducted. Additionally, registries should be created that provide a repository of completed studies for meta-analytic researchers.

publication bias (Banks, Kepes, & McDaniel, 2012; Kepes et al., 2012). Furthermore, when meta-analytic studies do test for this bias, they typically use suboptimal methods. Finally, we discussed why the organizational sciences are not likely to be immune from the effects of publication bias. Specifically, reporting correlation matrices, testing multiple hypotheses, and conducting thorough systematic searches in meta-analytic reviews are unlikely to completely prevent the occurrence of publication bias. Many other prevention techniques should be used to mitigate the threat. By better educating researchers on the definition, causes, detection, and prevention of this bias, as a field we should be more able to assess and mitigate its effects.

Note

1 Consistent with the publication bias literature, we use the word "suppression" to refer to studies that are not published or otherwise readily available (Kepes & McDaniel, 2013). This use of the word "suppression" does not imply deceit.

References

American Psychological Association. (2008). Reporting standards for research in psychology: Why do we need them? What might they be? *American Psychologist, 63*, 839–851.

American Psychological Association. (2010). *Publication manual of the American Psychological Association (6th ed.)*. Washington, DC: American Psychological Association.

Ariely, D. (2012). *The (honest) truth about dishonesty: How we lie to everyone—especially ourselves*. New York, NY: HarperCollins.

Banks, G. C., Batchelor, J. H., & McDaniel, M. A. (2010). Smarter people are (a bit) more symmetrical: A meta-analysis of the relationship between intelligence and fluctuating asymmetry. *Intelligence, 38*, 393–401.

Banks, G. C., Batchelor, J. H., Seers, A., O'Boyle, E. H., Pollack, J. M., & Gower, K. (2014). What does team-member exchange bring to the party? A meta-analytic review of team and leader social exchange. *Journal of Organizational Behavior, 35*, 273–295.

Banks, G. C., Kepes, S., & Banks, K. P. (2012). Publication bias: The antagonist of meta-analytic reviews and effective policy making. *Educational Evaluation and Policy Analysis, 34*, 259–277.

Banks, G. C., Kepes, S., & McDaniel, M. A. (2012). Publication bias: A call for improved meta-analytic practice in the organizational sciences. *International Journal of Selection and Assessment, 20*, 182–196.

Banks, G. C., & McDaniel, M. A. (2011). The kryptonite of evidence-based I-O psychology. *Industrial and Organizational Psychology: Perspectives on Science and Practice, 4*, 40–44.

Banks, G. C., & O'Boyle, E. H. (2013). Why we need I-O psychology to fix I-O psychology. *Industrial and Organizational Psychology: Perspectives on Science and Practice, 6*, 291–294.

Becker, B. J. (1994). Combining significance levels. In H. Cooper & L. V. Hedges (Eds.), *The handbook of research synthesis* (pp. 215–230). New York, NY: Russell Sage Foundation.

Becker, B. J. (2005). The failsafe N or file-drawer number. In H. R. Rothstein, A. J. Sutton, & M. Borenstein (Eds.), *Publication bias in meta analysis: Prevention, assessment, and adjustments* (pp. 111–126). West Sussex, UK: Wiley.

Begg, C. B., & Mazumdar, M. (1994). Operating characteristics of a rank correlation test for publication bias. *Biometrics, 50*, 1088–1101.

Bennett, A. A., & Miao, C. (2013). How do we know truth? Extensions and examples from similar academic fields. *Industrial and Organizational Psychology: Perspectives on Science and Practice, 6*, 276–278.

Berlin, J. A., & Ghersi, D. (2005). Preventing publication bias: Registries and prospective meta-analysis. In H. R. Rothstein, A. J. Sutton, & M. Borenstein (Eds.), *Publication bias in meta analysis: Prevention, assessment, and adjustments* (pp. 35–48). West Sussex, UK: Wiley.

Biemann, T. (2013). What if we were Texas sharpshooters? Predictor reporting bias in regression analysis. *Organizational Research Methods, 16*, 335–363.

Blackwell, S. C., Thompson, L., & Refuerzo, J. (2009). Full publication of clinical trials presented at a national maternal-fetal medicine meeting: Is there a publication bias? *American Journal of Perinatology, 26*, 679–682.

Borenstein, M., Hedges, L. V., Higgins, J. P., & Rothstein, H. R. (2009). *Introduction to meta-analysis*. West Sussex, UK: Wiley.

Bosco, F. A., Field, J. G., & Pierce, C. A. (2012, August). *Accomodational plasticity in organizational science: Impact of hypothesis framing on effect size.* Paper presented at the annual meeting of the Academy of Management, Boston, MA.

Briner, R. B., & Rousseau, D. M. (2011). Evidence-based I-O psychology: Not there yet. *Industrial and Organizational Psychology: Perspectives on Science and Practice, 4*, 3–22.

Chalmers, I., & Dickersin, K. (2013). Biased under-reporting of research reflects biased under-submission more than biased editorial rejection. *F1000Research, 2*, 1–6.

Chan, A.-W. (2008). Bias, spin, and misreporting: Time for full access to trial protocols and results. *PLoS Medicine, 5*, e230.

60 George C. Banks et al.

Chan, A.-W., & Altman, D. G. (2005). Identifying outcome reporting bias in randomised trials on PubMed: Review of publications and survey of authors. *British Medical Journal, 330,* 753–756.

Chiaburu, D. S., Peng, A. C., Oh, I.-S., Banks, G. C., & Lomeli, L. C. (2013). Employee organizational cynicism antecedents and outcomes: A meta-analysis. *Journal of Vocational Behavior, 83,* 181–197.

Cooper, H., DeNeve, K., & Charlton, K. (1997). Finding the missing science: The fate of studies submitted for review by a human subjects committee. *Psychological Methods, 2,* 447–452.

Curfman, G. D., Morrissey, S., & Drazen, J. M. (2006). Expression of concern reaffirmed. *New England Journal of Medicine, 354,* 1193.

Dalton, D. R., Aguinis, H., Dalton, C. M., Bosco, F. A., & Pierce, C. A. (2012). Revisiting the file drawer problem in a meta-analysis: An assessment of published and nonpublished correlation matrices. *Personnel Psychology, 65,* 221–249.

De Angelis, C., Drazen, J. M., Frizelle, F. A., Haung, C., Hoey, J., Horton, R., Kotzin, S. . . . Van Der Weyden, M. B. (2004). Clinical trial registration: A statement from the International Committee of Medical Journal Editors. *New England Journal of Medicine, 351,* 1250–1251.

Dickersin, K. (2005). Publication bias: Recognizing the problem, understandings its origins and scope, and preventing harm. In H. R. Rothstein, A. J. Sutton, & M. Borenstein (Eds.), *Publication bias in meta analysis: Prevention, assessment, and adjustments* (pp. 11–34). West Sussex, UK: Wiley.

Duval, S. J. (2005). The "trim and fill" method. In H. R. Rothstein, A. J. Sutton, & M. Borenstein (Eds.), *Publication bias in meta analysis: Prevention, assessment, and adjustments* (pp. 127–144). West Sussex, UK: Wiley.

Duval, S. J., & Tweedie, R. L. (2000a). A nonparametric "trim and fill" method of accounting for publication bias in meta-analysis. *Journal of the American Statistical Association, 95,* 89–98.

Duval, S. J., & Tweedie, R. L. (2000b). Trim and fill: A simple funnel-plot-based method of testing and adjusting for publication bias in meta-analysis. *Biometrics, 56,* 455–463.

Dwan, K., Altman, D. G., Arnaiz, J. A., Bloom, J., Chan, A.-W., Cronin, E., Decullier, E. . . . Williamson, P. R. (2008). Systematic review of the empirical evidence of study publication bias and outcome reporting bias. *PloS One, 3,* e3081.

Easterbrook, P. J., Gopalan, R., Berlin, J. A., & Matthews, D. R. (1991). Publication bias in clinical research. *The Lancet, 337,* 867–872.

Egger, M., Smith, G. D., Schneider, M., & Minder, C. (1997). Bias in meta-analysis detected by a simple, graphical test. *British Medical Journal, 315,* 629–634.

Emerson, G. B., Warme, W. J., Wolf, F. M., Heckman, J., Brand, R. A., & Leopold, S. S. (2010). Testing for the presence of positive-outcome bias in peer review: A randomized controlled trial. *Archives of Internal Medicine, 170,* 1934–1939.

Epstein, W. M. (1990). Confirmational response bias among social work journals. *Science, Technology, and Human Values, 15,* 9–37.

Etter, J. F., & Stapleton, J. (2009). Citations to trials of nicotine replacement therapy were biased toward positive results and high-impact-factor journals. *Journal of Clinical Epidemiology, 62,* 831–837.

Evans, S. (1996). Statistician's comment (to Misleading meta-analysis: "Fail safe N" is a useful mathematical measure of the stability of results by R. Persaud). *British Medical Journal, 312,* 125.

Fanelli, D. (2012). Negative results are disappearing from most disciplines and countries. *Scientometrics, 90,* 891–904.

Ferguson, C. J., & Brannick, M. T. (2012). Publication bias in psychological science: Prevalence, methods for identifying and controlling, and implications for the use of meta-analyses. *Psychological Methods, 17*, 120–128.

Gerber, A., & Malhotra, N. (2008a). Do statistical reporting standards affect what is published? Publication bias in two leading political science journals. *Quarterly Journal of Political Science, 3*, 313–326.

Gerber, A. S., & Malhotra, N. (2008b). Publication bias in empirical sociological research: Do arbitrary significance levels distort published results? *Sociological Methods & Research, 37*, 3–30.

Greenhouse, J. B., & Iyengar, S. (2009). Sensitivity analysis and diagnostics. In H. Cooper, L. V. Hedges, & J. C. Valentine (Eds.), *The handbook of research synthesis and meta-analysis* (2nd ed., pp. 417–433). New York, NY: Russell Sage Foundation.

Greenwald, A. G. (1975). Consequences of prejudice against the null hypothesis. *Psychological Bulletin, 82*, 1–20.

Hahn, S., Williamson, P. R., Hutton, J. L., Garner, P., & Flynn, E. V. (2000). Assessing the potential for bias in meta-analysis due to selective reporting of subgroup analyses within studies. *Statistics In Medicine, 19*, 3325–3336.

Harrison, J. S., Banks, G. C., Pollack, J. M., O'Boyle Jr., E. H., & Short, J. C. (in press). Publication bias in strategic management research. *Journal of Management*.

Hartshorne, J., & Schachner, A. (2012). Tracking replicability as a method of post-publication open evaluation. *Frontiers in Computational Neuroscience, 6*, 8.

Hedges, L. V., & Vevea, J. L. (2005). Selection methods approaches. In H. R. Rothstein, A. Sutton, & M. Borenstein (Eds.), *Publication bias in meta analysis: Prevention, assessment, and adjustments* (pp. 145–174). West Sussex, UK: Wiley.

Higgins, J. P., & Green, S. (Eds.). (2011). *Cochrane handbook for systematic reviews of interventions; Version 5.1.0 [updated March 2011]*: The Cochrane Collaboration. Available from www.cochrane-handbook.org

Hopewell, S., Clarke, M., & Mallett, S. (2005). Grey literature and systematic reviews. In H. R. Rothstein, A. J. Sutton, & M. Borenstein (Eds.), *Publication bias in meta analysis: Prevention, assessment, and adjustments* (pp. 48–72). West Sussex, UK: Wiley.

Hunter, J. E., & Schmidt, F. L. (2004). *Methods of meta-analysis: Correcting error and bias in research findings.* Newbury Park, CA: Sage.

Ioannidis, J. (2008). Interpretation of tests of heterogeneity and bias in meta-analysis. *Journal of Evaluation in Clinical Practice, 14*, 951–957.

Ioannidis, J., & Doucouliagos, H. (2013). What's to know about the credibility of empirical economics? *Journal of Economic Surveys, 27*, 997–1004.

Jick, T. D. (1979). Mixing qualitative and quantitative methods: Triangulation in action. *Administrative Science Quarterly, 24*, 602–611.

Kepes, S., Banks, G. C., McDaniel, M. A., & Whetzel, D. L. (2012). Publication bias in the organizational sciences. *Organizational Research Methods, 15*, 624–662.

Kepes, S., Banks, G. C., & Oh, I. S. (2014). Avoiding bias in publication bias research: The value of "null" findings. *Journal of Business and Psychology, 29*, 183–203.

Kepes, S., Bennett, A., & McDaniel, M. A. (2014). Evidence-based management and the trustworthiness of our cumulative scientific knowledge: Implications for research, teaching, and practice. *Academy of Management Learning & Education, 13*, 446–466.

Kepes, S., & McDaniel, M. A. (2013). How trustworthy is the scientific literature in I-O psychology? *Industrial and Organizational Psychology: Perspectives on Science and Practice, 6*, 252–268.

62 George C. Banks et al.

Kepes, S., McDaniel, M. A., Banks, G. C., Hurtz, G. M., & Donovan, J. J. (2011, April). *Big five validity and publication bias: Conscientiousness' validity is lower than assumed.* Paper presented at the annual meeting of the Society for Industrial and Organizational Psychology, Chicago, IL.

Kepes, S., McDaniel, M. A., Brannick, M. T., & Banks, G. C. (2013). Meta-analytic reviews in the organizational sciences: Two meta-analytic schools on the way to MARS. *Journal of Business and Psychology, 28,* 123–143.

Kerr, N. L. (1998). HARKing: Hypothesizing after the results are known. *Personality and Social Psychology Review, 2,* 196–217.

Kicinski, M. (2013). Publication bias in recent meta-analyses. *PLoS One, 8,* e81823.

Kirkham, J. J., Riley, R. D., & Williams, P. R. (2011). A multivariate meta-analysis approach for reducing the impact of outcome reporting bias in systematic reviews. *Statistics in Medicine, 31,* 2179–2195.

Leavitt, K., Mitchell, T. R., & Peterson, J. (2010). Theory pruning: Strategies to reduce our dense theoretical landscape. *Organizational Research Methods, 13,* 644–667.

Lipsey, M. W., & Wilson, D. B. (1993). The efficacy of psychological, educational, and behavioral treatment: Confirmation from meta-analysis. *American Psychologist, 48,* 1181–1209.

Mahoney, M. J. (1977). Publication prejudices: An experimental study of confirmatory bias in the peer review system. *Cognitive Therapy & Research, 1,* 161–175.

Mazar, N., Amir, O., & Ariely, D. (2008). The dishonesty of honest people: A theory of self-concept maintenance. *Journal of Marketing Research, 45,* 633–644.

McDaniel, M. A. (2009, April). *Cumulative meta-analysis as a publication bias method.* Paper presented at the annual meeting of the Society for Industrial and Organizational Psychology, New Orleans, LA.

McDaniel, M. A., & Kepes, S. (in press). An evaluation of Spearman's hypothesis by manipulating g-saturation. *International Journal of Selection and Assessment.*

McDaniel, M. A., McKay, P., & Rothstein, H. (2006, April). *Publication bias and racial effects on job performance: The elephant in the room.* Paper presented at the annual meeting of the Society for Industrial and Organizational Psychology, Dallas, TX.

McDaniel, M. A., Rothstein, H. R., & Whetzel, D. L. (2006). Publication bias: A case study of four test vendors. *Personnel Psychology, 59,* 927–953.

McGauran, N., Wieseler, B., Kreis, J., Schuler, Y. B., Kolsch, H., & Kaiser, T. (2010). Review reporting bias in medical research—a narrative. *Trials, 11,* 1–15.

McKay, P. F., & McDaniel, M. A. (2006). A reexamination of black–white mean differences in work performance: More data, more moderators. *Journal of Applied Psychology, 91,* 538–554.

Murtaugh, P. A. (2002). Journal quality, effect size, and publication bias in meta-analysis. *Ecology, 83,* 1162–1166.

O'Boyle, E. H., Banks, G. C., & Gonzalez-Mule, E. (in press). The chrysalis effect: How ugly data metamorphosize into beautiful articles. *Journal of Management.*

O'Boyle, E. H., Rutherford, M., & Banks, G. C. (in press). Publication bias in entrepreneurship research: An examination of dominant relations to performance. *Journal of Business Venturing.*

Olson, C. M., et al. (2002). Publication bias in editorial decision making. *Journal of the American Medical Association, 287,* 2825–2828.

Orwin, R. G. (1983). A fail-safe N for effect size in meta-analysis. *Journal of Educational Statistics, 8,* 157–159.

Palmer, T. M., Peters, J. L., Sutton, A. J., & Moreno, S. G. (2008). Contour-enhanced funnel plots for meta-analysis. *Stata Journal, 8,* 242–254.

Peters, J. L., Sutton, A. J., Jones, D. R., Abrams, K. R., & Rushton, L. (2008). Contour-enhanced meta-analysis funnel plots help distinguish publication bias from other causes of asymmetry. *Journal of Clinical Epidemiology, 61*, 991–996.

Rosenthal, R. (1979). The file drawer problem and tolerance for null results. *Psychological Bulletin, 86*, 638–641.

Rothstein, H. (2012). Accessing relevant literature. In H. M. Cooper (Ed.), *APA handbook of research methods in psychology: Vol. 1. Foundations, planning, measures, and psychometrics* (pp. 133–144). Washington, DC: American Psychological Association.

Rothstein, H. R., & Hopewell, S. (2009). Grey literature. In H. M. Cooper, L. V. Hedges, & J. C. Valentine (Eds.), *The handbook of research synthesis and meta-analysis* (2nd ed., pp. 103–126). New York, NY: Russell Sage Foundation.

Rothstein, H. R., Sutton, A. J., & Borenstein, M. (2005). Publication bias in meta-analyses. In H. R. Rothstein, A. J. Sutton, & M. Borenstein (Eds.), *Publication bias in meta analysis: Prevention, assessment, and adjustments* (pp. 1–7). West Sussex, UK: Wiley.

Sackett, P. R., & Larson, J. R. (1990). Research strategies and tactics in industrial and organizational psychology. In M. D. Dunnette & L. M. Hough (Eds.), *Handbook of industrial and organizational psychology* (Vol. 1, pp. 419–489). Palo Alto, CA: Consulting Psychologists Press.

Schmidt, F., & Oh, I. S. (2013). Methods for second-order meta-analysis and illustrative applications. *Organizational Behavior and Human Decision Processes, 121*, 204–218.

Schmidt, F. L., & Hunter, J. E. (2014). *Methods of meta-analysis: Correcting error and bias in research findings* (3rd ed.). Newbury Park, CA: Sage.

Schmidt, F. L., Hunter, J. E., Pearlman, K., Hirsh, H. R. (1985). Forty questions about validity generalization and meta-analysis. *Personnel Psychology, 38*, 697–798.

Simonsohn, U., Nelson, L. D., & Simmons, J. P. (2014). P-curve: A key to the file drawer. *Journal of Experimental Psychology: General, 143*, 534–547.

Song, F., et al. (2010). Dissemination and publication of research findings: An updated review of related biases. *Health Technology Assessment, 14*, 1–220.

Sterling, T. D., & Rosenbaum, W. L. (1995). Publication decisions revisited: The effect of the outcome of statistical tests on the decision to publish and vice versa. *American Statistician, 49*, 108–112.

Sterne, J. A., Gavaghan, D., & Egger, M. (2005). The funnel plot. In H. R. Rothstein, A. J. Sutton, & M. Borenstein (Eds.), *Publication bias in meta analysis: Prevention, assessment, and adjustments* (pp. 75–98). West Sussex, UK: Wiley.

Sterne, J.A.C., Sutton, A. J., Ioannidis, J. P., Terrin, N., Jones, D. R., Lau, J., Carpenter, J. . . . Higgins, J. P. (2011). Recommendations for examining and interpreting funnel plot asymmetry in meta-analyses of randomised controlled trials. *British Medical Journal, 343*, d4002.

Strech, D. (2011). The ethics of a restrictive regulation of trial registration. *Ethik in Der Medizin, 23*, 177–189.

Sutton, A. J. (2009). Publication bias. In H. Cooper, L. V. Hedges, & J. C. Valentine (Eds.), *The handbook of research synthesis and meta-analysis* (2nd ed., pp. 435–452). New York, NY: Russell Sage Foundation.

Sutton, A. J., & Pigott, T. D. (2005). Bias in meta-analysis induced by incompletely reported studies. In H. R. Rothstein, A. J. Sutton, & M. Borenstein (Eds.), *Publication bias in meta analysis: Prevention, assessment, and adjustments* (pp. 223–240). West Sussex, UK: Wiley.

Tate, B. W., & McDaniel, M. A. (2008, August). *Race differences in personality: An evaluation of moderators and publication bias.* Paper presented at the annual meeting of the Academy of Management, Anaheim, CA.

Terrin, N., Schmid, C. H., Lau, J., & Olkin, I. (2003). Adjusting for publication bias in the presence of heterogeneity. *Statistics in Medicine, 22*, 2113–2126.

Turner, E. H., Matthews, A. M., Linardatos, E., Tell, R. A., & Rosenthal, R. (2008). Selective publication of antidepressant trials and its influence on apparent efficacy. *New England Journal of Medicine, 358*, 252–260.

Vevea, J. L., Clements, N. C., & Hedges, L. V. (1993). Assessing the effects of selection bias on validity data for the General Aptitude Test Battery. *Journal of Applied Psychology, 78*, 981–987.

Vevea, J. L., & Woods, C. M. (2005). Publication bias in research synthesis: Sensitivity analysis using a priori weight functions. *Psychological Methods, 10*, 428–443.

Weinhandl, E. D., & Duval, S. (2012). Generalization of trim and fill for application in meta-regression. *Research Synthesis Methods, 3*, 51–67.

Wertil, M. M., Schob, M., Brunner, F., & Steurer, J. (2013). Incomplete reporting of baseline characteristics in clinical trials: An analysis of randomized controlled trials and systematic reviews involving patients with chronic low back pain. *PLos One, 8*, e58512.

Whetzel, D. L. (2006, April). *Publication bias of studies on the validity of customer service measures: A review of Frei and McDaniel's (1998) Meta-analytic results.* Paper presented at the annual meeting of the Society for Industrial and Organizational Psychology, Dallas, TX.

Williamson, P. R., & Gamble, C. (2007). Application and investigation of a bound for outcome reporting bias. *Trials, 8*, 9.

Zarin, D. A., Tse, T., & Ide, N. C. (2005). Trial registration at ClinicalTrials.gov between May and October 2005. *New England Journal of Medicine, 353*, 2779–2787.

Zarin, D. A., Tse, T., Williams, R. J., Califf, R. M., & Ide, N. C. (2011). The ClinicalTrials.gov results database: Update and key issues. *New England Journal of Medicine, 364*, 852–860.

PART II
Design Issues

3

RED-HEADED NO MORE

Tipping Points in Qualitative Research in Management

Anne D. Smith, Laura T. Madden and Donde Ashmos Plowman

The proscriptive debate between qualitative and quantitative research designs is a familiar discussion in the management discipline (Eby, Hurst, & Butts, 2008). Much research from both sides has been dedicated to the relative merits of their preferred research designs as well as to instruction about how to successfully design, conduct, and publish studies with these designs (Creswell, 1998; Ketchen & Ireland, 2010; Smith, 2002). In regard to qualitative research specifically, this attention has generated a rich discussion of creating methodological fit (Edmondson & McManus, 2007), ensuring construct validity (Lincoln, Lynham, & Guba, 2011), and emphasizing theoretical contributions (Gephart, 2004; Ghoshal, 2005; Langley, 1999).

Despite the wealth of conversation about qualitative research, the number of published articles that use qualitative research designs is growing more slowly than some would like (Podsakoff & Dalton, 1987), particularly in mainstream management journals. In fact, quantitative review studies and cautionary advice from experienced qualitative researchers indicate that qualitative research remains at the margins of management research, lending to a perception of qualitative research as the "red-headed stepchild" (Eby et al., 2008, p. 219).

In this chapter, we address this perception or myth by exploring trends in the publication rates of qualitative research. Using a quantitative look at qualitative publication trends from the past 23 years in three mainstream U.S. management journals—*Academy of Management Journal (AMJ)*, *Administrative Science Quarterly (ASQ)*, and *Organization Science (OS)*—we document trends in qualitative research over the past two decades and discuss the implication of these trends for the future

68 Anne D. Smith et al.

of qualitative research. In contrast to previous reviews of qualitative research (e.g., Daft, 1980; Locke & Golden-Biddle, 1997; Podsakoff & Dalton, 1987; Van Maanen, 1998), we find signs that qualitative research has reached a tipping point (Gladwell, 2000) and address the factors that contribute to these encouraging trends.

By doing so, we offer several contributions. First, we contribute a new lens on the discussion of the perceived legitimacy of qualitative research in the management discipline. Second, our specific content-analysis procedure allows a more fine-grained approach for identifying qualitative versus nonqualitative designs, which creates a more holistic picture of the state of qualitative research in mainstream management journals. Finally, our discussion of tipping points indicates a positive future for qualitative research as well as an understanding of which factors will continue the upward trends we identify.

Qualitative Research at the Margins

Two sets of literature reviews related to research methods provide a backdrop for this study. First, we describe quantitative reviews reported in the management literature and focus on three particularly relevant reviews to this paper: Podsakoff and Dalton (1987), Scandura and Williams (2000), and Eby and colleagues (2008). We then examine a second set of literature in which qualitative authors voice their concerns about qualitative methods in management. We suggest that our focal myth—qualitative research as red-headed stepchild—has been perpetuated by both quantitative reviews and musings by qualitative researchers.

Quantitative Reviews

More than two decades ago, Podsakoff and Dalton (1987, p. 433) observed that research published in management journals rarely used qualitative methods and suggested that the lack of exemplars meant that these "nontraditional" methods "if adopted at all, would be adopted very slowly." In their review of the research methods used in 193 articles published in 1985 in five journals—*AMJ, ASQ, Journal of Applied Psychology (JAP), Journal of Management (JOM)*, and *Organizational Behavior and Human Decision Processes (OBHDP)*—qualitative methods of data collection and analysis barely appeared at all. In regard to this curious absence, the authors noted only that "research that could be included even broadly in such a [qualitative or ethnographic] category was rarely seen in these journals during the year examined" (Podsakoff & Dalton, 1987, p. 436).

Similarly, Scandura and Williams (2000) reviewed and categorized all *ASQ, AMJ*, and *JOM* publications between 1985 and 1987 and 1995 and 1997 using McGrath's (1982) eight research strategies: formal theory/literature review, sample survey, laboratory experiment, experimental simulation, field study, field experiment, judgment task, and computer simulation. Although some might consider qualitative methods a form of primary field study (e.g., Miles & Huberman, 1994), the description of that category is unclear about whether Scandura and Williams (2000) included qualitative studies. Thus, no explicit reference to qualitative research appeared in their review.

During the last decade, several researchers trained in the traditional quantitative paradigm have noted the minor role for papers with qualitative methods, stating that "qualitative research does not frequently appear in mainstream, high-impact social science journals" and "the adoption of qualitative approaches has proceeded at a snail's pace" (Eby et al., 2008, p. 242). In a parallel field of research noted by Eby and colleagues (2008), Kidd (2002) conducted a quantitative review of 454 articles across 15 American Psychological Association journals and identified only 1% that were qualitative; further, 33% of the journals reviewed had never published a qualitative study. Likewise, Eby and colleagues (2008) found that about 3% of the articles published in nine top applied psychology, management,[1] and social science journals from 1990 to 2005 could be classified as qualitative or mixed. As seen across these quantitative reviews, qualitative research is being adopted slowly by management journals and thus remains at the margins, which perpetuates our central myth.

Qualitative Advice

Another popular area related to qualitative research concerns the design and execution of the methodology. Within this literature stream, many experienced qualitative researchers offer their guidance, and several well-recognized qualitative researchers document the substantial considerations involved in conducting qualitative research. In a recent series of "From the Editor" essays in *AMJ*, some of the field's best qualitative researchers (Dutton & Dukerich, 2006; Eisenhardt & Graebner, 2007; Gephart, 2004; Siggelkow, 2007; Suddaby, 2006; Weick, 2007) reflect on their own experiences conducting qualitative research or reviewing and editing qualitative journal submissions, and each noted how challenging qualitative research is to perform. For instance, Gephart (2004, pp. 460–461) cautions that qualitative research is often "more difficult and time consuming to create than good quantitative research." In addition, Suddaby (2006, p. 633) notes his continual surprise at the "profound misunderstanding of what constitutes qualitative research" and likened qualitative research to a "high-risk expedition."

In the same vein, Pratt's (2008) survey of qualitative researchers uncovers frustration and discouragement within the journal review process because of a lack of agreed-upon evaluation criteria for qualitative research. From this research, Pratt (2008, p. 494) concludes that it is "exceedingly difficult for qualitative researchers to have all the detail necessary to meet the evaluative standards while at the same time meeting format standards (e.g., page lengths) required by the journals." This frustrating lack of criteria is compounded by a fundamental question about what qualitative research is. In fact, both factors act as barriers to efforts to enhance the status and availability of qualitative research. Johnson, Buehring, Cassell, and

70 Anne D. Smith et al.

Symon (2007, p. 24) note this status divide: "qualitative research has attained an often begrudging acceptance as a legitimate, yet *usually subordinate* form of research in management disciplines" (emphasis added).

These comments provide a daunting picture of the process of conducting and publishing qualitative research. In fact, the advice gleaned paints an uphill battle for qualitative research to gain legitimacy in management research. Coupled with the findings from the quantitative reviews of high-impact journals, these warnings unfortunately encourage the myth that qualitative research is the red-headed stepchild of management research.

Our Approach to Assessing Qualitative Publications

Although many quantitative reviews have been conducted, the previous studies of qualitative publication trends offer an incomplete picture by relying on only a few years' worth of data (Podsakoff & Dalton, 1987; Scandura & Williams, 2000) or using data from only one journal (Van Maanen, 1998). Our study builds on these studies and extends other research (e.g., Daft, 1980; Locke & Golden-Biddle, 1997; Podsakoff & Dalton, 1987; Van Maanen, 1998) to assess the state of qualitative research. In contrast to earlier work, we use a quantitative content-analysis approach to review 23 years of data from three mainstream U.S. management journals: *AMJ*, *ASQ*, and *OS*.

We purposefully chose these journals and years for several reasons. First, following Locke and Golden-Biddle (1997), we selected at least a 20-year period in order to identify patterns in the state of qualitative research. We considered 1990 an appropriate starting point because *OS* was initiated in this year and because several seminal pieces on this topic were published in the late 1980s (e.g., Barley, 1986; Eisenhardt, 1989a, 1989b; Eisenhardt & Bourgeois, 1988; Sutton, 1987). We brought the articles up to date to year-end 2012 and thus extended the study period beyond more recent reviews (e.g., Eby et al., 2008).

Second, we chose *AMJ*, *ASQ*, and *OS*, all of which were on the *Financial Times* list of top academic publication outlets, because management journals are distinctive from psychology or sociology journals, and we wanted to glean insights into this group specifically. Although other research (Plowman & Smith, 2011) has identified a significantly higher rate of qualitative research in European journals such as *Journal of Management Studies*, in which almost 50% of the empirical publications from 1986 through 2008 were qualitative research, we chose to focus our inquiry on U.S. journals. Additionally, we excluded other high-ranking management journals after literature reviews uncovered severely limited traditions of publishing qualitative research. For instance, we did not include the *Strategic Management Journal (SMJ)* after Molina-Azorin (2009) identified a scant 5% of papers between 1997 through 2006 that used qualitative methods. At its peak rate in 2000, *SMJ* published just nine qualitative articles (Molina-Azorin, 2009). Further, the *Journal of Management (JOM)* mentioned the word "qualitative" only once in its 2006 30-year retrospective and was thus excluded from our analysis.

To determine what constitutes a significant level of qualitative publications, we followed the method used in Van Maanen's (1998) 40-year review of qualitative studies published in *ASQ*. According to Van Maanen, 158, or 15%, of the articles published during that period used qualitative methods. He observed that qualitative studies comprised 28% of the publications in the first decade, 8% in the second decade, and 12% and 16% in the last two decades respectively. Likewise, we consider the rate of publication of qualitative research to be significant, and therefore not at the margins, if it meets a 10% threshold level for a journal. We additionally assess whether the ratio of qualitative papers as compared to total papers for a journal was significantly different than zero.

Methodology

Because qualitative research is a wide umbrella (Van Maanen, 1979) and qualitative methods are noted for their inventiveness (Buchanan & Bryman, 2007), we followed a careful procedure to determine whether an article was qualitative in nature. We first reviewed each article to determine if it contained a description of its methodology. Special-issue introductions, book reviews, essays, and editor forum articles were removed from further evaluation. We then considered whether each of the remaining articles fit Locke and Golden-Biddle's (2002) criteria for selection as a qualitative approach: (a) the research took place in a natural setting and the primary data were obtained through observation, interviewing, corporate or organizational texts or documents, and images, and (b) conclusions were derived by working with the verbal language rather than numerical analysis. Following Locke and Golden-Biddle (1997) and Johnson and colleagues' (2007) advice about the complementary nature of qualitative and quantitative research, we included wholly qualitative studies as well as mixed-methods studies that included substantial qualitative and quantitative components. Similar to Van Maanen's survey (1998, p. xix), the mixed-methods articles we included had an "emphasis on the qualitative materials." In coding, we interpreted that to mean that qualitative data analysis was clearly discussed and not subordinate to the quantitative analysis.

Finally, we reviewed each article to determine its fit with published categories of qualitative research designs (Creswell, 1998; Gephart, 1999; Lee, 1999; Locke & Golden-Biddle, 1997; Suddaby, 2006; Van Maanen, 1998). Almost all qualitative articles in our study were clearly linked to at least one qualitative research tradition. We referred to all other empirical articles that did not meet the criteria for inclusion in our sample as "nonqualitative" studies. Using these guidelines, two authors coded articles in the three journals as qualitative or nonqualitative. We reviewed our codes, in which we had more than 80% agreement. Where we found disagreement, we reviewed the article and made a joint decision about its categorization. Our coding procedure resulted in 441 qualitative articles. To delve further into trends, we used cross-tabulation tables using a two-tailed Pearson chi-square statistical test.

Findings

Our results show an overall upward trend in the last 23 years for qualitative publications as compared to nonqualitative publications as well as an increasing absolute number of qualitative publications across all three journals (see Figure 3.1). During our study period, qualitative publications made up 18% of the papers published in the three journals, as seen in Table 3.1. The trend line of qualitative publications to nonqualitative publications in Figure 3.1 shows that qualitative papers make up almost 25% of total publications in 2002 and 27% of total publications in 2009, up from around 13% in 1990. The actual number and proportion of qualitative papers published in each journal varied, with *OS* at almost 30% of papers and *ASQ* at 22%. We calculated the slope of the proportion line between 1990 and 2012 and found them to be positive and significant ($B = .57$; $t = 4.8$; $p < .001$). These numbers show that qualitative publications are a significant presence in these journals and therefore not at the margins of mainstream management research.

In a more fine-grained analysis to address the trends in each journal, we compared three periods of time: the first 9 years of our study period (1990–1998); the subsequent 7 years, which culminated when the Eby and colleagues (2008) study

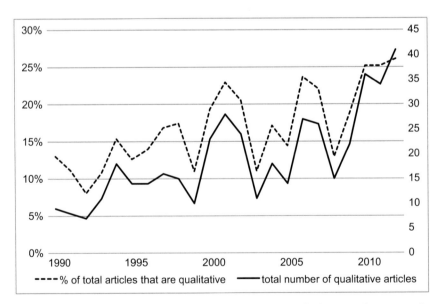

FIGURE 3.1 Proportion of Qualitative and Nonqualitative Articles by Year, Three Journals, 1990–2012

Red-Headed No More 73

TABLE 3.1 Paper Types from Three Journals, 1990–2012

	Qualitative	% Qualitative	Nonqualitative	% Nonqualitative	Total	% Total
Academy of Management	135	10%	1181	90%	1316	100%
Administrative Science Quarterly	99	22%	352	78%	451	100%
Organization Science	207	29%	516	71%	723	100%
TOTAL PAPERS	441	18%	2049	82%	2490	100%

TABLE 3.2 Growth Trends in Qualitative Publishing, Three Journals, 1990–2012

	AMJ			ASQ			OS		
	Total Papers	Qual. Papers	% Qual/ Total	Total Papers	Qual. Papers	% Qual/ Total	Total Papers	Qual. Papers	% Qual/ Total
9-year Period: 1990–1998	495	26	5%	198	41	21%	146	45	31%
7-year period: 1999–2005	415	40	10%	135	33	24%	201	55	27%
7-year period: 2006–2012	406	69	17%	118	25	21%	376	107	29%

ended (1999–2005); and the most recent 7 years of our study period (2006–2012). As seen in Table 3.2, the contrast between *ASQ* and *AMJ* is stark. Even though both of these journals started around the same time (1956 and 1958, respectively), *AMJ* had a much lower number of qualitative papers. In addition, their proportion of qualitative to total publications is around 5% as compared to *ASQ*'s 21%. *OS*, which was founded in 1990 with a mission to publish nontraditional research (Daft & Lewin, 1990), was closer to the 28% rate of qualitative publications of *ASQ* during its first decade (Van Maanen, 1998). Although *AMJ* had the lowest initial publication rate of qualitative research among the three journals in our study, this journal has noted the greatest increase in both actual qualitative papers published and as a percentage of total publications. During the 2006 to 2012 period, qualitative publications in *AMJ* grew to 17% of all publications. Although *ASQ* had a much higher overall rate of publishing qualitative papers as compared to *AMJ*, with 21% of publications as qualitative in the 1990 to 1998 period, *ASQ* was the only journal in our study that slightly decreased in both the number and the

74 Anne D. Smith et al.

proportion of qualitative papers published between 1999 and 2005 (24% of total papers) and 2006 and 2012 (21% of total papers). OS increased its number of published qualitative papers and as a proportion of total papers during the last two 7-year periods: 1999 to 2005 (27%) to 2006 to 2012 (29%). Only *ASQ* has maintained a significant level of qualitative publications at more than 20% of total publications across our 23-year study period. These trends at *AMJ* and OS indicate a higher than "snail's pace" growth for qualitative research in management publications.

We wanted to dig deeper to understand the overall and proportional rise in qualitative publications. During our coding, we noted that many qualitative papers were published in special issues. To explore this possible connection, we compared publication rates of qualitative research in regular versus special issues (see Table 3.3). In total, 24% of all qualitative papers are found in special issues, whereas only 16% of

TABLE 3.3 Qualitative Trends: Papers in Special Issues by Journal, 1990–2012

Academy of Management Journal	Qualitative		Nonqualitative		Total	
Regular Issue	96	71%	1013	86%	1109	86%
Special Issue	39	29%	168	14%	207	14%
TOTAL *AMJ* PAPERS	135		1181		1316	
Regular Issue vs. Special Issue	Chi-Square	19.7			p < .0001	
Administrative Science Quarterly	Qualitative		Nonqualitative		Total	
Regular Issue	91	92%	341	97%	432	97%
Special Issue	8	8%	11	3%	19	3%
TOTAL *ASQ* PAPERS	99		352		451	
Regular Issue vs. Special Issue	Chi-Square	4.7			p < .05	
Organization Science	Qualitative		Nonqualitative		Total	
Regular Issue	150	72%	362	70%	512	71%
Special Issue	57	28%	154	30%	211	29%
TOTAL OS PAPERS	207		516		723	
Regular Issue vs. Special Issue	Chi-Square				n.s.	
TOTAL PAPERS	Qualitative		Nonqualitative		Total	
Regular Issue	337	76%	1716	84%	2053	84%
Special Issue	104	24%	333	16%	437	16%
TOTAL PAPERS	441		2049		2490	
Regular Issue vs. Special Issue	Chi-Square	13.5			p < .0001	

nonqualitative are published in special issues, which represents a significant overall relationship for our study journals ($\chi^2 = 13.5, p < .0001$). Although this pattern held across *AMJ* and *ASQ* in our study, in *OS*, special issues were just as likely to have qualitative as quantitative papers in special issues.

Another trend we noted by individually coding each journal article was that fewer sole-authored qualitative papers appeared in our sample over time. We wondered if more teams of authors might be aiding the growth of qualitative publishing by improving construct validity (e.g., Eby et al., 2008); providing positive effects from relationships among qualitative researchers (Dutton & Dukerich, 2006); dividing the work among other researchers; and/or adding a theory expert.[2] Although multiple authors do not necessarily mean multiple qualitative researchers, we decided to examine the authorship structure of qualitative research as a possible amplifying condition. In Table 3.4, we compared team authorship for the

TABLE 3.4 Paper Authorship: Single-Authored or Teams by Journal, 1990–2012

Academy of Management Journal	*Qualitative*		*Nonqualitative*		*Total*
Single-Authored	33	24%	207	18%	240
Teams	102	76%	974	82%	1076
TOTAL *AMJ* PAPERS	135		1181		1316
AMJ: Single-Authored vs. Team Papers	Chi-Square	3.9			*p* < .05
Administrative Science Quarterly	*Qualitative*		*Nonqualitative*		*Total*
Single-Authored	38	38%	129	37%	167
Teams	61	62%	223	63%	284
TOTAL ASQ PAPERS	99		352		451
ASQ: Single-Authored vs. Team Papers	Chi-Square	n.s.			*n.s.*
Organization Science	*Qualitative*		*Nonqualitative*		*Total*
Single-Authored	72	35%	102	23%	174
Teams	135	65%	414	77%	549
TOTAL OS PAPERS	207		516		723
OS: Single-Authored vs. Team Papers	Chi-Square	18.2			*p* < .001
TOTAL PAPERS	*Qualitative*		*Nonqualitative*		*Total*
Single-Authored	143	32%	438	24%	581
Teams	298	68%	1611	76%	1909
TOTAL PAPERS FROM 3 JOURNALS	441		2049		2490
TOTAL: Single-Authored vs. Team Papers	Chi-Square	17.2			*p* < .0001

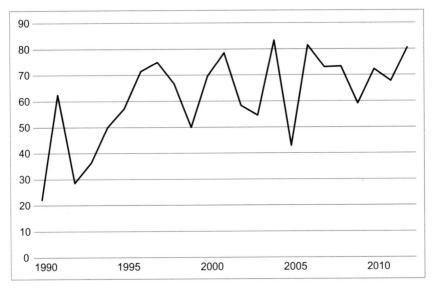

FIGURE 3.2 Trends in Qualitative Authorship: Teams, Three Journals, 1990–2012

441 qualitative articles to that of the 2,049 nonqualitative articles to determine whether qualitative research was conducted in teams more often than nonqualitative research was. Our results show that authorship teams comprised 68% of qualitative papers but 76% of nonqualitative papers, providing a significant difference ($\chi^2 = 17.2$; $p < .0001$). This relationship between author composition and type of methodology held for every journal except for *ASQ*. However, the trend of authorship over time (see Figure 3.2) is positive and significantly different from zero ($b = 1.48$; $t = 3.38$; $p < .01$), which indicates that qualitative research is increasingly being conducted in teams.

Our main finding from this study indicates that qualitative research is a significant part of these three management journals, thus busting the red-headed stepchild myth that qualitative research is at the margins of the management discipline. However, the small decline in *ASQ* qualitative publications during the last 7 years provides a kernel of truth to the myth about the growth of qualitative research. In the next section, we discuss the tipping points for qualitative research suggested by these findings.

Discussion

We began this study hoping to clarify the status of qualitative research and its growth trend. From our 23-year review of three management journals, we identified overall growth in the actual number of qualitative publications and in the proportion of journal space dedicated to qualitative research. We recognize that our analysis is missing other mainstream journals with lower rates of qualitative publication, which offers a kernel of truth to the red-headed myth, but the results of our analysis provide a strong foundation that bodes well for the future of qualitative publications.

We also looked deeper into why qualitative research is becoming more mainstream. We use Gladwell's (2000) tipping point framework to understand the factors that have contributed to the growth in qualitative research and discuss how these factors can continue to help. Gladwell (2000) defines a tipping point as the moment in time when change occurs rapidly and identifies three factors that help a trend "tip": the law of the few, context, and stickiness. We address each of this factors in the context of qualitative research in the management discipline to provide an explanation for the trends we observe.

The Law of the Few: Editors

Ideas become mainstream and thus reach their tipping point, according to Gladwell (2000), when influential, connected people champion them. In this context, journal editors are influential people who wield tremendous power to shape an academic journal during their tenure (Ketchen & Ireland, 2010). In each of the three journals, trends in qualitative publications can be traced to tenures for influential journal editors and their connections to other researchers. For instance, in his new role as *AMJ* editor, Tom Lee committed the journal to increasing its qualitative publications (Lee, 2001), at which point the number of editorial board members versed in qualitative research began to grow. This trend culminated in the appointment in 2011 of two associate editors to assess qualitative research specifically. These associate editors stated, "The fact that two associate editors are now dedicated exclusively to managing qualitative papers through the review process—one for micro submissions (Kevin) and the other for macro submissions (Tima)—is strong evidence of that commitment" (Bansal & Corley, 2011, p. 233).

Similarly, the initiating statement by the *OS* founding editors Daft and Lewin (1990, p. 2) addresses field studies:

> Our hopes for the journal are it will: play a role in enhancing research relevance, weaken the barriers to fresh methods and topics about organizations, incorporate ideas and methods from other disciplines, help loosen the buckles on the normal science straitjacket in which we believe the field of organization studies finds itself.

This trend can also be seen at *ASQ*. In fact, one of *ASQ*'s editorial board members (1978–1990 and 1993–2000), John Van Maanen, is often credited for bringing qualitative research into the mainstream literature with a watershed *ASQ* special issue in 1979 (e.g., Sutton, 1997). This evidence shows that clear signals from

78 Anne D. Smith et al.

influential editors have helped qualitative research "tip" and develop a significant presence in management journals.

The Power of the Context: Special Issues

The second factor in Gladwell's (2000) framework for tipping points suggests that small variations in context can have a magnifying effect on a trend. We see a parallel between the power of context and creation of special issues. Special issues provide a context in which to initiate conversations about promising new topics or reinvigorate conversations about topics that have received less contemporary research focus (Mowday, 2006; Priem, 2006; Rynes, 2003). Likewise, qualitative methods are best suited for exploring new topics and building theory (Eisenhardt & Graebner, 2007; Yin, 1994). As such, they provide a fit with special issues, which are designed (a) to attract finished or nearly finished manuscripts in a nascent area of scholarly interest; (b) to stimulate new research that would not have been conducted without the special-issue call for papers; and (c) to make the soliciting journal seem more interesting to readers because it highlights cutting-edge research (Rynes, 2003). Authors' and readers' interest in special issues may stem from evidence that special issues improve the knowledge development in a field by both speeding up the timeline to publication and producing more influential papers with higher citation counts (Olk & Griffith, 2004). Because qualitative methods are best suited for exploring new topics and building theory (Edmondson & McManus, 2007; Eisenhardt & Graebner, 2007), special issues create a beneficial context for qualitative research.

The Stickiness Factor: Winning Publications

Gladwell's (2000) third factor, stickiness, refers to the ability for an idea or phenomenon to influence behavior and stand out in memory. Qualitative research is exemplified as containing rich stories (Rynes, 2003) that can provide context for theories and carry an authenticity to the audience. The stickiness of these memorable stories may be part of the reason that qualitative papers in *AMJ* and *ASQ* are disproportionately selected as annual best paper winners. As seen in Table 3.5, the list of winners includes a much larger proportion of qualitative papers than is reflected in the proportion of total published papers. For instance, at *AMJ*, of the 24 award-winning papers published between 1986 and 2011, 11 were qualitative or mixed methods studies with a strong qualitative component. At *ASQ*, the same pattern held; of all 19 award-winning papers published on the *ASQ* site, 9 were qualitative. These percentages of winning papers, 42% and 47% respectively, are far higher than *AMJ*'s 17% and *ASQ*'s 21% during the last 7 years.

Qualitative research is not without its challenges, but our data suggest that qualitative research has reached a tipping point from which we can expect qualitative research to continue to increase from its current 17% of total publications in the

TABLE 3.5 *AMJ* and *ASQ* Award Winners[1]: Qualitative in Bold

	AMJ (11 qualitative out of 27 winning papers)	ASQ (9 qualitative out of 19 winning papers)
2011	**James R. Detert & Amy C. Edmondson[2]**	
2010	David R. Hekman, Karl Aquino, Bradley P. Owens, Terence R. Mitchell, Pauline Schilpzand, & Keith Leavitt	
2009	**Melissa E. Graebner**	
2008	Michael L. Barnett & Andrew A. King	
2007	**Donde Ashmos Plowman, Lakami T. Baker, Tammy E. Beck, Mukta Kulkarni, Stephanie Thomas Solansky, & Deandra Villarreal Travis**	Luis R. Gómez-Mejia, Katalin Takács Haynes, Manuel Núñez-Nickel, Kathyrn J. L. Jacobson, & José Moyano-Fuentes
2006	**Royston Greenwood & Roy Suddaby**	**Katherine J. Klein, Jonathan C. Ziegert, Andrew P. Knight, & Yan Xiao**
2005	**Clark G. Gilbert**	**Roy Suddaby & Royston Greenwood**
2005	**Ewan Ferlie, Louise Fitzgerald, Martin Wood, & Chris Hawkins**	
2004	Rajshree Agarwal, Raj Echambadi, April M. Franco, & M.B. Sarkar	**Kevin G. Corley & Dennis A. Gioia**
2003	**Kimberly D. Elsbach & Roderick M. Kramer**	Martha S. Feldman & Brian T. Pentland (theory)
2002	Peter D. Sherer & Kyungmook Lee	**Nicolaj Siggelkow**
2001	Scott E. Seibert, Marie L. Kraimer, & Robert C. Liden	**Robin J. Ely & David A. Thomas**
2000	Shaker A. Zahra, R. Duane Ireland, & Michael A. Hitt	Jesper B. Sørensen & Toby E. Stuart
1999	Walter J. Ferrier, Ken G. Smith, & Curtis M. Grimm	Morten T. Hansen
1998	Harry G. Barkema & Freek Vermeulen	**Mark J. Zbaracki**
1997	Anne S. Tsui, Jone L. Pearce, Lyman W. Porter, & Angela M. Tripoli	**Brian Uzzi**
1996	Danny Miller & Jamal Shamsie	Walter W. Powell, Kenneth W. Koput, & Laurel Smith-Doerr
1995	Mark A. Huselid	Kathleen M. Eisenhardt & Behnam N. Tabrizi
1994	Eric Abrahamson & Choelsoon Park	Jane E. Dutton, Janet M. Dukerich, & Celia V. Harquail (theory)
1993	D. Harold Doty, William H. Glick, & George P. Huber	**James R. Barker**
1992	Luis R. Gomez-Mejia & David B. Balkin	Anne S. Tsui, Terri D. Egan, & Charles A. O'Reilly III

(Continued)

80 Anne D. Smith et al.

TABLE 3.5 (Continued)

	AMJ *(11 qualitative out of 27 winning papers)*	*ASQ* *(9 qualitative out of 19 winning papers)*
1991	**Jane E. Dutton & Janet M. Dukerich**	Jennifer A. Chatman
1990	**Lynn A. Isabella**	**Rebecca Henderson & Kim B. Clark**
1989	**Connie J. G. Gersick**	Charles A. O'Reilly III, David F. Caldwell, & William P. Barnett
1988	**Robert I. Sutton & Anat Rafaeli**	
1987	Gareth R. Jones	
1986	Toby D. Wall, Nigel J. Kemp, Paul R. Jackson, & Chris W. Clegg	

[1] We could not find a similar list of paper winners for *Organization Science*. The award-winning papers were found on the *AMJ* and *ASQ* websites.

[2] This paper was one of the most difficult to categorize as qualitative, mixed method, or nonqualitative. In the end, after discussion among authors, we decided to code it as mixed method given the rich interview data were analyzed and displayed in the paper, qualitative results complemented their quantitative study 2, and the qualitative research was not subservient to the quantitative studies.

journals we reviewed. We hope that addressing the legend about this particular methodology will hearten current qualitative researchers and encourage those contemplating the use of qualitative methods.

Conclusions

Although quantitative research methodologies continue to dominate management journals, qualitative methodologies have become much more common than even a decade ago. Podsakoff and Dalton (1987) were correct that time would help qualitative research come into its own. We hope that clarifying thinking about qualitative research will help increase its presence across the top management journals. Ghoshal's (2005) criticism of management theories developed out of business schools with an overly narrow scientific approach to studying real-world organizations is evidence that opportunities for qualitative methods abound. Our evidence suggests that qualitative research is not nearly the outlier it once was.

Our study is not without limitations. First, we only evaluated published papers. Had our analysis been based on the total set of papers submitted for review, perhaps different patterns would have emerged. However, in a 2013 CARMA talk, *AMJ* associate editor Tima Bansal identified an increasing submission rate of qualitative research (at 13.4%) between 2010 and 2013 and concluded that the percentage of qualitative published papers should increase in the future (Bansal, 2013). Second, we categorized all authors of an article classified according to our definition of qualitative as qualitative researchers. This decision probably overstates the number of qualitative authors. Third, we did not assess the relative strength of the relationships we identified, only that a relationship between two variables existed and was not by chance.

We recognize the irony of using quantitative methods to examine qualitative issues, but we aimed to uncover significant patterns. Future study using qualitative methods could build on the findings reported here and delve deeper into *how* qualitative research is making inroads into journals and *why* authors choose the methodologies they do. We recognize that our myth of qualitative research at the margin is not completely debunked given the exclusion of certain journals, but, perhaps in a third edition of this methodological myths book, we might see tipping-point elements reflected in growth of qualitative research in *SMJ* and *JOM*. In the end, we hope that our findings will encourage researchers—young and old, trained in qualitative methods or not, working together or alone—to pursue qualitative methods and open management theory to new lenses, ideas, and provocative insights. We see a bright future ahead for qualitative research in management. It truly is "coming of age" (Bansal & Corley, 2011, p. 233) and becoming a part of the management research family.

Acknowledgments

We appreciate the help of Laura D'Oria and Blake Mathias (both doctoral students at the University of Tennessee Knoxville) for some coding in this paper.

Notes

1 This extremely low percentage of qualitative articles in management may result from Eby and colleagues' approach to identifying qualitative research. They used search terms instead of an article-by-article review and categorization, which is seen with some reviews with a higher percentage of qualitative research in management (Locke & Golden-Biddle, 1997; Plowman & Smith, 2011). It also appears that Eby and colleagues (2008) may not have included terms such as "inductive" or "field studies" in their search, further dampening the number of identified qualitative articles. The qualitative paper categorization approach used in this paper was to review each published paper and categorize it, an approach we believe should be used by researchers of future review pieces. We are willing to share our list of qualitative papers in order to maintain an apples-to-apples comparison in the future.

2 Qualitative research can generate findings about theoretical directions unanticipated at the beginning of a study. Some authors are brought into a qualitative project to offer theoretical expertise to expedite revisions and movement toward publication.

References

Bansal, T. (2013). *Tips and traps for publishing qualitative research: An editor's perspective.* CARMA talk April 19, 2013, http://carma.wayne.edu/VideoLibrary.asp

82 Anne D. Smith et al.

Bansal, T., & Corley, K. (2011). The coming of age for qualitative research: Embracing the diversity of qualitative methods. *Academy of Management Journal, 54*, 233–237.

Barley, S. R. (1986). Technology as an occasion for restructuring: Evidence from observations of CT scanners and the social order of radiology departments. *Administrative Science Quarterly, 31*, 78–108.

Buchanan, D. A., & Bryman, A. (2007). Contextualizing methods choice in organizational research. *Organizational Research Methods, 10*, 483–501.

Creswell, J. (1998). *Qualitative inquiry and research design: Choosing among five traditions.* Thousand Oaks, CA: Sage Publications.

Daft, R. L. (1980). The evolution of organization analysis in *ASQ*, 1959–1979. *Administrative Science Quarterly, 25*, 623–636.

Daft, R. L., & Lewin, A. Y. (1990). Can organization studies begin to break out from the normal science straightjacket? An editorial essay. *Organization Science, 1*, 1–11.

Dutton, J. E., & Dukerich, J. M. (2006). The relational foundation of research: An underappreciated dimension of interesting research. *Academy of Management Journal, 49*, 21–26.

Eby, L. T., Hurst, C. S., & Butts, M. M. (2008). Qualitative research: The redheaded stepchild in organizational and social science research? In C. E. Lance & R. J. Vandenberg (Eds.), *Statistical and methodological myths and urban legends: Doctrine, verity and fable in organizational and social sciences* (pp. 219–246). New York, NY: Routledge.

Edmondson, A. C., & McManus, S. E. (2007). Methodological fit in management field research. *Academy of Management Review, 32*, 1155–1179.

Eisenhardt, K. M. (1989a). Building theories from case study research. *Academy of Management Review, 14*, 532–550.

Eisenhardt, K. M. (1989b). Making fast decisions in high-velocity environments. *Academy of Management Review, 32*, 543–576.

Eisenhardt, K. M., & Bourgeois, L. J. (1988). Politics of strategic decision making in high-velocity environments: Toward a midrange theory. *Academy of Management Journal, 31*, 737–770.

Eisenhardt, K. M., & Graebner, M. E. (2007). Theory building from cases: Opportunities and challenges. *Academy of Management Journal, 50*, 25–32.

Gephart, R. (1999). *Paradigms and research methods.* Paper presented at the annual meeting of the Academy of Management, Chicago, IL.

Gephart, R. (2004). Qualitative research and the *Academy of Management Journal*. *Academy of Management Journal, 47*, 454–462.

Ghoshal, S. (2005). Bad management theories are destroying good management practices. *Academy of Management Learning & Education, 4*, 75–91.

Gladwell, M. (2000). *The tipping point: How little things can make a big difference.* New York, NY: Little Brown.

Johnson, P., Buehring, A., Cassell, C., & Symon, G. (2007). Defining qualitative management research: An empirical investigation. *Qualitative Research in Organizations and Management: An International Journal, 2*, 23–42.

Ketchen, D. J., & Ireland, R. D. (2010). Upon further review: A survey of the *Academy of Management Journal*'s editorial board. *Academy of Management Journal, 53*, 208–271.

Kidd, S. A. (2002). The role of qualitative research in psychological journals. *Psychological Methods, 7*, 126–138.

Langley, A. (1999). Strategies for theorizing from process data. *Academy of Management Review, 24*, 691–710.

Lee, T. W. (1999). *Using qualitative methods in organizational research.* Thousand Oaks, CA: Sage Publications.

Lee, T. W. (2001). On qualitative research at *AMJ. Academy of Management Journal, 44*(2), 215–216.

Lincoln, Y. S., Lynham, S. A., & Guba, E. G. (2011). Paradigmatic controversies, contradictions, and emerging confluences, revisited. In N. K. Denzin & Y. S. Lincoln (Eds.), *The SAGE handbook of qualitative research* (pp. 97–128). Thousand Oaks, CA: Sage.

Locke, K., & Golden-Biddle, K. (1997). Constructing opportunities for contribution: Structuring intertextual coherence and "problematizing" in organizational studies. *Academy of Management Journal, 40*, 1023–1062.

Locke, K., & Golden-Biddle, K. (2002). An introduction to qualitative research: Its potential for industrial and organizational psychology. In S. G. Rogelberg (Ed.), *Handbook of research methods in IO psychology* (pp. 99–117). Malden, MA: Blackwell Publishers.

McGrath, J. (1982). Dilemmatics: The study of research choices and dilemmas. In J. E. McGrath, J. Martin, & R. A. Kulka (Eds.), *Judgment calls in research* (pp. 69–102). Newbury Park, GA: Sage.

Miles, M. B., & Huberman, A. M. (1994). *Qualitative data analysis: A sourcebook of new methods* (2nd ed.). Beverly Hills, CA: Sage.

Molina-Azorin, J. F. (2009). Understanding how mixed methods research is undertaken within a specific research community: The case of business studies. *International Journal of Multiple Research Approaches, 3*, 47–57.

Mowday, R. T. (2006). If special issues of journals are not so special, why has their use proliferated? *Journal of Management Inquiry, 15*, 389–393.

Olk, P., & Griffith, T. L. (2004). Creating and disseminating knowledge among organizational scholars: The role of special issues. *Organization Science, 15*, 120–129.

Plowman, D. A., & Smith, A. D. (2011). The gendering of organizational research methods. *Qualitative Research in Organizations and Management, 6*, 64–82.

Podsakoff, P. M., & Dalton, D. R. (1987). Research methodology in organizational studies. *Journal of Management, 13*, 419–441.

Pratt, M. G. (2008). Fitting oval pegs into round holes: Tensions in evaluating and publishing qualitative research in top-tier North American journals. *Organizational Research Methods, 11*, 481–509.

Priem, R. L. (2006). What happens when special issues just aren't "special" anymore? *Journal of Management Inquiry, 15*, 383–388.

Rynes, S. (2003). From the editors: Special research forums: Past, present, and future. *Academy of Management Journal, 46*, 535–537.

Scandura, T. A., & Williams, E. A. (2000). Research methodology in management: Current practices, trends, and implications for future research. *Academy of Management Journal, 43*, 1248–1264.

Siggelkow, N. (2007). Persuasion with case studies. *Academy of Management Journal, 50*, 20–24.

Smith, A. D. (2002). From process data to publication: A personal sensemaking. *Journal of Management Inquiry, 11*, 383–406.

Suddaby, R. (2006). From the editors: What grounded theory is not. *Academy of Management Journal, 49*, 633–642.

Sutton, R. (1987). The process of organizational death: Disbanding and reconnecting. *Administrative Science Quarterly, 32*, 542–569.

Sutton, R. I. (1997). The virtues of closet qualitative research. *Organization Science, 8*, 97–106.

Van Maanen, J. (1979). Reclaiming qualitative methods for organizational research: A preface. *Administrative Science Quarterly, 24*, 520–526.

Van Maanen, J. (1998). *Different strokes: Qualitative research in the* Administrative Science Quarterly *from 1956 to 1996.* Thousand Oaks, CA: Sage Publications.

Weick, K. E. (2007). The generative properties of richness. *Academy of Management Journal, 50*, 14–19.

Yin, R. K. (1994). *Case study research: Design and methods.* Thousand Oaks, CA: Sage Publications.

4

TWO WAVES OF MEASUREMENT DO NOT A LONGITUDINAL STUDY MAKE

Robert E. Ployhart and William I. MacKenzie Jr.

Anyone who has ever faced the "who started it" question with arguing children (or adults, for that matter) knows that two waves of data are insufficient for answering it. The simple action–consequence observation is often misleading, as the real "event" that caused the arguing has occurred earlier (sometimes much earlier) and for reasons very different than currently recognized. Every parent thus knows that we do not live in a two-wave world and certainly not a cross-sectional world. More broadly, every person, group, organization, and culture has an ongoing history that determines its present state. This history and present state, in turn, influence how we view the future, the manner in which we interpret the world around us, and the choices we make. If we do not understand the history of a particular situation, then it becomes difficult to understand what is occurring and why it is occurring. Trying to make sense of our world is nearly impossible when viewed from a cross-sectional lens. Observing an event at "Time 1" and seeing the consequence at "Time 2" might offer a bit more insight than a cross-sectional perspective, but not much more.

A truly longitudinal perspective is needed to appreciate the evolution and change of natural and organizational phenomena. Longitudinal research designs are fundamentally intended to strengthen causal inferences and enhance understanding of how phenomena, constructs, and processes change over time. It is widely recognized that research employing longitudinal designs is preferable to cross-sectional designs (Mitchell & James, 2001; Roe, 2008; Rogosa, 1995). Although it is certainly true that longitudinal designs can be more difficult to conduct, there is not much debate that longitudinal designs are generally more informative. What is ironic is that the field lacks a clear sense as to what a longitudinal design really is. As we explain in this chapter, many studies fashion themselves to be longitudinal in nature, yet they rely on only two waves of data. If one

86 Robert E. Ployhart et al.

accepts the premise that a longitudinal design should enhance our understanding of change over time, then longitudinal designs must contain a minimum of three waves of repeated data on the same variable.

We develop this point in the sections that follow. We first define longitudinal research and provide a brief overview of the kinds of benefits that such designs provide over cross-sectional studies. We then present the myth of interest in this chapter: that any study with two measurement occasions is a longitudinal study. We deconstruct this myth to identify its key features and examine the extent to which the extant literature embraces it. We then consider the kernel of truth that has breathed life into the myth. We conclude with the contemporary status of this myth, how to eliminate it, and how to advance the field in a manner that appreciates all designs while making clear that two waves of measurement do not a longitudinal study make.

Longitudinal Research: Definitions and Benefits

Ployhart and Vandenberg (2010, p. 97) define longitudinal research as "research emphasizing the study of change and containing at minimum three repeated observations (although more than three is better) on at least one of the substantive constructs of interest." This definition captures many of the prior arguments made by methodologists specializing in longitudinal research (Chan, 1998; Rogosa, 1995; Singer & Willett, 2003).

First, the definition emphasizes the *study of change*. A complete understanding of constructs, processes, relationships, or phenomena cannot occur without knowing how they change, unfold, or evolve over time. As Roe (2008, p. 37) so eloquently noted, "no form of behavior could possibly be defined without reference to time, and no behavior could be observed if the time interval were limited to zero." Pitariu and Ployhart (2010) further argued that most theories propose simple bivariate relationships absent any consideration of time or change and, hence, lead to the development of weak hypotheses that are difficult to falsify. Cohen, Cohen, West, and Aiken (2003, p. 569) state, "When data are gathered without reference to the timing of changes in variables, . . . our inferences about the functional relationships that give rise to the observations are bound to be correspondingly weak." Thus, if we need to study a phenomenon over time to truly understand it, there is no substitute for longitudinal designs.

Second, the definition recognizes that for any given variable, *three waves* of data collected repeatedly on the same observations *is the minimum number* of measurement occasions needed to adequately model change. The minimum number of waves of measurement is the key to differentiating a study that explores change over time from one that does not. Two waves of repeated measures data cannot adequately inform questions of change and hence are not a longitudinal study.

Overall, the use of longitudinal research designs offers many theoretical and empirical benefits. First, longitudinal designs can provide stronger inferences of causality (Singer & Willett, 2003). Second, longitudinal designs offer better estimates of relationships and better tests of mediation (Maxwell & Cole, 2007). Third, longitudinal designs enable more falsifiable hypotheses (Pitariu & Ployhart, 2010). Fourth, longitudinal designs reduce concerns about common method variance (at least to the extent such biases exist; Podsakoff, MacKenzie, Lee, & Podsakoff, 2003). Finally, longitudinal designs allow unique insights into the nature of how constructs and processes evolve over time (Roe, 2008). Given that most theory in management and the social sciences is fundamentally concerned with understanding the nature of relationships over time (Mitchell & James, 2001; Roe, 2008), the use of longitudinal research designs and analyses is absolutely vital to the advancement of the management and applied psychology professions (George & Jones, 2000).

Despite the many benefits, longitudinal research and designs also carry a host of unique conceptual, methodological, and analytical challenges that are often rarely understood (Ployhart & Vandenberg, 2010; Singer & Willett, 2003). Outside of some specializations (e.g., developmental psychology), there has traditionally been little systematic training provided to help students understand these challenges. As a result, and through no fault of their own, many researchers have a misunderstanding of some key issues underlying longitudinal research. One of the most pervasive of these misunderstandings is how many waves of data are needed to conduct a longitudinal study that informs questions of change.

The Myth: Two Waves of Data Make a Longitudinal Study

The myth we examine in this chapter is that two waves of data make a longitudinal study. There are two broad ways to conceptualize a two-wave study, and these are illustrated in Figures 4.1a and 4.1b. The first and most common approach is to have an independent variable (X) measured at Time 1 and a dependent variable (Y) measured at Time 2 (Figure 4.1a). For example, a researcher may examine job attitudes at Time 1 and job performance at Time 2 and *claim* to be studying the relationship between job attitudes and performance longitudinally. The second and less common approach is to have two repeated measurements on the same variable, where X1 and X2 represent the measurement of variable X at Times 1 and 2, respectively. For example, a researcher may examine job attitudes at Time 1 and then again at Time 2. In this example, the purpose of the study will be focused on changes in job attitudes.

However, regardless of whether the form taken is in Figure 4.1a or Figure 4.1b, two waves of data cannot adequately address questions of change. There are several reasons (see Rogosa, 1988, 1995; Rogosa, Brandt, & Zimowski, 1982). First, with two waves of measurement, the only form of change that can be studied is a straight line, and hence it is impossible to identify any curvilinear changes or trends. Given that many if not most phenomena likely change in a curvilinear manner over extended periods of time (George & Jones, 2000; Roe, 2008), it means

88 Robert E. Ployhart et al.

a. Two waves of measurement, two different variables. Cannot adequately inform questions of change.

b. Two waves of measurement, one variable. Cannot adequately inform questions of change.

c. Three waves of measurement, three different variables. Cannot adequately inform questions of change.

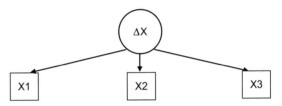

d. Three waves of measurement, one variable. The minimum necessary to adequately inform questions of change. The "Δ" symbol refers to change.

FIGURE 4.1 Examples of Designs that Include Time. X = independent variable, Y = dependent variable; M = mediating variable. The number refers to the timing of measurement.

that a two-wave study could greatly confuse or even misestimate the true nature of change taking place. For example, the solid line in Figure 4.2 shows a curvilinear pattern of change in the form of a U-shaped curve. There are no two time periods a researcher may pick that can adequately represent the nature of this curvilinear change. Stated more simply, any two-wave representation of the data in Figure 4.2 is, in the broader nature of the trend, wrong.

Second, it is only possible to examine the gain or difference between the two time periods. Such effects may be relevant for studies that emphasize pre-post group mean differences, such as the implementation of training and similar interventions. However, the two-wave study has great potential for misestimating effect sizes and reliability (Rogosa, 1995; Willett, 1989). It cannot adequately assess heterogeneity in change rates between observations.

Third, separating measurement occasions may help reduce method bias effects, but such an approach does not constitute a longitudinal study. First, the study is

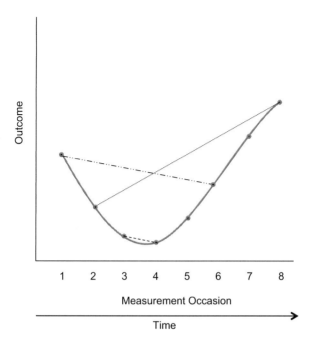

FIGURE 4.2 Example Showing How Two Waves of Measurement Will Misinform Questions of Change. In any given line between two data points, the form of change fails to capture the true trajectory. The different dashed lines illustrate three such connections between two data points. The solid line illustrates the true trend line.

not intended to inform questions of change but rather to address concerns about method bias. Second, there are no repeated measurements on any variable. Figure 4.1a illustrates this clearly, showing there is no form of change that can be modeled because every variable is only measured once. The design shown in Figure 4.1a is therefore only slightly better than a cross-sectional design.

Finally, even though the separation of measurement occasions may enhance inferences of cause and effect, temporal separation—by itself—says nothing about change. One of the reasons people believe two-wave studies are longitudinal is because they separate the timing of the two measures. Time is certainly a characteristic of longitudinal research, but the simple presence of temporal separation between the measurement of variables is not the defining feature of a longitudinal study. The most fundamental concern is that relying only on temporal separation between two variables masks or distorts the nature of dynamic relationships. For example, Ployhart and Hale (2014) apply Roe's (2008) framework to illustrate how different human resource interventions may differ in their onset, duration, and offset. The implementation of most human resource interventions will have some temporal lag that occurs before effects are noticeable (e.g., Birdi et al., 2008). The problem is that the literature says almost nothing about how long these lagged

90 Robert E. Ployhart et al.

effects may be, and it is nearly impossible to detect the effects without multiple repeated waves of data on the same variables. Thus, even though a meaningful period of time is needed to observe effects (George & Jones, 2000; Mitchell & James, 2001; Singer & Willett, 2003), there is no way questions of onset, duration, or offset can be observed without multiple waves of data.

To summarize, longitudinal studies are intended to inform questions of change (Cohen et al., 2003; Cronbach & Furby, 1970; Singer & Willett, 2003). Consequently, three waves of repeated measurement on the focal variable are minimally needed to allow a reasonable examination of change (Rogosa, 1995; Rogosa et al., 1982). Anything less than three waves of repeated data on the same variable will (a) limit the examination to cross-sectional relationships, (b) confound measurement error with systematic variance related to substantive change, and/or (c) produce potentially misleading estimates of the average amount of change observed (Rogosa, 1988, 1995; Singer & Willett, 2003).

Evidence and Variations of the Myth

Although it has been known for more than 30 years (e.g., Rogosa et al., 1982) that a minimum of three waves of repeated data is needed to understand change, the myth lives on. For example, Cohen and colleagues (2003, p. 569) suggested, "In the vast majority of published longitudinal studies in psychology and other behavioral sciences, data are collected at two points in time." We have considered two such examples in Figures 4.1a and 4.1b, but there are other manifestations of the myth. Most notable is Figure 4.1c, which presents a set of mediated relationships. Each measure (X, mediator M, and Y) is measured only once, and as we discuss shortly, cannot address questions of change (Maxwell & Cole, 2007). Only the relationships in Figure 4.1d can address questions of change, and hence only Figure 4.1d is an example of a longitudinal study.

To substantiate the various manifestations of the myth shown in Figures 4.1a, 4.1b, and 4.1c, we selectively review the literature to show that many studies claiming to be longitudinal simply are not. These studies are not longitudinal because they do not contain three repeated measures of the same variable. As we identify these studies, we do not intend to criticize the authors. Publishing is a difficult job and always conducted within one's scope of understanding. It is unfair to criticize authors for issues a reasonable person would not have known about or to criticize them on points that were not central to the purposes of their research. Therefore, to ensure readers understand that we are not above such criticism, we use our own earlier research (from when we were less familiar with longitudinal research) as examples whenever possible. We now consider each of the exemplars shown in Figure 4.1.

First, Figure 4.1a illustrates a study with two different variables measured at two different time periods. An example of this type of study describing itself as longitudinal but using only two waves of data (X and Y) is provided by Ployhart and

Ryan (1998). They simulated a selection process and measured fairness perceptions prehire (Time 1) and intentions posthire (Time 2). Another example is provided by Dulac, Coyle-Shapiro, Henderson, and Wayne (2008), who examined perceived organizational support and leader–member exchange at one time period and psychological breach and various work outcomes at a later time period. While both studies describe themselves as longitudinal, they actually are not because each variable is only measured once. This design does little to inform questions of change given that with only a single observation, there is nothing in which to observe change. We do not mean to be overly critical of this type of design because it has many benefits. First, it may help reduce concerns about method bias (Podsakoff et al., 2003). Second, it may offer stronger causal inferences than a cross-sectional study. Third, if the measurement occasions are substantively important, then it may offer practical implications as well (e.g., Time 1 is the start of college, Time 2 is the end of college). However, it is not a longitudinal study in the sense that it doesn't inform change. In fact, there is nothing that can change because each variable is only measured once.

Second, Figure 4.1b illustrates a study where scores on X1 are related to scores on X2. This is the classic pre-post design, but because it is limited to two repeated observations, is also limited to an examination of gain or difference scores (Cronbach & Furby, 1970). Ployhart and Ryan (1998) again provide an example, where even though fairness perceptions were measured both prehire and posthire, only two waves of measurement were used. This design has some value in the sense that it perhaps controls for prior scores, but it is of limited applicability for understanding change (Rogosa, 1995). First, it confounds different sources of variance. Second, the only line that can fit two waves is a straight line. Finally, high stability between Times 1 and 2 will produce low reliability (Cronbach & Furby, 1970). Therefore, this design is not one that provides adequate insight into change over time.

Third, studies that examine mediation using three (or more) waves of data with no repeated measures do not inform questions of change. Figure 4.1c illustrates a common example, such as X at Time 1 leads to a mediator (M) at Time 2, which leads to Y at Time 3. Like the design shown in Figure 4.1a, this design helps reduce concerns about method bias. It may also help reduce concerns about contemporaneous relationships, and it offers stronger insights about causality than a cross-sectional design. But it is not a design that will inform questions of change, because again, there are no repeated measurements on any of the variables. Indeed, Maxwell and Cole (2007) make the strong demonstration that mediation implies temporal precedence among variables that are related over time. Ignoring temporal issues may severely bias mediation tests and estimates, even to the point where the sign of effect sizes can reverse. An empirical example of a study claiming to be longitudinal but corresponding to Figure 4.1c is provided by Langfred (2007). This study examined task (X1a) and relationship conflict (X1b; both at Time 1) leading to trust (M2; Time 2), leading to autonomy (Y3a) and interdependence (Y3b; both at Time 3). Despite the term "longitudinal" appearing in the title, it is not a study that can inform questions of change in any of the constructs. Another example is provided by Nifadkar, Tsui, and Ashforth (2012). They examined newcomer affect and studied relationships among four different sets of variables, with each set measured at a different time (thus, two sets of mediated relationships). Separating the timing of the measures was important for both theoretical and methodological considerations, but the fact that each variable was measured only once precludes it from answering questions about change, and hence it is not a longitudinal study.

In contrast, Figure 4.1d shows the minimum longitudinal design necessary to inform questions of change. There are three repeated measurement occasions on a single variable, and so it is possible to model intraobservation change over time. More measurement occasions are to be preferred, because they enhance statistical power, provide greater precision around the estimation of the trend, and have greater reliability (Ployhart & Vandenberg, 2010; Willett, 1989). Therefore, three or more waves of data helps reduce many of the limitations of the two-wave study noted by Cronbach and Furby (1970).

A Kernel of Truth

The purpose of conducting a longitudinal study is to understand change (Chan, 1998; Cohen et al., 2003; Cronbach & Furby, 1970; Ployhart & Vandenberg, 2010; Singer & Willett, 2003). There is a kernel of truth underlying the myth that two waves of data make a longitudinal study. Actually, there are two kernels.

First, technically speaking and in the most narrow way, it is possible to study differences over time using two waves of repeated measures data (Rogosa, 1988). As Rogosa (1995, p. 8) himself notes, "A more exact statement of the myth would be that two observations are presumed to be adequate for studying change." But we have noted that there are a host of conceptual and methodological problems associated with trying to understand two-wave differences, and for this reason trying to understand change with two waves of repeated data is generally to be avoided (Chan, 1998; Cronbach & Furby, 1970; Singer & Willett, 2003). It is also for this reason that we use the term "differences" rather than "change" when discussing two waves of repeated data. Thus, the first kernel of truth is not true except under the most optimistic (i.e., unrealistic) conditions.

Second, the term "longitudinal" has historically been equated with research "design." Again, Rogosa (1995, p. 8) notes that this myth's origin was "inspired by the dominance of pre-test, post-test longitudinal designs in the methodological and empirical work of the behavioral and social sciences." Prior to the 1980s, most any study with two waves of temporally separated data that were also based on the same observations was called a longitudinal study (e.g., Berdie, 1955; McClelland, 1965; Van Maanen, 1975). Even more recently, Kirk (1995, p. 11) states, "The term longitudinal study refers to any research strategy in which the same individuals are observed at two or more times." However, scholars began to broaden their thinking of change from group mean differences to intraobservation differences over time. Early work in this tradition was prompted by Rao (1958) and Tucker (1958), who independently proposed growth curve methodologies. Growth curves are methods designed to fit a trend to a set of repeated data for each person (or whatever the unit of observation may be, such as insects or organizations). The term "growth" was used because much of this early work focused on biological growth or developmental growth in infants; however, these curves were also examined within the context of learning (e.g., "learning curves," Tucker, 1966). An analysis of growth curves in these early studies focused on how a given observation *changes* over time; hence the labeling of "intraobservation" change. The emphasis on intraobservation change really took off in the 1980s. First, Rogosa and colleagues (1982) effectively shifted the conversation of change from group mean pre-post differences to an intraobservation growth curve framework and an emphasis on within-observation change over time. Then a convergence of methods, software, and publications enabled the implementation and testing of a growth-curve framework (e.g., Bryk & Raudenbush, 1987; Laird & Ware, 1982; McArdle & Epstein, 1987; Meredith & Tisak, 1990; Tisak & Meredith, 1990; Willett & Sayer, 1994).

Since this earlier work, nothing less than a paradigm shift has occurred within the social sciences, with numerous applications, extensions, and integrations of growth curve models being proposed (Bliese & Ployhart, 2002; Chan, 1998; Curran, 2003; Lance, Mead, & Williamson, 2000; Singer & Willett, 2003). Today, our focus is squarely on intraobservation change and between-observation differences (interobservation differences) in intraobservation change (Curran & Bauer, 2011; Ployhart & Vandenberg, 2010). We see, then, that as methodologies advanced from simple pre-post group mean differences to the modeling of intraobservation change via growth curves, scholars began to adopt such methods and develop theories using the opportunities that those methods provided.

Thus, as scholars broadened their thinking about change from pre-post group mean differences to intraobservation differences over time, the term "longitudinal" did not evolve in a corresponding manner. The term "longitudinal" has remained overly inclusive, perhaps even stretched, to the point where it means different things to different scholars. Yet these kernels of truth should not be mistaken for truth, and moving past the myth is the focus of the final section of this chapter.

Moving Past the Myth

It should now be clear that having two waves of repeated-measures data is not the same as a longitudinal design in the sense that a longitudinal design is intended to understand change over time and that three measurement occasions from the same observations are necessary to provide such insights. To move past the myth and develop a more common form of communication and understanding, we make the following recommendations.

94 Robert E. Ployhart et al.

First, research should stop using the term "longitudinal" to describe studies illustrated in Figures 4.1a, 4.1b, and 4.1c, simply because they are not cross-sectional. To use the term "longitudinal" confers a number of strengths and perceptions of methodological rigor, such as stronger inferences of causality, examination of change, and higher reliability. These benefits are simply not warranted unless the study design employed is (minimally) like that shown in Figure 4.1d.

Second, studies that separate the timing of measures to reduce method bias are not longitudinal and should not refer to themselves as such. Examples of these kind of studies are shown in Figures 4.1a and 4.1c. The separation of measurement occasions may help strengthen inferences of causality, but it is certainly not able to inform questions of change. Rather, it was done primarily to reduce concerns about method bias. A longitudinal study may reduce concerns about method bias, but reducing method bias does not necessarily make for a longitudinal study.

Third, research should stop treating cross-sectional studies as the villain. We see this happen fairly frequently, such as when a study employs a design as shown in Figure 4.1a and claims it offers more insight than a cross-sectional design. We agree, but with the caveat, *not that much more insight.* This claim is like the supposed benefits of using low-nicotine cigarettes: yes, compared to regular cigarettes the low-nicotine ones are better, but not much, and certainly not better than avoiding smoking in the first place. Claiming to be more rigorous than a cross-sectional study is a pretty weak argument for the benefits of a study's design, and we suggest authors focus directly on the benefits or limitations rather than beating the stuffing out of the poor cross-sectional straw man!

Fourth, "box-and-arrow" models may imply a longitudinal process, but they are poor representations of it (Ployhart & Hale, 2014; Roe, 2008; Wright & Haggerty, 2005). For example, a study such as that shown in Figure 4.1c may certainly note it is a strength to have separated the timing of measurement occasions. Indeed, it might be argued that temporal separation is necessary to capture temporal lags between cause and effect. But the design in Figure 4.1c is awfully close to a cross-sectional study for any given relationship considered. That is, the arrow between any two variables does not imply change, growth, time, timing, or duration. Arrows mask temporal processes, and box-and-arrow models that have become so common in publications are often quite poor at explicating processes of growth, change, or development. It is what happens "within the arrow" that is important to understand because that is where change is occurring.

Fifth, and relatedly, we need to push theory development to emphasize change over time (Mitchell & James, 2001; Roe, 2008). As Roe (2008) notes, we know almost nothing about how long a phenomenon or effect lasts (duration), when it begins (onset), or when it will end (offset). We have echoed this concern, having argued that one can take nearly any phenomenon or process of interest and ask questions about how it originates, changes, and evolves or transforms over time and likely make a significant contribution to the existing literature (e.g., Ployhart & Hale, 2014). Answers to these kinds of questions also increase the practical relevance of our research. For example, how long do perceptions of injustice last? When one experiences a shock at work, how long does it take before one starts to look for a new job? If one goes on a vacation, is there a positive or negative effect when returning to work, and for how long does that effect occur? As we noted at the start of this chapter, we don't live in a cross-sectional world any more than we live in a two-wave world. Adopting a longitudinal perspective provides an opportunity to revisit prior theories and established findings and to examine the extent to which they may hold over time.

Sixth, while we firmly believe that methods should be applied to test theories, we also believe that methods offer the opportunity to challenge theories by operationalizing them in more specific ways. The relationship between methods and theory should be symbiotic, not unidirectional, as both are necessary to advance science. We encourage the development of even more refinements and extensions to longitudinal modeling. For example, one particularly important development involves the examination of discontinuous growth curve models. Lange and Bliese (2009) applied a discontinuous growth curve model to study the effects of cognitive ability on adaptation to unexpected task changes. They showed that those with higher cognitive ability actually demonstrated a greater reduction in performance at the time when the task changes. Such an insight would be obscured without modeling the discontinuous nature of change in this setting and hence leads to new theoretical insights that might not have otherwise been identified.

Seventh, journal editors and reviewers must take ownership of this issue. We have encountered many instances in which reviewers who are well intentioned and trying to be constructive use the term "longitudinal" in a manner inconsistent with the examination of change over time. For example, they may not recognize the differences between repeated-measures designs, longitudinal designs, and studies that emphasize change. This is oftentimes through no fault of their own because, as we have seen, the myth is quite hard to identify, contains a kernel of truth, and many scholars are not trained in longitudinal methods. Yet in our opinion, rather than letting the myth slide, the editor must take a more active role. When editors see reviewers misapplying the term "longitudinal," they should clarify the term for the benefit of the author and reviewer. Editors should ensure authors are using the terms correctly, even if the issue is not raised by reviewers.

Eighth, as a profession, we need to do a better job of training doctoral students about longitudinal methods. Training in longitudinal research methods is something that appears to be increasing, but is still not very common or systematic across graduate programs. Usually, the training tends to occur if the department or program happens to have a faculty member who engages in longitudinal research. More common is to have a first-year class on regression and ANOVA and have repeated-measures designs be part of the ANOVA sequence. However, it should now be clear that this type of training (e.g., ANOVA repeated-measures models) is insufficient for informing questions of intraindividual change. There needs to be consistent training on this topic, and training that is consistent in its use of the

96 Robert E. Ployhart et al.

term "longitudinal." Given the largely idiosyncratic nature of graduate programs, it may take systematic efforts from organizations such as the Center for the Advancement of Research Methods and Analysis (CARMA) to produce the kind of large-scale change necessary.

To sum it up, let's reserve the use of the term "longitudinal" to refer only to the study of change over time. Studies like those shown in Figures 4.1a, 4.1b, or 4.1c do not inform change and are not longitudinal. Reserve the use of the term "longitudinal" for designs that are intended to study change processes, use a minimum of three repeated waves of data on at least one of the variables of interest, and are intended to study intraobservation change over time. Use terms such as "repeated measures" for designs such as shown in Figure 4.1b and terms such as "temporal separation" for designs such as shown in Figures 4.1a and 4.1c. These terms are closer to the actual purpose and operationalization of the study—so let's leave the term "longitudinal" out of it.

. . . And if the Myth Continues?

One might reasonably question, "So what if the myth continues?" We believe myths such as the one examined in this chapter serve no immediate harm. However, in the long run, they are quite damaging because they provide a false sense of rigor. Widespread acceptance of this myth conveys the impression that the field is advancing as a science that understands change and temporal processes, when in fact we know little more than what is offered in cross-sectional studies. And oftentimes, we don't know any more than cross-sectional studies, because the identical logic, theory, and hypotheses are used in both cross-sectional and repeated-measures studies (Ployhart & Vandenberg, 2010). But there are other concerns.

First, as noted, misuse of the term "longitudinal" fails to appropriately describe the study. This can cause problems when conducting literature reviews or trying to make sense of the literature. In our preparation of this chapter, we were rather shocked to find so many different types of studies referring to themselves as longitudinal—and we knew what we were looking for. Now, imagine a scholar trying to learn about an area, but with little training or appreciation for the nuances of longitudinal research and methods. This poor individual is going to be confronted with numerous types of designs, statistical methods, and inferences, all under the generic heading "longitudinal." Clear and consistent use of the term "longitudinal" enhances understanding and communication.

Second, and relatedly, overuse or misuse of the term "longitudinal" can cause problems when conducting meta-analyses. The meta-analyst must review the primary studies and code them according to various attributes. Overusing or misusing the term "longitudinal" adds uncertainty into the coding process or, at a minimum, greater rater judgment. This, in turn, may decrease interrater agreement and reliability. Further, imagine trying to explain why Study A was excluded and Study B was not when both refer to themselves as longitudinal. Clearly it is possible to explain the rationale, but such explanations certainly complicate the process in an unnecessary and counterproductive manner.

Conclusion

Longitudinal designs are intended to inform questions of change, and informing questions of change requires a minimum of three repeated measures on the same variable for the same observations. It is a myth that two waves of data make a longitudinal study and inform questions of change, and we are fooling ourselves and hurting the advancement of our science if we allow this myth to continue. Our theories, research, practice, and personal lives unfold over time, and to allow this myth is to deny a reality we all experience.

Acknowledgments

Author Note: We wish to thank Bob Vandenberg, Chuck Lance, Ormonde Cragun, and Donnie Hale for their helpful comments and suggestions on earlier versions of this chapter.

References

Berdie, R. F. (1955). Aptitude, achievement, interest, and personality tests: A longitudinal comparison. *Journal of Applied Psychology, 39*, 103–114.

Birdi, K., Clegg, C., Patterson, M., Robinson, A., Stride, C. B., Wall, T. D., & Wood, S. J. (2008). The impact of human resource and operational management practices on company productivity: A longitudinal study. *Personnel Psychology, 61*, 467–501.

Bliese, P. D., & Ployhart, R. E. (2002). Growth modeling using random coefficient models: Model building, testing, and illustration. *Organizational Research Methods, 5*, 362–387.

Bryk, A. S., & Raudenbush, S. W. (1987). Application of hierarchical linear models to assessing change. *Psychological Bulletin, 101*, 147–158.

Chan, D. (1998). The conceptualization and analysis of change over time: An integrative approach incorporating longitudinal mean and covariance structures analysis (LMACS) and multiple indicator latent growth modeling (MLGM). *Organizational Research Methods, 1*, 421–483.

Cohen, J., Cohen, P., West, S. G., & Aiken, L. S. (2003). *Applied multiple regression/correlation analysis for the behavioral sciences* (3rd ed.). Hillsdale, NJ: Erlbaum.

Cronbach, L. J., & Furby, L. (1970). How should we measure "change"—or should we? *Psychological Bulletin, 74*, 68–80.

Curran, P. J. (2003). Have multilevel models been structural equation models all along? *Multivariate Behavioral Research, 38*, 529–569.

Curran, P. J., & Bauer, D. J. (2011). The disaggregation of within-person and between-person effects in longitudinal models of change. *Annual Review of Psychology, 62*, 583–619.

Dulac, T., Coyle-Shapiro, J. A., Henderson, D. J., & Wayne, S. J. (2008). Not all responses to breach are the same: The interconnection of social exchange and psychological contract processes in organizations. *Academy of Management Journal, 51*, 1079–1098.

George, J. M., & Jones, G. R. (2000). The role of time in theory and theory building. *Journal of Management, 26,* 657–684.

Kirk, R. E. (1995). *Experimental design.* Pacific Grove, CA: Brooks Cole.

Laird, N. M., & Ware, J. H. (1982). Random-effects models for longitudinal data. *Biometrics, 38*(4), 963–974.

Lance, C. E., Meade, A. W., & Williamson, G. M. (2000). We *should* measure change—and here's how. In G. M. Williamson & D. R. Shaffer (Eds.), *Physical illness and depression in older adults: Theory, research, and practice* (pp. 201–235). New York, NY: Plenum.

Lang, J. W., & Bliese, P. D. (2009). General mental ability and two types of adaptation to unforeseen change: Applying discontinuous growth models to the task-change paradigm. *Journal of Applied Psychology, 94,* 411.

Langfred, C. W. (2007). The downside of self-management: A longitudinal study of the effects of conflict on trust, autonomy, and task interdependence in self-managing teams. *Academy of Management Journal, 50,* 885–900.

Maxwell, S. E., & Cole, D. A. (2007). Bias in cross-sectional analyses of longitudinal mediation. *Psychological Methods, 12,* 23–44.

McArdle, J. J., & Epstein D. (1987). Latent growth curves within developmental structural equation models. *Child Development, 58,* 110–133.

McClelland, D. C. (1965). N achievement and entrepreneurship: A longitudinal study. *Journal of Personality and Social Psychology, 1,* 389–392.

Meredith, W., & Tisak, J. (1990). Latent curve analysis. *Psychometrika, 55,* 107–122.

Mitchell, T. R., & James, L. R. (2001). Building better theory: Time and the specification of when things happen. *Academy of Management Review, 26,* 530–547.

Nifadkar, S., Tsui, A. S., & Ashforth, B. E. (2012). The way you make me feel and behave: Supervisor-triggered newcomer affect and approach-avoidance behavior. *Academy of Management Journal, 55,* 1146–1168.

Pitariu, A. H., & Ployhart, R. E. (2010). Explaining change: Theorizing and testing dynamic mediated longitudinal relationships. *Journal of Management, 36,* 405–429.

Ployhart, R. E., & Hale, D. Jr. (2014). Human resource management is out of time. In A. Shipp & Y. Fried (Eds.), *Time and work* (pp. 76–96). New York: Psychology Press.

Ployhart, R. E., & Ryan, A. M. (1998). Applicants' reactions to the fairness of selection procedures: The effects of positive rule violations and time of measurement. *Journal of Applied Psychology, 83,* 3–16.

Ployhart, R. E., & Vandenberg, R. J. (2010). Longitudinal research: The theory, design, and analysis of change. *Journal of Management, 36,* 94–120.

Podsakoff, P. M., MacKenzie, S. B., Lee, J. Y., & Podsakoff, N. P. (2003). Common method biases in behavioral research: A critical review of the literature and recommended remedies. *Journal of Applied Psychology, 88,* 879.

Rao, C. R. (1958). Some statistical methods for comparison of growth curves. *Biometrics, 14,* 1–17.

Roe, R. A. (2008). Time in applied psychology: The study of "what happens" rather than "what is." *European Psychologist, 13,* 37–52.

Rogosa, D. R. (1988). Myths about longitudinal research. In K. W. Schaie, R. T. Campbell, W. M. Meredith, & S. C. Rawlings (Eds.), *Methodological issues in aging research* (pp. 171–209). New York, NY: Springer Publishing Company,

Rogosa, D. R. (1995). Myths and methods: "Myths about longitudinal research" plus supplemental questions. In J. M. Gottman (Ed.), *The analysis of change* (pp. 3–66). Mahwah, NJ: Lawrence Erlbaum Associates.

Rogosa, D., Brandt, D., & Zimowski, M. (1982). A growth curve approach to the measurement of change. *Psychological Bulletin, 92*, 726–748.

Singer, J. D., & Willett, J. B. (2003). *Applied longitudinal data analysis.* New York, NY: Oxford University Press.

Tisak, J., & Meredith, W. (1990). Descriptive and associated developmental models. In von Eye A (Ed.), *Statistical methods in longitudinal research* (Vol. 2, pp. 387–406). San Diego, CA: Academic Press.

Tucker, L. R. (1958). Determination of parameters of a functional relation by factor analysis. *Psychometrika, 23*, 19–23.

Tucker, L. R. (1966). Learning theory and multivariate experiment: Illustration of generalized learning curves. In R. B. Cattell (Ed.), *Handbook of multivariate experimental psychology* (pp. 476–501). Chicago, IL: Rand McNally.

Van Maanen, J. (1975). Police socialization: A longitudinal examination of job attitudes in an urban police department. *Administrative Science Quarterly, 20*, 207–228.

Willett, J. B. (1989). Some results on reliability for the longitudinal measurement of change: Implications for the design of studies of individual growth. *Educational and Psychological Measurement, 49*, 587–602.

Willett, J. B., & Sayer, A. G. (1994). Using covariance structure analysis to detect correlates and predictors of individual change over time. *Psychological Bulletin, 116*, 363–381.

Wright, P. M., & Haggerty, J. J. (2005). Missing variables in theories of strategic human resource management: Time, cause, and individuals. *Management Revue, 16*, 164–173.

5

THE PROBLEM OF GENERATIONAL CHANGE

Why Cross-Sectional Designs Are Inadequate for Investigating Generational Differences

Brittany Gentile, Lauren A. Wood, Jean M. Twenge, Brian J. Hoffman and W. Keith Campbell

As one of the largest and most influential generations, the Baby Boomers, begins to retire, organizations are increasingly looking for the best ways to integrate, motivate, and retain younger generations of workers. Both business practitioners and researchers have focused attention on generational differences among workers and their possible impact on important work constructs. This is a critical issue, because to the extent that younger generations differ from workers of older generations, managers and organizations have been advised to tailor their policies to better recruit, retain, and motivate their increasingly Millennial workforce (e.g., Ahmed, 2013; D'Amato & Herzfeldt, 2008; Hunter, 2013; Lub, Bijvank, Bal, Blomme, & Schalk, 2012; Meiser, 2013; Wilson, Squires, Widger, Cranley, & Tourangeau, 2008). However, most of these recommendations hinge on data that do not allow for the inference of generational differences. Specifically, these recommendations are commonly made on the basis of cross-sectional designs where responses on one or more psychological variables are collected from a sample of individuals (representing multiple generational groups) at the same point in time. Using this design, researchers have made such recommendations as, "We recommend managers take a more generation-specific approach to managing their workforce" (Lub et al., 2012, p. 566) and "The findings suggest an approach of generation-specific HR practices for talent retention" (D'Amato & Herzfeldt, 2008, p. 929).

The urban legend this chapter addresses is that cross-sectional designs can provide meaningful information about generational differences. To expose this myth, we first provide a brief overview of the concept of generations in order to clarify the type of data and analyses needed to understand differences in generations. We then discuss the common methodological designs used to study generational differences with particular attention to cross-sectional designs and time-lag designs. Third,

The Problem of Generational Change **101**

highlighting the impact of this urban legend, we briefly demonstrate that results and substantive conclusions differ depending on which design is used. Finally, we discuss the best practices for future research exploring generational differences.

Common Conceptualizations of Generations

The idea of generations as a cohort of individuals who share common characteristics comes from sociology and the work of Karl Mannheim (1928/1952). Mannheim theorized that individuals who grew up around the same time would exhibit characteristic traits and behaviors in adulthood by virtue of their shared cultural experiences during key, developmental years of early childhood and adolescence. As culture changed, each successive cohort of individuals would exhibit somewhat different characteristics from those of previous generations, the four most recent of which have been the primary focus of generational research: the Silent Generation (born approximately between 1925–1945), the Baby Boomers or Boomers (born approximately between 1946–1965), Generation X or GenX (born approximately between 1965–1981), and the Millennials (aka Generation Me, GenMe, GenY, nGen, and iGen; born approximately between 1982–1999; Strauss & Howe, 1991). Although categories of generations are commonly imposed, this is not necessary, as generations can be examined either as a categorical value or as a continuous one (Twenge, 2010).

Methodological Approaches to Generational Research

Three common methodological designs are used to examine changes across time: cross-sectional, time-lag, and longitudinal. These designs differ in the sources of time-related variation (i.e., age effects, cohort effects, and period effects; Schaie, 1965), with each design holding one effect constant, such that change over time must be attributable to the other two (Table 5.1). In generational research, cohort (or generational) effects are the effects of interest. Cross-sectional designs hold constant the effects of time period, while generation and age are confounded. In time-lag studies, age effects are held constant, while generation and period are confounded. Longitudinal designs hold constant the effect of generation and therefore are functionally uninteresting for examining generational differences.

TABLE 5.1 Experimental Designs and Their Associated Effects

Design	Effects Allowed to Vary	Effect Held Constant
Longitudinal	Age/Period	Cohort
Cross-Sectional	Age/Cohort	Period
Time-Lag	Cohort/Period	Age

Note: Cohort effects (i.e., generational effects) are the effects of interest in the study of generational change.

102 Brittany Gentile et al.

Because of this, a discussion of longitudinal designs falls outside the scope of this chapter. In what follows, we discuss cross-sectional and time-lag designs as they relate to generational research goals.

Cross-Sectional Designs

Cross-sectional designs are by far the most prevalent found throughout the organizational literature, and, as indicated by the surge of recent articles (e.g., Cennamo & Gardner, 2008; D'Amato & Herzfelt, 2008; Dries, Pepermans, & De Kerpel, 2008; Lester, Standifer, Schultz, & Windsor, 2012; Tang, Cunningham, Frauman, Ivy, & Perry, 2012; Wong, Gardiner, Lang, & Coulon, 2008), these designs have been heavily used of late to investigate generational differences in the workplace. Cross-sectional designs have become so popular that their utility for examining differences between generations often goes unquestioned. However, the popularity of this design should not be taken as evidence that cross-sectional designs are ideally suited (or even *acceptable*) for the investigation of generational change. As we will discuss, the usefulness of cross-sectional designs to investigate generational changes is in reality a myth, one that has likely propagated erroneous conclusions regarding generational differences much better explained by age.

The typical cross-sectional design found throughout the generational literature samples a group of employees at one time point, categorically groups these employees based on generational membership (i.e., birth year), and assesses differences between these generational groups on variables of interest (e.g., Cennamo & Gardner, 2008; Lub et al., 2012; Nelson, 2012; Wilson et al., 2008). For example, Cennamo and Gardner invited 1,422 employees of eight different organizations to participate; those who consented were divided into one of three generational groups (i.e., Baby Boomers, Generation X, or Millennials) based on birth year in order for comparison between groups to be made. Although this method provides a relatively easy way to sample multiple generations at one time, the nature of the design does not allow for inferences about generational differences to be made. Rather, the results and substantive conclusions from cross-sectional studies attempting to assess generational differences will inevitably be contaminated by the effects of age. Specifically, because the data are collected at one point in time, earlier generations are represented by older employees whereas more recent generations consist of a younger employee sample. To illustrate, consider a research scenario in which we wish to compare two generations (i.e., Baby Boomers and Generation X) on some variable. If we obtain a large enough sample, we could have participants who were born across the full span of the generation (e.g., Baby Boomers ranging birth years of 1946–1965 and Generation X ranging from birth years of 1966–1981). This means that the oldest Baby Boomer in our sample is 35 years older than the youngest Generation Xer. Furthermore, if we were to add Millennials to the study, the oldest Baby Boomer could be 53 years older than the youngest Millennial.

Some cross-sectional studies have attempted to isolate the effects of generation by controlling for age (e.g., Benson & Brown, 2011); however, this does not remove all of the variance introduced by age effects. Age effects are a consequence of being at a certain stage in life (or in one's career) and broadly encompass both biological (i.e., physical effects due to the process of aging) and psychosocial (i.e., psychological effects due to the employee's internalization of getting older) changes (Rhodes, 1983). In other words, the effects of age are far reaching, including correlates such as tenure, organizational level, job knowledge, work motivation, and work experience. Consequently, in cross-sectional studies, the difference between older generations and younger ones is not just mean age differences. The samples will also differ in correlates of age, with older generations likely more experienced and more tenured, for example, and younger generations generally less so. Continuing with the example from Cennamo and Gardner (2008), their sample of Baby Boomers had a significantly longer tenure with their organization compared to the younger generational groups, not surprisingly. Therefore, cross-sectional studies perfectly confound generation with age, making it impossible to separate the effects of generation from those of age.

In sum, by comparing older workers' responses to those of younger workers on variables assessed at the same point in time, any identified differences may be misattributed to those of generational membership rather than the often more likely effects of age. Because cross-sectional designs confound age effects with those of generation, there is no way to make founded conclusions about differences in generations. Therefore, the use of cross-sectional designs is inadequate if the research goal is to assess true generational changes over time.

Time-Lag Designs

The best design for the study of generational differences is the time-lag design (Rhodes, 1983; Twenge, 2010). The ideal time-lag design, a cohort-sequential design, follows multiple cohorts longitudinally over time beginning at a young age (Schaie, 1965). This allows the researcher to examine longitudinal (i.e., developmental) changes within a cohort as well as to examine differences between cohorts. However, the difficulty of collecting such data has largely made this method unfeasible. More common is a simplified time-lag design in which samples of the same-aged individuals are collected at different points in time (e.g., Baby Boomers at age 30 sampled in the 1970s could be compared to Millennials at age 30 sampled in the 2010s). For example, Twenge, Campbell, Hoffman, and Lance (2010) examined high school seniors' work values with their sample of Baby Boomers assessed in 1976, Generation X in 1991, and Millennials in 2006. Due to the time-lag nature of their sampling strategy, individuals representing each generation were asked the same questions when they were the same age. The time-lag approach is well suited for the examination of generational differences because, unlike cross-sectional designs, in which generation and age are confounded, time-lag studies effectively control for age effects.

104 Brittany Gentile et al.

As can be seen in Table 5.1, however, time-lag studies confound the effects of generation and time period. However, this confound with time period is much less of a concern compared to the generation–age confound of cross-sectional studies (Twenge, 2010). Period effects are a consequence of living through a particular historical period or event that is not dependent on age (e.g., September 11, 2001; D-Day; assassination of President Kennedy), and thus these effects are common across all generations exposed to the event (Rhodes, 1983). Because the formation of most perceptions and traits occurs early in life (e.g., Jin & Rounds, 2012; Johnson & Monserud, 2012; McCrae & Costa, 1996), older generations are less likely to change in response to later cultural shifts. For these reasons, period effects are considered the weakest of the three effects (Low, Yoon, Roberts, & Rounds, 2005; Schaie, 1965; Twenge, 2010).

To elucidate the differences between cross-sectional and time-lag designs, we present some hypothetical data. Table 5.2 depicts several different age groups at 10-year intervals, their birth year, and the year in which data were collected. All three approaches to studying change (i.e., cross-sectional, time-lag, and longitudinal) are depicted in the table for comparison. Cross-sectional data are portrayed in the diagonally bordered cells; the bordered row in the table depicts time-lag data, and longitudinal data are depicted in the bordered column. As can be seen from the table, what is being held constant versus what is assessed varies depending on which research design is utilized. For example, the developmental question underlying cross-sectional data is the existence of age and individual differences on a trait. Therefore, in this case, the mean difference between any two cells in the diagonal will be a mix of age and cohort (i.e., generational) differences. The bordered row in the table depicts time-lag data, in which data from individuals of the same age from different generations are collected at different time points. The developmental question of interest is the effect of cultural change on a trait. Since age is held constant, the mean difference between any two columns, holding row constant, will be a mix of generation and period differences. Thus, the time-lag design controls for age effects, allowing for the examination of possible

TABLE 5.2 Differences in Time-Lag, Cross-Sectional, and Longitudinal Data Collection Designs

Age	Year of Measurement					
50	2000	2010	2020	2030	2040	2050
40	1990	2000	2010	2020	2030	2040
30	1980	1990	2000	2010	2020	2030
20	1970	1980	1990	2000	2010	2020
10	1960	1970	1980	1990	2000	2010
Birth Year	1950	1960	1970	1980	1990	2000

Note: Cross-sectional data are represented in the diagonally bordered cells; time-lag data are depicted in the bordered row; longitudinal data are depicted in the bordered column.

generational effects; therefore, the time-lag approach should be the design of choice when conducting research on generational differences.

Discussion

The urban legend that cross-sectional designs are appropriate for assessing generational change is nothing more than a myth. However, as with all urban legends, there is a kernel of truth. In our urban legend, the kernel of truth is that cross-sectional designs can be used to examine cohort effects; however, because this design confounds cohort and age, their utility for answering questions specifically about generational differences is limited (Baltes, 1968; Buss, 1974; Schaie, 1965). This is not to say that just because a study uses cross-sectional data the results are not driven by true generational effects. In fact, cross-sectional and time-lag studies sometimes draw similar conclusions. However, in instances where they disagree, the problem is most likely due to differences in method, and the findings of cross-sectional studies especially should be treated with caution. This is of particular concern with regard to workplace attitudes and behaviors, which may be largely driven by age (i.e., work experience, career stage). The result is that differences between older and younger employees may be incorrectly attributed to their generational group when stage of life or organizational level is a more likely explanation. However, this is not the case with time-lag designs, which effectively control for age effects. In general, time-lag designs are able to draw much more reliable conclusions regarding the existence of generational differences.

Implications of Cross-Sectional versus Time-Lag Designs: Two Examples

With notable exceptions, the literature has often failed to recognize the difference between cross-sectional and time-lag designs, instead treating them as an analogous means of comparing generations, and, thus fueling the myth behind this urban legend. Although generational differences are studied in a number of fields, this myth is perhaps most prevalent in the workplace literature where popular speculation on the topic greatly dwarfs the empirical literature. I/O researchers, in an attempt to find empirical evidence for popular claims of generational differences, have often turned to readily available cross-sectional data. Taken together, the conclusions drawn from generational research represent both fact and fiction. The fiction stems from research attempting to draw conclusions about generational differences from cross-sectional designs, which may produce spurious results and, at minimum, should be interpreted with care. In contrast, the fact stems from research examining generational differences through the use of time-lag designs, which are able to generate a much more accurate representation of true generational differences. We briefly illustrate that cross-sectional designs used to investigate cohort effects may provide misleading conclusions by way of two examples from recent literature.

Example 1—Generational Differences in Work Attitudes

Cross-sectional studies have examined generational differences on various work attitudes (e.g., Benson & Brown, 2011; Beutell & Wittig-Berman, 2008; Cennamo & Gardner, 2008; Lub et al., 2012; Nelson, 2012; Tang et al., 2012; Wilson et al., 2008). These cross-sectional works tend to paint a gloomy picture of more recent generations' work attitudes. For example, a recent meta-analysis using only cross-sectional, primary studies examined pairwise comparisons between all possible combinations of generational groups on common work attitudes (Costanza, Badger, Fraser, Severt, & Gade, 2012). The authors found some support for Millennials' greater dissatisfaction and intent to turnover compared to older generational groups. Given the nature of the data, this trend is not surprising. Since age and cohort effects cannot be separated in cross-sectional designs, age is an equally plausible explanation for the supposed generational differences. Age and tenure are positively correlated with job satisfaction (Hunt & Saul, 1975; Kacmar & Ferris, 1989; Ng & Feldman, 2010), providing an alternative interpretation of the findings (Costanza et al., 2012). In stark contrast to the cross-sectional findings (even Benson & Brown, 2010, who controlled for age), time-lag data tell a different story. A recent time-lag study, using data from the WorkTrends™ survey (a national survey collecting yearly or biyearly data since 1985) found just the opposite—Millennials reported higher levels of job satisfaction and security than Generation Xers and Baby Boomers (Kowske, Rasch, & Wiley, 2010). Based on these results, it seems many cross-sectional studies attempting to study generational differences in work attitudes can misattribute the effects of age. From this, it seems that previously suggested recommendations directed toward increasing younger generations' job satisfaction and job security (e.g., Lub et al., 2012; Wilson et al., 2008) are likely unfounded.

Example 2—Generational Differences in Work Values

Cross-sectional studies have also been used to examine differences in work values (e.g., Leiter, Jackson, & Shaughnessy, 2009; Lester et al., 2012; Real, Mitnick, & Maloney, 2010; Wong et al., 2008). Recent cross-sectional work in this area tends to produce contradictory results, with some studies not supporting hypothesized value shifts and others findings changes in values that go against popular opinion (e.g., Real et al., 2010; Wong et al., 2008). A recent review of the generational work value literature reported, "The evidence is at best mixed, with as many studies failing to find differences between generations as finding them. Those differences that are found are not consistent, with a number of authors finding differences that contradict the popular stereotypes of Baby Boomers, Generation X and Generation Y" (Parry & Urwin, 2011, p. 88). Compared to cross-sectional study conclusions, time-lag studies have produced more consistent results. For example, using archival data from the national Monitoring the Future database, Twenge and colleagues

(2010) examined high school seniors' work values in 1976 (Baby Boomers), 1991 (Generation Xers), and 2006 (Millennials) and found evidence for small to moderate generational shifts in four out of the five work values they assessed (i.e., leisure, extrinsic, social, intrinsic). Twenge and colleagues' findings were consistent with Smola and Sutton's (2002) earlier time-lag value comparison between older and younger cohorts from 1974 and 1999. Thus, despite the mixed findings of cross-sectional research, there do seem to be generational shifts in values as evidenced by time-lag research.

Discussion

In conclusion, the two examples presented stress the necessity of using time-lag designs to examine generational change. Both examples demonstrate that the results from cross-sectional research compared to those of time-lag studies can differ. Although there is some truth to the myth in that cross-sectional designs can sometimes come to the same conclusions as time-lag research, we strongly advise against taking cross-sectional results and interpretations as evidence of true generational change. Next, we briefly discuss best practices in conducting time-lag research.

Best Practices for Generational Differences Research

In the present chapter, we have outlined various pitfalls of assessing generational changes using cross-sectional data. Although the urban legend does contain a kernel of truth, using cross-sectional designs to examine true differences between generations is ill advised. As should now be apparent, the preferred method for conducting generational research is the time-lag design. In order to further future research efforts, we present recommendations on the best ways to utilize the time-lag methodology.

The most challenging aspect researchers face when conducting a time-lag study is obtaining the cross-temporal data. Briefly, we review the two predominant methods of obtaining time-lag data sources. The first source is national datasets, which are useful for examining generational differences, as they often examine like-aged samples over a long period of time. To date, three national datasets have been used for this purpose: the Monitoring the Future (MTF) dataset, the Cooperative Institutional Research Program (CIRP) Freshman Survey, known more commonly as the American Freshman Survey (AFS), and the General Social Survey (GSS), run by the National Opinion Research Center (NORC). However, these are by no means the only datasets, and we encourage future researchers to explore other available options.

National datasets offer a number of advantages. They provide a representative sample of the population of interest and survey a diverse array of topics for study. Additionally, most can be readily downloaded from the Internet at no cost. However,

108 Brittany Gentile et al.

national datasets also have several limitations that should be noted. First, not all datasets go back far enough in time to be able to draw meaningful conclusions about generational differences. Even among those that do, there may be inconsistent data collection leading to missing years of data, as is the case with the GSS. Second, the presentation of survey items is not always consistent, with some items being reworded over time or dropped entirely to make room for new items that are more temporally relevant. Even items that are included year after year may not always be presented in the same way (e.g., shifts in item wording, scaling variations). As a result, piecing together the data from year to year can sometimes be a tedious process. Third, generational differences can only be examined for the age groups included in the survey. Some surveys, like MTF or AFS, which are limited to adolescents and young adults, may not be as useful for examining generational differences in adult roles such as in the workplace.

A second source of time-lag data is to use archival research and conduct a cross-temporal meta-analysis (CTMA). CTMA uses data from journal articles to investigate generational differences. Twenge (e.g., Twenge, 1997, 2000; Twenge & Campbell, 2001) developed the method as a way to assess mean-level changes in traits across successive cohorts of individuals over time. CTMA proceeds in much the same way as a traditional meta-analysis in terms of locating studies. However, rather than focusing on effect size metrics, sample means and year of data collection are collected. Data are then weighted by sample size or inverse variance and analyzed using regression. The potential confound of age is controlled for by conducting separate analyses for each age group (e.g., young employees: aged 20–35; mid-life employees: aged 36–50; older employees: aged 50+). Using this method, it is possible to get two types of information regarding mean level change over time. First, using the correlations between mean levels of a construct and year, it is possible to examine whether the construct has increased or decreased across cohorts. Second, it is possible to obtain an estimate of the proportion of variance accounted for by birth-cohort at the level of the individual. This can be calculated by using the regression equation to take the difference between mean scores for the first and last year of data collection and dividing by the average standard deviation of the individual samples. Although this is only a brief summary, we direct the interested reader to more complete primers for further reading (i.e., Twenge, Campbell, & Gentile, in press).

As with national datasets, there are several advantages and disadvantages to using CTMA to examine generational differences. One benefit is that CTMA often spans a greater period of time than national datasets, although this is dependent on what year the measure of interest was created. It is also sometimes possible with CTMA to examine change in a greater variety of age groups than are typically the target of national surveys. CTMA primarily uses full measures rather than a few survey items, thus avoiding the necessity of having to combine potentially disparate items into a workable scale. Since CTMA is dependent on archival data, the limitations of this method are similar to those of any meta-analysis, although there are some important differences. For instance, whether or not a CTMA can even be conducted is dependent on the number of primary studies available using the self-report measure of interest. Since CTMA is a time-lag method, however, the articles also need to span a significant portion of time (e.g., 22 years is the average span of one generation; Strauss & Howe, 1991). Likewise, as with traditional meta-analysis, the interpretation of results is constrained by the available samples, which may or may not cover the population of interest. Additionally, as these samples are not nationally representative, the results cannot be confidently extrapolated to the general population or used to make epidemiological claims about the normative level of a construct. That being said, CTMA can be used to answer relational questions, such as how a given construct is related to birth cohort within the groups studied (e.g., young Millennials and young Baby Boomers; older Millennials and older Baby Boomers).

Going forward, we encourage future researchers of generational differences to employ one of the methods discussed earlier for obtaining time-lag data rather than relying on readily available cross-sectional data. Although more difficult to obtain, time-lag data offer the most accurate means of investigating generational differences. It should be noted that much of the data for time-lag studies have only recently become available as the technology for collecting and sharing large data-sets has improved and will likely continue to improve in the coming years. In particular, crowdsourcing offers a promising avenue for future time-lag research. Crowdsourcing is the process of distributing a task among many people through online mechanisms. Websites like CrowdFlower and Amazon's Mechanical Turk can be utilized by researchers to collect survey data cheaply and easily from a diverse group of adult Internet users, lessening the difficulty of collecting adequate samples of time-lag data.

Concluding Thoughts

In this chapter we have reviewed, and hopefully debunked, the myth that cross-sectional designs are adequate for studying generational differences. The wide-spread use of these designs, particularly in the I/O literature, has unfortunately led to confusion concerning the impact of generational group on employee behavior in the workplace. While rarer, time-lag designs offer an improved way of examining these trends. It is hoped that future research will bear these observations in mind when choosing a method for examining generational differences.

References

Ahmed, A. (2013, April). How the millennial generation is transforming the workplace. *Arbitrage Magazine*. Retrieved from www.arbitragemagazine.com/topics/business/millennial-generation-transforming-workplace/

Baltes, P. B. (1968). Longitudinal and cross sectional sequences in the study of age and generation effects. *Human Development, 11*, 145–171.

Benson, J., & Brown, M. (2011). Generations at work: Are there differences and do they matter? *The International Journal of Human Resource Management, 22*, 1843–1865.

Beutell, N. J., & Wittig-Berman, U. (2008). Work–family conflict and work–family synergy for generation X, baby boomers, and matures—generational differences, predictors, and satisfaction outcomes. *Journal of Managerial Psychology, 23*, 507–523.

Buss, A. R. (1974). Generational analysis: Description, explanation, and theory. *Journal of Social Issues, 30*, 55–71.

Cennamo, L., & Gardner, D. (2008). Generational differences in work values, outcomes and person–organization values fit. *Journal of Managerial Psychology, 23*, 891–906.

Costanza, D. P., Badger, J. M., Fraser, R. L., Severt, J. B., & Gade, P. A. (2012). Generational differences in work-related attitudes: A meta-analysis. *Journal of Business Psychology, 27*, 375–394.

D'Amato, A., & Herzfeldt, R. (2008). Learning orientation, organizational commitment and talent retention across generations. *Journal of Managerial Psychology, 23*, 929–953.

Dries, N., Pepermans, R., De Kerpel, E. (2008). Exploring four generations' beliefs about career—is "satisfied" the new "successful"? *Journal of Managerial Psychology, 23*, 907–928.

Hunt, J. W., & Saul, P. N. (1975). The relationship of age, tenure, and job satisfaction in males and females. *The Academy of Management Journal, 18*, 690–702.

Hunter, M. (2013, March). How to manage older workers. *Management Today*. Retrieved from www.managementtoday.co.uk/news/1174842/

Jin, J., & Rounds, J. (2012). Stability and change in work values: A meta-analysis of longitudinal studies. *Journal of Vocational Behavior, 80*, 326–339.

Johnson, M. K., & Monserud, M. A. (2012). Work value development from adolescence to adulthood. *Advances in Life Course Research, 17*, 45–58.

Kacmar, K. M., & Ferris, G. R. (1989). Theoretical and methodological considerations in the age–job satisfaction relationship. *Journal of Applied Psychology, 74*, 201–207.

Kowske, B. J., Rasch, R., & Wiley, J. (2010). Millennials' (lack of) attitude problem: An empirical examination of generational effects on work attitudes. *Journal of Business Psychology, 25*, 265–279.

Leiter, M. P., Jackson, N. J., & Shaughnessy, K. (2009). Contrasting burnout, turnover intention, control, value congruence and knowledge sharing between Baby Boomers and Generation X. *Journal of Nursing Management, 17*, 100–109.

Lester, S. W., Standifer, R. L., Schultz, N. J., & Windsor, J. M. (2012). Actual versus perceived generational differences at work: An empirical examination. *Journal of Leadership and Organizational Studies, 19*, 341–354.

Low, K.S.D., Yoon, M., Roberts, B. W., & Rounds, J. (2005). The stability of vocational interests from early adolescence to middle adulthood: A quantitative review of longitudinal studies. *Psychological Bulletin, 131*, 713–737.

Lub, X. D., Bijvank, M. N., Bal, P. M., Blomme, R., & Schalk, M.J.D. (2012). Different or alike? Exploring the psychological contract and commitment of different generations of hospitality workers. *International Journal of Contemporary Hospitality Management, 24*, 553–573.

Mannheim, K. (1952). The problem of generations. In K. Mannheim (Ed.), *Essays on the sociology of knowledge* (pp. 276–322). London: Routledge & Kegan Paul. (Original work published 1928).

McCrae, R. R., & Costa, P. T., Jr. (1996). Toward a new generation of personality theories: Theoretical contexts for the five-factor model. In J. S. Wiggins (Ed.), *The five-factor model of personality* (pp. 51–87). New York, NY: Guilford Press.

Meiser, J. (2013, June). The Boomer-Millennial workplace clash: Is it real? *Forbes*. Retrieved from www.forbes.com/sites/jeannemeister/2013/06/04/the-boomer-millennial-workplace-clash-is-it-real/

Nelson, S. A. (2012). Affective commitment of generational cohorts of Brazilian nurses. *International Journal of Manpower, 33*, 804–821.

Ng, T.W.H., & Feldman, D. C. (2010). The relationships of age with job attitudes: A meta-analysis. *Personnel Psychology, 63*, 677–718.

Parry, E., & Urwin, P. (2011). Generational differences in work values: A review of theory and evidence. *International Journal of Management Reviews, 13*, 79–96.

Real, K., Mitnick, A. D., & Maloney, W. F. (2010). More similar than different: Millennials in the U.S. building trades. *Journal of Business Psychology, 25*, 303–313.

Rhodes, S. R. (1983). Age-related differences in work attitudes and behavior: A review and conceptual analysis. *Psychological Bulletin, 93*, 328–367.

Schaie, K. W. (1965). A general model for the study of developmental problems. *Psychological Bulletin, 64*, 92–107.

Smola, K. W., & Sutton, C. D. (2002). Generational differences: Revisiting generational work values for the new millennium. *Journal of Organizational Behavior, 22*, 363–382.

Strauss, W., & Howe, N. (1991). *Generations: The history of America's future, 1584 to 2069.* New York, NY: William Morrow and Company, Inc.

Tang, T. L., Cunningham, P. H., Frauman, E., Ivy, M. I., & Perry, T. L. (2012). Attitudes and occupational commitment among public personnel: Differences between Baby Boomers and Gen-Xers. *Public Personnel Management, 41*, 327–360.

Twenge, J. M. (1997). Changes in masculine and feminine traits over time: A meta-analysis. *Sex Roles, 36*, 305–325.

Twenge, J. M. (2000). The age of anxiety? Birth cohort change in anxiety. *Journal of Personality and Social Psychology, 79*, 1007–1021.

Twenge, J. M. (2010). A review of the empirical evidence on generational differences in work attitudes. *Journal of Business Psychology, 25*, 201–210.

Twenge, J. M., Campbell, S. M., Hoffman, B. J., & Lance, C. E. (2010). Generational differences in work values: Leisure and extrinsic values increasing, social and intrinsic values decreasing. *Journal of Management, 36*, 1117–1142.

Twenge, J. M., & Campbell, W. K. (2001). Age and birth cohort differences in self-esteem: A cross-temporal meta-analysis. *Personality and Social Psychology Review, 5*, 321–344.

Twenge, J. M., Campbell, W. K., & Gentile, B. (in press). Birth cohort differences in personality. In R. J. Larsen and M. L. Cooper (Eds.), *Handbook of personality processes and individual differences*. Washington, DC: American Psychological Association.

Wilson, B., Squires, M., Widger, K., Cranley, L., & Tourangeau, A. (2008). Job satisfaction among a multigenerational nursing workforce. *Journal of Nursing Management, 16*, 716–723.

Wong, M., Gardiner, E., Lang, W., & Coulon, L. (2008). Generational differences in personality and motivation—do they exist and what are the implications for the workplace? *Journal of Managerial Psychology, 23*, 878–890.

6

NEGATIVELY WORDED ITEMS NEGATIVELY IMPACT SURVEY RESEARCH

Dev K. Dalal and Nathan T. Carter

The most common method of measuring psychological constructs is the Likert-style (1932) multi-item scale. With these measures, items are written to tap the extreme end of an attribute, respondents indicate their level of agreement on a graded scale, and their standing on the construct of interest is indexed by summing observed responses across items. A common practice in the construction of Likert scales is the inclusion of negatively worded items in hopes of reducing response styles—systematic response tendencies that are independent of item content. Examples include general tendencies to agree to items (i.e., acquiescence), to disagree to items (i.e., nay-saying), and to provide extreme responses (see Cohen & Swerdlik, 2005; Podsakoff, MacKenzie, Lee, & Podsakoff, 2003; Swain, Weathers, & Niedrich, 2008; van Sonderen, Sanderman, & Coyne, 2013).

Items are considered negatively worded when they are written in the opposite direction of the dominant pole of the construct of interest and whose observed responses are reversed before computing attribute standing. Examples of two types of negatively worded items include *polar opposite* and *negated regular* items (Schriesheim & Eisenbach, 1995; Schriesheim, Eisenbach, & Hill, 1991; these correspond to what van Sonderen and colleagues, 2013, label *reverse wording* and *reverse oriented*, respectively). For example, if a regular item measuring conscientiousness is "I am always on time," the polar opposite (reverse wording) version of this item is "I am always late" and the negated regular (reverse oriented) version is "I am not always on time." Observed responses to these items would need to be reverse-scored, since agreeing to these items should be indicative of low conscientiousness. As noted, a widely held belief is that the inclusion of these types of items will reduce bias resulting from response styles. This practice is widespread in organizational science (e.g., Idaszak & Dragow, 1987; Schmitt & Stults, 1985; Spector, Van Katwyk, Brannick, & Chen, 1997), as well as in other fields, including education

Negatively Worded Items **113**

(e.g., Roszkowski & Soven, 2010; Weems, Onwuegbuzie, Schreiber, & Eggers, 2003), marketing (e.g., Swain et al., 2008; Weijters & Baumgartner, 2012), and medicine (e.g., Stewart & Frye, 2004).

In general, the practice of including negatively worded items rests on four assumptions: (1) including negatively worded items will eliminate or help identify respondents engaging in response styles; (2) negatively worded items will *not* impact scale quality; (3) negatively worded items will *not* change validity conclusions (Schriesheim & Eisenbach, 1995); and (4) negatively worded and positively worded items measure the same construct. That these four assumptions have been generally accepted has resulted in a methodological urban legend: Namely, mixed-item scales—that is, scales that include both positively worded and negatively worded items—will eliminate response styles without impairing scale properties. For example, in constructing a Need Satisfaction Scale, Van den Broeck, Vansteenskiste, De Witte, Soenens, and Lens (2010) state, "Finally, both positive (i.e., need satisfaction) and negative (i.e., need frustration) items were included . . . to avoid that an acquiescence bias . . . would contaminate participants' answers" (pp. 989–990). McCarthy and Goffin (2004), in their measure of Interview Anxiety, state that "A mix of positively and negatively keyed items was also included to control for acquiescent responding" (p. 616).

The goal of this chapter is to demonstrate that, although the first assumption may hold, the last three assumptions, contrary to popular belief, are not guaranteed. To this end, we begin by establishing the practice of incorporating negatively worded items to reduce response styles as an urban legend and identify the kernel of truth to this urban legend. We then detail how assumptions (2), (3), and (4) outlined earlier are, in fact, myths of this urban legend. We conclude by offering practical recommendations on the use of negatively worded items, when it is necessary, and we offer alternative approaches to identifying invalid data.

The Urban Legend and Kernel of Truth

As noted, the urban legend we address is that using mixed-items scales will eliminate invalid responding without adversely impacting scale properties. The kernel of truth to this legend is that using negatively worded items *was*, in fact, originally suggested as a method to reduce or identify invalid responding. In his original monograph, Likert (1932) suggests,

> To avoid any . . . tendency to a stereotyped response it seems desirable to have the different statements worded that about one-half of them have one end of the attitude continuum corresponding to the *left* or *upper* part of the reaction alternatives and the other half have the same end of the attitude continuum corresponding to the *right* or *lower* part of the reaction alternatives.

> *(p. 46, italics in original)*

114 Dev K. Dalal and Nathan T. Carter

This "tendency to a stereotyped response" refers to what Cronbach (1942, 1946, 1950) later termed a *response set*. Cronbach (1942) showed that different respondents tended to react differently to *true-false* items. Specifically, he demonstrated that, when unsure about a question, a subset of students tended to respond *true*—he labeled this tendency acquiescence. Cronbach (1946) further warned that validity could suffer as a result of response set, noting, "Since a response set permits persons with the same knowledge or attitude or ability to receive different scores, response sets always lower the logical validity of a test" (p. 484).

Later (e.g., Rorer, 1965), *response sets* would be differentiated from *response styles*. The distinguishing features of these two response tendencies differ with respect to the relation between item content and responding. That is, whereas responding according to response sets is thought to be related to item content, responding according to a response style is independent of item content (van Sonderen et al., 2013). An example of a response set is social desirability wherein observed responses are determined by item content so as to allow the respondent to be viewed favorably. In contrast, acquiescence—the tendency to say yes to all items—does not depend on the item content.[1]

Although some (e.g., Rorer, 1965) have questioned whether response styles are at all problematic, popular psychometrics texts (e.g., Allen & Yen, 1979; Anastasi, 1982; Nunnally, 1978) and articles (e.g., Jackson & Messick, 1958; Messick, 1962; Podsakoff et al., 2003) have generally advocated for attempting to reduce the occurrence of response styles—frequently, the recommended solution has been including negatively worded items. Since some respondents have the tendency to fall into response styles when items are phrased in a consistent way, mixing item types has been thought to curb this automatic responding. As Podsakoff and colleagues (2003) put it, negatively worded items are meant to be "cognitive 'speedbumps'" (p. 884) that prevent respondents from falling into a set, automatic pattern of responding. In line with assumption (1) described earlier, then, the use of negatively worded items can reduce response styles if respondents' automatic responding is interrupted. Moreover, inspection of inconsistent responding to negatively worded items can be used to identify individuals who are engaging in a response set (Swain et al., 2008).

The practice of including negatively worded items has become so commonplace, that many academics, practitioners, and students include negatively worded items in their scales without specifying why, as if to suggest that the practice is so well known that describing their rationale is not necessary. Indeed, in a review of scale development articles published in the top (Zickar & Highhouse, 2001) organizational research journals since 2000 (see Table 6.1), 19 of the 50 (38%) utilized negatively worded items but only 10 (20%) described why. Of the articles that did include a rationale, the two most frequently stated reasons for including negatively worded items were (1) that items were based off of past scales that included negatively worded items (40%) and (2) to reduce response styles (30%).

Negatively Worded Items **115**

TABLE 6.1 Review of Scale Development Papers

Journal	Used negatively worded items	Number offering a reason	Did not use negatively worded items	Number offering a reason
Academy of Management Journal	1	1	4	0
Journal of Applied Psychology	8	3	11	0
Journal of Management	3	3	8	2
Organizational Behavior and Human Decision Processes	0	N/A	2	0
Organizational Research Methods	3	2	2	1
Personnel Psychology	4	1	4	1
Summary:	19 (38%)	10 (20%)	31 (62%)	3 (6%)

Notes: (1) Review of scale development articles published since 2000. (2) Articles with a focus other than scale development were excluded.

Stated differently, researchers who included negatively worded items in their scales appear to do so under the belief that they will alleviate response styles or simply because "others did it." Indeed, Sauley and Bedeian (2000) state that they created a mixed-item scale because the "use of positive and negative wording can lessen mono-method bias and acquiescence by varying the presentation of items" (p. 906). Moreover, Sanders (2010) advises that "Items that need reverse scoring are recommended for scales because it encourages the respondent to respond to each item in turn . . ." (p. 186).

Although the original purpose for using negatively worded items is clear, there is a general inconsistency in the use of these types of items. This general inconsistency is seen when comparing the distinct approaches to scale development taken in four papers from the same journal (*Journal of Management*). On the one hand, although both Ferris and colleagues (2005) and Linderbaum and Levy (2010) exclude negatively worded items, only Linderbaum and Levy describe their rationale (i.e., avoiding negative aspects of mixed-item types, p. 1376). On the other hand, Dahling, Whitaker, and Levy (2009) and Sauley and Bedeian (2000) included negatively worded items in their scales, but neither discussed their rationale for including these items. Our purpose here is not to single out these studies as inappropriate; indeed, we have certainly engaged in this practice as well. Rather, our goal is to demonstrate the general trend that we have observed with respect to the use of negatively worded items—simply stated, we argue that not enough attention is being paid to the rationale for including or excluding negatively worded items.

116 Dev K. Dalal and Nathan T. Carter

Importantly, we believe the numbers presented in Table 6.1 are actually *underestimates* of the current state of the practice given our review only looked at studies whose main objective was to introduce a new scale. That is, our review excluded (1) studies wherein scale development was not a main focus or were conducted before 2000, (2) studies that utilize scales developed prior to 2000, and (3) scales developed for study-specific purposes.

In addition to journal articles, research methods textbooks (e.g., Cozby & Bates, 2012; Goodwin, 2010; Morling, 2012; Pelham & Blanton, 2012; Sanders, 2010; Shaughnessy, Zechmeister, & Zechmeister, 2012) suggest that negatively worded items should be included in scales. Further, popular published pieces on scale development (e.g., Hinkin, 1995, 1998) outline some of the negative aspects of including negatively worded items but still suggest that if appropriate care is taken, it is okay to include these items. Finally, in informal surveys of graduate students across disciplines, the first author has observed that nearly 100% of students were taught to include negatively worded items in their scales. The majority of these students further state that this practice was to curb response styles, yet very few reported that they actually checked their data for such patterns! This tendency is seen in published works as well. For example, although Dahling and colleagues (2009), McCarthy and Goffin (2004), Reeve and Smith (2001), and Sauley and Bedeian (2000) all included negatively worded items in their scales, none of these authors note whether respondents were removed due to response styles. Although it is possible that these authors do not mention anything about removing individuals from their sample due to response styles because no one responded with one, this seems unlikely.

In sum, the kernel of truth to this urban legend is that negatively worded items were originally recommended to help eliminate or detect response styles. However, this original recommendation belies the fact that using mixed-item scales can negatively impact scale quality; that is, three of the assumptions upon which this practice rests are not guaranteed. More specifically, the assumptions that negatively worded items (1) will not impact scale quality (2) will not change validity conclusions and (3) that negatively worded and positively worded items measure the same construct are actually myths to this urban legend. We detail these myths next.

The Myths

As just noted, there are three either implicitly or explicitly held beliefs regarding the use of negatively worded items that we delineate as myths. Indeed, in our review of the published literature (Table 6.1), only 8% of the studies acknowledged the potential negative psychometric issues associated with mixed-items scales. None of the authors note the issues with validity conclusions and/or construct misspecification. In the following, we provide evidence that suggests, in most instances, these assumptions are not met.

Myth #1: No Impairment in Psychometric Properties

A myriad of studies have shown that mixed-item scales are less reliable or have more measurement error than positively worded or negatively worded–only scales (e.g., Barnette, 2000; Cronbach, 1942; 1946; 1950; Pilotte & Gable, 1990; Rozkowski & Soven, 2010; Schriesheim & Eisenbach, 1995; Schriesheim et al., 1991; Schriesheim & Hill, 1981; Stewart & Frye, 2004; van Sonderen et al., 2013). In addition, a series of studies have shown that mixed-item scales result in an unexpected factor associated with the negatively worded items (e.g., Cordery & Sevastos, 1993; DiStefano & Motl, 2006; Idaszak & Drasgow, 1987; Magazine, Williams, & Williams, 1996; Marsh, 1996; McGee, Ferguson, & Seers, 1989; Pilotte & Gable, 1990; Roszkowski & Soven, 2010; Schmitt & Stults, 1985; Schriesheim & Eisenbach, 1995; Spector et al., 1997). Next we describe the findings regarding the reliability and factor structure of mixed-item scales in turn.

Negatively worded items load on a separate factor. Using exploratory factor analyses (EFA), confirmatory factor analyses (CFA), and multitrait-multimethod (MTMM) data, researchers (e.g., DiStefano & Motl, 2006; Magazine et al., 1996; Marsh, 1996; Schmitt & Stults, 1985; Spector et al., 1997) have consistently demonstrated that, on mixed-item scales, the negatively worded items tend to load on a separate factor. Although some have questioned whether this factor is a spurious method factor or a substantive construct (e.g., Lance, Baranik, Lau, & Sharlau, 2009), it is clear that negatively worded items share variance with each other that is not shared with the underlying construct; this form of systematic bias in observed responses occurs when mixed-item scales are used. In particular, observed responses to mixed-item scales may be modeled in the following CFA framework (Chan, 2009):

$$X_i = \lambda_T \xi_T + \lambda_{SB} \xi_{SB} + \delta \tag{1}$$

where X_i is the observed response to the ith item, ξ_T is the latent trait factor, ξ_{SB} is the latent trait reflective of the systematic bias introduced by negatively worded items, λ_T and λ_{SB} are the factor loadings relating the latent factors (trait and systematic bias, respectively) to the observed responses, and δ is the uniqueness or residual variance of the item. This model suggests that two different latent traits are needed to explain observed scores and has been found to show better model–data fit than a unidimensional model by several authors (e.g., DiStefano & Motl, 2006; Idaszak & Drasgow, 1987; Marsh, 1996). Different explanations have been offered for why negatively worded items share variance and therein produce ξ_{SB}, such as carelessness (Schmitt & Stults, 1985), respondent ability (Cordery & Sevastos, 1993), or tendencies to respond similarly to like items (Spector et al., 1997). Irrespective of the particular reason, in mixed-item scales, the negatively worded items share variance that results in a second factor, namely ξ_{SB}, that influences observed responses to those items. Stated differently, observed responses to mixed-item scales can be

118 Dev K. Dalal and Nathan T. Carter

contaminated by systematic bias resulting from combining negatively and positively worded items on the same scale.

Importantly, this systematic bias factor is only related to negatively worded items. Indeed, researchers (e.g., DiStefano & Motl, 2006; Marsh, 1996) have tried to model a systematic bias factor associated with positively worded items; however, these models have not fit the data, suggesting that the positively worded items are not sharing variance like the negatively worded items. Therefore, on scales with only positively worded items, there is no systematic bias to impact observed scores. On scales with *only* negatively worded items, the influence of the bias (i.e., ξ_{SB}) will actually be modeled in the trait factor (i.e., ξ_T) as a form of common method variance (e.g., Magazine et al., 1996) or substantive trait variance (e.g., Lance et al., 2009) depending on the construct being investigated. On mixed-item scales, however, the systematic bias will impact only the negatively worded items. If ignored, this systematic bias will be treated as item uniqueness (i.e., anything in the observed responses not explicitly modeled), thereby increasing measurement error (Bollen, 1989; Mulaik, 1972).

Mixed-item scales have more measurement error. The general trend in the aforementioned studies is that reliability estimates (i.e., Cronbach's α) are highest for scales with only positively worded items, followed by scales with only negatively worded items, and lowest for mixed-item scales (e.g., Schriesheim & Eisenbach, 1995; Schriesheim et al., 1991; van Sonderen et al., 2013). From equation (1), however, this finding is not unexpected. Recall that δ is variance that is not explained by the factors in the model and is composed of two components: a random and a systematic component (Bollen, 1989). Whereas the former is the result of unreliability of measurement, the latter is item-specific variance not captured by ξ_T (see also Kline, 2005). ξ_{SB} is a form of systematic variance independent of the trait, ξ_T, and, as noted in the previous section, can result from negatively worded items. Therefore, the differences in measurement error between scales with only positively worded items and scales with only negatively worded items is attributable to the differences in the systematic component of δ.

More specifically, on scales with only positively worded items, ξ_{SB} is nonexistent. That is, the systematic bias due to negative wording has no effect on responses to positively worded items. Therefore, this systematic bias factor cannot influence the systematic component of δ for positively worded–only scales. On scales with only negatively worded items, and if ξ_{SB} is not modeled, the systematic component of δ contains the variance due to the systematic bias factor. Therefore, because the systematic component of δ is greater due to ξ_{SB} not being modeled, the negatively worded items–only scales will have more measurement error than the positively worded items–only scales (Bollen, 1989; Mulaik, 1972).

On a mixed-item scale, however, the inclusion of both negatively and positively worded items can increase the amount of systematic error *and* random error in δ. The systematic component will increase, as just noted, when ξ_{SB} not being modeled. The random error component will increase due to the difficulties with mixing item types. As examples, Guion (2011) notes that random error variance can result from test-taker ability differences (see also Cordery & Sevastos, 1993) or individual differences in reactions to test content (II.A, p. 167; see also DiStefano & Motl, 2006), specific items on a scale (II.B, p. 167), and/or bias or carelessness while taking the measure (V.C, p. 168). When negatively worded items are mixed with positively worded items, the negatively worded items can be difficult to understand. Unless respondents are paying close attention, random error can increase due to carelessness (see also Schmitt & Stultz, 1985). Moreover, Pelham and Blanton (2012) note that negative statements tend to be misinterpreted, introducing another source of random error (see also, Swain et al., 2008; van Sonderen et al., 2013). Finally, when item types are mixed, respondents' frames of reference are suddenly changed and can result in confusion (e.g., Cohen & Swerdlik, 2005; Podsakoff et al., 2003) or actually assess a new construct altogether (e.g., Cacioppo, Gardner, & Berntson, 1997; Pilotte & Gable, 1990). Regardless of the specific source(s) of error, the result is an increase in both systematic error variance and random error variance, leading to the most measurement error in a mixed-item condition.

Although understanding the source of error variance (e.g., over time, across items, across raters) is important (Guion, 2011; Zickar, Cortina, & Carter, 2010), the differences in the amount of error variances discussed explains why coefficient-α is lower for mixed-items scales than for only positively worded or only negatively word item scales. An equation for Cronbach's coefficient-α, adapted from Cortina (1993), is:

$$\alpha = \frac{N^2 \times \overline{COV}}{\Sigma(VAR, COV)} \tag{2}$$

where N is the number of items, $\overline{COV}$ is the average of the interitem covariances, and $\Sigma(VAR, COV)$ is the sum of the item variances and interitem covariances. To the extent that item commonalties are high and uniqueness low, α will be high; however, random and systematic error will result in higher item uniqueness. As outlined, scales with only positively worded items have some systematic and random error; scales with only negatively worded items have increased systematic error due to the negatively worded items and random error. Mixed-item scales, however, will not only have increased systematic error resulting from negatively worded items but will also have increased random error due to mixing positive and negative items. In other words, the use of mixed-item scales introduces not only systematic bias due to the negatively worded items but also more random error due to the difficulty of interpreting negatively worded items when placed within positively worded items.

Importantly, because alpha is not a measure of unidimensionality (Cortina, 1993), it is possible to observe a high α even in the presence of a strong second factor perhaps masking the fact that such a factor is present. Indeed, Cortina (1993) shows that if interitem correlations average .30 within two orthogonal factors, reliability could be as high as .75 with 18 items. This value is not only above commonly cited cutoffs (see Lance, Butts, & Michels, 2006) but will likely be higher if the negatively worded items factor correlates even somewhat with the substantive trait being measured. Incidentally, this finding further demonstrates the limited value of heavy reliance on coefficient-α for understanding scale quality (see Sijtsma, 2009). Moreover, these findings from classical test theory approaches to reliability assessment have been recently (Sliter & Zickar, 2014) corroborated by item response theory indices of measurement precision (i.e., item discrimination, item information) showing negatively worded items have more measurement error than positively worded items.

In sum, negatively worded items tend to share variance with each other that is not related to the construct being measured. This extra factor not only impacts item responses but also represents systematic variance that is not caused by the construct of interest, thereby increasing systematic measurement error. When item types are mixed, random error due to mixing positive and negative items increases, further compounding measurement error; the result is scales that have more measurement error than positively worded–only scales.

From this evidence, we conclude that the inclusion of negatively worded items does in fact have an adverse impact on scale quality. Unfortunately, this finding seems to have gone largely unnoticed in recent scale development works. Indeed, of the 19 studies that included negatively worded items (Table 6.1), only one study (Lewis, 2003) acknowledged the negative impact of including negatively worded items on the scale. Interestingly, of the 31 studies that excluded negatively worded items, only three cited the negative psychometric impact of mixed-item scales as the reason for avoiding negatively worded items.

Myth #2: Using Mixed-Item Scales Does Not Change Validity Evidence

A second myth surrounding the practice of including negatively worded items on scales is that scale scores from mixed-item scales are as valid as scale scores from non–mixed-item scales. Given the relation between reliability and validity, however, this is unlikely to be true. As the well-known mantra taught to most researchers early in their training states: Reliability is the upper bound of validity (Allen & Yen, 1979). That is, a scale can be no more valid than it is reliable. As just detailed, reliability of mixed-item scales tends to be lower than either positively or negatively worded scales. Therefore, scores from mixed-item scales will tend to be less valid than positively worded or negatively worded scales. In some instances, the reliability of a mixed-item scale may appear adequate. Because of the increased systematic and random error, however, this scale is still likely to be less reliable than if the scale contained only positively or negatively worded items. More importantly, although the reliability of the scale may appear high, the systematic bias introduced with negatively worded items suggests that observed responses are being influenced by things other than the construct of interest.

Indeed, the introduction of systematic bias resulting from negatively worded items will cause observed scores to be a misrepresentation of the construct of interest. That is, the observed scores on the scale are not being caused solely by the construct of interest—in such cases, a scale cannot be considered valid (e.g., Borsboom, Mellenbergh, & van Heerden, 2004). In a series of studies, Schriesheim and colleagues (Schriesheim & Eisenbach, 1995; Schriesheim et al., 1991; Schriesheim & Hill, 1981) directly tested the accuracy of responses to positively worded, negatively worded, and mixed-item scales. The researchers had participants read hypothetical descriptions of leaders and then complete scales with different formats and item types. Across the experimental studies, they found that accuracy of observed responses was lowest in the mixed-item scales. Conditions in which only positively worded items were administered showed the most accuracy, lending further support to the argument that the increased error is due to difficulty with understanding negatively worded items.

Finally, some have asked if the systematic bias introduced by negatively worded items may actually introduce common method variance, thereby inflating correlations among scales (e.g., Magazine et al., 1996). If this is the case, validity evidence tainted with common method bias would be artificially high, leading to the same conclusion that observed scores from mixed-item scales are indeed invalid. Independent of whether the systematic bias increases measurement error (thereby deflating validity coefficients) or increases common method variance (thereby inflating validity coefficients), using mixed-item scales can have serious implications for validity conclusions.

Based on the results of past studies and basic tenets of psychometric theory, the assumption of equivalent validity of mixed-item and positively worded items–only scales is a myth. Further, inferences about validity may be misguided in that common method variance among negatively worded items can make validity coefficients appear artificially higher than if this method variance were taken into account. Clearly, this assumption of using negatively worded items is also suspect, and scale developers must consider these validity implications when developing measurement instruments.

Myth #3: Positively Worded and Negatively Worded Items Measure the Same Construct

The final myth we discuss in this chapter is the implicit belief that negatively worded and positively worded items measure the same construct. As detailed earlier, negatively worded items form their own factor when factor analyzed. Although some (e.g., DiStefano & Motl, 2006; Idaszak & Drasgow, 1987; Magazine et al., 1996; Spector et al., 1997) consider this factor a method or measurement artifact, others (e.g., Marsh, 1996; McGee et al., 1989; Lance et al., 2009) have argued that this secondary factor may be a substantive construct representing a different attribute. Importantly, both explanations could potentially be considered correct depending on the nature of the construct and the quality and type of negatively worded items.

For example, Cacioppo and colleagues (1997) argue that attitudes do not lie on a bipolar continuum of positive to negative but instead in a bidimensional space. In this space, an individual can simultaneously hold strong positive and negative attitudes (attitudinal ambivalence) or weak positive and negative attitudes (attitudinal indifference). According to this conceptualization, then, the factor associated with negatively worded items is not a method effect but is in fact a substantive *negative attitudes* construct. Marsh (1996) makes a similar argument with respect to self-esteem. In particular, Marsh argued that the negative items on the Rosenberg Self-Esteem Scale were actually indicative of *negative self-esteem*—a substantive construct of interest—though he did not find support for this conceptualization (see also DiStefano & Motl, 2006). Finally, a similar conceptualization is made with respect to positive and negative affect (Watson, Clark, & Tellegen, 1988) wherein the systematic factor underlying the negative-affect items is not a wording-type bias but a substantive construct on which individuals can vary.

Furthermore, the type of negatively worded items used is crucial for determining if the negatively worded items factor is method or substantive. In particular, it is possible that respondents may appear to be responding inconsistently to negatively worded items (i.e., saying *Strongly Agree* when they should have said *Strongly Disagree*), when, in fact, they are actually expressing an accurate sentiment. For example, agreeing to the items "My work is exciting" and "My work is boring" may appear contradictory, but it is possible to envision a job wherein some aspects of the job are exciting whereas others are boring. Take, for instance, the job of a police officer; on the one hand, patrolling the streets might represent a relatively exciting aspect of the job. Filing paperwork, on the other hand, could be quite boring. Therefore, responding *Agree* to both of these items may not be a response style but an accurate representation of a person's job satisfaction. In an attempt to increase the breadth of the construct covered while keeping the number of items small, researchers may be tempted to include negatively worded items that are slight variations of the positively worded items. In such instances, however, disentangling a method factor from a substantive construct or a response set from meaningful responses is difficult.

Clearly, whether or not the negatively worded items factor is trait or method must be judged by individual researchers given their particular constructs and types of negative items. These findings raise doubt about the tenability of the third assumption surrounding the use of negatively worded items. In echoing Lance and colleagues (2009), our point is to dissuade researchers from assuming (1) that their negatively and positively worded items necessarily measure the same construct and (2) that the negatively worded items factor is necessarily a method factor—such practices can have serious validity implications.

Recommendations

In light of this discussion, researchers may be wondering whether they should include negatively worded items in their scales. Unfortunately, a simple *yes* or *no* is not possible because, like most of social science research, it depends; specifically, it depends on the purpose for the negatively worded items. If, on the one hand, the purpose of negatively worded items is to measure a substantive trait (e.g., anxiety, negative attitudes), then negatively worded items are necessary. However, much care and attention to detail are necessary to ensure that the items are written clearly. If, on the other hand, the purpose is to control or identify response styles, this practice is not appropriate in light of alternative approaches.

Identifying Invalid Response Data

Newer means for controlling and identifying response sets have been presented and can generally fall into two broad categories: methodological and statistical. Table 6.2 presents some of the methodological interventions researchers have developed to help curb invalid responding, a brief description of how the approach works, and a reference where readers can obtain more information. Although we do not discuss all of these methods in detail here, we highlight a few that have proven to be effective.

First, Barnette (2000) suggests creating bidirectional-response scales rather than reversing item content to break respondents from automatic responding. That is,

TABLE 6.2 Examples of Methodological Approaches to Stopping Invalid Responding

Method	*Description*
Instructed Response Items	Inclusion of items that instruct the respondent to respond with a particular option (e.g., To ensure you are paying careful attention, please mark "strongly disagree" to this item). Flags respondents who give answers that are not according to the instructions (e.g., Meade & Craig, 2012).
Bogus Items	Inclusion of items to which respondents would not agree and/or disagree (e.g., The Sun revolves around the Earth). Flags respondents who give impossible answers to these items (e.g., Beach, 1989).
Self-Report Response Quality	Inclusion of one or more items that ask to what extent respondents put effort into their responses and/or that asks respondents if their data should be used. Flags respondents who self-report that they did not put in much effort and/or if their data should not be used (e.g., Meade & Craig, 2012).
Bidirectional Response Scales	Inclusion of mixed-response scales such that for half of the items, the response scale is arranged from *Strongly Disagree* to *Strongly Agree* but the response scale is arranged *Strongly Agree* to *Strongly Disagree* for the other half of the items. Breaks respondents' automatic responses since the response scale varies (e.g., Barnette, 2000).
Identified Responses	Responses are not made anonymously but confidentially. Increases the accountability for responses and therefore increases the motivation to respond more carefully (e.g., Meade & Craig, 2012).

124 Dev K. Dalal and Nathan T. Carter

for half of the items, the response scale would be ordered *Strongly Disagree* to *Strongly Agree*; for the other half of the items, the response scale would be ordered *Strongly Agree* to *Strongly Disagree*. Because the item content does not change (i.e., all positively worded), the negative aspects of negatively worded items are avoided. Because the response scales are altered, however, respondents cannot fall into response styles. Barnette created six different versions of an attitude scale toward year-round schooling that differed with respect to the items (i.e., all positively worded items or mixed items) and the nature of the response scale offered (i.e., *strongly disagree— strongly agree; strongly agree—strongly disagree;* bidirectional-response scale). Barnette found that the most reliable (as judged by coefficient α) version of the scale was the version with all positively worded items and bidirectional-response scale (p. 368). Although straightforward, this method may begin to confuse respondents in longer surveys, thereby increasing respondent frustration, fatigue, and possibly attrition.

A second straightforward approach is to simply include quality-check items intermixed among the scale items. These include bogus items (i.e., items respondents should not endorse) and/or instructed response items (i.e., items that tell the respondent how to respond). For example, respondents might be asked to what extent they agree to the item "The Sun revolves around the Earth" or asked "To ensure you are paying close attention, please respond *Strongly Agree* to this item." If a respondent agreed to the former item or did not agree to the latter item, this could suggest the respondent is not paying close attention to the items. Meade and Craig (2012) showed that the number of these types of items respondents incorrectly endorsed correlated with other indices of invalid responding and were able to successfully predict latent class membership (wherein latent classes corresponded to validity of response data). Moreover, these types of items have been recommended when conducting studies with crowd-sourced (e.g., Amazon Mechanical Turk) participants to identify invalid responding (Barger, Behrend, Sharek, & Sinar, 2011), and, in general, have been used successfully (e.g., Huang, Curran, Keeney, Poposki, & DeShon, 2012). A limitation to this approach, however, is that respondents may become frustrated if many of these types of items are included in studies; therefore, researchers must strive to strike a balance between wanting to check for invalid responses and frustrating respondents.

In addition to these methodological approaches, statistical approaches to identifying invalid data are also available. These approaches are designed to help researchers flag individuals who may have responded invalidly. Again, although we only highlight a few, Table 6.3 provides some examples. One methodology that has been used with some success is Mixed-Model Item Response Theory (MM-IRT), which can be used to identify unobservable, latent classes of respondents that use the response scale differently. For example, Carter, Dalal, Lake, Lin, and Zickar (2010) found three latent classes in a sample of respondents taking the Job Descriptive Index (JDI) measure of job satisfaction. One class was most likely to use the *Yes* response, one more likely to use *No*, and one more likely to use the *?*

response, *regardless* of their job satisfaction. It was found that membership in the class that relied heavily on the *?* was associated with lower Trust in Management, showing how systematic error can be problematic for the validity of a measure, as this evidence might suggest contamination due to the fear of potential retaliation. In application, MM-IRT can be a useful tool for detecting large groups of persons employing aberrant response sets as well as the reasons those response sets might emerge.

Another IRT methodology attempts to identify aberrant responding at the person level: *person fit* statistics. In this approach, the responses of each person are compared to what would have been expected by the calibrated model (Meijer & Sijtsma, 2001); misfitting persons can be flagged by significance tests and their response patterns can be examined and compared to what would be expected by the model. Such an approach could be helpful in identifying and eliminating respondents responding in a way that is inconsistent with the response theory. Indeed, a line of research concerned with identifying causes for person misfit (e.g., Emons, Sijtsma, & Meijer, 2004, 2005; Ferrando, 2012) could be of use to researchers and practitioners involved in large-scale surveys. One limitation to these IRT approaches that should be noted, however, is the need for larger sample sizes to allow for accurate estimation of model parameters.

In addition to IRT-based approaches, researchers (e.g., Meade & Craig, 2012) have demonstrated the efficacy for consistency measures. Consistency indices compute within-person correlations between two similar items (determined based on content, observed relation, or direct repetition). The logic of this method is that respondents who are responding carefully should show consistency in their responses to similar items. To the extent that this correlation is small, respondents are flagged as responding carelessly. In short, these consistency measures assess the extent to which respondents are *inconsistent* when they *should be* consistent.

Consistency indices have also been developed to determine if respondents are too consistent. With these indices, a within-person correlation is computed between pairs of dissimilar items (again, determined based on content or observed relation), and respondents are flagged to the extent this correlation is too high. That is, these indices assess the extent to which respondents are *consistent* when they *should not be*. Meade and Craig (2012) showed that these methods were, in general, successful at identifying invalid responders; the consistency indices based on similar items, however, were slightly better (see also Huang et al., 2012).

Some issues researchers will need to consider with these methods, however, include the need to use multiple indicators and the need to determine an appropriate cutoff for many of them. That is, the different statistical approaches outlined in Table 6.3 may need to be used together to ensure that all invalid responders are flagged. For example, whereas consistency indices from similar items can show when respondents are not being consistent, these indices would miss those individuals who are being *too* consistent in their responding—consistency indices for dissimilar items would be needed to flag these latter responders (Meade & Craig,

126 Dev K. Dalal and Nathan T. Carter

TABLE 6.3 Examples of Statistical Approaches to Identify Invalid Responding

Method	Description
Mixed-Model IRT	Statistical procedure that uses respondents' item response processes to determine latent classes of response scale usage. Allows the researcher to determine if certain classes of individuals are likely to respond with response sets (e.g., Carter, Dalal, Lake, Lin, & Zickar, 2010).
Person-Level IRT Fit	Statistical procedure that assesses to what extent the respondent does *not* fit the calibrated IRT model. Responses from misfitting respondents can be further scrutinized for inclusions (e.g., Meijer & Sijtsma, 2001).
Consistency Indices—Similar	Comparison of responses to *similar* pairs of items—determined empirically or based on content—to assess consistency in responding. May also include the same item asked twice. Flags respondents who are *not* consistent when they *should* be consistent (Johnson, 2005).
Consistency Indices—Dissimilar	Comparison of responses to *dissimilar* pairs of items—determined empirically or based on content—to assess consistency in responding. Flags respondents who are *too* consistent when they *should not* be consistent (e.g., Johnson, 2005).
Outlier Indices	Univariate or multivariate indices of the distance between a respondent's responses and the average responses. Flags individuals whose responses would be considered outliers (e.g., Meade & Craig, 2012).
Observed Response Patterns	Computing the number of times the same response option is used by each respondent. Flags the individuals who have used the same response option (e.g., *4*) more than would be expected (e.g., Costa & McCrae, 2008).
Response Time	Calculating the amount of time each respondent took to complete the scale/survey/study. Flags individuals who completed the survey extraordinarily quickly (e.g., Wise & Kong, 2005).

2012). In addition, many of these measures are continuous, which raises difficulties surrounding determining cutoffs for these indices that are sensitive enough to ensure that invalid responders are not missed but not so sensitive as to result in false positives.

Recommendations with Existing Scale Data

These suggestions should be considered in the process of new scale development, even if the scales are study specific. Many researchers, however, may already have scales and/or data with negatively worded items; we suggest researchers take four important steps before using the scale or data. First, consider the original rationale for including negatively worded items. If the purpose is to measure the negative pole of the construct, the researcher needs to consider how to score the two item types. It is more likely, however, that the negative items were included to reduce response styles. In such instances, our second step is to carefully review the type and quality of the negatively worded items. If the items are confusing or unclear in any way, researchers should be concerned about the possibility of a method effect. Third, researchers who are using negatively worded items to control for response styles should check to see if responses are invalid based on observed responses to the negatively worded items. Again, the use of negatively worded items does not automatically control response styles—we recommend that researchers include a check for response styles as a part of their data-cleaning process (Swain et al., 2008). Fourth, like Hinkin (1998), we suggest that researchers check not just the reliability of their mixed-item scales but also the factor structure to determine if a negatively worded items factor is present. If such a factor is present, researchers can conduct their substantive analyses with scale scores that use *and* exclude the negatively worded items to determine if the negatively worded items are influencing conclusions.

When Negatively Worded Items Are Necessary

Finally, there are instances when negatively worded items are not only appropriate but necessary. First, researchers creating bidimensional scales (Cacioppo et al., 1997) will need to include negatively worded items in their scales. In addition to care with writing negatively worded items, attention must be paid to scoring such scales. Indeed, a single summative score of the positively worded and negatively worded items would not be appropriate; a separate score for the positively and negatively worded items would be needed.

Second, negatively worded items are necessary when creating ideal-point or Thurstone scales (Thurstone, 1928). According to the ideal-point response process, respondents endorse items whose content matches their level of the attribute. Therefore, in order to scale extreme-positive, extreme-negative, and moderate attribute standing, items tapping these levels of the trait are necessary (Dragow, Chernyshenko, & Stark, 2010; Roberts, Donoghue, & Laughlin, 2000). As such, negatively worded items are necessary to tap negative attribute standing on ideal-point scales. It is important to note, therefore, that our discussion applies only to scales constructed under dominance (i.e., Likert) assumptions, which have recently been called into question for some constructs (e.g., Carter & Dalal, 2010; Dragow et al., 2010; Tay, Dragow, Rounds, & Williams, 2009). In each of these situations, however, extreme care must be taken to ensure the negatively worded items are clear and measuring the construct of interest.

Conclusions

As the review presented in Table 6.1 shows, researchers and practitioners continue to include negatively worded items on scales measuring psychological constructs. Here, we have argued that, because researchers do so under assumptions that are not guaranteed, this practice has become an urban legend. Unfortunately, using mixed-item scales can introduce a factor upon which only the negatively worded items load, can increase the amount of systematic and random error in responses, can change validity conclusions, and can even measure distinct constructs. Our goal was to caution researchers on the myths surrounding this practice so they can carefully consider the appropriateness of negatively worded items for their purposes. To this end, we remind researchers to critically evaluate negatively worded items in light of the nature of the construct being measured, the type of scale used, and the quality of the negatively worded items. Indeed, the "take-home" conclusions from this chapter are that response styles will not necessarily be prevented by simply including negatively worded items on one's scale, and these items may actually introduce new problems for researchers and practitioners.

Acknowledgments

The authors would like to thank Xiaoyuan (Susan) Zhu for her contribution to this chapter and Dalia L. Diab for her comments on earlier drafts of this chapter.

Note

1 We note that, although response sets and response styles are considered distinct phenomena by some, researchers have used different terms when referring to response styles including *response bias* (e.g., DiStefano & Motl, 2006), *response set* (e.g., Spector et al., 1997), *method effect*, and *halo effect* (e.g., Marsh, 1996). Our discussion centers on the urban legend of use of negatively worded items to mitigate bias in responses that result from responses that are independent of scale content and not about resolving terminology differences. Therefore, although we utilize the term *response style* throughout, our discussion extends to the same issues discussed by these researchers.

References

Allen, M. J., & Yen, W. (1979). *Introduction to measurement theory.* Monterey, CA: Brooks/Cole.

Anastasi, A. (1982). *Psychological testing* (5th ed.). New York, NY: Macmillan.

Barger, P., Behrend, T. S., Sharek, D. J., & Sinar, E. F. (2011). IO and the crowd: Frequently asked questions about using Mechanical Turk for research. *The Industrial-Organizational Psychologist, 49*, 11–17.

Barnette, J. J. (2000). Effects of stem and Likert response option reversals on survey internal consistency: If you feel the need, there is a better alternative to using those negatively worded stems. *Educational and Psychological Measurement, 60*, 361–370.

Beach, D. A. (1989). Identifying the random responder. *The Journal of Psychology, 123*, 101–103.

Bollen, K. A. (1989). *Structural equations with latent variables.* New York, NY: Wiley.

Borsboom, D., Mellenbergh, G. J., & van Heerden, J. (2004). The concept of validity. *Psychological Review, 111*, 1061–1071.

Cacioppo, J. T., Gardner, W. L., & Berntson, G. G. (1997). Beyond bipolar conceptualizations and measures: The case of attitudes and evaluative space. *Personality and Social Psychology Review, 1*, 3–25.

Carter, N. T., & Dalal, D. K. (2010). An ideal point account of the JDI Work Satisfaction Scale. *Personality and Individual Differences, 49*, 743–748.

Carter, N. T., Dalal, D. K., Lake, C. J., Lin, B. C., & Zickar, M. J. (2011). Using mixed-model item response theory to analyze organizational survey responses: An illustration using the job descriptive index. *Organizational Research Methods, 14*, 116–146.

Chan, D. (2009). So why ask me? Are self-report data really that bad? In C. E. Lance & R. J. Vandenberg (Eds.), *Statistical and methodology myths and urban legends: Doctrine, verity, and fable in organizational and social sciences* (pp. 309–336). New York, NY: Routledge.

Cohen, R. J., & Swerdlik, M. E. (2005). *Psychological testing and assessment: An introduction to tests and measurement* (6th ed.). New York, NY: McGraw-Hill.

Cordery, J. L., & Sevastos, P. P. (1993). Responses to the original and revised Job Diagnostic Survey: Is education a factor in responses to negatively worded items? *Journal of Applied Psychology, 78*, 141–143.

Cortina, J. M. (1993). What is coefficient alpha? An examination of theory and applications *Journal of Applied Psychology, 78*, 98–98.

Costa, P. T., Jr., & McCrae, R. R. (2008). The Revised NEO Personality Inventory (NEO-PI-R). In D. H. Saklofske (Ed.), *The SAGE handbook of personality theory and assessment. Vol. 2: Personality measurement and testing* (pp. 179–198). Thousand Oaks, CA: Sage.

Cozby, P. C., & Bates, S. C. (2012). *Methods in behavioral research* (11th ed.). New York, NY: McGraw-Hill.

Cronbach, L. J. (1942). Studies of acquiescence as a factor in the true-false test. *Journal of Educational Psychology, 33*, 401.

Cronbach, L. J. (1946). Response sets and test validity. *Educational and Psychological Measurement, 6*, 475–494.

Cronbach, L. J. (1950). Further evidence on response sets and test design. *Educational and Psychological Measurement, 10*, 3–31.

Dahling, J. J., Whitaker, B. G., & Levy, P. E. (2009). The development and validation of a new Machiavellianism scale. *Journal of Management, 35*, 219–257.

DiStefano, C., & Motl, R. W. (2006). Further investigating method effects associated with negatively worded items on self-report surveys. *Structural Equation Modeling, 13*, 440–464.

Drasgow, F., Chernyshenko, O. S., & Stark, S. (2010). 75 years after Likert: Thurstone was right! *Industrial and Organizational Psychology: Perspectives on Science and Practice, 3*, 465–476.

Emons, W.H.M., Sijtsma, K., & Meijer, R. R. (2004). Testing hypotheses about the person response function in person-fit analyses. *Multivariate Behavioral Research, 39*, 1–35.

Emons, W.H.M., Sijtsma, K., & Meijer, R. R. (2005). Global, local, and graphical person-fit analyses using person response functions. *Psychological Methods, 10*, 101–119.

Ferrando, P. J. (2012). Assessing inconsistent responding in E and N measures: An application of person-fit analyses in personality. *Personality and Individual Differences, 52*, 718–722.

Ferris, G. R., Treadway, D. C., Kolodinsky, R. W., Hochwarter, W. A., Kacmar, C. J., Douglas, C., & Frink, D. D. (2005). Development and validation of the political skill inventory. *Journal of Management, 31*, 126–152.

Goodwin, C. J. (2010). *Research in psychology: Methods and design* (6th ed.). Hoboken, NJ: Wiley.

Guion, R. M. (2011). *Assessment, measurement and prediction for personnel decision* (2nd ed.). New York, NY: Routledge.

Hinkin, T. R. (1995). A review of scale development practices in the study of organizations. *Journal of Management, 21*, 967–988.

Hinkin, T. R. (1998). A brief tutorial on the development of measures for use in survey questionnaires. *Organizational Research Methods, 1*, 104–121.

Huang, J. L., Curran, P. G., Keeney, J., Poposki, E. M., & DeShon, R. P. (2012). Detecting and deterring insufficient effort responding to surveys. *Journal of Business and Psychology, 27*, 99–114.

Idaszak, J. R., & Drasgow, F. (1987). A revision of the Job Diagnostic Survey: Elimination of a measurement artifact. *Journal of Applied Psychology, 72*, 69–74.

Jackson, D. N., & Messick, S. (1958). Content and style in personality assessment. *Psychological Bulletin, 55*, 243–252.

Johnson, J. A. (2005). Ascertaining the validity of individual protocols from web-based personality inventories. *Journal of Research in Personality, 39*, 103–129.

Kline, R. B. (2005). *Principles and practice of structural equation modeling* (2nd ed.). New York, NY: Guilford Press.

Lance, C. E., Baranik, L. E., Lau, A. R., & Scharlau, E. A. (2009). If it ain't trait it must be method: (Mis)application of multitrait-multimethod design in organizational research. In C. E. Lance & R. J. Vandenberg (Eds.), *Statistical and methodology myths and urban legends: Doctrine, verity, and fable in organizational and social sciences* (pp. 337–360). New York, NY: Routledge.

Lance, C. E., Butts, M. M., & Michels, L. C. (2006). The sources of four commonly reported cutoff criteria: What did they really say? *Organizational Research Methods, 9*, 202–220.

Lewis, K. (2003). Measuring transactive memory systems in the field: Scale development and validation. *Journal of Applied Psychology, 88*, 587–604.

Likert, R. (1932). A technique for the measurement of attitudes. *Archives of Psychology, 140*, 5–55.

Linderbaum, B. A., & Levy, P. E. (2010). The development and validation of the Feedback Orientation Scale (FOS). *Journal of Management, 36*, 1372–1405.

Magazine, S. L., Williams, L. J., & Williams, M. L. (1996). A confirmatory factor analysis examination of reverse coding effects in Meyer and Allen's affective and continuance commitment scales. *Educational and Psychological Measurement, 56*, 241–250.

Marsh, H. W. (1996). Positive and negative global self-esteem: A substantively meaningful distinction or artifactors? *Journal of Personality and Social Psychology, 70*, 810–819.

McCarthy, J., & Goffin, R. (2004). Measuring job interview anxiety: Beyond weak knees and sweaty palms. *Personnel Psychology, 57*, 607–637.

McGee, G. W., Ferguson Jr., C. E., & Seers, A. (1989). Role conflict and role ambiguity: Do the scales measure these two constructs?. *Journal of Applied Psychology, 74*, 815–818.

Meade, A. W., & Craig, S. B. (2012). Identifying careless responses in survey data. *Psychological Methods, 17*, 437–455.

Meijer, R. R., & Sijtsma, K. (2001). Methodology review: Evaluating person-fit. *Applied Psychological Measurement, 25*, 107–135.

Messick, S. (1962). Response style and content measures from personality inventories. *Educational and Psychological Measurement, 22*, 41–56.

Morling, B. (2012). *Research methods in psychology: Evaluating a world of information.* New York, NY: W. W. Norton & Company, Inc.

Mulaik, S. A. (1972). *The foundations of factor analysis.* New York, NY: McGraw-Hill.

Nunnally, J. C. (1978). *Psychometric theory.* New York, NY: McGraw-Hill.

Pelham, B. W., & Blanton, H. (2012). *Conducting research in psychology: Measuring the weight of smoke* (4th ed.). Belmont, CA: Wadsworth/Thompson Learning.

Pilotte, W. J., & Gable, R. K. (1990). The impact of positive and negative item stems on the validity of a computer anxiety scale. *Educational and Psychological Measurement, 50*, 603–610.

Podsakoff, P. M., MacKenzie, S. B., Lee, J. Y., & Podsakoff, N. P. (2003). Common method biases in behavioral research: A critical review of the literature and recommended remedies. *Journal of Applied Psychology, 88*, 879–903.

Reeve, C. L., & Smith, C. S. (2001). Refining Lodahl and Kejner's job involvement scale with convergent evidence approach: Applying multiple methods to multiple samples. *Organizational Research Methods, 4*, 91–111.

Roberts, J. S., Donoghue, J. R., & Laughlin, J. E. (2000). A generalized item response theory model for unfolding unidimensional polytomous responses. *Applied Psychological Measurement, 24*, 3–32.

Rorer, L. G. (1965). The great response-style myth. *Psychological Bulletin, 63*, 129–156.

Roszkowski, M. J., & Soven, M. (2010). Shifting gears: Consequences of including two negatively worded items in the middle of a positively worded questionnaire. *Assessment & Evaluation in Higher Education, 35*, 113–130.

Sanders, L. D. (2010). *Discovering research methods in psychology: A student's guide.* Malden, MA: Blackwell.

Sauley, K. S., & Bedeian, A. G. (2000). Equity sensitivity: Construction of a measure and examination of its psychometric properties. *Journal of Management, 26*, 885–910.

Schmitt, N., & Stults, D. M. (1985). Factors defined by negatively keyed items: The result of careless respondents? *Applied Psychological Measurement, 9*, 367–373.

Schriesheim, C. A., & Eisenbach, R. J. (1995). An exploratory and confirmatory factor-analytic investigation of item wording effects on the obtained factor structures of survey questionnaire measures. *Journal of Management, 21*, 1177–1193.

Schriesheim, C. A., Eisenbach, R. J., & Hill, K. D. (1991). The effect of negation and polar opposite item reversals on questionnaire reliability and validity: An experimental investigation. *Educational and Psychological Measurement, 51*, 67–78.

Schriesheim, C. A., & Hill, K. D. (1981). Controlling acquiescence response bias by item reversals: The effect on questionnaire validity. *Educational and Psychological Measurement, 41*, 1101–1114.

Shaughnessy, J. J., Zechmeister, E. B., & Zechmeister, J. S. (2012). *Research methods in psychology* (9th ed.). New York, NY: McGraw-Hill.

Sijtsma, K. (2009). On the use, the misuse, and the very limited usefulness of Cronbach's alpha. *Psychometrika, 74*, 107–120.

Sliter, K. A., & Zickar, M. J. (2014). An IRT examination of the psychometric functioning of negatively worded personality items. *Educational and Psychology Measurement, 74*, 214–226.

Spector, P. E., Van Katwyk, P. T., Brannick, M. T., & Chen, P. Y. (1997). When two factors don't reflect two constructs: How item characteristics can produce artifactual factors. *Journal of Management, 23*, 659–677.

Stewart, T. J., & Frye, A. W. (2004). Investigating the use of negatively phrased survey items in medical education settings: Common wisdom or common mistake? *Academic Medicine, 79*, S18–S20.

Swain, S. D., Weathers, D., & Niedrich, R. W. (2008). Assessing three sources of misreponse to reversed Likert items. *Journal of Marketing Research, 45*, 116–131.

Tay, L., Drasgow, F., Rounds, J., & Williams, B. A. (2009). Fitting measurement models to vocational interest data: Are dominance models ideal? *Journal of Applied Psychology, 94*(5), 1287.

Thurstone, L. L. (1928). Attitudes can be measured. *The American Journal of Sociology, 33*, 529–554.

Van den Broeck, A., Vansteenkiste, M., De Witte, H., Soenens, B., & Lens, W. (2010). Capturing autonomy, competence, and relatedness at work: Construction and initial validation of the Work-Related Basic Need Satisfaction scale. *Journal of Occupational and Organizational Psychology, 83*, 981–1002.

van Sonderen, E., Sanderman, R., & Coyne, J. C. (2013). Ineffectiveness of reverse wording of questionnaire items: Let's learn from cows in the rain. *PLOS ONE, 8*, e68967.

Watson, D., Clark, L. A., & Tellegen, A. (1988). Development and validation of brief measures of positive and negative affect: The PANAS scales. *Journal of Personality and Social Psychology, 54*, 1063–1070.

Weems, G. H., Onwuegbuzie, A. J., Schreiber, J. B., & Eggers, S. J. (2003). Characteristics of respondents who respond differently to positively and negatively worded items on rating scales. *Assessment & Evaluation in Higher Education, 28*, 587–606.

Weijters, B., & Baumgartner, H. (2012). Misresponse to reversed and negated items in surveys: A review. *Journal of Marketing Research, 49*, 737–747.

Wise, S. L., & Kong, X. (2005). Response time effort: A new measure of examinee motivation in computer-based tests. *Applied Measurement in Education, 18*, 163–183.

Zickar, M. J., Cortina, J. M., & Carter, N. T. (2010). Evaluation of measures: Sources of error, sufficiency, and contamination. In J. L. Farr & N. T. Tippins (Eds.), *Handbook of Employee Selection* (pp. 399–415). New York, NY: Routledge.

Zickar, M. J., & Highhouse, S. (2001). Measuring prestige of journals in industrial–organizational psychology. *The Industrial-Organizational Psychologist, 38*, 29–36.

7

MISSING DATA BIAS

Exactly How Bad Is Pairwise Deletion?

Daniel A. Newman and Jonathan M. Cottrell

When conducting social science research, missing data are a ubiquitous practical difficulty (Anseel, Lievens, Scollaert, & Choragwicka, 2010; Peugh & Enders, 2004; Roth, 1994). Under missing data conditions, it is necessary for the data analyst to choose from among several available missing data techniques, including (a) listwise deletion, (b) pairwise deletion, (c) single imputation, (d) maximum likelihood (ML), and (e) multiple imputation (MI) approaches. That is, when facing missing data, *abstinence is not an option*—one of these missing data techniques must be used, and all are imperfect. Thus, the issue of selecting a missing data technique is a matter of choosing the lesser of evils.

By far, the most common advice offered by methodologists (Enders, 2001, 2010; Graham, 2009; Little & Rubin, 2002; Newman, 2003, 2009; Schafer & Graham, 2002) is to employ state-of-the-art missing data techniques, namely *maximum likelihood* (ML; e.g., EM algorithm; Dempster, Laird, & Rubin, 1977; Little & Rubin, 1987; or Full Information Maximum Likelihood/FIML; see Enders, 2001) or *multiple imputation* (MI; Little & Rubin, 1987; Schafer, 1997). This research and advice has led to an urban legend that *pairwise deletion is almost never appropriate* (see Newman, 2009). Indeed, the APA Task Force on Statistical Inference (Wilkinson & Task Force on Statistical Inference, 1999) advised, "The two popular methods for dealing with missing data that are found in basic statistics packages—listwise and pairwise deletion of missing values—are among the worst methods available for practical applications" (p. 598).

But if a researcher chooses to use a subpar (or ad hoc) missing data technique (e.g., pairwise deletion) instead of a state-of-the-art missing data technique (e.g., ML, MI), then what exactly are the consequences? That is, how bad a problem does one create by choosing pairwise deletion? In describing missing data difficulties, Newman (2009) has summarized two primary problems caused by missing data: (a) decreased statistical power (i.e., larger sampling error, more Type II errors of

134 Daniel A. Newman and Jonathan M. Cottrell

inference) and (b) biased parameter estimates (e.g., systematic over- or underesti-mation of correlations, variances, and means). The current chapter will focus on one specific missing data issue: calculating the amount of *bias in parameter estimates* that is due to *pairwise deletion*.

The Notion of Statistical and Methodological Myths and Urban Legends

The current edited volume contains a collection of chapters about so-called statis-tical and methodological myths and urban legends (see also Lance, 2011; Lance & Vandenberg, 2009; Vandenberg, 2006). Before we proceed to situate the pairwise deletion bias problem by reviewing several types of missing data mechanisms and their corresponding missing data treatments, it might be useful for us to first make a few opening remarks about methodological urban legends in general.

We therefore begin by speculating that the source of many (if not most) meth-odological urban legends is *binary thinking*—that is, converting a natural contin-uum into a false dichotomy. Lance, Butts, and Michels (2006) discussed several prominent examples of binary thinking: Cronbach's α > .70 → acceptable reli-ability; James, Demaree, and Wolf's (1984) $r_{WG(J)}$ > .70 → justifiable aggregation of individual responses to represent group-level properties; GFI > .90 → good fit for a structural equation model; and eigenvalue > 1.0 → factor is worth retaining in factor analysis. Lance and colleagues' (2006) review revealed large flaws in both the origins and the common citations of these rules of thumb. We also note that in each instance, the rule of thumb was being used to carve a continuous reality (e.g., reliability, within-group agreement, model fit, and eigenvalues) into a dichot-omy (e.g., adequate vs. inadequate reliability, good vs. bad fit, retainable factor vs. factor not worth retaining). These false dichotomies are rooted in researchers' inherent *desire to use research methods for making decisions.*

Our position in the current chapter is that such dichotomous decisions will be better informed if the researchers understand the underlying continuum that is being carved by the rule of thumb. For example, the decision that Cronbach's α = .52 denotes inadequate reliability for a particular measurement application should be founded on a good understanding of the specific magnitude of the consequences of using a measure with reliability = .52—and not based merely on the rule of thumb that .52 < .70 automatically denotes that a measure is "unreliable."

Similarly, the idea that *pairwise deletion is almost never appropriate* (e.g., Newman, 2009; Wilkinson & Task Force on Statistical Inference, 1999) is also a rule of thumb that reveals dichotomous thinking. This rule of thumb has the potential to gain trac-tion as an urban legend, because it helps researchers to *make decisions* about which missing data technique to use (e.g., pairwise deletion vs. multiple imputation). But, similar to the examples above, we believe that decision making about which missing data technique to use will be better informed if there is a good understanding of the specific *magnitude* of the consequences of using pairwise deletion. That is, in the

Missing Data Bias **135**

current work, we seek to estimate the exact magnitude of missing data bias that is due to pairwise deletion rather than simply declaring, "pairwise deletion is bad."

A Brief Overview of Missing Data Problems and Solutions

Table 7.1 provides an overview of missing data problems (bias and error), missing data techniques (listwise deletion, pairwise deletion, single imputation, ML, MI), and missing data mechanisms (MCAR, MAR, MNAR). Although we believe that Table 7.1 is fairly self-explanatory, we want to highlight a few issues described in the table. First, listwise deletion can greatly impair statistical power and increase Type II errors of inference (i.e., failing to detect effects that really do exist). Second, both listwise deletion and pairwise deletion are *unbiased* techniques only under the narrow condition in which the missingness mechanism is missing completely at random (MCAR). Under all other (and much more realistic) conditions [i.e., systematic missingness patterns known as missing at random (MAR) and missing not at random (MNAR)], listwise deletion and pairwise deletion will tend to yield biased estimates (e.g., over- or underestimated correlations, variances, and means). Finally, state-of-the-art missing data techniques (ML and MI) are unbiased under both MCAR and MAR missingness mechanisms, meaning that ML and MI techniques will render less biased estimates than do pairwise and listwise deletion, especially when the data are systematically missing according to the MAR mechanism (Schafer & Graham, 2002). For example, one sort of research design that has a lot of MAR missingness is a longitudinal design, in which the same variable is measured repeatedly but attrition grows across measurement occasions (Newman, 2003). We present the nutshell overview of missing data terminology in Table 7.1 for the purpose of illustrating the narrow focus of the current chapter. That is, we will focus here on missing data *bias* under *pairwise deletion*.

TABLE 7.1 Missing Data Overview

	Definition or Description
Missing Data Problems	
I. Missing Data *Bias*	**Bias** *in parameter estimates*: systematic over- or underestimation of parameters/effect sizes (e.g., correlations, means, variances, regression coefficients)
II. Missing Data *Error*	**Errors** *of statistical inference* (hypothesis testing): - *Low statistical power*: Failure to detect true effects - *Inaccurate* (often larger) *standard errors*—p-values are wrong for statistical significance tests
Missing Data Mechanisms	
I. Random missingness (MCAR)	*Missing completely at random (MCAR)*: the probability that data are missing on a variable is *unrelated* to all variables, observed and unobserved $[p(\text{missing} \mid \text{complete data}) = p(\text{missing})]$

(Continued)

TABLE 7.1 (Continued)

	Definition or Description
II. Systematic missingness (MAR*, MNAR)	*Missing at random (MAR)*: the probability that data are missing on a variable is related to observed variables (observed data) only **[p(missing | complete data) = p(missing | observed data)]** *Missing not at random (MNAR)*: the probability that data are missing on a variable is related to the unobserved/missing variables (missing data) **[p(missing | complete data) ≠ p(missing | observed data)]**

Missing Data Techniques

I. Listwise deletion	Deleting all persons for whom any data are missing, then proceeding with the analysis **Problems**: *Lowest power*: large standard errors (SEs); *biased* estimates whenever missing data are not missing completely at random (MCAR)
II. Pairwise deletion	Calculating summary estimates (means, SDs, correlations) using all persons who provided data relevant to each estimate, then proceeding with analysis based on these estimates **Problems**: Different correlations based on different subsamples—corr. matrix can be *not positive definite*; also, *no single sample size* (N) makes sense for the entire corr. matrix (some SEs too big, some SEs too small); *biased* estimates whenever missing data are not missing completely at random (MCAR); usually less biased than listwise deletion
III. Single imputation	Imputing/replacing each missing datum with a "guess" (e.g., the variable mean, person mean, a random value, a predicted value from regression, a predicted value from regression with error added in), then proceeding with analysis as though the data were complete **Problems**: Using complete-data N (as though data were complete) leads to *underestimating SEs* (gives p-values that are too low; false positive conclusions); *biased* estimates, even when data are missing completely at random (MCAR)! (single imputation can create bias) One technique—*stochastic regression imputation*—is relatively unbiased (but SEs are still too small).
IV. Multiple imputation (MI)	Imputing/replacing each missing datum with a "guess" (e.g., a predicted value from regression with error added in), then proceeding with analysis as though the data were complete. Then, repeating this process multiple times (e.g., 5 to 20 times). Then, combining the results from the multiple imputations in such a way that the uncertainty involved in each single imputation gets included in the standard errors, making the standard errors and significance tests more accurate.

	Advantages: *Higher power, accurate SEs* (more accurate hypothesis tests), *unbiased* under completely random missingness (*MCAR*) and also *unbiased* under one form of systematic missingness (*MAR*) Can improve estimation by including *auxiliary variables* in the imputation model that are not part of the theoretical model being tested
	Disadvantages: *Biased* estimates whenever data are systematically missing not at random (MNAR); assumes an *imputation model* (e.g., multivariate normal, etc.); gives *slightly different estimates each time* (due to the random aspect of the imputation process); with SEM it yields *more nonconvergences* (because analysis must be successfully performed 40 times for 40 imputations), might have difficulty handling over 100 variables at once
V. Maximum likelihood (ML)	Direct estimation of parameters and standard errors by choosing estimates that maximize the probability of the observed data
	Advantages: *Higher power, accurate SEs* (more accurate hypothesis tests); *unbiased* under completely random missingness (*MCAR*) and also *unbiased* under one form of systematic missingness (*MAR*) (ML and MI results converge as N increases), ML results improve as N increases; avoids criticism from those who have a philosophical (not statistical) problem with imputation-based procedures like MI
	Disadvantages: *Biased* estimates whenever data are systematically missing not at random (MNAR); *assumes multivariate normality* (kurtosis can bias SEs); might have difficulty handling more than 100 variables at once

Note: See Rubin (1976); Little & Rubin (1987, 2002); Enders (2001, 2010); Schafer & Graham (2002); Newman (2003, 2009); Graham (2009).

* As noted by Schafer and Graham (2002), Rubin's (1976) use of the term "missing at random" (MAR) to refer to a systematic missingness mechanism is an unfortunate source of confusion. This confusing nomenclature is an artifact of the difference between how statisticians use the word *random* (i.e., to mean probabilistic instead of deterministic) versus how psychologists use the word *random* (i.e., to mean unpredictable or unrelated to the variables in the analysis).

Quantifying Missing Data Bias under Pairwise Deletion (i.e., Biased Correlations)

The goal of the current chapter is to quantify missing data *bias*. That is, we will attempt to show by *how much the observed correlation between two variables, x and y, is over- or underestimated using pairwise deletion*, when some of the data are missing from x, y, or both variables. First, we will classify 11 distinct *missing data selection mechanisms*. Second, we will derive equations—based upon manipulating and modifying

138 Daniel A. Newman and Jonathan M. Cottrell

some classic and lesser-known formulas for range restriction—that pinpoint by how much the correlation between x and y is likely to be biased under various missing data conditions (including the 11 missing data selection mechanisms, across a range of missing data amounts/response rates). Third, we will use these newly derived equations to pinpoint areas where bias due to pairwise deletion is likely to be small or relatively inconsequential. As such, we will evaluate the urban legend that "pairwise deletion is always bad, because it leads to problematic amounts of missing data bias."

Missing Data Selection Mechanisms

Case 1: Completely Random Missingness. The first missing data selection mechanism (Case 1 in Table 7.2) is *Completely Random Missingness*, which corresponds to Rubin's (1976) mechanism of missing completely at random (MCAR). In this mechanism, data on variable x, variable y, or both x and y are missing; and the missingness is due to a completely random process (like tossing a coin). Because the missing data are MCAR, pairwise deletion will yield an *unbiased* correlation (no missing data bias; i.e., the bias correction formula ultimately involves no correction at all: $r_{xy(comp)} = r_{xy(resp)}$).

Cases 2a and 2b: Direct Range Restriction. The second type of missing data selection mechanism is *Direct Range Restriction*, which involves both missing data on variable y that were selected (or, technically, screened out) on the basis of variable x (Case 2a) and also missing data on variable x that were selected out on the basis of variable y (Case 2b). An example of Case 2a is the traditional personnel selection scenario, in which we are interested in the predictive validity correlation between a predictor score x (e.g., a preemployment test battery, on which we have defined a cut score above which everyone was hired and below which no one was hired) and a criterion score y (e.g., supervisor ratings of job performance). Because we do not have job performance ratings (y) for those applicants who were never hired (i.e., who scored below the cut score on x), we have missing data on y because "y was selected on x." This pattern is illustrated by comparing Figure 7.1a (complete data on x and y) against Figure 7.1b (direct range restriction, where y is selected on x, and everyone who scores below the cut score on x ends up with missing data on y). The x-y correlation will be smaller in Figure 7.1b than in Figure 7.1a due to missing data bias (in this case, direct range restriction). As an aside, we note that direct range restriction is an MAR missingness mechanism according to Rubin's (1976) typology of missing data mechanisms (Table 7.2). The correction formula for removing missing data bias in the x-y correlation under direct range restriction was derived long ago by Pearson (1903). This direct range restriction correction formula is:

$$r_{xy(comp)} = r_{xy(resp)} \Big/ \sqrt{(1-u^2)r_{xy(resp)}^2 + u^2}, \qquad \text{(Eq. 1)}$$

where $r_{xy(comp)}$ is the *unbiased* correlation between x and y (with no missing data bias: i.e., the correlation that would have been observed under complete-data

TABLE 7.2 Missing Data Bias in the Correlation Under 11 Missing Data Selection Mechanisms

Missing Data Selection Mechanism	Rubin's (1976) Mechanism	Selection variable z	Bias Correction Formula	
(1) *Completely Random Missingness* (y and/or x selected randomly)	MCAR	$z = e$	$r_{xy(comp)} = r_{xy(resp)}$	
(2a) *Direct Range Restriction* (y selected on x)	MAR	$z = x$	$r_{xy(comp)} = r_{xy(resp)} / \sqrt{(1 - u^2)r^2_{xy(resp)} + u^2}$	(Eq. 1)
(2b) *Direct Range Restriction* (x selected on y)	MAR	$z = y$	Same as Equation 1	
(3a) *Stochastic Direct Range Restriction* (y probabilistically selected on x)	MAR	$z = x + je$	$r_{xy(comp)} = r_{xy(resp)} \sqrt{(1 + v)} / \sqrt{(1 + r^2_{xy(resp)}v)}$	(Eq. 6)
(3b) *Stochastic Direct Range Restriction* (x probabilistically selected on y)	MAR	$z = y + je$	Same as Equation 6	
(4) *Indirect Range Restriction* (y and/or x selected on z; z is observed)	MAR	$z = z$	$r_{xy(comp)} = \dfrac{r_{xy(resp)} + r_{zx(resp)}r_{zy(resp)}(1/u^2 - 1)}{\sqrt{(1/u^2 - 1)r^2_{zx(resp)} + 1}\sqrt{(1/u^2 - 1)r^2_{zy(resp)} + 1}}$	(Eq. 8)
(5a) *Direct Range Restriction* (x selected on x)	MNAR	$z = x$	Same as Equation 1	
(5b) *Direct Range Restriction* (y selected on y)	MNAR	$z = y$	Same as Equation 1	
(6a) *Stochastic Direct Range Restriction* (x probabilistically selected on x)	MNAR	$z = x + je$	Same as Equation 6	
(6b) *Stochastic Direct Range Restriction* (y probabilistically selected on y)	MNAR	$z = y + je$	Same as Equation 6	
(7) *Indirect Range Restriction* (y and/or x selected on z; z is unobserved)	MNAR	$z = z$	Same as Equation 8 above. [But need $r_{zx(resp)}$ and $r_{zy(resp)}$, and don't have them.]	

Note: $r_{xy(comp)} = r_{xy}$ correlation in complete data (i.e., no missing data bias), $r_{xy(resp)} = r_{xy}$ correlation among respondents only (incomplete data; with missing data bias), $u^2 = s_z^2 / S_z^2$, $s_z^2 = $ variance of z among respondents, $s_z^2 = $ variance of z in complete data (including respondents and nonrespondents), $u^2 = $ variance ratio for range restriction (should always be ≤ 1.0; u^2 is a function of the response rate, assuming normality of z), let $v = \left(\frac{1}{u^2} - 1\right) / (j + 1)$, $j = $ random variance multiplier, $e = $ random error term.

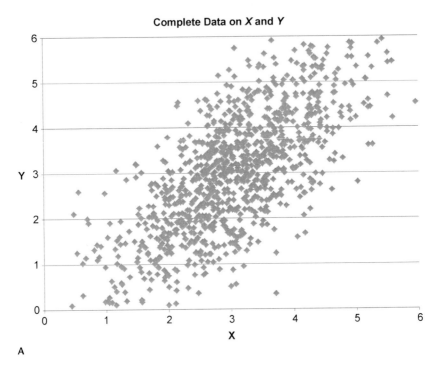

A

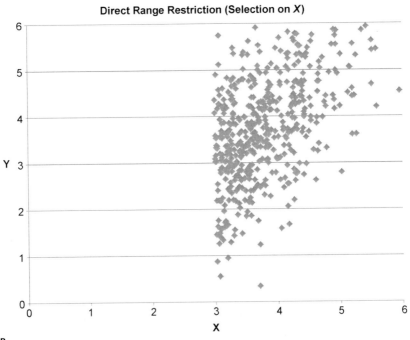

B

FIGURE 7.1 Missing Data Bias (Continued)

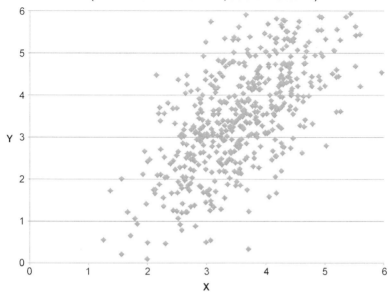

C

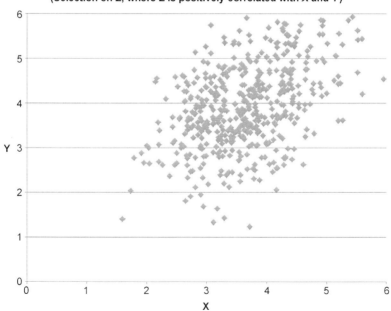

D

FIGURE 7.1 (Continued)

142 Daniel A. Newman and Jonathan M. Cottrell

conditions), $r_{xy(resp)}$ is the range-restriction *biased* correlation between x and y (due to missing data bias: i.e., the pairwise-deleted correlation that was observed based on the subset of respondents whose data were available for both x and y), and u^2 is the variance ratio of restricted (respondents-only) variance to unrestricted (complete-data) variance (i.e., $u^2 = s_x^2/S_x^2$). Equation 1 requires the traditional assumptions of homoscedasticity and linearity of the x-y relationship but does not assume normality (see review by Sackett & Yang, 2000; and Lawley, 1943).

We further note that, if we now add the assumption of distributional normality, the variance ratio u^2 can be expressed as a function of the response rate. To show this, we will modify an equation by Dobson (1988), which is based upon Schmidt, Hunter, and Urry's (1976) expression for the variance of a truncated normal distribution, and approximates u^2 as a function of the selection ratio:

$$u^2 = 1 + c_{x_z}\phi_c/p_c - (\phi_c/p_c)^2 \qquad \text{(Eq. 2)}$$

where u^2 is still the variance ratio of the restricted group divided by the unrestricted group, c_{x_z} is the selection cut-score in standard score (z-score) form, ϕ_c is the ordinate (i.e., height of the normal curve) at c_{x_z}, and p_c is the selection ratio (i.e., proportion of population sampled). Notice that p_c can be alternatively thought of as the *response rate* for the selected variable. We note here that for a standard normal curve, $\phi_c = 1/\sqrt{2\pi e^{c^2}}$, which can be substituted into Equation 2 to yield:

$$u^2 = 1 + c_{x_z}/p_c\sqrt{2\pi e^{c^2}} - (1/p_c^2 2\pi e^{c^2}). \qquad \text{(Eq. 3)}$$

Equation 3 thus estimates u^2 as a function of the response rate only (p_c), assuming normality. We should mention that the cut score c_{x_z} is also a function of the response rate only, although rather than attempting to estimate the cut score using a closed-form equation or using a z-table from the appendix of a statistics textbook, we will instead use the more precise and handy Microsoft Excel function to approximate c_{x_z} as "$= -$ NORMSINV('response rate')."

To visualize the relationship between the response rate and the variance ratio u^2, see Figure 7.2. Figure 7.2 shows that, as the response rate decreases (from .999 [~100%] to .001 [~0%]), the variance ratio also decreases, monotonically (from .990 to .068). That is, greater amounts of missing data yield smaller variance ratios, as described by Equation 3.

Now, to calculate the amount of missing data bias under direct range restriction, we begin with the missing data bias formula:

$$\text{Missing Data Bias} = r_{xy(resp)} - r_{xy(comp)} \qquad \text{(Eq. 4)}$$

When *Missing Data Bias* is negative, it means that $r_{xy(resp)}$ provides either an underestimate or a larger negative estimate of $r_{xy(comp)}$. When *Missing Data Bias* is positive, it means that $r_{xy(resp)}$ provides either an overestimate or a smaller negative

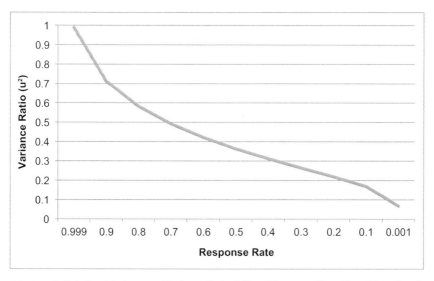

FIGURE 7.2 Relationship between Variance Ratio (u^2) and Response Rate (from Equation 3)

estimate of $r_{xy(comp)}$. By substituting Equation 1 into Equation 4, we can get a direct estimate of *missing data bias under direct range restriction*:

$$\text{Missing Data Bias} = r_{xy(resp)} - r_{xy(resp)} / \sqrt{(1-u^2)r^2_{xy(resp)} + u^2}$$

$$= r_{xy(resp)}\left(1 - 1/\sqrt{(1-u^2)r^2_{xy(resp)} + u^2}\right) \quad \text{(Eq. 5a)}$$

Equation 5a can also be expressed as a function of the complete-data correlation $r_{xy(comp)}$:

$$\text{Missing Data Bias} = \pm\sqrt{u^2 / \left(\frac{1}{r^2_{xy(comp)}} - 1 + u^2\right)} - r_{xy(comp)}, \quad \text{(Eq. 5b)}$$

where the sign of the square-rooted term (+ or −) is set to the sign of $r_{xy(comp)}$.

To understand Equation 5b, one can inspect Figure 7.3. Figure 7.3 illustrates the correspondence between the amount of missing data (i.e., response rate) and the amount of missing data bias in the observed correlation. For example, when the response rate = .999 (i.e., ~100% response rate, or no missing data), the amount of missing data bias is zero. However, as the response rate decreases from 100% toward zero, the amount of *missing data bias* under direct range restriction increases (i.e., more missing data → more missing data bias). Note that the missing data bias always decreases the magnitude of the correlation, meaning that a *positive* correlation between *x* and *y* is *underestimated* (negative bias) due to missing data under direct range restriction, and a *negative* correlation between *x* and *y* is positively

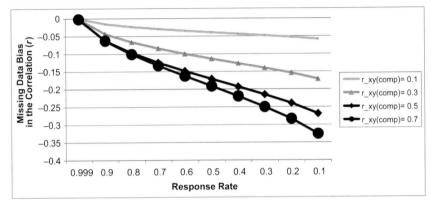

FIGURE 7.3 Missing Data Bias under Direct Range Restriction (from Equation 5b)

biased due to missing data under direct range restriction. Finally, Figure 7.3 shows that under direct range restriction, the amount of missing data bias gets larger when the underlying complete-data correlation is larger.

Cases 3a and 3b: Stochastic Direct Range Restriction. The third type of missing data selection mechanism is *Stochastic Direct Range Restriction*, or *probabilistic* direct range restriction. The case of direct range restriction (Case 2), in which missing data on variable *y* are based upon strict top-down referral on variable *x*, is a very special case of missing data that will not apply across a wide range of scenarios. That is, it would be rare to find that everyone with scores below a particular cutoff point on *x* had missing data on *y*, while everyone who scored above the cut point on *x* had observed (nonmissing) scores on *y*—this direct range restriction pattern only tends to appear under particular hiring/admissions scenarios, where *x* is a preemployment test and *y* is a criterion such as job performance (e.g., Figure 7.1b). A somewhat more general missing data mechanism—that applies beyond the somewhat limited employee selection examples—is stochastic direct range restriction.

In the missing data mechanism of *stochastic direct range restriction* (Case 3a), missingness on variable *y* is *partly* based on *x*, and partly random (see Figure 7.1c). This sort of missing data pattern has been simulated in missing data research by Switzer, Roth, and Switzer (1998) and Newman (2003). This missingness pattern is typically invoked in Monte Carlo simulations by creating a missing data cut score, which is a composite variable of *x* plus a random error term, *e*. If an individual scores above a certain threshold on this (*x* + error) composite cut score, then that person's data on variable *y* are retained; otherwise that person's data on *y* are deleted (i.e., simulated as missing). One substantive example of stochastic direct range restriction (see more examples in what follows) is a pattern in which those would-be respondents who have low job satisfaction are systematically less likely to respond to an employee survey.

Indeed, stochastic direct range restriction is a much more realistic version of Rubin's (1976) MAR missing data mechanism, because it only dictates that individuals with lower scores on variable x are probabilistically less likely to respond to the survey measure of y. Some empirical data also suggest that stochastic direct range restriction is more realistic than direct range restriction. In a review of empirical respondent–nonrespondent comparison studies, Newman (2009) summarized the d_{miss} index (i.e., the standardized mean difference between respondents and nonrespondents; see Newman & Sin, 2009) to be of small to moderate magnitude, showing that missingness is often related to—but not entirely dependent upon—the variable being studied. For example, for justice perceptions ($d_{miss} = -.44$), for satisfaction ($d_{miss} = -.15$), and for conscientious personality ($d_{miss} = -.38$), all three constructs were probabilistically related to survey nonresponse, summarizing primary studies conducted by Rogelberg and colleagues (Rogelberg, Luong, Sederburg, & Cristol, 2000; Spitzmuller, Glenn, Barr, Rogelberg, & Daniel, 2006). That is, an individual with a conscientious personality is probabilistically more likely to respond to an organizational survey, but there is not some magical cut point on conscientiousness above which everyone will respond and below which everyone will be missing. In sum, empirical evidence suggests that organizational survey research suffers from stochastic direct range restriction on the following selection variables: justice perceptions, satisfaction, and conscientiousness (Newman, 2009; Rogelberg et al., 2000; Spitzmuller et al., 2006). Thus, any organizational research involving these variables will likely suffer missing data bias under the stochastic direct range restriction pattern.

Stochastic direct range restriction is illustrated in Figure 7.1c. In Figure 7.1c, individuals with a low score on x will probabilistically *tend* to be missing data on y, according to a linear probability function (the lower one's score on x, the more likely one is to be missing data on y). That is, data on y are selected (i.e., not missing) according to $x + e$, rather than being directly selected according to x alone.

To quantify the *missing data bias* in the correlation coefficient that is likely to obtain under *stochastic direct range restriction*, we will again refer to Pearson's (1903) range restriction formula, but this time we will use a stochastic selection term ($x + $ error) instead of selecting on x alone. We can thus derive the stochastic direct range restriction correction formula:

$$r_{xy(comp)} = r_{xy(resp)} \sqrt{(1+v)} \Big/ \sqrt{(1+r^2_{xy(resp)}v)}, \tag{Eq. 6}$$

where $r_{xy(comp)}$ is still the *unbiased* correlation between x and y (with no missing data bias), $r_{xy(resp)}$ is still the range-restriction *biased* correlation between x and y (due to missing data bias: i.e., the pairwise-deleted correlation that was observed based on the subset of respondents whose data were available for both x and y), v is a term defined as $v = \left(\dfrac{1}{u^2} - 1 \right) \Big/ (j+1)$, u^2 is still the variance ratio of restricted to unrestricted variance (which can be approximated from the response rate; see

146 Daniel A. Newman and Jonathan M. Cottrell

Equation 3), and j is a random variance multiplier, which is the ratio of the variance of the random error term to the variance of x.

To elaborate on what j is, we note that data are selected on a stochastic selection term $x + je$, where e is a random variable with the same variance as x and j is an integer that determines how random (vs. systematic) the missingness pattern is. When $j = 0$, there is no random component in the missingness mechanism, and we have direct range restriction. When $j = 1$, the random component in the missingness mechanism is equal to the systematic component (because there is selection on $x + e$, and e has the same variance as x). By extension, when $j = 20$, missingness is almost completely random, because there is selection on $x + 20e$, so the random error component (i.e., $20e$) has 20 times as much variance as the systematic component x. The stochastic direct range restriction formula thus converts the notion of range restriction into a continuum between completely systematic missingness ($j = 0$) and completely random missingness ($j = \infty$), where the extent to which a missingness pattern is random is governed by the parameter j (the random variance multiplier). The larger j is, the more random the missingness mechanism is. The derivation of Equation 6 will be discussed in more detail later, when we describe indirect range restriction.

Now, to calculate the amount of missing data bias under stochastic direct range restriction, we begin with the missing data bias formula (Equation 4) but substitute Equation 6 into Equation 4 to get an estimate of *missing data bias under stochastic direct range restriction*:

$$\text{Missing Data Bias} = r_{xy(resp)} - \left(r_{xy(resp)} \sqrt{(1+v)} \Big/ \sqrt{(1 + r^2_{xy(resp)}v)} \right)$$

$$= r_{xy(resp)} \left(1 - \sqrt{(1+v)} \Big/ \sqrt{(1 + r^2_{xy(resp)}v)} \right) \qquad \text{(Eq. 7a)}$$

Equation 7a can also be expressed as a function of the complete-data correlation $r_{xy(comp)}$:

$$\text{Missing Data Bias} = \frac{r_{xy(comp)}}{\sqrt{1 + v - r^2_{xy(comp)}v}} - r_{xy(comp)} \qquad \text{(Eq. 7b)}$$

To understand Equation 7b, look at Figures 7.4 and 7.5. Figure 7.4 shows the correspondence between the amount of missing data (i.e., response rate) and the amount of missing data bias in the observed correlation under stochastic direct range restriction (i.e., when $j = 1$, thus the missingness mechanism is equal parts systematic and random). When the response rate = .999 (i.e., ~100%), the amount of missing data bias is zero. However, as the response rate decreases from 100% toward zero, the amount of *missing data bias* under stochastic direct range restriction increases (i.e., more missing data → more missing data bias). Note the missing data bias again always decreases the magnitude of the correlation under stochastic direct range restriction (e.g., a *positive* correlation between x and y is *negatively biased* due to missing data, and a *negative* correlation between x and y is *positively biased* due to missing data under stochastic direct range restriction). The missing data bias due to stochastic direct range restriction is thus similar to missing data bias under direct range restriction (see earlier), except that—because stochastic direct range restriction is more random than ordinary direct range restriction—the missing data bias is smaller in magnitude under the stochastic restriction mechanism. Figure 7.4 and Equation 7b further show that under stochastic direct range restriction, the magnitude of missing data bias gets larger when the underlying complete-data correlation is larger.

Also note that the amount of missing data bias under stochastic direct range restriction (Figure 7.4) is smaller than the amount of missing data bias under direct range restriction (Figure 7.3). The trend is that, as the missingness mechanism becomes more random and less systematic (as j increases), the amount of missing data bias decreases. To illustrate a more extreme example of this, Figure 7.5 shows

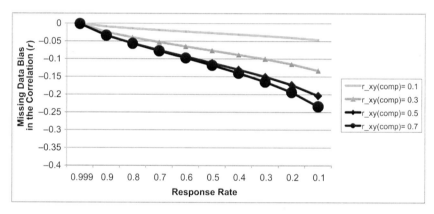

FIGURE 7.4 Missing Data Bias under Stochastic Direct Range Restriction ($j = 1$: missingness is 1/2 systematic and 1/2 random) [from Equation 7b]

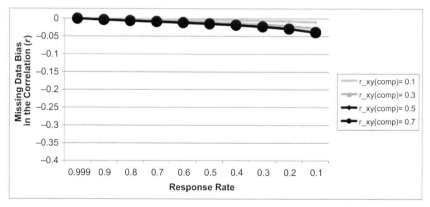

FIGURE 7.5 Missing Data Bias under Stochastic Direct Range Restriction ($j = 20$: missingness is 1/21 systematic and 20/21 random) [from Equation 7b]

148 Daniel A. Newman and Jonathan M. Cottrell

that when $j = 20$ (i.e., data on y are selected on the stochastic selection term $x + 20e$—so the missingness mechanism is almost completely random, because it is due to 20 parts random variance e and only 1 part systematic variance x), then missing data bias is tiny. Indeed, as the missingness mechanism becomes more and more random (as j increases), then the degree of missing data bias converges to zero. Recall that under completely random missingness (MCAR), there is no missing data bias.

Case 4: Indirect Range Restriction. The fourth type of missing data selection mechanism is *Indirect Range Restriction* (Case 4), which occurs when missing data on variable x and/or y are based upon strict top-down referral on a third variable z, and z is correlated with x and/or y. This missing data scenario is typically known as Thorndike Case 3 (Thorndike, 1949; see Sackett & Yang, 2000), and the well-known correction formula for this scenario is:

$$r_{xy(comp)} = \frac{r_{xy(resp)} + r_{zx(resp)}r_{zy(resp)}(1/u^2 - 1)}{\sqrt{(1/u^2 - 1)r_{zx(resp)}^2 + 1}\sqrt{(1/u^2 - 1)r_{zy(resp)}^2 + 1}}, \tag{Eq. 8}$$

where $r_{xy(comp)}$ is still the *unbiased* correlation between x and y (with no missing data bias), $r_{xy(resp)}$ is still the range-restriction *biased* correlation between x and y (due to missing data bias: i.e., the pairwise-deleted correlation that was observed based on the subset of respondents whose data were available for both x and y), $r_{zx(resp)}$ is the range-restricted correlation between z and x, $r_{zy(resp)}$ is the range-restricted correlation between z and y, and u^2 is the variance ratio of restricted (respondents-only) variance to unrestricted (complete-data) variance, for the third variable z (i.e., $u^2 = s_z^2/S_z^2$). Figure 7.1d illustrates a scatterplot from an indirect range restriction scenario in which both r_{zx} and r_{zy} are positive (i.e., when the missing data selection variable z is positively correlated with both x and y).

To calculate *missing data bias under indirect range restriction*, we can use the formula:

$$\text{Missing Data Bias} = r_{xy(resp)} - \frac{r_{xy(resp)} + r_{zx(resp)}r_{zy(resp)}q}{\sqrt{qr_{zx(resp)}^2 + 1}\sqrt{qr_{zy(resp)}^2 + 1}} \tag{Eq. 9a}$$

where we let $q = (1/u^2 - 1)$. Equation 9a can also be expressed as a function of the complete-data correlation $r_{xy(comp)}$:

$$\text{Missing Data Bias} = r_{xy(comp)}\sqrt{qr_{zx(resp)}^2 + 1}\sqrt{qr_{zy(resp)}^2 + 1} - r_{zx(resp)}r_{zy(resp)}q - r_{xy(comp)}$$

$$= r_{xy(comp)}\left(\sqrt{qr_{zx(resp)}^2 + 1}\sqrt{qr_{zy(resp)}^2 + 1} - 1\right) - r_{zx(resp)}r_{zy(resp)}q \tag{Eq. 9b}$$

To explain Equation 9b, we refer to Figures 7.6, 7.7, and 7.8. Figures 7.6 through 7.8 show missing data bias in the pairwise deleted correlation between x

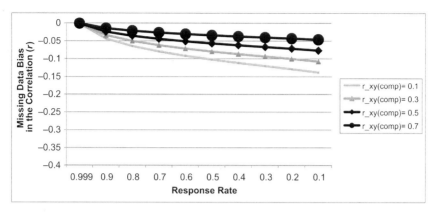

FIGURE 7.6 Missing Data Bias under Indirect Range Restriction (from Equation 9b; $r_{zx(comp)} = .40$ [positive] and $r_{zy(comp)} = .40$ [positive])

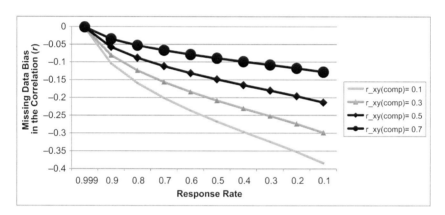

FIGURE 7.7 Missing Data Bias under Indirect Range Restriction (from Equation 9b; $r_{zx(comp)} = .60$ [positive] and $r_{zy(comp)} = .60$ [positive])

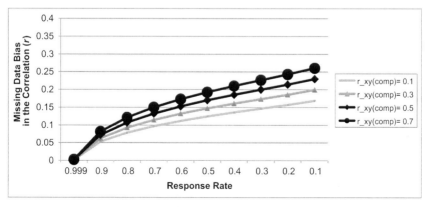

FIGURE 7.8 Missing Data Bias under Indirect Range Restriction (from Equation 9b; $r_{zx(comp)} = .40$ [positive] and $r_{zy(comp)} = -.40$ [negative])

150 Daniel A. Newman and Jonathan M. Cottrell

and y under *indirect range restriction* (where x and/or y were selected on a third variable z, which is correlated with x and/or y). In Figure 7.6, both x and y are positively correlated with z, such that $r_{zx(comp)} = .40$ and $r_{zy(comp)} = .40$ (also see Figure 7.1d). As the amount of missing data increases, the amount of missing data bias increases.

In Figure 7.7, we see a scenario in which both x and y are very strongly positively correlated with z, such that $r_{zx(comp)} = .60$ and $r_{zy\ (comp)} = .60$. By comparing Figure 7.7 with Figure 7.6, we see that when the selection variable z is more strongly correlated with x and/or y, then there is more missing data bias (Figure 7.7, where r_{zx} and r_{zy} both $= .60$, has more missing data bias than Figure 7.6, where r_{zx} and r_{zy} both $= .40$). To restate, when the selection mechanism z is more strongly correlated with x and/or y, then there is more missing data bias in the x-y correlation.

Finally, Figure 7.8 depicts a scenario in which $r_{zx(comp)} = .40$ (positive) and $r_{zy(comp)} = -.40$ (negative). When r_{zx} and r_{zy} differ in sign (i.e., have opposite signs), then the missing data bias can produce a *larger* correlation (i.e., $r_{xy(comp)}$ is bigger in magnitude than $r_{xy(comp)}$). Indirect range restriction with r_{zx} and r_{zy} having opposite signs is the only scenario we have covered in which missing data bias causes a correlation to grow in absolute value.

Completely Random Missingness, Direct Range Restriction, and Stochastic Direct Range Restriction as Special Cases of Indirect Range Restriction

Earlier, we reviewed four major types of missing data selection mechanisms: (a) Case 1: *Completely Random Missingness*, (b) Cases 2a and 2b: *Direct Range Restriction*, (c) Cases 3a and 3b: *Stochastic Direct Range Restriction*, and (d) Case 4: *Indirect Range Restriction*. Cases 1, 2, and 4 are well known in the personnel selection literature (see Sackett & Yang, 2000; Thorndike, 1949), and the stochastic direct range restriction formulas (Cases 3a and 3b) are original and were derived for the current chapter.

At this point, we will now demonstrate that *all* of the missing data selection mechanisms (see Table 7.2) are special cases of indirect range restriction. That is, all of the bias correction formulas (Table 7.2) can be expressed as constrained versions of Equation 8. First, *Completely Random Missingness* is a special case of Equation 8 in which the selection variable $z = e$, and thus $r_{zx} = 0$ and $r_{zy} = 0$ (that is, the selection variable z is unrelated to both x and y). With these two constraints, Equation 8 simplifies to $r_{xy(comp)} = r_{xy(resp)}$, demonstrating that there is no missing data bias when $r_{zx} = 0$ and $r_{zy} = 0$.

Second, for *Direct Range Restriction*, the selection variable $z = x$ (i.e., selection on x), which is a special case of Equation 8, where $r_{zx} = 1.0$ and $r_{zy} = r_{xy}$ (because the selection variable $[z]$ *is* x itself). With these two constraints, Equation 8 simplifies to Equation 1 (that is, *direct range restriction* is a special case of *indirect range restriction* in which the selection variable z is x [or y]).

Third, *Stochastic Direct Range Restriction* involves selection on $z = x + je$ (i.e., selection on x [or y] plus random error). Equation 6 is also a special case of Equation 8 (indirect range restriction) in which $r_{zx} = 1/\sqrt{(j+1)}$ and $r_{zy} = r_{xy}/\sqrt{(j+1)}$. These two expressions for r_{zx} and r_{zy} are derived from the formulas for composite correlations (Ghiselli, Campbell, & Zedeck, 1981), specifically the correlation between x and $x + je$ and the correlation between y and $x + je$. With these two constraints (on r_{zx} and r_{zy}), Equation 8 simplifies to Equation 6. Note also that, because $r_{zx} = 1/\sqrt{(j+1)}$, which can never be negative, then r_{zx} and r_{zy} can only be opposite in sign when r_{xy} is negative. Therefore, we have demonstrated mathematically that stochastic direct range restriction (similar to ordinary direct range restriction) typically will not increase the magnitude of an observed correlation—that is, missing data bias will always bring the correlation closer to zero.

Finally, as a technical note, when implementing constraints on Equation 8 in order to estimate missing data bias (i.e., if one wants to plot Figures 7.3 through 7.8 using the constrained version of Equation 8 rather than plotting them directly via Equations 5b and 7b), one should remember that Equation 8 operates on the *restricted* r_{zx} and r_{zy}. So if graphing Figure 7.3 using Equation 8 and the constraints $r_{zx} = 1.0$ and $r_{zy} = r_{xy}$, it will be necessary to first restrict r_{xy} using the formula

$$r_{xy(resp)} = \sqrt{u^2 \bigg/ \left(\frac{1}{r^2_{xy(comp)}} - 1 + u^2 \right)}$$ (see Equation 5b). Likewise, if graphing Figures 7.4 and 7.5 using Equation 8 and the constraints $r_{zx} = 1/\sqrt{(j+1)}$ and $r_{zy} = r_{xy}/\sqrt{(j+1)}$, it will be necessary to first restrict r_{xy} using the formula

$$r_{xy(resp)} = r_{xy(comp)} \bigg/ \sqrt{1 + v - r^2_{xy(comp)}v}$$ (see Equation 7b). Finally, when graphing Figures 7.6 through 7.8 using Equation 8, it is necessary to first restrict both $r_{zx(comp)}$

and $r_{zy(comp)}$ using the formula $r_{zx(resp)} = \sqrt{u^2 \bigg/ \left(\frac{1}{r^2_{zx(comp)}} - 1 + u^2 \right)}$ (cf. Equation 5b).

Maximum Likelihood (ML) and Multiple Imputation (MI) remove all Missing Data Bias under MAR Range Restriction. Before proceeding, we note that—aside from Case 1: Missingness Completely at Random (MCAR)—all of the other missingness selection mechanisms we have reviewed up to this point (Cases 2a, 2b, 3a, 3b, and 4 in Table 7.2) are instances of MAR missingness. Recall that MAR missingness (which stands for "missing at random"; Rubin, 1976) is actually a *systematic* form of missingness. (The MAR mechanism has a confusing name; because MAR is a *systematic* missingness mechanism and is not *random* in the conventional sense of the word—only MCAR is a *random* missingness mechanism; see Table 7.1 footnote.)

As reviewed in Table 7.1, MAR missingness refers to a circumstance in which the probability that data are missing on a variable is possibly related to the observed variables (observed data) but is not related to the missing data itself.

152 Daniel A. Newman and Jonathan M. Cottrell

Mathematically, MAR missingness satisfies the equation: p(missing | complete data) = p(missing | observed data) (see Schafer & Graham, 2002). Note that this MAR equation holds for Case 2a (i.e., Direct Range Restriction where y is selected on x), because the probability that y is missing given the complete data on x and y is the same as the probability that y is missing given the observed data on x. In other words, because y is missing based upon an observed variable (i.e., based upon x, in this case), then the missingness mechanism is MAR. Case 3a (Stochastic Direct Range Restriction, where y is selected on $x + je$) also satisfies the MAR equation: p(missing | complete data) = p(missing | observed data). The probability that y is missing given the complete data on x is the same as the probability that y is missing given the observed data on x. Case 4 (Indirect Range Restriction, where x and/ or y are selected on z, and z *is observed*) is also an MAR missingness mechanism. Whenever the selection variable z is observed, or partly observed and partly random, then the missing data are MAR.

Because the missing data selection mechanisms in Cases 2a, 2b, 3a, 3b, and 4 are all MAR, they have a very special, and very useful, property: under MAR, it is possible to recover *unbiased* estimates of the correlation by using the state-of-the-art missing data techniques of maximum likelihood (ML) and multiple imputation (MI; Schafer & Graham, 2002). So for missing data Cases 2a, 2b, 3a, 3b, and 4 in Table 7.2, despite the missing data bias in the pairwise-deleted correlation that can be described by Equations 5b, 7b, and 9b, there is *no bias* in the ML estimates or MI estimates of the correlation.

To illustrate that this is true (i.e., that ML missing data techniques are unbiased under MAR), we conducted a simulation of missing data under the MAR mechanism (i.e., Cases 2a, 2b, 3a, 3b, and 4). For the simulation, we simply generated data from a multivariate normal distribution in which x was correlated with y at $r_{xy(comp)} = .40, r_{z_1x(comp)} = .30, r_{z_1y(comp)} = .30, r_{z_2x(comp)} = .30, r_{z_2y(comp)} = -.30$, and e is a random variable that is uncorrelated with x, y, z_1, and z_2. Because the current chapter focuses on missing data *bias*, we did not want the results to be confounded with sampling *error*, so we generated an extremely large number of cases ($N = 500,000$). We then deleted data according to Cases 2a, 2b, 3a, 3b, and 4 from Table 7.2, and at three different response rates (75%, 50%, and 25%). For example, to simulate the 25% response rate under stochastic direct range restriction (Case 3a), we first calculated a cut score $x + e$, then sorted all persons on $x + e$, and then deleted y for those who scored in the bottom 75% on the cut score $x + e$. Missing data bias (Equation 4) was then estimated under two missing data treatments: pairwise deletion and ML estimation (the ML estimation was implemented using the EM algorithm in SAS Proc MI, SAS version 9.1). Results are presented in the top half of Table 7.3.

The top half of Table 7.3 demonstrates several findings about pairwise deletion bias. First, pairwise deletion is unbiased (bias = .00) under completely random missingness (Case 1, MCAR). Second, pairwise deletion is strongly biased under direct range restriction (Cases 2a and 2b), and the bias increases as the response

TABLE 7.3 Missing Data Bias under Pairwise Deletion vs. ML Estimation for 11 Missing Data Selection Mechanisms ($r_{xy(oup)} = .40$)

Missing Data Selection Mechanism	Rubin's (1976) Mechanism	Selection variable z	Pairwise Deletion Bias			ML Estimation Bias		
			75%	50%	25%	75%	50%	25%
(1) *Completely Random Missingness* (y and/or x selected randomly)	MCAR	$z = e$	.00	.00	.00	.00	.00	.00
(2a) *Direct Range Restriction* (y selected on x)	MAR	$z = x$	−.10	−.14	−.19	.00	.00	.00
(2b) *Direct Range Restriction* (x selected on y)	MAR	$z = y$	−.09	−.14	−.19	.01	.01	.00
(3a) *Stochastic Direct Range Restriction* (y probabilistically selected on x) [$j = 1$]	MAR	$z = x + e$	−.04	−.06	−.07	.00	.00	.00
(3b) *Stochastic Direct Range Restriction* (x probabilistically selected on y) [$j = 1$]	MAR	$z = y + e$	−.04	−.06	−.07	.00	.01	.01
(3a) *Stochastic Direct Range Restriction* (y probabilistically selected on x) [$j = 10$]	MAR	$z = x + 10e$	.00	.00	.00	.00	.00	.00
(3b) *Stochastic Direct Range Restriction* (y probabilistically selected on y) [$j = 10$]	MAR	$z = y + 10e$	.00	.00	.00	.00	.00	.01
(4) *Indirect Range Restriction* (y and/or x selected on z; z is observed) r_{zx} & r_{zy} have [same sign] {opposite signs}	MAR	$z = \tilde{z}, r_{zx} = .3$ [$r_{zy} = .3$] {$r_{zy} = -.3$}	[−.02] {+.06}	[−.03] {+.08}	[−.04] {+.10}	[.00] {.00}	[.00] {.00}	[.00] {.00}
(5a) *Direct Range Restriction* (x selected on x)	MNAR	$z = x$	−.10	−.14	−.19	−.08	−.13	−.18
(5b) *Direct Range Restriction* (y selected on y)	MNAR	$z = y$	−.09	−.14	−.19	−.08	−.13	−.17
(6a) *Stochastic Direct Range Restriction* (x probabilistically selected on x) [$j = 1$]	MNAR	$z = x + e$	−.04	−.06	−.07	−.04	−.05	−.06
(6b) *Stochastic Direct Range Restriction* (y probabilistically selected on y) [$j = 1$]	MNAR	$z = y + e$	−.04	−.06	−.07	−.04	−.05	−.06
(7) *Indirect Range Restriction* (y and/or x selected on z; z is unobserved) r_{zx} & r_{zy} have [same sign] {opposite signs}	MNAR	$z = \tilde{z}, r_{zx} = .3$ [$r_{zy} = .3$] {$r_{zy} = -.3$}	[−.02] {+.06}	[−.03] {+.08}	[−.04] {+.10}	[−.02] {+.06}	[−.03] {+.08}	[−.04] {+.10}

Note: Simulation results based upon $N = 500,000$; response rates = 75%, 50%, and 25%; MCAR = missing completely at random, MAR = missing at random (i.e., a type of systematic missingness, with a confusing label; Rubin, 1976), MNAR = missing not at random. Pairwise deletion is unbiased under MCAR, while ML estimation is unbiased under MCAR and MAR. ML estimation implemented via the EM algorithm. j = random variance multiplier; e = random error term.

154 Daniel A. Newman and Jonathan M. Cottrell

rate falls (bias grows from −.09 to −.19 as the response rate falls from 75% to 25%). Third, pairwise deletion is modestly biased under stochastic direct range restriction with $j = 1$ (Cases 3a and 3b, where $j = 1$; the bias grows from −.04 to −.07 as the response rate falls from 75% to 25%). Fourth, pairwise deletion is virtually unbiased under stochastic direct range restriction with $j = 10$ (Cases 3a and 3b, where $j = 10$; bias = .00), because with a random variance multiplier of $j = 10$, the missingness mechanism becomes essentially a random mechanism. Fifth, under indirect range restriction (Case 4) where r_{zx} and r_{zy} have the same sign (e.g., both are positive), pairwise deletion creates a small amount of underestimation bias (bias grows from −.02 to −.04 as the response rate falls from 75% to 25%). Sixth, under indirect range restriction in which r_{zx} and r_{zy} have opposite signs (e.g., one positive and the other negative), pairwise deletion creates considerable overestimation bias (bias grows from +.06 to +.10 as the response rate falls from 75% to 25%). Recall that the condition in which r_{zx} and r_{zy} have opposite signs is the only case under which pairwise deletion produces an overestimate of the correlation—otherwise, the correlation will be underestimated. To summarize, pairwise deletion leads to biased correlations under systematic MAR missingness. The only case in which pairwise deletion did not bias the observed correlation was under stochastic direct range restriction when the random term $j = 10$ was so large that the missingness mechanism was essentially MCAR.

In contrast to pairwise deletion, the top half of Table 7.3 also demonstrates the extent of missing data bias under ML estimation. In short, there is none. ML estimation uniformly recovers the complete-data correlation in an unbiased fashion (bias ranges from .00 to .01) whenever the missing data mechanism is MAR (i.e., in Cases 2a, 2b, 3a, 3b, and 4). The ML missing data technique removes missing data bias (i.e., is unbiased) under all these missing data scenarios.

Missing Data Bias under MNAR Range Restriction: Cases 5a, 5b, 6a, 6b, and 7. Finally, we discuss a set of missing data scenarios (missingness selection mechanisms) that are neither MCAR nor MAR. This last type of missing data mechanism, called missing not at random (MNAR), is defined when the probability that data are missing on a variable is related to the unobserved/missing data themselves. The MNAR mechanism satisfies the equation: [p(missing | complete data) ≠ p(missing | observed data)]. In Table 7.2, Cases 5a, 5b, 6a, 6b, and 7 are all MNAR missingness mechanisms. For instance, in Case 5b, y is selected on y itself, meaning that for any individual who scores below some cut score on y, the y data are missing. An unfortunate reality is that the MNAR missingness mechanism can be difficult to detect, because doing so would typically require the researcher to compare the observed scores on y to the missing scores on y—and the missing scores on y are not available.

The MNAR missing data selection mechanisms (Cases 5a, 5b, 6a, 6b, and 7) are parallel to the Cases 2a, 2b, 3a, 3b, and 4 (elaborated earlier), except that the previously discussed Cases 2a through 4 were all MAR, not MNAR. The MAR patterns

(Cases 2a through 4) and MNAR patterns (Cases 5a through 7) in Table 7.2 are the same with regard to the amount of missing data bias in the pairwise deleted correlation, but they are different with regard to whether ML and MI techniques can recover the unbiased correlation estimates. Recall that both ML and MI missing data approaches are *unbiased* under MCAR *and* MAR conditions, whereas pairwise deletion is only unbiased under MCAR conditions. Both pairwise deletion and the ML and MI techniques are still biased under MNAR conditions. To illustrate this point, we refer again to Table 7.3. In the bottom half of Table 7.3 (i.e., Cases 5a through 7, the MNAR conditions), we see a pattern of missing data bias under pairwise deletion that is the same as the bias pattern we observed under the MAR conditions (i.e., Cases 2a through 4). That is, pairwise deletion is equally ill equipped to handle MAR as MNAR missingness. Further, we also see that the ML estimation approach performs poorly under MNAR conditions. In fact, ML estimation is just as biased as pairwise deletion when the data are MNAR (see Cases 5a, 5b, 6a, 6b, and 7 in Table 7.3).

So neither pairwise deletion nor ML estimation can yield unbiased estimates under the MNAR missingness mechanism (see Table 7.3, bottom half). As such, MNAR data are often analyzed with either selection models (Heckman, 1979; Puhani 2000; Winship & Mare, 1992) or pattern mixture models (Glynn, Laird, & Rubin, 1986; Little, 1993; Rubin, 1987; see review by Enders, 2010). Unfortunately, selection models and pattern mixture models must be based upon assumptions about the missing data mechanism that are potentially errant and largely untestable; therefore, these alternatives often perform worse than ML estimation or MI estimation (see Enders, 2010).

At the bottom line, we do not know whether a given incomplete dataset suffers from MAR versus MNAR missingness. If the missingness happens to be MAR, then ML and MI approaches will consistently outperform pairwise deletion. If the missingness happens to be MNAR, then ML and MI will perform equally as poorly as pairwise deletion. Thus, there is no instance in which pairwise deletion is to be preferred over ML and MI missing data approaches.

Further, we note that MAR and MNAR patterns can be thought of as residing along a continuum (Graham, 2009), where the key issue is whether the selection variable z—or other variables that are correlated with the selection variable z (Graham, 2003)—can be incorporated into the ML estimation or multiple imputation model. Indeed, the key difference between Case 4 and Case 7 in Tables 7.2 and 7.3 is not the missing data selection process itself, but rather whether the selection variable z was observed. *If either the selection variable z or covariates of z can be observed, then the circumstance transforms from an MNAR (Case 7) scenario into an MAR (Case 4) scenario. Whenever the selection variable z or its covariates can be observed (which is typically the case, to some extent), then ML and MI approaches will tend to outperform pairwise deletion.* Whenever z and its covariates cannot be observed (strict MNAR: i.e., a rare situation), then ML and MI approaches will be somewhat biased but still perform just as well as pairwise deletion.

156 Daniel A. Newman and Jonathan M. Cottrell

Conclusion and Future Research

The current chapter marks an early attempt to answer the question, "How bad is pairwise deletion?" Doing so will hopefully enable a better assessment of the boundary conditions for the urban legend that "pairwise deletion should never be used." The equations and examples will point the way toward a more intuitive understanding of the complicated issue of discerning when missing data bias creates a big problem, versus when it creates only a very minor problem.

We provide a list of summary statements in Table 7.4. Whereas pairwise deletion is preferable to listwise deletion, because pairwise deletion follows the "fundamental principle of missing data analysis" to "use all of the available data" (Newman, 2009, p. 11), we have shown that pairwise deletion nonetheless typically creates an underestimation bias in the correlation coefficient. This missing data bias is estimable as a function of (a) the amount of missing data and (b) the systematic missing data selection mechanism (see Table 7.2, and Equations 5b, 7b, and 9b). When the missing data mechanism is MAR (Cases 2a, 2b, 3a, 3b, and 4), then ML estimation and multiple imputation can provide unbiased estimates of the correlation, thereby removing the missing data bias that would have been suffered under pairwise deletion. On the other hand, when the missing data mechanism is strictly MNAR (Cases 5a, 5b, 6a, 6b, and 7), little can be done to improve upon pairwise deletion. However, an MNAR mechanism can be converted into an MAR mechanism to the extent that the missing data selection variable z or its correlates can be observed and then included in the imputation model.

TABLE 7.4 Summary Statements About Pairwise Deletion Bias

(1) Missing data are a common problem that necessitates a choice from among several alternative missing data treatments: listwise deletion, pairwise deletion, single imputation, multiple imputation (MI), or maximum likelihood estimation (ML). The researcher must choose one of these missing data treatments—abstinence is not an option.

(2) Listwise deletion and single imputation are almost universally recognized as inferior alternatives due to errors of inference they engender. Listwise deletion tends to create Type II errors (due to small sample size/low statistical power), and single imputation tends to create Type I errors (it overstates the actual sample size by imputing data then treating the sample as complete when it is not, and can thus underestimate standard errors and p-values). So the remaining and more commonly defended techniques are pairwise deletion, ML, and MI.

(3) The blanket advice offered by methodologists is that researchers should avoid using pairwise deletion and should instead use either ML or MI approaches for missing data. This advice is based on the concept that pairwise deletion leads to missing data bias (e.g., systematic over- or underestimation of the correlation, mean, and/or standard deviation).

(4) The *exact amount* of missing data bias to be expected under pairwise deletion is not well known by social science researchers. We therefore present a set of equations to estimate the magnitude of missing data bias in the x-y correlation under pairwise deletion.

(5) Missing data can be thought of as a selection mechanism, where for each incomplete variable (x and/or y) there exists a selection variable (z), with a cut score below which data are missing and above which data are not missing. We thus identify 11 missing data selection mechanisms (Table 7.2), which are all special cases of indirect range restriction. We can then adapt range restriction formulas to estimate missing data bias under pairwise deletion as a function of the response rate (amount of missing data) and the missingness mechanism (see the 11 mechanisms described in Table 7.2).

(6) These 11 missing data mechanisms range from *completely random missingness* (MCAR) to completely systematic missingness (i.e., *direct range restriction*). In between these two extremes are *stochastic direct range restriction* and *indirect range restriction*.

(7a) Pairwise deletion produces no missing data bias when the data are *missing completely at random* (MCAR).

(7b) Pairwise deletion can produce relatively extreme missing data bias under *direct range restriction*, as described by *Equation 5b* (e.g., at 50% response rates, the correlation is 30–40% underestimated and is likely underestimated by $r = .2$ or less).

(7c) Pairwise deletion produces less extreme missing data bias under *stochastic direct range restriction*, as described by *Equation 7b* (e.g., at 50% response rates, the correlation is likely underestimated by $r = .1$ or less).

(7d) Pairwise deletion typically leads to *underestimation* of the observed correlation and will only overestimate an x-y correlation in the rare case that the selection variable z is correlated positively with x and negatively with y (or vice versa; i.e., when r_{zx} and r_{zy} have opposite signs). This is described by *Equation 9b*.

(8a) There are cases in which using pairwise deletion vs. ML or MI missing data techniques doesn't matter. Under MCAR (i.e., Case 1 in Tables 2 and 3), none of these three techniques is biased. Under MNAR (i.e., Cases 5a, 5b, 6a, 6b, and 7 in Tables 7.2 and 7.3), all three of these techniques are equally biased. So under MCAR and MNAR missing data mechanisms, pairwise deletion is no worse than the alternatives.

(8b) There are also cases in which ML and MI are better than pairwise deletion (i.e., MAR mechanisms: Cases 2a, 2b, 3a, 3b, and 4 in Tables 2 and 3). Under MAR, maximum likelihood (ML) and multiple imputation (MI) will give *unbiased* estimates of the correlation, whereas pairwise deletion will provide *biased* estimates of the correlation. This statistical fact is the source of methodologists' advice to avoid pairwise deletion in favor of ML and MI approaches.

(8c) In no case is pairwise deletion less biased than ML and MI approaches.

(8d) Noting that ML and MI approaches will be much less biased than pairwise deletion to the extent that the missing data are MAR (i.e., systematically missing under Rubin's [1976] MAR pattern), it becomes useful for the researcher to know how to convert an MNAR scenario into an MAR scenario. Missing data are MAR to the extent that the selection variable z is (a) observed/measured *or* (b) made up of two components, one part observed and the other part random/uncorrelated with x and y.

That is, an MNAR mechanism can be converted into more of an MAR mechanism if the researcher can measure variables that are correlated with the selection variable z. When this is the case, then pairwise deletion will become considerably worse than ML and MI techniques, which are unbiased under MAR.

(9) Pairwise deletion bias is sometimes large and sometimes small. Whether the bias is large enough to be problematic is a matter of judgment. This bias is a function of (a) the amount of missing data and (b) the missing data selection mechanism, as described in Equations 5b, 7b, and 9b. Pairwise deletion bias can typically be reduced by using ML or MI missing data techniques (to the extent that we have observed variables that are correlated with the selection variable z).

158 Daniel A. Newman and Jonathan M. Cottrell

In short, the urban legend that "you should not use pairwise deletion" has turned out to be an overgeneralization. There are no known circumstances in which pairwise deletion will produce more accurate results than ML or MI approaches. As ML and MI missing data routines become increasingly easy to use, the number of reasons to rely upon potentially biased pairwise deletion will dwindle. Equations 5a, 7a, and 9a now provide handy ways to estimate the magnitude by which a pairwise deleted correlation is biased. Of course, whether a correlation bias of −.06 is problematic is a matter of judgment. The advancement here is a set of estimation formulas to gauge the magnitude of this missing data bias (Table 7.2).

To restate, there are some cases in which the choice to use pairwise deletion versus ML and MI missing data routines does not matter (i.e., under MCAR and MNAR missingness mechanisms). On the other hand, there are also cases in which ML and MI techniques are clearly better/less biased than pairwise deletion (i.e., under the MAR missingness mechanism). The natural question that ensues is whether a given missing data pattern is the result of an MAR mechanism (where pairwise deletion is inferior to ML and MI techniques) versus an MCAR or MNAR mechanism (where pairwise deletion performs equally to ML and MI techniques). This distinction between MAR and the other missingness mechanisms hinges entirely upon whether one has observed any variables that are correlated with the selection variable z. Nonetheless, pairwise deletion is never better than (less biased than) ML and MI techniques.

Another practical problem that arises when attempting to estimate pairwise deletion bias is the difficulty in determining—in the face of a real dataset with some missing data—which of the 11 selection mechanisms (Table 7.2) actually gave rise to the missingness. Although there is an extent to which this question is impossible to fully answer—unless the researcher has created the missing data herself, as in the case of personnel selection on an observed variable x (Thorndike, 1949), or planned missingness designs (Graham, Taylor, Olchowski, & Cumsille, 2006)—the best way to gain confidence about the missing data selection mechanism is to collect data from both respondents and nonrespondents on some variables that correlate with the selection variable z (thus creating an MAR pattern).

If no data are available on the nonrespondents in the sample at hand, then one possibility is to use nonlocal meta-analytic data on the differences between respondents and nonrespondents for the variables x and y. For example, Rogelberg and colleagues (Rogelberg et al., 2003; Spitzmuller et al., 2006) have compared survey respondents to survey nonrespondents on a variety of constructs, and Newman (2009) meta-analyzed this work to show that $d_{miss} = -.38$ ($N = 399$) for conscientious personality and $d_{miss} = -.44$ ($N = 608$) for procedural justice perceptions. If one were interested in estimating missing data bias in the observed correlation between conscientiousness (x) and procedural justice perceptions (y), then we could roughly estimate that $r_{zx} = d_{miss(x)} \Big/ \sqrt{d^2_{miss(x)} + \frac{1}{p(1-p)}}$, where p is the response rate. Using this formula, we would find that for a response rate of 50%, $r_{zx} = -.38 \big/ \sqrt{(-.38)^2 + \frac{1}{.5(1-.5)}} = -.187$ for conscientiousness and $r_{zx} = -.44 \big/ \sqrt{(-.44)^2 + \frac{1}{.5(1-.5)}} = -.215$ for procedural justice. If the observed correlation between conscientiousness and procedural justice perceptions were $r_{xy(resp)} = .10$ (e.g., Burnett, Williamson, & Bartol, 2009), then we could estimate, using Equation 8, the complete data correlation $r_{xy(comp)} = .159$. That is, we would estimate that the missing data bias due to pairwise deletion would be $-.059$ (Equation 9a). Depending upon the generalizability of our input estimates of d_{miss} (i.e., the standardized mean difference between respondents and nonrespondents) for conscientiousness and procedural justice, we could conduct a sensitivity analysis to determine whether our theoretical inference based on the observed correlation between conscientiousness and justice might remain supported if the response rates had been 100% (i.e., under complete-data conditions). That is, we can use meta-analytic prior estimates of d_{miss} to correct for missing data bias.

Finally, our presentation was limited to missing data bias in the bivariate correlation. The same logic could be extended and applied to structural equation model/ multiple regression model parameters, which are a function of correlations (see Newman 2009). For example, we could estimate missing data bias in the *indirect effect* from a mediation hypothesis by noting that the product of the X → M path and the M → Y path suffers missing data bias by an amount that can be calculated from Equations 5a, 7a, and/or 9a. One potential drawback to this approach is the possibility that correlation matrices constructed under pairwise deletion might be nonpositive definite (Marsh, 1998).

In conclusion, we have offered a set of formulas that can be used to estimate the precise magnitude of pairwise deletion bias. This bias is a function of the amount of missing data and the strength of the systematic missingness mechanism. We have further demonstrated that pairwise deletion bias can be completely remedied by ML and MI missing data techniques (Rubin, 1976; Schafer & Graham, 2002) unless the selection variable z is unobserved. Thus, our advice for future missing data treatment would be to (a) use ML and MI missing data techniques and (b) attempt to measure the selection variable z or its correlates and then include z (or its covariates) in the imputation model (Collins, Schafer, & Kam, 2001; Graham, 2003).

References

Anseel, F., Lievens, F., Schollaert, E., & Choragwicka, B. (2010). Response rates in organizational science, 1995–2008: A meta-analytic review and guidelines for survey researchers. *Journal of Business and Psychology, 25*, 335–349.

Burnett, M. F., Williamson, I. O., & Bartol, K. M. (2009). The moderating effect of personality on employees' reactions to procedural fairness and outcome favorability. *Journal of Business and Psychology, 24*, 469–484.

Collins, L. M., Schafer, J. L., & Kam, C. M. (2001). A comparison of inclusive and restrictive strategies in modern missing data procedures. *Psychological Methods, 6*, 330–351.

Dempster, A. P., Laird, N. H., & Rubin, D. B. (1977). Maximum likelihood from incomplete data via the EM algorithm. *Journal of the Royal Statistical Society, B39*, 1–38.

Dobson, P. (1988). The correction of correlation coefficients for restriction of range when restriction results from the truncation of a normally distributed variable. *British Journal of Mathematical and Statistical Psychology, 41*, 227–234.

Enders, C. K. (2001). A primer on maximum likelihood algorithms for use with missing data. *Structural Equation Modeling, 8*, 128–141.

Enders, C. K. (2010). *Applied missing data analysis.* New York, NY: Guilford.

Ghiselli, E. E., Campbell, J. P., & Zedeck, S. (1981). *Measurement theory for the behavioral sciences.* San Francisco, CA: W. H. Freeman & Co.

Glynn, R. J., Laird, N. M., & Rubin, D. B. (1986). Selection modeling versus mixture modeling with nonignorable nonresponse. In H. Wainer (Ed.), *Drawing inferences from self-selected samples* (pp. 115–142). New York, NY: Springer-Verlag.

Graham, J. W. (2003). Adding missing-data-relevant variables to FIML-based structural equation models. *Structural Equation Modeling, 10*, 80–100.

Graham, J. W. (2009). Missing data analysis: Making it work in the real world. *Annual Review of Psychology, 60*, 549–576.

Graham, J. W., Taylor, B. J., Olchowski, A. E., & Cumsille, P. E. (2006). Planned missing-data designs in psychological research. *Psychological Methods, 11*, 323–343.

Heckman, J. T. (1979). Sample selection bias as a specification error. *Econometrica, 47*, 153–161.

James, L. R., Demaree, R. G., & Wolf, G. (1984). Estimating within-group interrater reliability with and without response bias. *Journal of Applied Psychology, 69*, 85–98.

Lance, C. E. (2011). More statistical and methodological myths and urban legends. *Organizational Research Methods, 14*, 279–286.

Lance, C. E., Butts, M. M., & Michels, L. C. (2006). The sources of four commonly reported cutoff criteria: What did they really say? *Organizational Research Methods, 9*, 202–220.

Lance, C. E., & Vandenberg, R. J. (Eds.). (2009). *Statistical and methodological myths and urban legends: Doctrine, verity and fable in the organizational and social sciences.* New York: Routledge.

Lawley, D. N. (1943). A note on Karl Pearson's selection formulae. *Proceedings of the Royal Society of Edinburgh, LXII—Part 1*(1), 28–30.

Little, R. J. A. (1993). Pattern mixture models for multivariate incomplete data. *Journal of the American Statistical Association, 88*, 125–134.

Little, R. J. A., & Rubin, D. B. (1987). *Statistical analysis with missing data.* New York, NY: Wiley.

Little, R. J. A., & Rubin, D. B. (2002). *Statistical analysis with missing data* (2nd ed.). New York, NY: Wiley.

Marsh, H. W. (1998). Pairwise deletion for missing data in structural equation models: Nonpositive definite matrices, parameter estimates, goodness of fit, and adjusted sample sizes. *Structural Equation Modeling: A Multidisciplinary Journal, 5*, 22–36.

Newman, D. A. (2003). Longitudinal modeling with randomly and systematically missing data: A simulation of ad hoc, maximum likelihood, and multiple imputation techniques. *Organizational Research Methods, 6*, 328–362.

Newman, D. A. (2009). Missing data techniques and low response rates: The role of systematic nonresponse parameters. In C. E. Lance & R. J. Vandenberg (Eds.), *Statistical and methodological myths and urban legends: Doctrine, verity, and fable in the organizational and social sciences* (pp. 7–36). New York, NY: Routledge.

Newman, D. A., & Sin, H. P. (2009). How do missing data bias estimates of within-group agreement? Sensitivity of SD_{WG}, CV_{WG}, $r_{WG(J)}$, $r_{WG(J)}$*, and ICC to systematic nonresponse. *Organizational Research Methods, 12*, 113–147.

Pearson, K. (1903). Mathematical contributions to the theory of evolution—XI. On the influence of natural selection on the variability and correlation of organs. *Philosophical Transactions*, CC.-A 321, 1–66.

Peugh, J. L., & Enders, C. K. (2004). Missing data in educational research: A review of reporting practices and suggestions for improvement. *Review of Educational Research, 74*, 525–556.

Puhani, P. A. (2000). The Heckman correction for sample selection and its critique. *Journal of Economic Surveys, 14*, 53–67.

Rogelberg, S. G., Conway, J. M., Sederburg, M. E., Spitzmuller, C., Aziz, S., & Knight, W. E. (2003). Profiling active and passive nonrespondents to an organizational survey. *Journal of Applied Psychology, 88*, 1104–1114.

Rogelberg, S. G., Luong, A., Sederburg, M. E., & Cristol, D. S. (2000). Employee attitude surveys: Examining the attitudes of noncompliant employees. *Journal of Applied Psychology, 85*, 284–293.

Roth, P. L. (1994). Missing data: A conceptual review for applied psychologists. *Personnel Psychology, 47*, 537–560.

Rubin, D. B. (1976). Inference and missing data. *Biometrika, 63*, 581–592.

Rubin, D. B. (1987). *Multiple imputation for nonresponse in surveys.* Hoboken, NJ: Wiley.

Sackett, P. R., & Yang, H. (2000). Correction for range restriction: An expanded typology. *Journal of Applied Psychology, 85*, 112–118.

Schafer, J. L. (1997). *Analysis of incomplete multivariate data.* New York, NY: Chapman & Hall.

Schafer, J. L., & Graham, J. W. (2002). Missing data: Our view of the state of the art. *Psychological Methods, 7*, 147–177.

Schmidt, F. L., Hunter, J. E., & Urry, V. W. (1976). Statistical power in criterion-related validation studies. *Journal of Applied Psychology, 61*, 473–485.

Spitzmuller, C., Glenn, D. M., Barr, C. D., Rogelberg, S. G., & Daniel, P. (2006). "If you treat me right, I reciprocate": Examining the role of exchange in survey response. *Journal of Organizational Behavior, 27*, 19–35.

Switzer, F. S., Roth, P. L., & Switzer, D. M. (1998). Systematic data loss in HRM settings: A Monte Carlo analysis. *Journal of Management, 24*, 763–779.

Thorndike, R. L. (1949). *Personnel selection: Test and measurement techniques.* New York, NY: Wiley.

Vandenberg, R. J. (2006). Introduction: Statistical and methodological myths and urban legends: Where, pray tell, did they get this idea?. *Organizational Research Methods, 9*, 194–201.

Wilkinson, L., & Task Force on Statistical Inference. (1999). Statistical methods in psychology journals: Guidelines and explanations. *American Psychologist, 54*, 594–604.

Winship, C., & Mare, R. D. (1992). Models for sample selection bias. *Annual Review of Sociology, 18*, 327–350.

8

SIZE MATTERS . . . JUST NOT IN THE WAY THAT YOU THINK

Myths Surrounding Sample Size Requirements for Statistical Analyses

Scott Tonidandel, Eleanor B. Williams and James M. LeBreton

When designing a new study, researchers frequently must answer the critical question, "How many participants do I need?" The adage "the more participants the better" does not provide a concrete suggestion for researchers to use as a guidepost. Numerous rules of thumb have been generated and used as simple heuristics by researchers when determining necessary sample sizes. Often, these rules of thumb specify minimum sample sizes for particular analyses (e.g., $N > 100$ for multiple regression) or they specify a ratio of the number of participants needed relative to other aspects of the analyses (e.g., ratio of # of participants to # of variables).

However, these rules of thumb are often fraught with shortcomings. First, for many analyses, the rules of thumb are so diverse that without much trouble, researchers can find a citation to justify virtually any sample size. For example, a researcher conducting a multiple regression analysis that includes three predictors could cite Tabachnick and Fidell (1989) to support a sample size of as few as 15 participants, or she could reference Cohen and Cohen's (1983) recommendation of more than 500. Second, it is not uncommon for researchers to ignore the context or qualifying statements that accompanied the original rules of thumb. This often results in inappropriate applications of the rules of thumb. Finally, sample size recommendations typically focus on statistical power and null hypothesis significance hypothesis testing, which may obscure what should be the true focus of determining the appropriate sample size: the precision of the estimate that results from running the analysis. The myth that we address in this chapter is really twofold. First, we intend to show that simple sample size rules of thumb are not appropriate for determining sample size across multiple types of analyses. In addition, we also debunk the myth that power analysis is the preferred alternative to these simpler heuristics.

Even though rules of thumb have problems, they also contain some degree of truth. It is, therefore, our intention not only to discuss some of the issues with these rules of thumb but also to unmask the "kernels of truth" hiding within these rules. We believe it is also instructive to examine a few illustrative examples that reveal how researchers often apply these rules of thumb. Although sample size issues arise in many areas, we focus on analyses using the traditional multiple regression model, the multilevel regression model (i.e., multilevel modeling or MLM), and the structural equation model (SEM). Though these are diverse topics, the following format serves as a guide throughout the chapter:

- What are the popular rules of thumb to which researchers refer when running these analyses?
- What are illustrative examples of how researchers invoke these rules of thumb when running these analyses?
- Why do we consider the "rules of thumb" approach to estimating sample size to be a statistical urban myth?
- And, are there any kernels of truth imbedded in the popular rules of thumb?

Finally, we discuss power analysis and why we believe recommendations for using power analysis to set minimum sample sizes represents a different type of statistical urban myth. We conclude by providing a set of alternative recommendations for estimating sample sizes to guide researchers in the future.

Multiple Regression

Although many statistical techniques are fraught with confusion over sample size requirements, multiple regression is a particularly salient example. Multiple regression analysis is one of the most widely used hypothesis testing techniques in the organizational sciences. In fact, from 1980 to 2000, multiple regression was the most frequently used statistical technique in the flagship journal for organizational psychologists, *Journal of Applied Psychology* (Austin, Scherbaum, & Mahlman, 2002). In the year 2000, 46.3% of the analyses were multiple regression. Given the popularity of multiple regression, it is no surprise that sample size requirements for regression have become a popular topic of debate.

Multiple regression is frequently taught to first-year graduate students, and these same students often rely on multiple regression for theses, dissertations, or other research projects. Thus, there are often—based on strictly anecdotal evidence—conversations between eager students wanting to run a study and their advisors: "How many participants do you think we will need in order to run a multiple regression?" The possible answers to this question are seemingly endless; thus, many professors turn to heuristics from the literature to guide students and colleagues. This reliance on heuristics commonly results in professors (ourselves

164 Scott Tonidandel et al.

included) citing a rule of thumb they have come across in the literature when choosing a sample size.

So, what are the sample size rules of thumb people are using for multiple regression and where do they come from? Is the professor giving good advice by using a particular rule of thumb in the given situation? In this section, we review common rules of thumb that researchers rely on and then discuss the kernels of truth within these heuristics by examining their original purpose and context.

Multiple Regression: The Rules of Thumb

In a review of the literature, we identified seven primary rules of thumb that researchers have invoked to justify minimum sample sizes for multiple regression. These include:

1. Harris's (1975) recommendation for a minimum sample size of $N \geq 50 + m$, where m is the number of predictor variables.
2. Nunnally's (1978) advice that if there are only two or three independent variables, 100 or more participants would be enough to create nonbiased regression weights. However, with 9 or 10 independent variables, 300 to 400 participants would be necessary to prevent substantial bias.
3. Green (1991) suggested a number of recommendations, but the simplest and most similar to those of Harris and Nunnally is $N \geq 104 + p$ or $N \geq 50 + 8p$, where p is the number of predictors.
4. Green (1991) offered an alternative recommendation that incorporated an estimate of effect size into the equation: For multiple correlation, he offered $N \geq L / f^2$ and the partial correlation $(8/f^2) + (m - 1)$, where f^2 equals the estimated effect size of $R^2/(1 - R^2)$, m is the number of predictors, and $L = .4 + 1.65m - 0.5m^2$ when $m < 11$ (pp. 502–504).
5. Tabachnick and Fidell (1989) recommended a ratio of participants to predictors of at least 5:1 but also stated a preference for a ratio of 20:1. Later, Tabachnick and Fidell (1996) suggested another ratio of 40:1 for some applications of multiple regression.
6. Maxwell (2000) lamented that simplistic sample size recommendations typically underestimate the sample sizes necessary for multiple regression. Although he cautioned researchers not to rely too heavily on such conventions, he nevertheless offered a table of minimum sample size ratios, ranging from 70:1 to 119:1.
7. Finally, many researchers base sample size recommendations on a power analysis. Researchers who invoke this strategy often cite Cohen and Cohen (1983), who provided power tables for determining the appropriate sample size as a function of alpha level, desired level of power, and anticipated effect size. Thus, although this approach is not a simple heuristic, it is nevertheless a popular choice for determining the minimum sample size.

Size Matters **165**

TABLE 8.1 Sample Sizes Produced by Rules of Thumb

Rule of Thumb	Number of Predictors			
	3	6	9	12
Harris (1975)	53	56	59	62
Nunnally (1978)	100+		300–400	500+
Green (1991)				
$\quad N \geq 104 + p$	107	110	113	116
$\quad N \geq 50 + 8p$	74	98	122	146
$\quad N \geq L / f^2$				
$\quad\quad$ Small Effect	70	55	40	95
$\quad\quad$ Medium Effect	10	8	6	13
$\quad\quad$ Large Effect	4	4	3	6
Tabachnick & Fidell (1989)	15	30	45	60
Tabachnick & Fidell (1996)	120	240	360	480
Maxwell (2000)	218	543	1,009	
Cohen & Cohen (1983)				
$\quad$ Small Effect	549	686	787	872
$\quad$ Medium Effect	77	95	109	120
$\quad$ Large Effect	36	43	49	54

Although this list is not meant to be exhaustive, it does capture the most commonly invoked rules of thumb for determining minimum sample sizes. Table 8.1 recapitulates these seven rules of thumb. In order to estimate the recommended sample sizes for Green (1991) and Cohen and Cohen (1983), we used f^2 of .02, .15, and .35 for small, medium, and large effects, respectively, as Cohen and Cohen suggested, and set desired power to .80, which is commonly done in the literature.

Multiple Regression: The Sample Size Myths

The published literature contains many applications of these rules of thumb. Our intention in presenting these examples here and in subsequent sections is not to criticize these authors for using such sample size rules of thumb. On the contrary, these authors looked to the literature for guidance and provided strong citations to support their decisions. We applaud the fact that they actually provided details on sample size estimation, as some articles simply fail to make any mention of sample size adequacy.

Instead, our intention is to illustrate how these rules of thumb have been used. For example, Goffin and Gellatly (2001) stated, "With respect to the multiple correlation analysis, our sample size exceeded common minimum recommendations (e.g., Darlington, 1990; Tabachnick and Fidell, 1989)" (p. 443). Presumably, Goffin

166 Scott Tonidandel et al.

and Gellatly were using Tabachnick and Fidell's 5:1 rule of thumb as justification for their sample size of 78 with six predictors, because Tabachnick and Fidell's larger ratio recommendations would not be met with such a sample size. Thus, although we do not know the issues surrounding their sample size choice, Goffin and Gellatly justified their chosen sample size with one of the smaller ratios from Table 8.1.

Another example of how rules of thumb are currently used comes from an article by Taormina (2009). Taormina acknowledged that the number of respondents used in the study, $N = 156$, "might be questioned in relation to the number of variables used in the regressions" (p. 671). The author went on to explain that Nunnally (1978) would have suggested as many as 400 respondents, whereas Maxwell (2000) would say, "such numbers may be unattainable" (p. 671). Interestingly, Maxwell's article focused on the idea that sample size recommendations have greatly underestimated adequate sample sizes; thus, it is not likely that he would react negatively to Nunnally's (1978) larger recommendation. To illustrate that his sample size was adequate, Taormina invoked Green's (1991) formulas of $N \geq 104 + p$ and $N \geq 50 + 8p$, which yielded minimum sample sizes of 117 and 154, respectively, to show that his sample of 156 exceeded those numbers. He concluded that "although larger samples are generally preferred, the sample size of this study may be considered adequate" (p. 671).

Clearly, there is a belief among authors that these rules of thumb are useful for determining an appropriate sample size, and the examples noted are simply meant to be illustrative—there are plenty of other examples one could pull from the extant literature. Although many authors are comfortable using one or more of the rules of thumb from Table 8.1, we consider the application of these rules to be perpetuating a statistical urban myth: There is a single, "correct" estimate of sample size that may be obtained using one of the formulae from Table 8.1.

As one can see from Table 8.1, there is actually not a single number but a very wide range of suggested sample sizes. For example, with nine predictor variables, a researcher could argue that only 45 participants are needed (Tabachnick & Fidell, 1989); however, the skeptical reviewer might wonder if 1,009 might be more appropriate (Maxwell, 2000). This large range is problematic for two main reasons. First, because there is no clear and unanimous sample size requirement, researchers could end up using too few or too many participants when estimating the parameters for a multiple regression analysis. Although we have been discussing the issues associated with having too few participants, having too many participants can also be problematic, as it may be a waste of time and resources and produce results that are statistically significant but lack practical significance (Cortina & Landis, 2009). Second, researchers, with very little effort, can justify virtually any sample size. Because of the many rules of thumb used to justify minimum sample sizes and their widely divergent values, it is a myth that these rules of thumb will lead researchers to choose the appropriate sample size.

Multiple Regression: Kernels of Truth

If we have many rules of thumb to choose from, all of which vary in their recommendations for sample sizes, can all of these rules of thumb be "right"? Is one rule of thumb "better" than the others? Or do different rules of thumb apply in different circumstances? In order to fully appreciate the value (or lack thereof) in these heuristics, one must appreciate the context and purpose that the original authors used to guide the development of each heuristic.

Harris (1975) began discussing sample size requirements for multiple regression by admitting, "there have been few empirical sampling studies of how large an N is needed for this robustness" (p. 50). Having qualified the readers with this fact, Harris (1975) *did* offer the rule of $N \geq 50 + m$. However, he explained that this rule should be the case for tests on individual regression coefficients where the Xs and Ys have grossly nonnormal distributions and $N - m$ is less than 50. Thus, his rule of thumb is simply a recommendation based on the "few empirical sampling studies of how large an N is needed" that were in existence at the time (p. 50). Overall, this rule of thumb is offered within a very specific context and based upon minimal existing research.

A few years after Harris's (1975) recommendation, Nunnally's (1978) offered his rule of thumb within the specific context of cross-validating the results from a regression analysis. Nunnally believed that if the researcher's goal was to select the best variables from as many as 10 possible variables, it would be wise to have a large number of participants, as many as 400 to 500, in the study. Why this large number? He stated,

> Whatever the sample size and amount of preselection among predictor variables, it is wise to look for information in subsequent studies that serves to cross-validate both the beta weights and the multiple correlation obtained in the initial investigation.
>
> *(p. 200)*

Thus, he recommended this large number of participants in order for the regression weights and the multiple correlation to cross-validate in subsequent investigations. Moreover, the real purpose of Nunnally's (1978) rule of thumb was to make a recommendation about the sample sizes needed to select variables to retain in future regression analyses.

In contrast, Tabachnick and Fidell (1989) had a different purpose in mind when they made their recommendations. In the first edition of their multivariate text, they suggested that the minimum number of participants for each predictor variable in a regression analysis should be 5:1. They made this recommendation with some hesitancy:

> If either standard multiple or hierarchical regression is used, one would like to have 20 times more cases than IVs. That is, if you plan to include 5 IVs,

168 Scott Tonidandel et al.

it would be lovely to measure 100 cases. In fact, power may be unacceptably low no matter what the cases-to-IVs ratio if you have fewer than 100 cases. However, a bare minimum requirement is to have at least 5 times more cases than IVs.

(p. 128)

This rule of thumb eventually suggests a "bare minimum requirement" of 5:1; researchers citing this bare minimum have conveniently ignored the prior sentence, which qualifies that minimum and actually suggests a minimum of at least 100 cases. Perhaps unsurprisingly, their recommendation of 5:1 is dropped in later editions of the text, where instead Tabachnick and Fidell (1996) offered a recommended a ratio of 40:1. However, like so many other rules of thumb, this latter recommendation should be used only in a certain situation: when a researcher is doing a statistical (stepwise) regression. Thus, each of these authors' rules of thumb was generated for a very unique situation, and these qualifiers are rarely considered when invoking the rules of thumb.

At first glance, it may appear that Green (1991) simply endorsed the rule of $N \geq 50 + 8p$, but in actuality, his recommendations were more complex. In the conclusion of his article, he explained that traditional rules of thumb, meaning those that are simplistic ratios like 5:1, are the simplest to use, but they are rarely in line with power analyses; thus, he felt that the aforementioned formula of $N \geq 50 + 8p$ is a better guideline for researchers than the simpler ratio alternatives. However, this formula works only if researchers are interested in a medium effect size and if their hypothesis uses a multiple correlation or one type of partial correlation. Moreover, this formula is most accurate if $p < 7$ (p. 504). If those circumstances are not met, he offered a more complex rule of thumb: $N \geq L / f^2$ for the multiple correlation and $8/f^2 + (m - 1)$ for the partial correlation. Another important caveat in Green's recommendation is that researchers really should conduct power analyses to gain the greatest accuracy and flexibility and disregard his aforementioned rule of thumb. However, because of the additional complexities in conducting a power analysis, Green reverted to his recommendation that his "more complex" rule of thumb (i.e., $N \geq 50 + 8p$) is a suitable simplified replacement for power analysis and is better than a more simplistic ratio. Overall, even though many researchers cite Green for the $N \geq 50 + 8p$ rule of thumb, his actual recommendations were much more nuanced, and those nuances are rarely considered by contemporary researchers.

Similar to Green (1991), Maxwell (2000) also lamented that the commonly used rules of thumb underestimate the sample size needed for a multiple regression analysis. He considered these rules of thumb too simplistic and thought they should be ignored; however, at the end of the article, he presented a table of ratios of sample size to predictors, which ranged from 70:1 to 119:1. Maxwell explicitly stated that this table should be used only "in the complete absence of any theoretical expectations and assuming that all zero-order correlations among variables of interest are 'medium'" (p. 453). This table is also appropriate only when researchers attempt to obtain a power of .80. Although this table was, in his view, more defensible than relying on a more "arbitrary" rule of thumb like some of the other simplistic, absolute sample size or ratio-type options, it should *not* be a table that researchers solely rely on when determining their sample size. Instead, he believed researchers should use alternate procedures based on several equations that he provided:

> The best approach of all might be to use several of the formulas [I have provided], even when the number of predictors is fixed at a single value. To the extent that the sample sizes suggested by the various formulas converge, the researcher can have added confidence that the suggested sample size is in fact appropriate from a variety of perspectives.
>
> *(p. 450)*

The kernel of truth in Maxwell's rule of thumb is that the smaller and simplistic ratios far underestimate the necessary sample size; researchers should ultimately ignore these rules of thumb. Nevertheless, researchers cite Maxwell (2000) as a rule of thumb to justify their sample size.

Unlike the previous rules of thumb, there are those authors who specifically advocate using a power analysis to determine the minimum sample size. For example, Cohen and Cohen (1983) provided power tables for determining the appropriate sample size. Although a reliance on power to determine sample size may seem most justifiable, concrete, and flexible, several steps are involved in making this decision:

1. Set the significance criterion to be used, $\propto$.
2. Set the desired power for the statistical test.
3. Obtain an L value from the tables in their appendix according to your $\propto$ value, number of predictors, and desired level of power.
4. Determine the population effect size of interest and the expected alternative-hypothetical value (Cohen & Cohen, 1983, p. 117).
5. Substitute L and f^2 in $n = L / f^2 + k + 1$, which will result in the number of cases necessary (f^2 is the population effect size of interest).

These steps provide what appears to be a relatively clear set of rules for determining adequate sample sizes across a wide range of situations. However, several unstated assumptions impact these five steps, making the application of power analysis more challenging than it may first appear. The most arbitrary of these assumptions is an estimate of the population effect size of interest (Step 4). Cohen and Cohen did offer, with some hesitation, a set of guidelines for small (.02), medium (.15), and large (.35) effect sizes; however, this set of guidelines is actually fraught with misunderstanding and misapplication (Cortina & Landis, 2009).

170 Scott Tonidandel et al.

Obviously one's choice of effect size will have a dramatic effect on the recommended sample size (see Table 8.1 above).

Although Cohen and Cohen (1983) provided an excellent set of guidelines based on statistical power, the application of this approach is not as objective as many researchers would like to think. Later we argue that power analysis, while superior to the common rules of thumb, is not the optimal approach for determining sample sizes because it focuses on statistical significance. In contrast, we recommend an alternative approach that emphasizes the accuracy of parameter estimation. Before elaborating on why it is a myth that power analysis is the best method for determining sample size and detailing the specifics of this alternative approach, we briefly review the sample size myths associated with MLM and SEM.

Multilevel Modeling

Over the last 15 years, the popularity of MLM has steadily increased (Kozlowski & Klein, 2000). One consistent theme mentioned in the literature is that sample sizes need to be adequately large to conduct MLM because the maximum likelihood estimation models often used in multilevel analysis are asymptotic (Maas & Hox, 2004). Outside of this broad generalization, many rules of thumb provide guidance for researchers designing multilevel studies. Our current focus is on selected salient examples of these rules of thumb, though researchers may encounter a variety of recommendations for numerous types of multilevel situations (e.g., Hedges & Hedberg, 2007; Moerbeek & Teerenstra, 2011; Raudenbush, 1997; Raudenbush, Martinez, & Spybrook, 2007).

MLM: The Rules of Thumb

The work that guides sample size recommendations in MLM for the most part has been simulation studies focusing on different aspects of the multilevel models, such as fixed effects and variance components. The main rules of thumb referenced by authors of empirical studies are found in Kreft (1996), Hox (2010; Maas & Hox, 2004, 2005), and Scherbaum and Ferreter (2009).

When researching rules of thumb in MLM, one inevitably comes across Kreft's (1996) 30/30 rule. Although Kreft did not carry out her own simulation studies, her research summarized earlier studies by Kim, by Bassiri, by Busing, and by van der Leeden and Busing. Based on this review, Kreft recommended 30 groups with 30 individuals per group should be a minimum sample size for MLM. This 30/30 rule is what researchers often strive for when designing their multilevel studies, and it is cited frequently as an MLM rule of thumb. For example, Cambré, Kippers, van Beldhoven, and De Witte (2012) examined group-level differences in job satisfaction within an organization. In order to justify their sample of 24 job groups, they referenced Kreft (1996), arguing that the number of groups "approaches the preferred number of at least 30 groups on the second level prescribed by some authors (Kreft, 1996; Maas and Hox, 2004)" (p. 211). The Cambré and colleagues paper is simply one of many papers that cited Kreft when describing minimum sample sizes needed for multilevel regression (for other examples, see Hecker & Violato, 2008; Major, Fletcher, Davis, & Germano, 2008).

Though Kreft intended for the 30/30 rule to apply to cross-level interactions, Hox (2010; Maas & Hox, 2004, 2005) instead believed it was sound advice only for certain fixed effects parameters. For cross-level interactions, Hox recommended a modification of Kreft's rule of 50/20 (50 groups with 20 individuals per group). Hox offered this rule based on his interpretation of the simulation studies that Kreft summarized, and he believed that 50/20 is a more appropriate recommendation for cross-level interactions.

As was true with multiple regression, some experts have encouraged researchers to use power analysis to estimate minimum sample sizes for MLM. Scherbaum and Ferreter (2009) are proponents of this type of calculation. Estimating sample sizes for the various parameters involves numerous formulas, which they included in their work. The general approach is to maximize power by determining optimal allocation of sample sizes to Level 1 and Level 2. Though this calculation may seem simple, this power analysis approach requires an understanding of some important caveats, which we will further explain in the kernel of truth section. However, first we think it is important to examine the similarities and differences in the sample size requirements obtained using these three rules of thumb (see Table 8.2).

MLM: The Sample Size Myths

All three rules of thumb are commonly cited in the literature. For example, Eisenberger and colleagues (2010) used Maas and Hox (2004, 2005) as justification for the sample size in their multilevel design. While admitting that their average number of subordinates per supervisor, 3.2, is small, these authors argued that their sample size "appears to be sufficiently high to produce accurate results" (p. 1092) based on the tradeoff between Level 2 and Level 1 units. Further, they highlighted their 79 supervisors as being a sufficient Level 2 sample size in accordance with

TABLE 8.2 Rules of Thumb for MLM

Author	Rule of Thumb
Kreft (1996)	30 groups with 30 individuals each
Hox (2010); Maas & Hox (2004, 2005)	50 groups with 20 individuals each
Scherbaum and Ferreter (2009)	Power analysis for fixed effects, variance components, and cross-level interactions in two level linear models

Maas and Hox's recommendation of at least 30 samples at the group level. As another example of how MLM rules of thumb are referenced in the literature, consider Major, Fletcher, Davis, and Germano (2008), who reached the threshold of 30 participants per group with their 916 employees, but lamented, "We sampled 10 organizations. . . . Simulation research suggests that a minimum level-2 sample size should be at least 30 (p. 892–893) (Hox, 2002; Kreft, 1996; Maas & Hox, 2004)" (p. 892–893).

In addition to the reliance on simple heuristics, we also encountered a surprising trend of authors justifying their sample size by noting other MLM studies with comparable or smaller sample sizes. This was true both in instances where the requirements of the rules of thumb are met and in instances where the sample size is not large enough to surpass the minimum thresholds of the rules of thumb. For example, Gentry and Sparks (2012) remarked, "our study has ample sample size at both [Level 1 and Level 2], as compared to the traditional rule-of-thumb of 30 groups with at least 30 people in each group" (p. 25). This is a typical comment showing that the sample size used in the study exceeds a rule of thumb in the literature. They went on to point out that "recent multilevel studies . . . all had sample sizes that were considerably less at both levels than this study. . . . The sample size in our study is also much greater than what is normally found in organizational research" (p. 25). Though this large sample size may be considered a relative strength of their study, other authors use similar arguments when they fail to reach the minimum rule of thumb thresholds. For example, some authors would reference Kreft (1996), among others, to suggest that 30 Level 2 observations would be optimal. Yet because their study consisted of fewer Level 2 observations, they would justify their limited sample by noting that they had "substantially more" groups than commonly found in other studies in the same domain, thus making their sample size seem reasonable in comparison to other similar studies. In sum, a number of authors of MLM studies invoked various sample size rules of thumb, even when they may have failed to achieve the required threshold, whereas other authors looked to other studies as providing the rule-of-thumb basis for justifying the sample sizes in their own study.

Clearly, authors believe that these simple heuristics can help guide them in their choice of sample size for multilevel studies. However, this is a myth. There is nothing magical about the recommended ratios suggested by Kreft (1996) and Hox (2010; Maas & Hox, 2004, 2005). The lack of agreement in the recommended number of participants at either level illustrates one of the problems. Moreover, the rules of thumb are not in line with the recommendations from a power analysis in many situations. This blind reliance on the rules of thumb neglects the particular context of one's own study, which may contrast the particular context in which the recommendations were made. To better understand why the use of these rules of thumb represents a statistical myth, it is instructive to first examine the kernels of truth linked to each rule and the specifics surrounding their development.

MLM: Kernels of Truth

The most widely cited rule of thumb we found, Kreft's (1996), was actually a recommendation based on a summary of earlier simulation studies. Kreft detailed the boundary conditions for each of these studies, revealing the kernel of truth behind her recommendations. First, Kim and Bassiri were solely focused on the fixed effects. The conclusion from both of these simulation studies was that "power for first level estimates depends on the total number of observations, while power of second level estimates depends on the number of groups" (p. 16). Kreft also reviewed Busing's two simulations that focused on the estimates of variance components and found that "the variance component is under estimated for all conditions, except for samples with 300 groups" (p. 18). Finally, in terms of cross-level interactions, Kreft summed up the work by Bassiri and by van der Leeden and Busing, who showed that 30 groups with 30 individuals each was sufficient for detecting cross-level interactions.

In sum, a closer examination of Kreft's work yields a more nuanced understanding of the rule of thumb for which she is so often cited. Researchers often reference Kreft for the aforementioned 30/30 rule, and they believe this rule applies to many different parameters of interest. In reality, the 30/30 rule is only applicable, in Kreft's view, to cross-level interactions. She came to different conclusions about fixed effects and variance components. It should also be noted that Kreft included another important caveat: "most [simulation studies] use low intra class correlations," meaning that these conclusions do not apply to situations in which people, or units, have intraclass correlations larger than $r = .25$ (p. 12). These are important caveats that are rarely acknowledged when citing Kreft for the 30/30 rule.

Even though Kreft's 30/30 rule is commonly cited in the MLM literature, it is interesting to note that her 1996 work is an unpublished manuscript. Moreover, all of the simulation studies that Kreft summarized are themselves unpublished manuscripts. In addition to these simulation studies being unpublished, they are somewhat old, and the combination of these two factors made them difficult to find; we were, with great difficulty, able to obtain Kreft's paper, but we were unable to track down the original simulation studies. Perhaps of more concern, though, is that many researchers utilizing MLM are justifying their sample sizes based on a series of simulation studies that are unpublished and have never undergone the peer-review process. This critique is not to say that the simulation studies and their resulting recommendations do not have merit, but rather that our field has been basing a critical design consideration on unpublished (and potentially dated) research.

The 50/20 rule attributed to Hox (2010) has its caveats as well. Recall that Hox recommended 50 groups with 20 individuals each for cross-level interactions. However,

> If there is strong interest in the random part, the variance and covariance components and their standard errors, the number of groups should be

174 Scott Tonidandel et al.

considerably larger, which leads to a 100/10 rule: about 100 groups with at least 10 individuals per group.

(p. 235)

Hox also noted that these rules are somewhat flexible in that if the number of groups increases, the number of individuals per group can be less, and vice versa. Hox's previous work with Maas provided further justification for and clarification on the rules of thumb he advises researchers to use. Specifically, Maas and Hox (2004, 2005) conducted a simulation of 27 conditions with 1,000 data sets each to determine the influence of different sample sizes on the accuracy of the estimates. They concluded that 50 groups are needed (and a later refinement becomes the 50/20 rule). They also explained, "if one is only interested in the fixed effects of the model, ten groups can lead to good estimates. . . . If one also wants correct estimates of the standard errors, at least 50 groups are needed" (p. 135). Overall, though Hox is most popularly cited for the 50/20 rule, a closer look at his work reveals a range of group sample size recommendations, conditional on the situation and goals of the research project.

Finally, power analysis again represents an alternative to simple rules of thumb for determining minimum sample sizes for MLM. However, unlike multiple regression, a power analysis for MLM is a much more cumbersome task because the computations involve a number of additional factors. Scherbaum and Ferreter (2009) provided one of the most comprehensive reviews of the factors that influence statistical power in multilevel models. First, the intraclass correlation (ICC) needs to be determined and is usually estimated a priori, which involves using more arbitrary heuristics as a guide for computing this quantity. Another important factor influencing power is the inclusion of Level 1 or Level 2 covariates; covariates can reduce between-group variance, and they can have a high cost associated with them (cost of sampling Level 2 units is generally higher than Level 1 units). The specific estimation method used for calculating the parameters can have an influence as well, and there is actually a lack of literature on the best method. Finally, the parameter of interest in the multilevel model is an important factor, meaning that the sample size needed to attain a specific level of statistical power will differ depending on whether one is estimating simple fixed effects, variance components, or cross-level interactions.

Overall, many researchers turn to familiar heuristics when designing a multilevel study. However, it is a statistical myth to believe that the use of any one heuristic or rule of thumb accurately captures the complexity of estimating minimum sample sizes for MLM. It is important that researchers understand the different factors that affect the necessary sample size for MLM and only then decide if one of the rules of thumb is appropriate in their given situation. Power analysis is a reasonable alternative to simpler rules of thumb for MLM, but we intend to argue that it is also a myth that power analysis is the best approach for determining sample size. At the end of our chapter, we offer an alternative suggestion for choosing an appropriate sample size that we hope researchers consider instead of performing a power analysis.

Structural Equation Modeling

A final technique that has gained immense popularity over the last 40 years (across many disciplines in the social and behavioral sciences) is structural equation modeling (SEM). Kenny (2005) explained this trend best when he wrote, "Researchers love SEM because it addresses the questions they want answered. Perhaps more than any other technique, SEM 'thinks' about research the way researchers do" (p. x). As was the case with the techniques discussed earlier, researchers have often relied on various rules of thumb when determining minimum sample sizes for use with SEM. And it is not surprising that the various SEM rules of thumb often yield a wide range of sample size recommendations resulting from a variety of factors, including those noted by Kline (2011): the complexity of the structural and measurement models, the method used to estimate parameters, and various characteristics of the data (e.g., distributional characteristics; level of measurement).

SEM: The Rules of Thumb

Researchers have suggested two categories or types of calculations that should be used to estimate appropriate SEM sample sizes. The first category consists of using a ratio of the number of cases to the parameters being estimated (Bentler & Chou, 1987; Jackson, 2003; Kline, 2005, 2011). The second category consists of power calculations being used to generate minimum sample size estimates (MacCallum, Browne, & Sugawara, 1996; Saris & Satorra, 1993).

In terms of ratio-type rules of thumb, Jackson (2003) advised researchers to think of sample size in terms of an $N:q$ ratio, that is, the ratio of cases (N) to the number of model parameters that require statistical estimation (q). Although Jackson did not recommend a specific numerical value, he is referenced in the literature as a jumping-off point for other ratio-type rules. One of those rules, from Bentler and Chou (1987), recommended a ratio of 5:1 (sample size to freely estimated parameters). Their recommendation arose from an exploration of practical issues in SEM. Namely, when advising researchers on sample size considerations, Bentler and Chou (1987) suggested that samples can be "small to moderate in size, and the question arises whether large sample statistical theory is appropriate in such situations" (p. 90). These authors reviewed previous Monte Carlo studies, which attempted to find the distribution of estimators and test statistics used in SEM. The Monte Carlo studies involved only a few types of models, sample sizes, and estimators, which resulted in a lack of definitive recommendations for the distribution of estimators and test statistics and, therefore, a lack of a definitive sample size recommendation. Nevertheless, Bentler and Chou (1987) offered an admittedly "oversimplified guideline that might serve as a rule of thumb," the 5:1 recommendation (p. 91).

176 Scott Tonidandel et al.

Another author who offered a ratio-type rule was Kline (2005, 2011). He suggested that "a desirable goal is to have the ratio of the number of cases to the number of free parameters be 20:1; a 10:1 ratio, however, may be more realistic. . . . If the ratio is less than 5:1, the statistical precision of the results may be doubtful" (2005, p. 111). Even though Kline did offer a ratio-type rule of thumb, he is more often referenced for his absolute sample size recommendation (e.g., Lei & Wu, 2007). Concerning this latter recommendation, Kline recognized that SEM is truly a large-sample technique, which requires a minimum of 200 cases based on his review of previous SEM sample sizes in the literature.

As with multiple regression and MLM, power analysis has also been suggested as an alternative to simple heuristics for determining sample size in SEM. In SEM, the power calculations differ depending on whether one is interested in testing individual parameters or the fit of the entire model. Saris and Satorra (1993) explained how to determine the sample size needed to detect an individual effect (parameter), whereas, MacCallum and colleagues (1996) provided a guide for researchers wanting to perform power analyses for SEM when testing hypotheses about the overall fit of a model. These popular rules of thumb are summarized in Table 8.3.

SEM: The Sample Size Myths

A number of recent studies provide examples of how these rules of thumb are used in the literature. For example, Parent and Moradi (2009) referenced three rules of thumb:

> The final sample size of 229 exceeded Kline's (2005) recommendation of at least 200 cases for CFA but did not meet Bentler and Chou's (1987) recommended minimum of five cases per parameter estimated. . . . Also, models with greater degrees of freedom require smaller sample sizes to achieve higher power than do models with fewer degrees of freedom (MacCallum et al., 1996).
>
> (p. 180)

Parent and Moradi justified their final sample size with a combination of absolute sample size and ratio-type rules of thumb, along with a reference to power

TABLE 8.3 Rules of Thumb for SEM

Author	Rule of Thumb
Jackson (2003)	N:q (cases: number of parameters that require estimates)
Bentler and Chou (1987)	5:1 (cases: parameters)
Kline (2005, 2011)	20:1 (cases: parameters); also offered 200-case minimum
Saris and Satorra (1993)	Power analysis for individual parameters
MacCallum et al. (1996)	Power analysis at the model level

analysis. Actually, Kline would likely advise that a 20:1 ratio of number of cases to parameters would be ideal in this situation, a 10:1 might be more realistic and sufficient, and that a ratio below 5:1 might not provide realistic results. Thus, in the present example, the sample size does indeed meet Kline's 200-case minimum recommendation, but it does not exceed Kline's other minimum ratio-type thresholds, nor does the sample meet the minimum 5:1 ratio offered by Bentler and Chou (1987).

Another study, by Silvester, Patterson, Koczwara, and Ferguson (2007), referenced Bentler and Chou (1987). The authors admitted that their sample size for the structural model was relatively small ($N = 90$) but that Bentler and Chou (1987) argued that a ratio of 5:1 is sufficient; thus, their ratio of 9:1 was justifiable. They do not mention the fact that the sample size is well below the popularly cited 200-cases rule. However, they did mention, "sample sizes equivalent to that reported here have been analyzed in a similar manner (see also Ferguson, James, O'Hehir, & Sanders, 2003; Martocchio & Judge, 1997)" (p. 523). Once again, this time in the SEM context, a seemingly small sample size was justified by referencing other work using a similar sample size.

This sampling of illustrative examples was selected simply to highlight evidence that researchers regularly use these rules of thumb for SEM. However, the use of these heuristics is simply perpetuating the myth that a simple equation can yield accurate sample size projections across a wide range of situations. In reality, the diverse set of rules of thumb yield widely varying sample size recommendations. Moreover, these recommendations can also differ greatly from estimates of power analysis depending on particular conditions. In fact, as with other analyses, the conditions under which these sample size recommendations were made are vital to consider, which brings us to the kernels of truth within the myth.

SEM: Kernels of Truth

Although the different types of rules of thumb result in a range of sample sizes, each recommendation contains a kernel of truth. For example, Kline (2005, 2011) believed that it might be helpful for readers to think about the recommended sample size for SEM in more absolute terms. Thus, based on the meta-analyses that previous researchers conducted, he offered that a typical sample size was approximately 200 cases. Kline took this further and concluded that sample sizes between 100 and 200 participants could be considered "medium," with those under 100 being "small" and those exceeding 200 being "large" (2005, p. 15). He also offered the ratio-type rule of thumb of 20:1 and advised researchers that this ratio, rather than an absolute minimum sample size, might be a more appropriate goal when choosing a sample size, especially if they are dealing with a complex model. Researchers should understand two additional notes about Kline's advice. First, he indicated that a sample size of "200 or even much larger may be necessary for a

178 Scott Tonidandel et al.

very complicated path model" (p. 110); thus, the rule of 200 may not even be large enough for some situations. Second, he advised readers that a more precise technique for estimating the correct sample size would be a power analysis.

Several Monte Carlo studies prior to Bentler and Chou (1987) tried to answer whether large-sample statistical theory could be applied to SEM. These studies were limited in what they included; as such, Bentler and Chou did not believe that they resulted in definitive recommendations. Thus, they offered researchers their own rule of thumb, an "oversimplified guideline" of a 5:1 ratio of sample size to number of free parameters under normal and elliptical theory (p. 90). They cautioned researchers that this guideline is appropriate only when there are "many indicators of latent variables and the associated factor loadings are large" (p. 91). The consequence of this qualification is that it necessitates large sample sizes. When the circumstances are different—for example, when the distribution is not normal—a ratio of at least 10:1 would more appropriate. However, these authors noted that this 10:1 recommendation was based on "even less experience" (p. 91). Overall, Bentler and Chou's (1987) recommendations of 5:1 and 10:1 are widely adopted even though they are based on relatively little empirical evidence.

Jackson (2003) also encouraged researchers to use a ratio-based technique for determining sample size in SEM. He recommended that researchers think of sample size in terms of $N{:}q$ (ratio of cases to the number of model parameters that require statistical estimates) even though the results from his simulation studies supporting this ratio were mixed. Further, Jackson determined that the absolute sample size had a more profound effect on the parameters of interest (namely the fit indices) than did the $N{:}q$ ratio, but he cautioned that an absolute sample size fails to consider the number of parameters being estimated. He did not want to advise researchers solely to depend on an absolute sample size, even though it heavily impacted the results. Thus, he concluded that an $N{:}q$ ratio may be useful in order to take into account the parameters being estimated, but he further reiterated that the overall sample size needs to be considered as well.

Jackson (2003) illustrated the importance of considering the number of estimated parameters when calculating the minimum sample size necessary for SEM. As such, some scholars have turned to power analysis, which takes into account the number of estimated parameters, along with other features of the design (e.g., the relationship between variables, alpha level, and desired level of power). However, researchers need to understand several additional caveats. First, as is evident in the work by Saris and Satorra (1993), using a power analysis to determine the necessary sample size involves several steps: (1) generate a predicted covariance matrix based on one's research model, (2) input these data into an SEM computer program, (3) analyze the data to obtain a sample size, and (4) consult a special table in order to ascertain the "estimated probability of detecting the added free parameter when testing for it" (Kline, 2011, p. 222).

Another approach to power analysis focuses on model-level fit and also involves several key assumptions. Specifically, MacCullum and colleagues (1996) based their approach on the root mean square error of approximation and non-central chi-square distributions and consider the overall level of model fit by testing a hypothesis of "close fit" or "exact fit." A known limitation of the chi-square test of model fit is that larger sample sizes actually increase the probability of concluding a lack of fit regardless of the true fit of the data to the model, whereas a poorly fitting model can produce a nonsignificant chi-square when sample sizes are small. This limitation is why their technique uses alternative fit indices whose inferences regarding model fit improve as N increases. Unlike the chi-square test, the formulas for determining required sample size under their technique utilize familiar inputs such as alpha, desired level of power, predicted effect size in terms of a discrepancy in model fit, and the number of parameters to be estimated. As with any power analysis, "there is an unavoidable element of arbitrariness" when one must make these input decisions (MacCallum et al., 1996, p. 138).

In sum, SEM is a technique requiring large sample sizes, yet researchers have looked to various rules of thumb to justify their often small to medium sample sizes. The belief in the adequacy of these rules is a myth. Moreover, though power analysis is clearly a better alternative, it is also a myth that power analysis is the best solution to the sample size–planning problem. For example, MacCallum and colleagues (1996) recognize that minimum sample size requirements could yield undesirable effects on other aspects of the SEM. Specifically, an N that is sufficiently large for model testing may not be sufficiently large for other applications. This adequacy might particularly be a problem for obtaining precise parameter estimates: the N could achieve the desired level of power for estimating model fit, but the model could still be insufficient with respect to parameter estimation. Thus, we close our chapter by introducing an alternative approach to determining minimum sample size that is based on accuracy of parameter estimation rather than statistical significance.

An Alternative to Power Analysis

The rules of thumb reviewed in this chapter have been used to guide decisions about minimum sample sizes and have largely focused on issues related to sample sizes needed to identify a statistically significant effect (if it exists). This focus is particularly apparent from those authors who recommend power analysis for determining an adequate sample size, but it is also often an unstated goal of the other rules of thumb. Though we have clearly illustrated that the belief in the rules of thumb for determining appropriate sample size should be considered a myth, we also argue that another myth exists concerning power analysis as the best alternative for determining sample size. Evidence for the existence of this myth can be found in the requirements set forth by most granting agencies expecting that authors conduct a power analysis to determine an adequate sample size. Additional anecdotal evidence for the existence of this myth can be found in the comments

180 Scott Tonidandel et al.

from an anonymous reviewer of a submission on rules of thumb and sample size. To paraphrase the reviewer,

> One myth that the first paper will [hopefully] work to dispel is that we should [not] be using these rules of thumb in the first place when power analyses and required sample sizes can be accurately and easily estimated.

Clearly, there is a shared perception that power analysis is the preferred alternative to rules of thumb for determining appropriate sample sizes, but we consider this belief to be a myth, which we hope to debunk in favor of an alternative method.

So, what is the power analysis myth? Essentially, whenever researchers contemplate how many participants are required to support their hypothesis, they are really asking a question about statistical power because they want to be able to detect a significant effect or relationship if one truly exists. However, a focus on statistical power is problematic because the results of a dichotomous significant/ nonsignificant decision do not address the magnitude of the population effect, which is our ultimate interest (for a more thorough discussion of this controversy, see Cohen, 1994, among others).

As a result of this and other shortcomings, we recommend researchers shift their focus from null hypothesis testing to what we call *precise parameter estimation* (PPE). There is a small but growing awareness that PPE should be the goal for research (Bonett & Wright, 2011; Kelley & Maxwell, 2003; Lai & Kelley, 2011). The PPE approach focuses on determining the number of participants that will lead to accurate or precise estimation of parameters, not solely statistically significant ones. Our recommended approach changes the focus of attention from statistical hypothesis testing to stabilizing parameter estimation. In any sample, a statistic will vary from the parameter (hence, the concept of sampling error); however, statistics obtained from studies using larger sample sizes will, in general, be less variable and yield more precise or accurate estimates of the population parameter. The accuracy with which we can precisely estimate a parameter is a function of the width of the confidence interval around a point estimate; the narrower the confidence interval, the more certain one can be that the observed estimate of a parameter approximates its corresponding population parameter.

This goal of obtaining a narrow confidence interval around a parameter estimate is fundamentally different from power analysis, whose goal is to obtain a confidence interval that correctly excludes the null value. The required sample size for power analysis depends on the value of the effect itself and will likely produce extremely large confidence intervals if the anticipated effects are large or extremely narrow confidence intervals if the anticipated effects are small. In the former example, despite knowing that an effect is nonzero, we would have little insight into the true population value of the effect because of an excessively large confidence interval. In contrast, the PPE approach does not focus on whether the confidence interval correctly excludes the null value; rather, our ultimate interest is simply in an accurate estimate of the population effect—irrespective of whether the true effect is close to or far from zero (or some other null value). Though both power analysis and PPE require similar inputs, the resulting precision of the parameter estimates can differ greatly. Whereas the PPE method ensures a confidence interval of a desired width regardless of the magnitude of the population coefficient, power analysis can recommend sample sizes whose resulting estimates may yield confidence intervals that are embarrassingly large.

The PPE approach draws from ideas originally introduced by Kelley and Maxwell (2003) as it relates to sample size planning for multiple regression and extends these notions to other analyses. For those researchers who are interested in the squared multiple correlation, Bonett and Wright (2011) presented a similar procedure to that of Kelley and Maxwell (2003). They also extended Kelley and Maxwell's (2003) work from standardized regression coefficients to unstandardized coefficients and included a simple method for approximating the required sample size to estimate unstandardized regression coefficients with a desired level of precision. Snijders and Bosker (1993) provide a framework for determining necessary sample size in MLM with a focus on parameter estimation. Finally, Lai and Kelley (2011) laid the initial groundwork for a discussion of planning sample sizes for SEM that focused more on precisely estimating parameters and less on null hypothesis significance testing. These authors suggested that our accumulation of knowledge would be improved if researchers reported confidence intervals rather than just the results of significance testing. The aforementioned authors provide the means to implement the PPE philosophy for sample size planning across a variety of analyses. Though we have presented these techniques for only three analyses, the PPE philosophy can be extended to any statistical tests via simple extensions of what we have already discussed.

In summary, we believe that the usefulness of existing sample size rules of thumb is a myth and the misapplications of these heuristics have generated a need for a different approach to sample size planning. Although power analysis is a more attractive candidate than using simple heuristics, we believe that it is also a myth that power analysis is the best alternative, because power analysis has the wrong focus. Power analysis focuses on correctly rejecting the null value, whereas researchers should actually be focused on having a sufficiently large sample size to yield reasonably precise estimates of the parameter of interest. Since power analysis and PPE require the researchers to provide similar inputs, we recommend using the PPE formulas to determine sample size requirements, because ultimately the focus should be on accuracy. In order to be a more productive science, we need to move away from our emphasis on statistical power toward the accuracy of the parameter of interest; this preferred approach is easily applicable for researchers when they are designing studies.

182 Scott Tonidandel et al.

References

Austin, J., Scherbaum, C. A., & Mahlman, R. A. (2002). History of research methods in industrial and organizational psychology: Measurement, design, analysis. In S. G. Rogelberg (Ed.), *Handbook of research methods in industrial and organizational psychology* (pp. 3–33). Malden, MA: Blackwell.

Bentler, P. M., & Chou, C. (1987). Practical issues in structural modeling. *Sociological Methods Research, 16*, 78–117.

Bonett, D. G., & Wright, T. A. (2011). Sample size requirements for multiple regression interval estimation. *Journal of Organizational Behavior, 32*, 822–830.

Cambré, B., Kippers, E., van Veldhoven, M., & De Witte, H. (2012). Jobs and organisations: Explaining group level differences in job satisfaction in the banking sector. *Personnel Review, 41*, 200–215.

Cohen, J. (1994). The earth is round ($p < .05$). *American Psychologist, 49*, 997–1003. http://dx.doi.org/10.1037//0003-066X.49.12.997

Cohen, J., & Cohen, P. (1983). *Applied multiple regression/correlation analysis for the behavioral sciences.* Hillsdale, NJ: Erlbaum.

Cortina, J. M., & Landis, R. S. (2009). When small effect sizes tell a big story. In C. E. Lance & R. J. Vandenberg (Eds.), *Statistical and methodological myths and urban legends* (287–308). New York, NY: Routledge.

Eisenberger, R., Karagonlar, G., Stinglhamber, F., Neves, P., Becker, T. E., & Gonzalez-Morales, M. G. (2010). Leader–member exchange and affective organizational commitment: The contribution of supervisor's organizational embodiment. *Journal of Applied Psychology, 95*, 1085–1103.

Gentry, W. A., & Sparks, T. E. (2012). A convergence/divergence perspective of leadership competencies managers believe are most important for success in organizations: A cross-cultural multilevel analysis of 40 countries. *Journal of Business Psychology, 27*, 15–30.

Goffin, R. D., & Gellatly, I. R. (2001). A multi-rater assessment of organizational commitment: Are self-report measures biased? *Journal of Organizational Behavior, 22*, 437–451.

Green, S. B. (1991). How many subjects does it take to do a regression analysis? *Multivariate Behavioral Research, 26*, 499–510.

Harris, R. J. (1975). *A primer of multivariate statistics.* New York, NY: Academic Press.

Hecker, K., & Violato, C. (2008). How much do differences in medical schools influence student performance? A longitudinal study employing hierarchical linear modeling. *Teaching and Learning in Medicine, 20*, 104–113.

Hedges, L. V., & Hedberg, E. C. (2007). Intraclass correlation values for planning group-randomized trials in education. *Educational Evaluation and Policy Analysis, 29*, 60–87.

Hox, J. J. (2010). *Multilevel analysis.* New York, NY: Routledge.

Jackson, D. L. (2003). Revisiting sample size and number of parameter estimates: Some support for the N:q hypothesis. *Structural Equation Modeling, 10*, 128–141.

Kelley, K., & Maxwell, S. E. (2003). Sample size for multiple regression: Obtaining regression coefficients that are accurate, not simply significant. *Psychological Methods, 8*, 305–321.

Kenny, D. (2005). Series editor's note. In R. B. Kline, *Principles and practice of structural equation modeling* (p. x). New York, NY: Guilford Press.

Kline, R. B. (2005). *Principles and practice of structural equation modeling.* New York, NY: Guilford Press.

Kline, R. B. (2011). *Principles and practice of structural equation modeling.* New York, NY: Guilford Press.

Size Matters **183**

Kozlowski, S. W., & Klein, K. J. (2000). A multilevel approach to theory and research in organizations: Contextual, temporal, and emergent processes. In K. Klein & S. Kozlowski (Eds.), *Multilevel theory, research, and methods in organizations: Foundations, extensions, and new directions* (pp. 3–90). San Francisco, CA: Jossey-Bass.

Kreft, I.G.G. (1996). *Are multilevel techniques necessary? An overview, including simulation studies.* Unpublished manuscript, California State University, Los Angeles, California.

Lai, K., & Kelley, K. (2011). Accuracy in parameter estimation for targeted effects in structural equation modeling: Sample size planning for narrow confidence intervals. *Psychological Methods, 16*, 127–148.

Lei, P., & Wu, Q. (2007). Introduction to structural equation modeling: Issues and practical considerations. *Educational Measurement: Issues and Practice, 26*, 33–43.

Maas, C.J.M., & Hox, J. J. (2004). Robustness issues in multilevel regression analysis. *Statistica Neerlandica, 58*, 127–137.

Maas, C.J.M., & Hox, J. J. (2005). Sufficient sample sizes for multilevel modeling. *Methodology, 1*, 86–92.

MacCallum, R. C., Browne, M. W., & Sugawara, H. M. (1996). Power analysis and determination of sample size for covariance structure modeling. *Psychological Methods, 1*, 130–149.

Major, D. A., Fletcher, T. D., Davis, D. D., & Germano, L. M. (2008). The influence of work-family culture and workplace relationships on work interference with family: A multilevel model. *Journal of Organizational Behavior, 29*, 881–897.

Maxwell, S. E. (2000). Sample size and multiple regression. *Psychological Methods, 5*, 434–458.

Moerbeek, M. N., & Teerenstra, S. (2011). Optimal design in multilevel experiments. In J. J. Hox and J. K. Roberts (Eds.), *Handbook of advanced multilevel analysis* (pp. 257–281). New York, NY: Routledge.

Nunnally, J. C. (1978). *Psychometric theory* (2nd ed.). New York, NY: McGraw-Hill.

Parent, M. C., & Moradi, B. (2009). Confirmatory factor analysis of the Conformity to Masculine Norms Inventory and development of the Conformity to Masculine Norms Inventory-46. *Psychology of Men and Masculinity, 10*, 175–189.

Raudenbush, S. W. (1997). Statistical analysis and optimal design for cluster randomized trials. *Psychological Methods, 2*, 173–185.

Raudenbush, S. W., Martinez, A., & Spybrook, J. (2007). Strategies for improving precision in group-randomized experiments. *Educational Evaluation and Policy Analysis, 1*, 5–29.

Saris, W. E., & Satorra, A. (1993). Power evaluations in structural equation models. In K. A. Bollen & J. S. Long (Eds.), *Testing structural equation models* (pp. 181–204). Newbury Park, CA: Sage.

Scherbaum, C. A., & Ferreter, J. M. (2009). Estimating statistical power and required sample sizes for organizational research using multilevel modeling. *Organizational Research Methods, 12*, 347–367.

Silvester, J., Patterson, F., Koczwara, A., & Ferguson, E. (2007). "Trust me . . .": Psychological and behavioral predictors of perceived physician empathy. *Journal of Applied Psychology, 92*, 519–527.

Snijders, T. A., & Bosker, R. J. (1993). Standard errors and sample sizes for two-level research. *Journal of Educational Statistics, 18*, 237–259.

Tabachnick, B. G., & Fidell, L. S. (1989). *Using multivariate statistics* (2nd ed.). Cambridge, MA: Harper & Row.

Tabachnick, B. G., & Fidell, L. S. (1996). *Using multivariate statistics* (3rd ed.). New York, NY: HarperCollins.

Taormina, R. J. (2009). Organizational socialization: The missing link between employee needs and organizational culture. *Journal of Managerial Psychology, 24*, 650–676.

PART III
Analytical Issues

9

WEIGHT A MINUTE . . . WHAT YOU SEE IN A WEIGHTED COMPOSITE IS PROBABLY NOT WHAT YOU GET!

Frederick L. Oswald, Dan J. Putka and Jisoo Ock

Organizational researchers are motivated by the idea that the data that we collect on workplace phenomena (e.g., data on employees, on teams, on the work environment) are ultimately supposed to provide better information and guidance than human intuition provides on its own. A considerable amount of empirical research has demonstrated experts are critically important for identifying variables and measures on which to collect data. Research has also shown that once experts identify variables and measures, a statistical combination of quantitative data (e.g., a simple sum or linear regression) is consistently superior to the judgments of a single expert. Remarkably, this conclusion is reached across a very diverse range of phenomena relevant to organizations, such as employee performance, training effectiveness, managerial success, achievement in school, and physical and psychological health (Dawes, Faust, & Meehl, 1989; Grove, Zald, Lebow, Snitz, & Nelson, 2000; Ostroff, 1991). The false belief that expert judgments trump algorithms is a stubborn one, for example in personnel selection practice (Highhouse, 2008). This is perhaps because the experts stand to gain financially from this belief by self-promoting it.

This superiority of statistical over expert reasoning is consistently achieved even when the data are combined in a relatively simple manner, such as through a linear composite. Examples of linear composite of variables include a simple unit-weighted sum or the predicted scores from a linear regression. Several examples of linear composite formation follow:

Real-World Examples

- A company might evaluate employees every 6 months on multiple dimensions of performance (e.g., 1–5 scores for customer service, task performance, teamwork, safety behavior), and all employees' scores are then multiplied by weights that the company believes reflect the relative importance of each dimension; finally, these weighted scores are added together to form an overall score for each employee. The company then makes use of that overall score when deciding on promotions, transfers, training, and termination.

- New employees might be required to enroll in and pass a number of training modules (e.g., knowledge of company policies, worker safety, diversity, teamwork). The grade in each module might be based on components such as homework, quizzes, and tests, and each one of these components might be counted as a differing percentage of the final grade based on their perceived importance or percentage of total effort required.

- U.S. military recruits take the Armed Services Vocational Aptitude Battery (ASVAB), from which an Armed Forces Qualification Test (AFQT) score is created. Specifically, the AFQT score is equal to the Arithmetic Reasoning scale score (AR), plus Math Knowledge (MK), plus two times the sum of Paragraph Comprehension (PC) and Word Knowledge (WK). Recruits are then selected on the basis of this weighted composite score.

Research-Based Examples

- When conducting a job analysis, each task for a job might be rated on its difficulty and weighted by a rating of its importance; these values could then be added up across all relevant tasks within jobs for the purposes of comparison across jobs or for estimating aspects of the utility of a job (e.g., the CREPID method; Cascio & Ramos, 1986).

- Multiple linear regression analysis is probably the most obvious and unvarnished practice of creating a weighted linear composite. In a typical and simple case, weights for multiple predictors are selected such that the correlation between the weighted composite and the criterion is maximized (i.e., the sum of squared errors of prediction are minimized).

- In exploratory factor analysis, each variable in the analysis is modeled as a linear composite of factor scores that are multiplied by their respective factor loadings (in addition to adding the model-defined residual). The loadings are the weights, and to determine appropriate loadings, modern software can adopt and apply a wide range of reasonable rotation criteria, such as varimax, oblimin, or others aimed at achieving simple structure (Bernaards & Jennrich, 2005).

- In meta-analysis, average results are often based on weighted linear composite of effect sizes (e.g., correlations): The weight for a given effect is larger to the extent the effect contributes more information to the meta-analysis (e.g., has a larger sample size, greater psychometric reliability, and less range restriction; Schmidt & Hunter, 2014).

You now are hopefully convinced that weighted linear composites abound in both real-world and research applications. Now we will dive into the actual computation of weighted linear composites as a prerequisite to introducing—and dispelling—four common urban legends that surround them.

Urban Legend 1

> **The Legend:** "Standardizing and summing variables means that each variable contributes equally to the composite."
>
> **Kernel of Truth:** This is only true when there are only two variables or all correlations between variables are equal (including all being equal to zero).
>
> **Full Truth:** With more than two variables, standardizing and summing variables almost never means that each variable contributes equally to the composite.

To understand and debunk this legend, it is useful to examine the formula for the variance of a composite. Consider a set of p variables that are standardized to z scores, so that the covariance matrix equals the correlation matrix shown in Table 9.1:

TABLE 9.1 Covariance Matrix Among Standardized Variables in a Unit-Weighted Composite

	Z_1	Z_2	Z_3	$\ldots$	Z_p
Z_1	1	r_{12}	r_{13}	$\ldots$	r_{1p}
Z_2	r_{21}	1	r_{23}	$\ldots$	r_{2p}
Z_3	r_{31}	r_{32}	1	$\ldots$	r_{3p}
$\ldots$	$\ldots$	$\ldots$	$\ldots$	$\ldots$	$\ldots$
Z_p	r_{p1}	r_{p2}	r_{p3}	$\ldots$	1

The subscripts here refer to the row and column of the variables, and therefore correlation (covariance) matrix is symmetric across the main diagonal (e.g., $r_{12} = r_{21}$). What is the total variance and covariance, $C(Z)$, represented in a unit-weighted composite of the variables in this correlation matrix? All you have to do is add up all of the elements (cells) of the matrix (Wang & Stanley, 1970):

$$C(Z) = 1 + r_{12} + r_{13} + \ldots + r_{1p} + r_{21} + 1 + r_{23} + \ldots + r_{2p} \ldots + r_{p1} + r_{p2} + r_{p3} + \ldots + 1, \text{ or simply:}$$
$$C(Z) = 2 \bullet (\text{sum of correlations on the lower diagonal}) + (\text{number of variables}),$$

190 Fred Oswald, Dan J. Putka, and Jisoo Ock

meaning that

$$C(Z) = 2\sum_{i>j} r_{ij} + p$$

The formula or some variation of it is often provided in textbooks as the variance of a composite of standardized variables (e.g., Ghiselli, Campbell, & Zedeck, 1981), and although it may not appear intuitive, it simply indicates that we are adding up all of the elements of a correlation matrix.

As will be discussed later, there are many ways to determine the contribution of each standardized variable to the variance of a composite. One simple (and, arguably, overly simplistic) way is to create p sums from the p columns of the correlation matrix above and assign each of the p sums to its respective variable (see Chase, 1960; Englehart, 1932; Pratt, 1987). This serves to assign all pairs of symmetric correlations fairly, giving one correlation to each variable in the pair being correlated. These p column sums also add up to the total variance of the composite, so to determine the percentage contribution of a given variable to the total, one takes its column sum and divides by the total composite variance. It is easy to see that by this definition of variable contribution, variable contributions to the composite will be unequal as long as there are multiple correlations (i.e., $p > 2$) and the correlations are also unequal (which is usually the case).

For a brief example, Table 9.2 shows a covariance matrix of four standardized variables, Z_1 to Z_4.

Given that the composite is the simple unit-weighted sum $C = Z_1 + Z_2 + Z_3 + Z_4$, then the total variance of the composite is simply 8.4, which is the sum of all the numbers within the covariance matrix (these are correlations because the variables are standardized). Then the proportion of a variable's contribution to the composite variance can simply be represented by each variable's column sum divided by this total: for example, for Z_2, the column sum is 2.5, and thus the contribution of Z_2 is $100(2.5/8.4) =$ about 30% of the composite variance. Thus, contrary to legend, simply standardizing and summing variables to form a composite does not mean that each of those variables will contribute equally to composite variance.

TABLE 9.2 Covariance Matrix Among four Standardized Variables in a Unit-Weighted Composite

	Z_1	Z_2	Z_3	Z_4
Z_1	1	.5	.3	.2
Z_2	.5	1	.6	.4
Z_3	.3	.6	1	.2
Z_4	.2	.4	.2	1
column sum	2.0	2.5	2.1	1.8
percent	23.8	29.8	25.0	21.4

Given standardization alone does not guarantee equal weighting, it is informative to extend the example to situations in which unstandardized (raw) variables are used to form a composite. Doing so will help establish a foundation for discussion of further urban legends around weighting. Determining the variance of a composite in this case is virtually the same as the case of standardized variables; the only difference here is that we are summing raw covariances instead of standardized covariances (i.e., correlations). The raw covariance between two variables X_i and X_j is simply $cov_{ij} = r_{ij}s_is_j$, where s_i and s_j are the respective standard deviations of the variables; this means that the covariance between a variable with itself is the variance, because the correlation between a variable and itself is $r_{ii} = 1$, $s_is_i = s_i^2$, and therefore $r_{ii}s_is_i = 1 \cdot s_i^2 = s_i^2$. Thus, the covariance matrix looks similar to the correlation matrix, as is shown in Table 9.3:

TABLE 9.3 Covariance Matrix Among Raw Variables in a Unit-Weighted Composite

	X_1	X_2	X_3	$\ldots$	X_p
X_1	s_1^2	$r_{12}s_1s_2$	$r_{13}s_1s_3$	$\ldots$	$r_{1p}s_1s_p$
X_2	$r_{21}s_2s_1$	s_2^2	$r_{23}s_2s_3$	$\ldots$	$r_{2p}s_2s_p$
X_3	$r_{31}s_3s_1$	$r_{31}s_3s_2$	s_3^2	$\ldots$	$r_{3p}s_3s_p$
$\ldots$	$\ldots$	$\ldots$	$\ldots$	$\ldots$	$\ldots$
X_p	$r_{p1}s_ps_1$	$r_{p2}s_ps_2$	$r_{p3}s_ps_3$	$\ldots$	s_p^2

(In matrix notation, this is **SRS**, where S is the $p \times p$ diagonal matrix of standard deviations and **R** is the $p \times p$ correlation matrix.) There is symmetry in the covariances across the main diagonal here as there was with the correlation matrix (e.g., $cov_{12} = cov_{21}$), and like the correlation matrix, the total variance and covariance in a composite of these variables, $C(X)$, is also represented by the sum of all elements in the matrix:

$$C(X) = s_1^2 + r_{12}s_1s_2 + r_{13}s_1s_3 + \ldots + r_{1p}s_1s_p + r_{21}s_2s_1 + s_2^2 + r_{23}s_2s_3 + \ldots$$
$$+ r_{2p}s_2s_p \ldots + r_{p1}s_ps_1 + r_{p2}s_ps_2 + r_{p3}s_ps_3 + \ldots + s_p^2, \text{ or simply}$$
$C(X) = 2 \cdot$(sum of covariances on the lower diagonal) + (sum of the variances of the variables)

meaning that

$$C(X) = 2\sum_{i>j} r_{ij}s_is_j + \sum_{i=1}^{p} s_i^2$$

Again, this latter formula (or some variant) is typically presented in textbooks for the variance of the composite, but many people find it inscrutable and therefore accept it on faith. The formula is more understandable once it is known that it is simply equal to the sum of all the elements in the covariance matrix.

192 Fred Oswald, Dan J. Putka, and Jisoo Ock

If we operationalize the contribution of each variable to the variance of this unstandardized composite as the sum of cells for each column in the covariance matrix (just as we did in the case for standardized variables), then it is obvious that the relative contribution of a variable is not only affected by the differences in correlations; it is also affected by the differences in standard deviations of each variable. This latter point makes sense conceptually and is often the reason we standardize in the first place: Annual income, test scores, and years of prior work experience might all be expressed on very different numeric scales, and if they are not standardized, then annual income would generally be the most influential variable simply by virtue of having the largest natural scale. Other times, we want the natural variation across variables to influence the importance of the composite, where variables in a composite with larger amounts of variance will generally be more important than variables with smaller amounts. Unfortunately this latter desire can usually only be fulfilled when the metrics of the variables are the same.

The illustrations serve to illustrate the importance of both covariance and variance of variables that contribute to a composite. We next turn our attention to issues of applying weights to variables in a composite to influence their relative contribution to the variance of the composite, which leads to a second urban legend.

Urban Legend 2

The Legend: "Weights that are given to variables reflect their relative contribution to the composite score."

Kernel of Truth: This can happen, but only under mathematical conditions of the sort that one would not anticipate (e.g., two uncorrelated standardized variables, original weights of 1 and $\sqrt{2}$, and the first weight is doubled).

Full Truth: This myth is generally false because nominal weights (the weights applied) are not the same as effective weights (the weights indicating the relative importance of variables in the composite).

It is a straightforward extension to show how weighting each variable affects composite variance—whether you are doubling the weight of a variable or otherwise. In general, weighting a variable means changing the variable's original standard deviation to the original standard deviation times the weight. Here is an example of weighting a variable: Take a variable X that has a standard deviation of $s_X = 5$. Now say that you would like a standard deviation of 10; this means multiplying each of the scores in X by the weight $w = 2$ so that the new standard deviation is $w{\cdot}s_X = 2{\cdot}5 = 10$. The reason this weighting effect is important to keep

Weight a Minute **193**

in mind is that, per the earlier illustration, the standard deviation of a variable plays a fundamental role in how much it contributes to composite variance.

If you have ever created z scores, then you have committed the act of weighting a variable: For example, let's take the variable X with a standard deviation of $s_X = 5$. Weighting the variable X with the weight $w = 1/5$ effectively divides each scores in X by 5, and thus the standard deviation of the new weighted variable will be $(1/5){\bullet}5 = (1/s_X){\bullet}s_X = 1$. As we showed before, the variable's original standard deviation is adjusted by a factor that is equal to the weight; the weight in this case just happens to be the inverse of the variable's original standard deviation, so the new standard deviation becomes 1 after weighting.

When there are multiple variables in a composite, how does changing a variable's weight affect its contribution to composite variance? To illustrate, let's return to Urban Legend 1 and consider what happens if we double the weight applied to one of the variables in our composite. Generally speaking, say that we weight X_1 by the value w, and therefore its standard deviation s_1 changes to s_1^*, where $s_1^* = w{\bullet}s_1$; then regarding the components of composite variance, the following highlighted cells in Table 9.4 will also change:

TABLE 9.4 Covariance Matrix Among Raw Variables in a Weighted Composite

	X_1	X_2	X_3	...	X_p
X_1	s_1^{*2}	$r_{12}s_1^*s_2$	$r_{13}s_1^*s_3$	...	$r_{1p}s_1^*s_p$
X_2	$r_{21}s_2s_1^*$	s_2^2	$r_{23}s_2s_3$	...	$r_{2p}s_2s_p$
X_3	$r_{31}s_3s_1^*$	$r_{31}s_3s_2$	s_3^2	...	$r_{3p}s_3s_p$
...	...	...	...	...	...
X_p	$r_{p1}s_ps_1^*$	$r_{p2}s_ps_2$	$r_{p3}s_ps_3$	...	s_p^2

As you can see, composite variance changes as a function of the standard deviation of X_1 changing on its own; however, all correlations involving X_1 and the other X variables in the composite are multiplied by this standard deviation as well, which is why changing the standard deviations of variables by weighting has a complex effect on composite variance whenever the variables in the composite are correlated.

In other words, people who create, apply, and interpret weights applied to variables in a linear composite often forget that a given weight does not only apply to a given variable; it also applies to all the other variables with which it correlates. In other words, as the title of the chapter indicates, the *nominal weights* that you see or use (i.e., the weights often thought to be the desired contributions of each variable in a composite) are usually not the same as the *effective weights* that result (i.e., the actual contribution of each variable in a composite; see Guion, 2011). These effective weights are often unknown and therefore rarely understood, which in turn could have important practical implications. For example, a company's use of weighted composites in high-stakes personnel decisions might be brought to legal

194 Fred Oswald, Dan J. Putka, and Jisoo Ock

challenge, such as in cases where the composite scores are used to compare people with one another (i.e., norm-referenced tests) or a composite cutoff score has to be justified (i.e., criterion-referenced tests). The legal context might further consider subgroup differences and adverse impact in the context of a selection system that involves weighting scores and setting cutoffs on composites or components thereof.

Now turning to the previous example with a composite of four standardized variables, Z_1 to Z_4, what if a company thought that the third variable was twice as important as the rest of the variables? That company might then naively decide to weigh that variable twice as much in a linear composite of the variables, such that $C = Z_1 + Z_2 + 2{\bullet}Z_3 + Z_4$. Given the previous discussion, this weighting makes the standard deviation of Z_3 equal to $w{\bullet}s_3 = 2{\bullet}1 = 2$, instead of 1 like the other standardized variables.

Taking this weighting into account, let us now look in Table 9.5 at the covariance matrix and the contribution of the variables to the composite in a similar way as we did previously with the unweighted composite:

TABLE 9.5 Covariance Matrix Among Four Standardized Variables in a Weighted Composite

	Z_1	Z_2	Z_3	Z_4
Z_1	1	.5	2${\bullet}$.3	.2
Z_2	.5	1	2${\bullet}$.6	.4
Z_3	2${\bullet}$.3	2${\bullet}$.6	2${\bullet}$1	2${\bullet}$.2
Z_4	.2	.4	2${\bullet}$.2	1
column sum	2.3	3.1	4.2	2.0
percent	19.8	26.7	36.2	17.2

The total variance of the linear composite (i.e., the sum of the variance-covariance matrix) becomes 11.6. The contribution of Z_3 to the linear composite variance was 25% before but is 36.2% now; thus, giving Z_3 a weight of 2 does not double its contribution, and in neither case is the contribution of each variable proportional to the weighted values.

Urban Legend 3

The Legend: "If one limits the number of points that each variable can contribute to the composite score, then the relative contribution of each variable to the composite is reflected in the proportion of points allocated to each variable."

Kernel of Truth: Allocating points to variables *does* limit the variables' contributions to the maximum possible composite *score*—but this is not the same as the variables' contributions to composite *variance*.

> **Full Truth:** Differences in points (nominal weights) given to variables, standard deviations, and correlations *together* drive the relative contribution of variables to composite variance.

This urban legend reflects a situation that we have often confronted in practice in which organizations attempt to force the relative influences on each variable by only allowing a certain number of points for each. For example, say that an organization is building a "promotion potential" composite formed from four variables: (a) personality scores (X_1), (b) ability test scores (X_2), (c) leadership training performance (X_3), and (d) past job performance (X_4). They decide they want to give past performance the most weight and the other variables less weight in determining the composite, so they rescale the four variables to have ranges from 0 to 10, 0 to 20, 0 to 30, and 0 to 40, respectively, and therefore the maximum score a person can get on the composite is 100 points. The incorrect belief or myth here is that this will allow them to conclude that the relative contribution of each variable to composite variance is 10%, 20%, 30%, and 40%, respectively.

The motivation for this approach is understandable, and certainly this is a very intuitive way for lay decision makers to think about weighting issue. Unfortunately, this approach completely disregards the fact that not only the caps on the scores (the nominal weights) affect the influence of the variables; the standard deviations and correlations for the variables also have critical influences in driving the relative contribution of each variable to composite variance. For example, if everyone allocating points agrees that the variable with the 40-point maximum is very important, there will be little variance in that variable, and therefore it will account for far less than 40% of composite variance.

To illustrate this more closely, let us say that in the example just described, the data collected on the variables X_1, through X_4 have the following standard deviations: 5, 7, 5, and 3, respectively. Furthermore, to keep things simple, assume that they all correlate .30, and unit nominal weights are applied when forming the composite score (i.e., the variables are just summed together). Table 9.6 presents the covariance matrix and the breakdown of their effective weights, which, again, simply reflect the sums of the columns.

As one can see, in terms of proportion of composite variance, X_4 accounts for far less than 40% of composite variance the organization had intended (12.4%), and the contributions of other variables are not in line with their intended contributions either. Thus, simply capping the number of points a variable can contribute to the composite is not sufficient for achieving a desired relative contribution for each variable—attention still needs to be given to the nominal weights applied to each variable, its standard deviation, and correlation with other variables.

With this caution in mind, then what is one to do? Fortunately, variables contributing to a composite vary in their correlations and variances, and then a simple

196 Fred Oswald, Dan J. Putka, and Jisoo Ock

TABLE 9.6 Covariance Matrix Among Four Raw Variables in a Weighted Composite

	X_1	X_2	X_3	X_4
X_1	5•5	.3•5•7	.3•5•5	.3•5•3
X_2	.3•7•5	7•7	.3•7•5	.3•7•3
X_3	.3•5•5	.3•5•7	5•5	.3•5•3
X_4	.3•3•5	.3•3•6	.3•3•5	3•3
column sum	47.5	76.3	47.5	24.3
percent	24.3	39.0	24.3	12.4
(intended contribution)	(10.0)	(20.0)	(30.0)	(40.0)

computer program can determine the nominal weights that will yield desired effective weights. Linear programming, for instance, can quickly find a set of positive weights that provide the desired variable contributions in a composite (i.e., the desired matrix column sums). The first component in a principal components analysis (PCA) finds weights that, when applied to the variables, maximize the variance of the linear composite. This might be a desirable criterion under the strong assumption that all of the unique variance of each variable in the component is reliable variance, because then the component potentially maximizes the validity of the composite.

Urban Legend 4

The Legend: "Effective weights accurately reflect the relative contribution of variables to composite variance."

Kernel of Truth: Wang and Stanley's (1970) longstanding concept of "effective weights" (i.e., the sum of a column in a weighted covariance matrix) provides just *one* way to index this relative contribution.

Full Truth: There are numerous indices that reflect a variable's relative contribution to a composite; each index provides a different perspective on the meaning of a variable's "contribution." Alternatives may be desirable. Suppressor effects can be problematic when using effective weights, for instance.

All of the urban legends mentioned illustrate common myths surrounding weighting in linear composites. They all represent variants on a common theme— the nominal weights applied to variables and the relative contribution of those variables to composite variance are often two very different things. From a practical perspective, what applied researchers and practitioners would ideally like to know is what set of nominal weights they *should* use to achieve a particular relative contribution of variables that is desired for their particular situation. Unlike the illustrations given, executing this is a particularly thorny issue. It is challenging on two fronts—one is computational, the other is conceptual.

From a computational perspective, linear programming, for instance, can quickly find a set of positive weights that provide the desired column sums (variable contributions) in the matrices based on standardized or unstandardized variables, such as those matrices we have presented. However, all of the illustrations are based on the notion that the sums of the columns in the weighted covariance matrix (i.e., the operational definition of "effective weights," per Wang & Stanley, 1970), provide accurate representation of the "contribution" of a given variable to a composite variance. As we will see, however, "the contribution" of each variable can change, even with a fixed pattern of standard deviations, correlations, and nominal weights, and this change depends on how one operationally defines "contribution." Depending on one's definition, one can come to different answers for what nominal weights are required to achieve the desired weighting. Thus, the first conceptual challenge researchers must confront when attempting to derive a set of nominal weights that will result in a target set of relative contributions for each variable will be defining precisely what is meant by "contribution."

One way to think about the options for each variable's "contribution" to composite variance is within the context of multiple linear regression (MLR), where standardized predictors $X_1, X_2, X_3 \ldots$ are weighted by regression coefficients b_1, b_2, b_3 to create the linear composite $b_1X_1 + b_2X_2 + b_3X_3. \ldots$. Regression weights are chosen to maximize the correlation between the composite and the standardized criterion Y to be predicted (i.e., the sum of squared errors of prediction is minimized). In the context of MLR, regression coefficients are nominal weights, not effective weights. MLR is thus a special case of the general formula for a weighted linear composite, $w_1X_1 + w_2X_2 + w_3X_3. \ldots$, regression weights in b are empirically informed by sample validities and predictor correlations, whereas the weights in $\mathbf{w}$ in a linear composite could be informed by anything (e.g., expert judgments, meta-analytic data). No matter how weights are derived, they can be empirically examined for how they affect the contribution of each variable (predictor in the case of MLR) to the composite that results.

In what ways might the "contribution" of a variable differ? One way is by considering *both* the validity and adverse impact of a composite rather than validity alone. Through a variety of simulations and applications, organizational researchers have found that varying variables' weights and their standard deviations[1] has a practical effect on the validity and adverse impact of a composite (Hattrup, Rock, & Scalia, 1997; Murphy & Shiarella, 1997; Schmitt, Rogers, Chan, Sheppard, & Jennings, 1997). These researchers have emphasized that no single set of weights is ideal: Weights that optimize validity across multiple criteria will not maximize validity for any particular criterion (Green, 1969), and typically, no set of weights can maximize validity and minimize adverse impact at the same time. This latter point is called the longstanding "validity-diversity dilemma" (Ployhart & Holtz, 2008; Sackett, Schmitt, Ellingson, & Kabin, 2001), where one has to select a desired and obtainable value of validity before being able to optimize adverse impact, or vice versa. Hopefully, some pair of validity and adverse impact values is desirable along this pareto-optimal frontier (De Corte, Lievens, & Sackett, 2007).

Other modern methods have provided alternative indices to effective weights for understanding the relative importance of each predictor. The indices could apply to any type of weights applied to variables in a composite, although they are generally derived and discussed in the regression (MLR) literature. For example, *dominance analysis* (Budescu, 1993; Chevan & Sutherland, 1991)[2] examines all possible MLR submodels and determines whether a predictor always contributes more unique variance across all submodels (i.e., shows complete dominance) or whether it contributes more unique variance on average across submodels (i.e., shows conditional dominance). Even without findings of complete or conditional dominance, examining the patterns of prediction across all possible subsets of MLR can be informative (Madden & Bottenberg, 1963). *Uniqueness coefficients* is one element of dominance analysis as well as commonality analysis (e.g., Mood, 1971; Nimon, Lewis, Kane, & Haynes, 2008), referring to the amount of variance that a variable contributes to a composite when it is entered last in a hierarchical MLR; a predictor is relatively more important if it has a larger uniqueness coefficient. *Relative weight analysis* (Fabbris, 1980; Genizi, 1993; Johnson, 2000) does not examine all MLR submodels but instead distributes the predictable variance (or R^2) from the regression model across the predictors as a joint function of their validities (i.e., independent contributions to the criterion) and intercorrelations (i.e., independent relationships with one another). The R code packages "yhat" (Nimon & Oswald, 2013) and "relaimpo" (Groemping, 2006) compute these relative importance indices as well as others, but it is not unexpected that such software needs to catch up with the research literature that has extended the fundamental problem of relative importance into domains involving multiple criteria (Huo & Budescu, 2009; LeBreton & Tonidandel, 2008), logistic regression (Azen & Traxel, 2008; Tonidandel & LeBreton, 2010), interaction and nonlinearity (LeBreton, Tonidandel, & Krasikova, 2013), multilevel modeling (Luo & Azen, 2012), and conditions in which the number of variables is large and might even exceed the sample size (Strobl, Malley, & Tutz, 2009; Zou, Hastie, & Tibshirani, 2007). It is an underappreciated fact that these methods can be applied without a criterion, where the weighted composite is used as the criterion instead (such that $R^2 = 1$ for the regression; see Scherbaum, Putka, Naidoo, & Youssefina, 2010). With this approach, one could determine how rational weights are aligned with a variety of variable importance weights.

A series of issues and challenges remain for estimating the contribution of a variable to a weighted linear composite. First, there is the problem of equifinality: Depending on the purpose to which composite scores are put, a wide range of variable weights can lead to the same practical outcomes. MLR yields a unique set of regression coefficients that maximize R^2 for a specific sample, but when the goal is to generalize beyond the sample into other samples, then it turns out that an infinite set of alternative weights (fungible weights) that yield an identical value of R^2 is possible (Waller, 2008), and some of these sets of weights might suggest a different ordering of the relative importance of the predictors than other sets of weights do. A similar phenomenon occurs for rational weighting without a criterion in the presence of correlated predictors, where composites with different weights are often correlated .90 and higher, which approaches the limit of the composites' psychometric reliabilities, suggesting similar outcomes in top-down selection decisions (Ree, Caretta, & Earles, 1998).

Second, there is the issue of suppressor effects. Suppressors are predictors in MLR that are important when they enhance the prediction of other predictors in the model (by suppressing variance in those variables that is unrelated to the criterion; in the personality domain, see Collins & Schmidt, 1997). Dominance analysis and other methods that examine all possible regression models can help identify the importance of a predictor as a suppressor. Suppressors are problematic for relative weights analysis and for other indices because the validity of a classic suppressor, and thus its relative importance, is zero; therefore, other approaches to determining relative importance in the presence of suppression effects is needed (Shieh, 2006).

The third issue to consider is the effects of measurement error variance: A variable with low reliability will have a weaker regression coefficient in MLR than if the variable was measured with high reliability. This is appropriate when the goal is practical: Variables in a predictor composite should be less important if they are less reliable. However, if the goal is theoretical—to understand the importance of latent variables predicting a latent outcome—then it might be important to estimate psychometric reliability of the predictors and criterion and then estimate the relative importance of the variables at the latent level. Although psychometric corrections for measurement reliability are often routinely applied (e.g., in meta-analysis), they are only fruitful to the extent that reliability coefficients successfully operationalize the structure of measurement error variance (DeShon, 1998; Jarjoura & Brennan, 1982). Note that psychometric corrections for measurement error variance are to improve one's *theoretical* understanding of variable relationships in a composite; corrections come with larger standard errors, and they will generally not improve the *practical* predictive power of individual scores on the weighted composite.

Fourth, variables may be under the psychometric influence of range restriction. For instance, selecting on a weighted composite itself can alter weights and correlations dramatically in the selected sample (Sackett, Lievens, Berry, & Landers, 2007), and selection on variables related to those variables in the composite can have similar effects. Thus, to understand the relative importance of variables in an unrestricted sample, it is helpful to have as much information on the unrestricted sample as possible (e.g., variances and covariances) and to have foreknowledge of the range restriction processes associated with the sample (Sackett & Yang, 2000).

As mentioned with regard to corrections for measurement error variance, range restriction corrections can be made to estimate variable importance in the population of interest; corrections here also will not serve to improve the prediction of individual cases. The systematic distorting effects of measurement error variance and range restriction on the relative importance of variables have long been acknowledged (e.g., Heilman, 1929), yet there is room for additional conceptual and empirical work to be conducted.

Fifth, a consideration of statistical power might guide when weighted composites are used: Empirically weighted variables in a composite (e.g., from MLR) might be most informative when they are developed on the basis of large and generalizable sample sizes (i.e., weights do not capitalize on random errors); it may also be helpful to analyze, examine, and deal with data that indicate nonnormal distributions and multivariate outliers. Alternatively, applying rational weights or unit weights may end up being the most useful (robust) for smaller sample sizes and without much marginal loss in many practical situations (Thorndike, 1986). The challenge might be to determine the common situation in which sample sizes seem to be in between these two extremes, which obviously will depend on the psychometric and conceptual nature of the variables and sample involved, whether a criterion is available to incorporate validity considerations into predictor weighting, the nature of judges providing rational weights, and so on. A recent example in the domain of biodata (Cucina, Caputo, Thibodeaux, & Maclane, 2012) indicates that moderate sample sizes (e.g., $N = 150$) can yield practical gains in prediction from empirical instead of rational weights applied to items in a scoring composite. In other cases, sample sizes often must be prohibitively large to reap the benefit of more complex scoring methods, or there may be no benefit at all, and unit weights remain sufficient (Bobko, Roth, & Buster, 2007; Schmidt, 1971). Weighting the more reliable variables in a composite can serve to improve validity, but only up to a point; overweighting the most reliable variables can reduce validity (Kane & Case, 2004).

Sixth might be to reverse the problem in some cases, similar to what was discussed in Urban Legend 3: Rather than weighting composite variables rationally or empirically with MLR, then determining the importance of the variables (i.e., specifying nominal weights to get effective weights), one might first determine the desired importance of each variable in the composite and then determine the variable weights that need to be applied in order to achieve or best approximate that goal (i.e., specifying effective weights to get desired nominal weights). This is an age-old problem (e.g., Dunnette & Hoggatt, 1957; Wilks, 1938) with some general solutions motivated by the factor analysis of groups of related variables (MacDonald, 1968). The general challenge is multifaceted because relative importance has been variously defined: For example, how might variables be weighted in a linear composite to achieve desired types of dominance in a dominance analysis, or how might variables be weighted in a linear composite to achieve desired relative weights? Understanding what these weights have to be can be illustrative; for instance, cognitive ability tests often have to be down-weighted much more than anticipated or reasonable to meet the desired goal of avoiding adverse impact (Sackett & Ellingson, 1997); or a similar conclusion is that adding noncognitive tests to a predictor composite containing a cognitive variable with a large mean subgroup difference typically does not have much of a useful effect (Potosky, Bobko, & Roth, 2005; Ryan, Ployhart, & Friedel, 1998).

Conclusion

The creation of weighted linear composites is ubiquitous in organizational practices such as performance appraisal, training assessment, and personnel selection, where variables are weighted and added together to form a linear composite. When there either are a large number of these variables or when there are fewer variables that are very highly correlated, the composite score may not be very sensitive to different weights that are selected. Alternatively, when there are a moderate number of variables that are conceptually distinct and there are enough data to support empirical distinctions, weighting variables may affect the composite as well as estimates of the variables' relative contributions to the composite.

This would not be a chapter worth reading if there weren't myths to be busted. The four myths we addressed center around a common theme: The weights applied to each variable in a linear composite—either by experts (SME weights), by statistical analysis (linear regression), or by default (unit weights)—are almost always different from the relative contribution of each variable in a composite, and yet weights are often viewed as a direct way to operationalize variable importance.

To complicate matters, there is not one form of "relative contribution." Even though we have demonstrated the contribution of weighted variables to composite, the fact that variables are usually correlated means that their contributions to a composite overlap, and we point out that multiple statistical methods exist for allocating shared contributions back to each variable and determining the variables' relative importance in a composite. Adding to these complications are factors both seen and unseen, both practical and psychometric. Practical factors include the issue of missing data, of unique or shifting expert opinion, and the use of criterion-referenced testing (where comparisons against a standard or cutoff are the focus) rather than comparisons between people. Psychometric factors include those that meta-analysis methods have sensitized organizational researchers to: measurement error variance, range restriction, and sampling error variance (Schmidt & Hunter, 2014). Some of these factors might be addressed through statistical correction; these corrections may lead to better estimates of variable importance but usually do not improve prediction or rank ordering afforded by a composite.

In conclusion, we hope this chapter has heighted awareness of how variable weighting exists everywhere in organizational research (regression analysis, job analysis, meta-analysis) and that a number of urban legends and myths surround

202 Fred Oswald, Dan J. Putka, and Jisoo Ock

the practice of creating and interpreting weighted composites. We believe that in large-sample data sets, it is valuable to explore multiple alternative approaches for understanding the nature of variances and covariances of variables in a weighted composite—the approaches that currently exist as well as approaches derived in the future. This process of exploration will yield more important insights than searching for a single mechanistic approach or definitive answer to the problem of weighting composites.

Notes

1 Although note that changing a standard deviation is the same as changing a weight (e.g., changing a variable's weight from 1 to 2 is the same as doubling its standard deviation).
2 Note that dominance analysis is mathematically identical to the Shapley value in economics (see Lipovetsky & Conklin, 2001; Shapley, 1953)

References

Azen, R., & Traxel, N. (2008). Using dominance analysis to determine predictor importance in multiple regression. *Journal of Educational and Behavioral Statistics, 34,* 319–347.

Bernaards, C. A., & Jennrich, R. I. (2005). Gradient projection algorithms and software for arbitrary rotation criteria in factor analysis. *Educational and Psychological Measurement, 65,* 676–696.

Bobko, P., Roth, P. L., & Buster, M. A. (2007). The usefulness of unit weights in creating composite scores: A literature review, application to content validity, and meta-analysis. *Organizational Research Methods, 10,* 689–709.

Budescu, D. V. (1993). Dominance analysis: A new approach to the problem of relative importance of predictors in multiple regression. *Psychological Bulletin, 114,* 542–551.

Cascio, W. F., & Ramos, R. A. (1986). Development and application of a new method for assessing job performance in behavioral/economic terms. *Journal of Applied Psychology, 71,* 20–28.

Chase, C. I. (1960). Computation of variance accounted for in multiple correlation. *Journal of Experimental Education, 28,* 265–266.

Chevan, A., & Sutherland, M. (1991). Hierarchical partitioning. *The American Statistician, 45,* 90–96.

Collins, J. M., & Schmidt, F. L. (1997). Can suppressor variables enhance criterion-related validity in the personality domain? *Educational and Psychological Measurement, 57,* 924–936.

Cucina, J. M., Caputo, P. M., Thibodeaux, H. F., & Maclane, C. N. (2012). Unlocking the key to biodata scoring: A comparison of empirical, rational, and hybrid approaches at different sample sizes. *Personnel Psychology, 65,* 385–428.

Dawes, R. M., Faust, D., & Meehl, P. E. (1989). Clinical versus actuarial judgment. *Science, 143,* 1668–1674.

De Corte, W., Lievens, F., & Sackett, P. R. (2007). Combining predictors to achieve optimal trade-offs between selection quality and adverse impact. *Journal of Applied Psychology, 92,* 1380–1393.

DeShon, R. P. (1998). A cautionary note on measurement error corrections in structural equation models. *Psychological Methods, 3,* 412–423.

Dunnette, M. D. & Hoggatt, A. C. (1957). Deriving a composite score from several measures of the same attribute. *Educational and Psychological Measurement, 17*, 423–434.

Englehart, M. D. (1932). The relative contributions of certain factors to individual differences in arithmetical problem solving ability. *Journal of Experimental Education, 1*, 19–27.

Fabbris, L. (1980). Measures of predictor variable importance in multiple regression: An additional suggestion. *Quality & Quantity, 4*, 787–792.

Genizi, A. (1993). Decomposition of R^2 in multiple regression with correlated regressors. *Statistica Sinica, 3*, 407–420.

Ghiselli, E. E., Campbell, J. P., & Zedeck, S. (1981). *Measurement theory for the behavioral sciences.* San Francisco, CA: Freeman & Company.

Green, B. F. (1969). Best linear composites with a specified structure. *Psychometrika, 34*, 301–318.

Groemping, U. (2006). Relative importance for linear regression in R: The package *relaimpo*. *Journal of Statistical Software, 17*.

Grove, W. M., Zald, D. H., Lebow, B. S., Snitz, B. E., & Nelson, C. (2000). Clinical vs. mechanical prediction: A meta-analysis. *Psychological Assessment, 12*, 19–30.

Guion, R. M. (2011). *Assessment, measurement, and prediction for personnel selection systems.* New York, NY: Routledge.

Hattrup, K., Rock, J., & Scalia, C. (1997). The effects of varying conceptualizations of job performance on adverse impact, minority hiring, and predicted performance. *Journal of Applied Psychology, 82*, 656–664.

Heilman, J. D. (1929). Factors determining grade achievement and grade location. *Pedagogical Seminary and Journal of Genetic Psychology, 36*, 435–457.

Highhouse, S. (2008). Stubborn reliance on intuition and subjectivity in employee selection. *Industrial and Organizational Psychology: Perspectives on Science and Practice, 1*, 333–342.

Huo, Y., & Budescu, D. V. (2009). An extension of dominance analysis to canonical correlation analysis. *Multivariate Behavioral Research, 44*, 688–709.

Jarjoura, D., & Brennan, R. L. (1982). A variance components model for measurement procedures associated with a table of specifications. *Applied Psychological Measurement, 6*, 161–171.

Johnson, J. W. (2000). A heuristic method for estimating the relative weight of predictor variables in multiple regression. *Multivariate Behavioral Research, 35*, 1–19.

Kane, M., & Case, S. M. (2004). The reliability and validity of composite scores. *Applied Measurement in Education, 17*, 221–240.

LeBreton, J. M, Tonidandel, S. (2008). Multivariate relative importance: Extending relative weight analysis to multivariate criterion spaces. *Journal of Applied Psychology, 93*, 329–345.

LeBreton, J. M., Tonidandel, S., & Krasikova, D. V. (2013). Residualized relative importance analysis: A technique for the comprehensive decomposition of variance in higher-order regression models. *Organizational Research Methods, 16*, 449–473.

Lipovetsky, S., & Conklin, M. (2001). Analysis of regression in game theory approach. *Applied Stochastic Models in Business and Industry, 17*, 319–330.

Luo, W., & Azen, R. (2012). Determining predictor importance in hierarchical linear models using dominance analysis. *Journal of Educational and Behavioral Statistics, 38*, 3–31.

MacDonald, R. P. (1968). A unified treatment of the weighting problem. *Psychometrika, 33*, 351–381.

Madden, J. M., & Bottenberg, R. A. (1963). Use of an all possible combination solution to certain multivariate regression problems. *Journal of Applied Psychology, 47*, 365–366.

Mood, A. M. (1971). Partitioning variance in multiple regression analyses as a tool for developing learning models. *American Educational Research Journal, 8*, 191–202.

Murphy, K. R., & Shiarella, A. H. (1997). Implications of the multidimensional nature of job performance for the validity of selection tests: Multivariate frameworks for studying test validity. *Personnel Psychology, 50*, 823–854.

Nimon, K., Lewis, M., Kane, R., & Haynes, R. M. (2008). An R package to compute commonality coefficients in the multiple regression case: An introduction to the package and a practical example. *Behavioral Research Methods, 40*, 457–466.

Nimon, K. F., & Oswald, F. L. (2013). Understanding the results of multiple linear regression: Beyond standardized regression coefficients. *Organizational Research Methods, 16*, 650–674.

Ostroff, C. (1991). Training effectiveness and scoring schemes: A comparison. *Personnel Psychology, 44*, 353–374.

Ployhart, R. E., & Holtz, B. C. (2008). The diversity-validity dilemma: Strategies for reducing racioethnic and sex subgroup differences and adverse impact in selection. *Personnel Psychology, 61*, 153–172.

Potosky, D., Bobko, P., & Roth, P. L. (2005). Forming composites of cognitive ability and alternative measures to predict job performance and reduce adverse impact: Corrected estimates and realistic expectations. *International Journal of Selection and Assessment, 13*, 304–315.

Pratt, J. W. (1987). Dividing the indivisible: Using simple symmetry to partition variance explained. In T. Pukilla & S. Duntaneu (Eds.), *Proceedings of the Second Tampere Conference in Statistics* (pp. 245–260). University of Tampere, Finland.

Ree, M. J., Carretta, T. R., & Earles, J. A. (1998). In top-down decisions, weighting variables does not matter: A consequence of Wilk's Theorem. *Organizational Research Methods, 1*, 407–420.

Ryan, A. M., Ployhart, R. P., & Friedel, L. A. (1998). Using personality testing to reduce adverse impact: A cautionary note. *Journal of Applied Psychology, 83*, 298–307.

Sackett, P. R., & Ellingson, J. E. (1997). The effects of forming multi-predictor composites on group differences and adverse impact. *Personnel Psychology, 50*, 707–721.

Sackett, P. R., Lievens, F., Berry, C. M., & Landers, R. N. (2007). A cautionary note on the effects of range restriction on predictor intercorrelations, *92*, 538–544.

Sackett, P. R., Schmitt, N., Ellingson, J. E., & Kabin, M. B. (2001). High-stakes testing in employment, credentialing, and higher education: Prospects in a post-affirmative-action world. *American Psychologist, 56*, 302–318.

Sackett, P. R., & Yang, H. (2000). Correction for range restriction: An expanded typology. *Journal of Applied Psychology, 85*, 112–118.

Scherbaum, C., Putka, D. J., Naidoo, L., & Youssefina, D. (2010). Key driver analyses: Current trends, problems, and alternative approaches. In S. Albrecht (Ed.), *Handbook of employee engagement: Models, measures, and practice* (pp. 182–196). Cheltenham, UK: Edward-Elgar Publishing House.

Schmidt, F. L. (1971). The relative efficiency of regression and simple unit predictor weights in applied differential psychology. *Educational and Psychological Measurement, 31*, 699–714.

Schmidt, F. L., & Hunter, J. E. (2014). *Methods of meta-analysis: Correcting error and bias in research findings* (3rd ed.). Thousand Oaks, CA: Sage.

Schmitt, N., Rogers, W., Chan, D., Sheppard, L., & Jennings, D. (1997). Adverse impact and predictive efficiency of various predictor combinations. *Journal of Applied Psychology, 82*, 719–730.

Shapley, L. S. (1953). A value for *n*-person games. In H. W. Kuhn & A. W. Tucker (Eds.), *Contributions to the theory of games* (vol. 2; pp. 307–317). Princeton, NJ: Princeton University Press.

Shieh, G. (2006). Suppression situations in multiple linear regression. *Educational and Psychological Measurement, 66*, 435–447.

Strobl, C., Malley, J., & Tutz, G. (2009). An introduction to recursive partitioning: Rationale, application, and characteristics of classification and regression trees, bagging, and random forests. *Psychological Methods, 14*, 323–348.

Thorndike, R. L. (1986). The role of general ability in prediction. *Journal of Vocational Psychology, 29*, 332–339.

Tonidandel, S., & LeBreton, J. M. (2010). Determining the relative importance of predictors in logistic regression: An extension of relative weights analysis. *Organizational Research Methods, 13*, 767–781.

Waller, N. G. (2008). Fungible weights in multiple regression. *Psychometrika, 73*, 691–703.

Wang, M. W., & Stanley, J. C. (1970). Differential weighting: A review of methods and empirical studies. *Review of Educational Research, 40*, 663–705.

Wilks, S. S. (1938). Weighting systems for linear functions of correlated variables when there is no dependent variable. *Psychometrika, 3*, 23–40.

Zou, H., Hastie, T., & Tibshirani, R. (2006). Sparse principle component analysis. *Journal of Computational and Graphical Statistics, 15*, 265–286.

10

DEBUNKING MYTHS AND URBAN LEGENDS ABOUT HOW TO IDENTIFY INFLUENTIAL OUTLIERS

Herman Aguinis and Harry Joo

An outlier is an individual, team, firm, or any other unit that deviates markedly from others. *Influential outliers* are units that deviate markedly from the rest and, in addition, their presence has a disproportionate impact on substantive conclusions regarding relationships among variables. Due to their disproportionate impact on substantive conclusions, influential outliers constitute one of the most enduring and pervasive methodological challenges in both micro- (Orr, Sackett, & DuBois, 1991) and macro-level (Hitt, Harrison, Ireland, & Best, 1998) organizational science research.

There are many examples of substantive conclusions that have been changed based on how just a handful of influential outliers were identified in the same data set (Aguinis, Gottfredson, & Joo, 2013). For example, Hollenbeck, DeRue, and Mannor (2006) reanalyzed data collected by Peterson, Smith, Martorana, and Owens (2003), who investigated the relationships among CEO personality, team dynamics, and firm performance. Hollenbeck and colleagues (2006) showed that, of the 17 statistically significant correlations reported by Peterson and colleagues (2003), only one was actually significant for all 17 sensitivity analyses, in which each of the 17 individual data points (i.e., 17 CEOs) was removed one at a time. In other words, Hollenbeck and colleagues (2006) demonstrated that substantive conclusions regarding relationships among CEO personality, team dynamics, and firm performance changed almost completely depending on which cases were identified as outliers.

In spite of their pervasiveness and importance, there is confusion, misunder-standing, and a lack of clear guidelines on how to identify influential outliers. In particular, researchers frequently rely on three myths and urban legends (MULs) to identify such data points. These three MULs are rooted in the commonly invoked yet incorrect assumption that a data point, by virtue of being located far from others, *necessarily* has a large influence on substantive results (e.g., regression coefficients, correlations). Although many researchers tend to assume that distance also means influence, this assumption often does not hold true because distance is a necessary but not sufficient condition for influence. To illustrate this point, consider Figure 10.1 (from Aguinis et al., 2013), which includes a scatter plot of a data set involving one predictor and one criterion. Regression analysis based on these data yields an R^2 of .73 when Cases #1, #2, and #3, which seem to be far from the rest, are excluded from the analysis. When Case #1, #2, or #3 is included one at a time, R^2 changes to .11, .95, or .17, respectively. So, the inclusion of each of these individual cases does change results regarding model fit in a substantive manner. Further, the inclusion of Case #1 or #3 reduces R^2 and also affects the model's parameter estimates (i.e., the intercept and/or slope). On the other hand, now consider Case #2, which is also far from the others—in terms of both the X and Y variable distributions. The inclusion of Case #2 in the analysis improves R^2 because of its location along the regression line. However, its inclusion or exclusion does not affect the intercept or slope parameter estimates. In short, although Case #2 is clearly far from other data points, it does not have influence on the

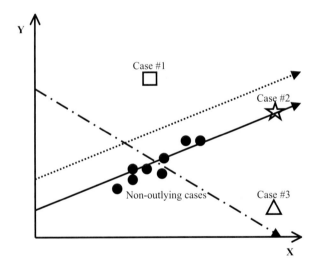

FIGURE 10.1 Scatter plot illustrating that distance is not necessarily the same as influence in the context of regression

208 Herman Aguinis and Harry Joo

parameter estimates of this model, which illustrates that distance is not necessarily the same as influence.

The goal of our manuscript is to debunk three MULs about how to identify influential outliers. For each of these three MULs, we explain their nature, the kernels of truth behind them, and how the kernels of truth have been misapplied over time to form the MULs. Also, we illustrate these MULs using published articles with one important caveat: The practices we refer to are so pervasive that we could have illustrated them with dozens of examples. So we chose some illustrations with the purpose of making our points, but we do not wish to single these articles out as being particularly special in any way. In addition, after the discussion of each of the three MULs, we offer best-practice recommendations regarding how to identify influential outliers in the analytic contexts of multiple regression, structural equation modeling (SEM), multilevel modeling, meta-analysis, and time series analysis. We chose to address these particular data-analytic approaches because they are among the most popular and frequently used in organizational science research (Aguinis, Pierce, Bosco, & Muslin, 2009).

Three Pervasive Myths and Urban Legends about How to Identify Influential Outliers

We identified the three MULs through a content analysis of how authors of articles published in substantive organizational science journals identify influential outliers, as well as a review of recommendations on how to identify influential outliers offered in methodological sources. First, we content analyzed journal articles that mentioned the topic of outliers identified by Aguinis and colleagues (2013). The literature review focused on the following journals covering the years 1991 through 2010: *Academy of Management Journal, Journal of Applied Psychology, Personnel Psychology, Strategic Management Journal, Journal of Management,* and *Administrative Science Quarterly.* This process resulted in a total of 232 articles. Second, we reviewed the References list of each of these journal articles to locate and examine methodological sources upon which they may have relied regarding the issue of outliers. For example, we reviewed several textbooks that are typically used in training doctoral students in the organizational sciences (e.g., Cohen, Cohen, West, & Aiken, 2003; Tabachnick & Fidell, 2007).

As a result, we uncovered that the following are the three most common MULs about how to identify influential outliers: (1) Univariate cutoffs (e.g., top and bottom 1% of cases, cases that are more than 2 or 3 standard deviation [SD] units away from the mean) are sufficient for identifying influential outliers; (2) inspection of visual plots (e.g., histograms, scatter plots, residual plots) is sufficient for identifying influential outliers; and (3) absolute cutoffs based on multivariate test statistics (e.g., standardized residuals beyond $\pm$ 3 SD units, Cook's D values greater than 1) are appropriate for identifying influential outliers.

Table 10.1 includes a summary of the results of our content analysis, which revealed that 94 (i.e., 40.5%) of the 232 published substantive journal articles in

TABLE 10.1 Summary of Myths and Urban Legends about How to Identify Influential Outliers: Their Nature, Pervasiveness, Kernels of Truth, and How the Kernels of Truth Have Been Misapplied

Myth and Urban Legend (MUL)	Pervasiveness of MUL (out of 138 articles that were transparent enough in reporting how influential outliers were identified)	Kernels of Truth Behind the MUL	How the Kernels of Truth Have Been Misapplied Over Time to Form the MUL
Univariate cutoffs are sufficient for identifying influential outliers.	64.49% (89 articles)	• Univariate cutoffs help identify distant cases, which are often influential outliers. • Authoritative methodological sources describe univariate cutoffs in detail.	• Many authors have come to misunderstand distance as not only a necessary but also a sufficient condition for influence. • Many authors seem to have jumped to the incorrect conclusion that because an authoritative methodological source describes univariate cutoffs, the inference is that such cutoffs are recommended as sufficient means for identifying influential outliers.
Inspection of visual plots is sufficient for identifying influential outliers.	12.32% (17 articles)	• Superior alternative procedures for identifying influential outliers did not exist or were not available for practical use before the early 1980s. • Authoritative methodological sources give detailed descriptions of a number of visual techniques.	• Many authors have continued to use visual plots alone to identify influential outliers, even though improvements in statistical methods and computing technology no longer justify the exclusive use of visual plots on practical grounds. • Many authors seem to have jumped to the incorrect conclusion that an authoritative methodological source describing visual plots means that visual plots are sufficient means for identifying influential outliers.

(Continued)

210 Herman Aguinis and Harry Joo

TABLE 10.1 (Continued)

Myth and Urban Legend (MUL)	Pervasiveness of MUL (out of 138 articles that were transparent enough in reporting how influential outliers were identified)	Kernels of Truth Behind the MUL	How the Kernels of Truth Have Been Misapplied Over Time to Form the MUL
Absolute cutoffs based on multivariate test statistics are appropriate for identifying influential outliers.	8.70% (12 articles)	• Authoritative methodological sources seem to approve of the use of absolute cutoffs based on multivariate test statistics to identify influential outliers.	• Many authors have continued to use such absolute cutoffs to identify influential outliers, even though evidence has accumulated pointing to the superiority of research design–based cutoffs. Research design–based cutoffs are superior because they can vary from study to study depending on the characteristics of the particular research context such as sample size and number of predictors. Specifically, the "bar" for considering a case as an influential outlier is higher as sample size decreases and the number of predictors increases in a model.

Note: Of the 232 journal articles included in our review, 94 (i.e., 40.5%) were not sufficiently transparent in their reporting for us to determine precisely how influential outliers were identified. So these percentages are based on a total of 138 articles that provided sufficient information. Out of those 138 articles, 111 (i.e., 80.43%) articles relied on at least one of the three MULs.

our literature review were not sufficiently transparent in their reporting for us to determine precisely how influential outliers were identified. For example, in an article published in *Strategic Management Journal* in 2009, the authors "ran regression diagnostics to look for outliers and removed seven observations that substantially skewed regression results, consistent with normal practice." In another article published in *Journal of Applied Psychology* in 2008, the authors noted that "on the basis of an outlier analysis, three cases were dropped from the U.S. sample, as they contributed most to departures of multivariate kurtosis." This lack of transparency is obviously an issue that needs to be addressed, and later in our manuscript we suggest that journal policies should motivate authors to include at least a few sentences on how they identified influential outliers. Of the remaining 138 articles that were sufficiently transparent in reporting how influential outliers were identified, 111 (i.e., 80.43%) relied on at least one of the three MULs. As a preview of the next sections, Table 10.1 offers a summary of each MUL, the kernels of truth behind each MUL, and how the kernels of truth have been misapplied over time.

Univariate Cutoffs Are Sufficient for Identifying Influential Outliers

According to this MUL, influential outliers are identified as cases that are far from others given a distribution of data points for a single variable. Among the 138 journal articles in our review that were sufficiently transparent in reporting how influential outliers were identified, 89 (i.e., 64.49%) relied on this MUL. As an example among micro-level studies, Stajkovic and Luthans (1997) conducted a meta-analysis, and "to estimate the relative stability of unbiased effect-size magnitudes . . . effect sizes positioned 1.5 to 3 lengths from the upper or lower edge of the 50 percent interquartile range . . . were considered outliers" (p. 1127). As an illustration in the macro domain, Henkel (2009) identified firms lying within the extreme 1% of the return on equity distribution and treated them as special cases "to restrict the influence of outliers" (p. 293). Note that our discussion here neither pertains to nor criticizes how researchers in these examples subsequently handled influential outliers. For example, Stajkovic and Luthans (1997) reported results with and without the influential outliers they identified—our focus is in on how outliers were identified.

There are two kernels of truth underlying this MUL—a conceptual-logical one and an authoritative one. First, the conceptual-logical kernel of truth is that univariate cutoffs help identify distant cases, which are often influential outliers. Specifically, univariate cutoffs "have some utility for identifying extreme cases" (Meade & Craig, 2012, p. 440). In turn, such "unusual cases that are far from the rest of the data . . . even one, can seriously jeopardize the results and conclusions of the regression analysis" (Cohen et al., 2003, p. 102). Accordingly, it seems logical to use "distance" as a proxy for "influence."

Second, the authoritative rationale used by some researchers is that the sources they cite describe univariate cutoffs in detail. For example, Cohen and colleagues (2003, chapter 4) discussed how to use boxplots and, in doing so, stated that "values of any outlying scores are displayed separately when they fall below $Q_1 - 3SIQR$ or above $Q_3 + 3SIQR$" (p. 108). Note that SIQR is the semi-interquartile range, or $(Q3 - Q1)/2$. Similarly, Tabachnick and Fidell (2007, chapter 4) stated that "cases with standardized scores in excess of 3.29 ($p < .001$, two-tailed test) are potential outliers" (p. 73). Other similarly influential and widely used textbooks that discuss univariate cutoffs to identify cases lying at a distance from others in a distribution include Tukey (1977) and Hildebrand (1986).

Unfortunately, the kernels of truth seem to have been misapplied over time in two ways. First, many authors have come to misunderstand distance as not only a necessary but also a sufficient condition for influence. Researchers using univariate cutoffs often produce false positives (i.e., deciding that a distant case is an influential outlier when it is not influential) and, sometimes, also false negatives (i.e., deciding that a case seemingly not far from others is not an influential outlier when it is influential; Aguinis et al., 2013). Thus, careful examination of data can reveal cases that are far from others but do not have influence on the results. For example, McCann and Vroom (2010) noted that a hotel had an unusually large number of rooms, yet further examination of that case revealed that its exclusion from the data set actually did not change any of the results in a substantive manner.

Second, many authors seem to have jumped to the incorrect conclusion that because an authoritative methodological source describes univariate cutoffs, the inference is that such cutoffs are recommended as sufficient means for identifying influential outliers. In fact, just because authoritative and widely used methodological sources describe univariate cutoffs, this does not mean that they have recommended that such cutoffs alone be used for identifying influential outliers. For example, although Cohen and colleagues (2003, chapter 4) described univariate cutoffs, they noted in the same chapter that outliers are given more detailed consideration later in chapter 10, in which they "encourage . . . the use of specialized statistics known as regression diagnostics which can greatly aid in the detection of outliers" (p. 394). Thus, Cohen and colleagues actually discouraged the sole use of univariate cutoffs to identify influential outliers.

Summary

The nature of the MUL: Univariate cutoffs are sufficient for identifying influential outliers. The kernels of truth: Univariate cutoffs help identify distant cases, which are often influential outliers. Also, authoritative methodological sources describe univariate cutoffs in detail. How the kernels of truth have been misapplied over time to form the MUL: Many authors have come to misunderstand distance as not only a necessary but also a sufficient condition for influence. Further, many authors seem to have jumped to the incorrect conclusion that an authoritative methodological source describing univariate cutoffs means that such cutoffs are recommended as sufficient means for identifying influential outliers.

Inspection of Visual Plots Is Sufficient for Identifying Influential Outliers

The second MUL involves using visual plots such as histograms, scatter plots, residual plots, and index plots as sufficient means for identifying influential outliers. Of the 138 articles in our review that were sufficiently transparent in reporting how influential outliers were identified, 12.32% (17 articles) relied on this MUL. Among these 17 studies, some used univariate visual plots (e.g., histograms), while others used multivariate visual plots. Multivariate visual plots include multiple variables (e.g., scatter plots) as well as plots of multivariate test statistics (e.g., residual plots, index plots). As an illustration in the micro domain, Blanton and colleagues (2009) examined a number of scatter plots "to determine visually if there were apparent outliers whose presence might have influenced the trend of the data within conditions" (p. 578). As an example in the macro domain, Bogert (1996) examined the data distributions of the dependent variables as the means to try to identify outliers that "unduly influenced the reported regression results" (p. 248). Note that our discussion here neither pertains to nor criticizes how researchers in these examples subsequently handled influential outliers. Specifically, Blanton and colleagues (2009) and Bogert (1996) reported results with and without influential outliers—which is a sound practice recommended by Aguinis and colleagues (2013).

There are four main reasons why the use of visual plots as a necessary and sufficient means for identifying influential outliers is inappropriate (Cohen et al., 2003; Iglewicz & Hoaglin, 1993; Ziegert & Hanges, 2009). First, similar to the first MUL, this practice relies on the incorrect logic that a case with a large distance from others necessarily means that the case also has a large influence on the study's results. Second, the determination of exactly which cases are identified as influential outliers in the same visual plot may vary from one researcher to another depending on a person's subjective judgment. Not surprisingly, some have described the practice as "a notoriously flawed approach for detecting outliers" (Ziegert & Hanges, 2009, p. 593) and "not a reliable way to identify potential outliers" (Iglewicz & Hoaglin, 1993, p. 9). Further, a cynical view is that researchers using visual plots are more likely to "find" influential outliers for the purpose of finding better support for one's hypothesis—an inappropriate practice that capitalizes on chance (Cortina, 2002) and borders on unethical research conduct (Bedeian, Taylor, & Miller, 2010). Third, visual plots used for identifying influential outliers "suffer in small samples because of the small number of comparators available" (Martin & Roberts, 2010, p. 258). In other words, the same cases may or may not be identified as outliers depending on the size of the sample. Fourth, the practice of using visual plots to identify influential outliers is usually accompanied by low transparency. Stated differently, replicating the decision of labeling a case as an outlier is difficult if a plot is not accompanied by a verbal description of exactly which cases were identified as influential outliers and why.

There are two kernels of truth underlying this MUL—a practical one and an authoritative one. First, in terms of practicality, superior methods (i.e., cutoffs based on multivariate test statistics that take into account the research design features of a study) simply did not exist or were not available for practical use before the early 1980s (Martin & Roberts, 2010). Accordingly, visual plots were a good practical alternative, although they only have limited ability to identify influential outliers.

The second kernel of truth is that authoritative methodological sources (e.g., textbooks) give detailed descriptions of a number of visual techniques, thereby possibly giving the impression that using them alone to identify influential outliers is acceptable. For example, Cohen and colleagues (2003, chapter 4) explained how to use a variety of visual techniques—although they do not state that using plots alone is the recommended procedure for identifying influential outliers.

Unfortunately, the kernels of truth have been misapplied over time in largely two ways. First, many authors have continued to use visual plots alone to identify influential outliers, even though there have been a number of developments that now make it practical to use better alternative procedures for identifying influential outliers. Specifically, seminal works by Cook (1977, 1979), Belsley, Kuh, and Welsch (1980), and Cook and Weisberg (1982) have provided more appropriate procedures (i.e., cutoffs based on multivariate test statistics that take into account research design features of a study). Another development is that high-speed computers have become more readily available, which have facilitated the implementation of these procedures. As a result, it is no longer justified on practical grounds to use visual plots as a sufficient means to identify influential outliers.

Second, many authors seem to have jumped to the incorrect conclusion that an authoritative methodological source describing visual plots means that visual plots are sufficient means for identifying influential outliers. In fact, just because authoritative methodological sources give detailed descriptions of a number of visual plots, this does not mean these sources recommend the use of visual plots as sufficient means for identifying influential outliers. Further, the same authoritative methodological sources (e.g., Cohen et al., 2003; Iglewicz & Hoaglin, 1993) describing various visual plots in detail also discourage the use of visual plots as sufficient means for identifying influential outliers, as noted in the discussion regarding the nature of the MUL.

Summary

The nature of the MUL: Inspection of visual plots is sufficient for identifying influential outliers. The kernels of truth: Superior alternative procedures for identifying influential outliers did not exist or were not available for practical use before the early 1980s. Also, commonly used methodological sources give detailed descriptions of a number of visual techniques. How the kernels of truth have been misapplied over time to form the MUL: Many authors have continued to use visual plots alone to identify influential outliers, even though improvements in statistical methods and computing technology no longer justify the exclusive use of visual plots on practical grounds. Further, many authors seem to have jumped to the incorrect conclusion that an authoritative methodological source describing visual plots means that visual plots are sufficient means for identifying influential outliers.

Absolute Cutoffs Based on Multivariate Test Statistics Are Appropriate for Identifying Influential Outliers

The third MUL involves using absolute cutoffs based on multivariate test statistics to identify influential outliers. According to this MUL, influential outliers are cases whose multivariate test statistic values exceed a numeric threshold, and this threshold is exactly the same regardless of a study's research design features such as sample size and number of variables investigated. As we will describe and illustrate later in our manuscript, considering research design features improves accuracy in the process of identifying influential outliers.

Of the 138 articles included in our review that were sufficiently transparent in reporting how influential outliers were identified, 8.70% (12 articles) relied on absolute cutoffs based on multivariate test statistics. As an example in the micro domain, Montes and Zweig (2009) looked for observations with standardized residuals beyond $\pm$ 3 SD units to identify data points that "might adversely affect the validity of the results" (p. 1249). As an illustration in the macro domain, Wright, Kroll, Krug, and Pettus (2007) looked for observations with residual values larger than 4 SD units to identify "firms that unduly influenced the regression results" (p. 86).

The kernel of truth behind this MUL seems to be based on the reliance on authoritative sources. For example, Belsley and colleagues (1980) actually did give credit to the utility of absolute cutoffs based on multivariate test statistics when they stated that "it is natural to say, at least to a first approximation, that any of the diagnostic measures is large if its value exceeds two in magnitude. Such a procedure defines what we call an absolute cutoff" (p. 28). Granted, Belsley and colleagues (1980, p. 28) also described and endorsed research design–based cutoffs based on multivariate test statistics—that is, cutoffs based on multivariate test statistics that take into account the research design features of a study. For example, observations with DFFITS values (i.e., similar to Cook's D but using a different scale) above or below $\pm 2\sqrt{\frac{(k+1)}{n}}$ are considered influential outliers, where k = number of predictors and n = sample size. But Belsley and colleagues (1980) do not seem to have stated explicitly that research design–based cutoffs are superior to absolute cutoffs based on multivariate test statistics. As another example of such ambiguity, Cohen and colleagues (2003, p. 404) stated that "a value of 1.0 or the critical value of the F distribution at α = .50 with $df = (k + 1, n - k - 1)$ is used" regarding Cook's D, thereby making it seem that it does not matter whether a researcher uses absolute or research design–based cutoffs based on multivariate test statistics. Thus, the apparent approval of absolute cutoffs based on multivariate test statistics—which can be used across studies regardless of their design features—subsequently seems to have led to the widespread use of such absolute cutoffs to identify influential outliers.

The kernel of truth has been misapplied because many authors have continued to use such absolute cutoffs to identify influential outliers, even though evidence has accumulated demonstrating that the process of identifying influential outliers must include research design considerations (Andrews & Pregibon, 1978; Chatterjee & Hadi, 1986; Martin & Roberts, 2010). In other words, research design–based cutoffs, compared to absolute cutoffs, assess influence more accurately, as we describe in the following two illustrations.

216 Herman Aguinis and Harry Joo

First, consider DFFITS, which assesses the influence that a data point has on all regression coefficients in a regression model as a whole. The cutoff value for DFFITS in a study with a sample size of 100 ($n = 100$) and 10 predictors ($k = 10$) is $\pm 2 \sqrt{(10 + 1)/100} = \pm 0.663$, the absolute value of which is about twice as large as that of ± 0.346 in a study with the same sample size ($n = 100$) but 2 predictors ($k = 2$). Through this adjustment in the cutoff values for DFFITS is based on number of predictors, one can assess influence more accurately because as the number of predictors increases, so does the number of regression coefficients as a whole that a data point must affect to be an influential outlier. This "increased bar" for a data point to be influential is therefore reflected in the higher cutoff value for DFFITS.

As a second illustration, once again referring to DFFITS, note that the cutoff value in a study where $k = 2$ and $n = 100$ is $\pm 2 \sqrt{\dfrac{2 + 1}{100}} = \pm 0.346$, the absolute value of which is substantially larger than that of ± 0.173 for a study where $k = 2$ but $n = 400$. Through this adjustment in the cutoff values for DFFITS based on sample size, one can assess influence more accurately, because even if two cases cause the same overall amount of change in the same regression coefficients, the case in the model with the smaller sample size (i.e., fewer "competitors") is less influential than the other case in the model with the larger sample size (i.e., more "competitors"). To account for these differences in terms of "competition," the cutoff value for DFFITS decreases as sample size increases.

Summary

The nature of the MUL: Absolute cutoffs based on multivariate test statistics are appropriate for identifying influential outliers. The kernel of truth: Authoritative methodological sources seem to approve of the use of absolute cutoffs based on multivariate test statistics to identify influential outliers. How the kernel of truth has been misapplied over time to form the MUL: Many authors have continued to use such absolute cutoffs to identify influential outliers, even though evidence has accumulated pointing to the superiority of research design-based cutoffs. Research design-based cutoffs are superior because they can vary from study to study depending on the characteristics of the particular research context such as sample size and number of predictors. Specifically, the "bar" for considering a case as an influential outlier is higher as sample size decreases and number of predictors increases in a model.

Best-Practice Recommendations on How to Identify Influential Outliers

In this section, we offer best-practice recommendations on how researchers should proceed in terms of identifying influential outliers. These recommendations are necessary in light of the pervasiveness of practices based on the three MULs that

TABLE 10.2 Summary of Best-Practice Recommendations on How to Identify Influential Outliers

Recommendation	Description
Follow Aguinis et al.'s (2013) three-step approach, regardless of the particular data-analytic context.	• Step 1: Identify error outliers. • Step 2: Identify interesting outliers. • Step 3: Identify influential outliers.
Identify two types of influential outliers—model fit outliers and prediction outliers—in the context of multiple regression, SEM, or multilevel modeling.	• When identifying model fit outliers, use a two-step process: (1) identify cases that exceed cutoffs based on suitable techniques, and (2) check whether the removal of each previously identified case changes model fit. • When identifying prediction outliers, identify cases that exceed cutoffs based on suitable techniques. • These various techniques and cutoffs, as well as practical implementation guidelines, used in multiple regression, SEM, or multilevel modeling, are discussed in Aguinis et al. (2013).
Use research design–based cutoffs to identify influential outliers.	• For example, for DFFITS (i.e., used to assess the influence that a data point has on all regression coefficients in a regression model as a whole), the recommended cutoff is $\pm 2\sqrt{\dfrac{(k+1)}{n}}$, where k = number of predictors and n = sample size. • As another example, for Cook's D values of cases, the recommended research design-based cutoff is: F distribution at $\alpha = .50$ with $df = (k + 1, n - k - 1)$.
Use visual techniques alone when there are no research design–based cutoffs available.	• For example, in SEM, it is acceptable to use index plots when using generalized Cook's D and single parameter influence. • An index plot includes case numbers on the X axis and test statistic values on the Y axis.
Identify influential outliers when using meta-analysis.	• Calculate the SAMD value for each primary-level study. • Regarding the recommended research design–based cutoff, use a scree plot of SAMD values, where SAMD values of primary studies are plotted from the highest to the lowest value on the Y-axis while the corresponding rank-ordered position of each primary-level study is denoted on the X-axis. Studies with SAMD values that lie above the "elbow" (i.e., the point that separates the steep slope from the gradual slope in the scree plot) are identified as influential outliers.
Identify influential outliers when using time series analysis.	• Use independent component analysis (ICA). • The recommended research design–based cutoff is: $\mu_i \pm 4.47\sigma_i$, where μ_i and σ_i are the mean and the standard error of the ith extracted component, respectively.

we described earlier. Table 10.2 offers a summary of the recommendations we discuss next, which also include illustrations of how these recommended procedures have been implemented in published articles.

Our first recommendation is to follow a sequential process consisting of three broad steps as identified by Aguinis and colleagues (2013). These three steps should be applied regardless of the particular data-analytic approach (e.g., regression, SEM, meta-analysis, multilevel modeling) used for assessing substantive questions and hypotheses. In the recommended sequential process, a researcher first needs to identify error outliers (i.e., outlying cases caused by undesirable reasons such as mistakes made in the research process), then interesting outliers (i.e., outlying cases caused not by mistakes but instead by potentially interesting substantive reasons) and, finally, influential outliers (i.e., outlying cases that are neither error nor necessarily interesting cases and that affect substantive conclusions of the study). Thus, identifying influential outliers in the third step of the process ensures that the cases identified as influential outliers are such, as opposed to other types of outliers.

In the particular context of multiple regression, SEM, and multilevel modeling, the third step in the aforementioned sequential process involves identifying two types of influential outliers: (1) model fit outliers (i.e., cases whose presence alters the fit of a model) and (2) prediction outliers (i.e., cases whose presence alters parameter estimates). When identifying model fit outliers, the researcher should first use suitable techniques and cutoffs as well as subsequently check whether model fit is changed by the removal of each identified case. This two-step process is necessary because the techniques suited for identifying model fit outliers assess the distance of a case from other cases instead of the influence of the case on model fit. When identifying prediction outliers, the researcher only needs to use suitable techniques and cutoffs and does not need to subsequently check whether model fit is changed by the removal of each identified case, because the techniques suited for identifying prediction outliers directly assess the influence of the case on parameter estimates. These various techniques and cutoffs, as well as practical implementation guidelines, used in multiple regression, SEM, or multilevel modeling are also discussed by Aguinis and colleagues (2013). For example, in line with Aguinis and colleagues' (2013) recommended two-step process for identifying model fit outliers, Baldridge, Floyd, and Markóczy (2004) first identified potential model fit outliers and subsequently checked whether each potential model fit outlier actually had influence on the fit of the model. As a result, Baldridge and colleagues (2004) found that three of the five potential model fit outliers were indeed model fit outliers. Had the researchers neglected the second step of checking whether each potential model fit outlier was in fact a model fit outlier, they would have erroneously identified two additional observations as influential outliers.

As an additional recommendation, we emphasize the importance of using research design–based cutoffs when using specific techniques to identify influential outliers. For example, Grant (2008) used *DFBETAS* (i.e., indicating whether the inclusion of a case leads to an increase or decrease in a single regression coefficient) and Cook's D to identify prediction outliers in his hierarchical regression model. For both techniques, Grant (2008) used research design–based cutoffs that take into account the number of cases and predictors in the model. As an illustration of model fit outlier identification in the analytic context of SEM, Goerzen (2007) first derived the Mahalanobis distance values (i.e., the length of the line segment between a data point and the centroid of the remaining cases), identified those cases that exceeded the research design–based cutoff used, and then checked whether the removal of the identified cases changed the fit of the tested models (though we recommend that such removal be done with one identified case at a time).

There are unique circumstances when it is appropriate to not use research design–based cutoffs and instead use visual techniques alone for identifying influential outliers (i.e., the second MUL we discussed). This recommendation applies to situations for which there are no research design–based cutoffs available for practical use. For example, in SEM, it is recommended that researchers use two techniques (i.e., multivariate test statistics)—generalized Cook's D and single parameter influence—to identify prediction outliers (Pek & MacCallum, 2011). Because there are no research design–based cutoffs available, it is acceptable to use index plots that include case numbers on the X axis and test statistic values on the Y axis.

Next, we offer recommendations for two additional data-analytic contexts: meta-analysis and time series analysis. Use of these two analytic techniques is fairly typical in organizational science research, yet recommendations on how to identify influential outliers in these contexts were not discussed by Aguinis and colleagues (2013). First of all, as mentioned earlier, the researcher must identify error and then interesting outliers before identifying influential outliers. To identify influential outliers in the context of meta-analysis, we recommend that researchers calculate the sample-adjusted meta-analytic deviancy (SAMD) statistic value for each observation, or the effect size estimate from each primary-level study included in the meta-analysis (Huffcutt & Arthur, 1995). This technique is recommended because an influential outlier is a function of both effect size and sample size, and SAMD takes into account both. The recommended research design–based cutoff involves using a scree plot of SAMD values, which are plotted from the highest to the lowest value on the Y-axis, while the corresponding rank-ordered position of each primary-level study is denoted on the X-axis (Arthur, Bennett, & Huffcutt, 2001). Primary-level studies with SAMD values that lie above the "elbow" (i.e., the point that separates the steep slope from the gradual slope in the scree plot) are identified as influential outliers. This cutoff takes research design features into consideration because the primary-level studies with SAMD values above the elbow are those that, compared to others, contribute substantially more to the variance across the primary-level studies in the particular meta-analytic data base at hand. So the exact location of the elbow varies from one meta-analysis to another. As an illustration

220 Herman Aguinis and Harry Joo

of the recent use of this approach, Taylor, Russ-Eft, and Taylor (2009) conducted a meta-analysis of the transfer of training literature and used a scree plot of SAMD values to identify influential outliers.

Finally, to identify influential outliers in the context of time series analysis, we recommend the use of independent component analysis (ICA), accompanied by the research design–based cutoff of "$\mu i \pm 4.47\sigma i$, where μi and σi are, respectively, the mean and the standard error of the ith extracted component" (Baragona & Battaglia, 2007, p. 1973). MATLAB code for implementing ICA to identify influential outliers is publicly available online and has been developed by Bell and Sejnowski (1995; www.sccn.ucsd.edu/eeglab/) and Hyvärinen and Oja (2000; www.cis.hut.fi/projects/ica/fastica/).

Concluding Comments

The presence of outliers seems to be an unavoidable fact of life when conducting organizational science research (Aguinis & O'Boyle, 2014; O'Boyle & Aguinis, 2012). Thus, it is important that researchers address influential outliers appropriately, as well as report how they dealt with such cases openly and transparently. Our content analysis of 232 substantive journal articles that mentioned the term "outlier" revealed that about 40% did not provide sufficient information for us to understand the procedures that were implemented to identify these particular cases. Among studies that reported sufficient information on how authors identified influential outliers, about 80% of them have fallen prey to at least one of the three myths and urban legends that we described in our manuscript. Each of these MULs is inappropriate because they are based on the commonly invoked but incorrect assumption that a case with a large distance from others also *necessarily* has a large influence on the study's results.

As noted by Aguinis and colleagues (2013),

> without a description of the identification techniques used, a skeptical scientific audience might raise doubts about a study's substantive conclusions . . . [because] . . . a cynical view is that outliers are treated in such a way that their inclusion or exclusion from a data set is not based on sound and standardized practices, but on whether results favor one's preferred hypotheses.
> *(pp. 292, 297)*

We hope our manuscript will allow researchers to critically revisit common practices about how to identify influential outliers, as well as encourage researchers to adopt more appropriate practices. Also, we would like to offer the proposal that journal editors and reviewers make a proactive effort to ensure transparent reporting practices regarding outliers. This can be done by requiring authors of manuscripts describing empirical research to include at least a few sentences on how they identified influential outliers—this material may be included in a separate section titled "Outlier Identification and Management." Overall, we hope our manuscript will lead to the use of more appropriate and transparent practices for identifying influential outliers in future research.

Acknowledgments

Some of the material included in this manuscript was presented as professional development workshops at the meetings of the Academy of Management in 2011 (San Antonio, TX), 2012 (Boston, MA), and 2013 (Orlando, FL). We thank Bob Vandenberg for his highly constructive and detailed feedback that allowed us to improve our manuscript substantially.

References

Aguinis, H., Gottfredson, R. K., & Joo, H. (2013). Best-practice recommendations for defining, identifying, and handling outliers. *Organizational Research Methods, 16*, 270–301.

Aguinis, H., & O'Boyle, E. (2014). Star performers in twenty-first-century organizations. *Personnel Psychology, 67*, 313–350.

Aguinis, H., Pierce, C. A., Bosco, F. A., & Muslin, I. S. (2009). First decade of *Organizational Research Methods*: Trends in design, measurement, and data-analysis topics. *Organizational Research Methods, 12*, 69–112.

Andrews, D. F., & Pregibon, D. (1978). Finding the outliers that matter. *Journal of the Royal Statistical Society, Series B*, 85–93.

Arthur, W., Jr., Bennett, W., Jr., & Huffcutt, A. I. (2001). *Conducting meta-analysis using SAS*. Mahwah, NJ: Erlbaum.

Baldridge, D. C., Floyd, S. W., & Markóczy, L. (2004). Are managers from Mars and academicians from Venus? Toward an understanding of the relationship between academic quality and practical relevance. *Strategic Management Journal, 25*, 1063–1074.

Baragona, R., & Battaglia, F. (2007). Outliers detection in multivariate time series by independent component analysis. *Neural Computation, 19*, 1962–1984.

Bedeian, A. G., Taylor, S. G., & Miller, A. N. (2010). Management science on the credibility bubble: Cardinal sins and various misdemeanors. *Academy of Management Learning and Education, 9*, 715–725.

Bell, A. J., & Sejnowski, T. J. (1995). An information-maximization approach to blind separation and blind deconvolution. *Neural Computation, 7*, 1129–1159.

Belsley, D. A., Kuh, E., & Welsch, R. E. (1980). *Regression diagnostics: Identifying influential data and sources of collinearity*. New York, NY: John Wiley & Sons, Inc.

Blanton, H., Jaccard, J., Klick, J., Mellers, B., Mitchell, G., & Tetlock, P. E. (2009). Strong claims and weak evidence: Reassessing the predictive validity of the IAT. *Journal of Applied Psychology, 94*, 567–582.

Bogert, J. D. (1996). Explaining variance in the performance of long-term corporate blockholders. *Strategic Management Journal, 17*, 243–249.

Chatterjee, S., & Hadi, A. S. (1986). Influential observations, high leverage points, and outliers in linear regression. *Statistical Science, 1*, 379–393.

Cohen, J., Cohen, P., West, S. G., & Aiken, L. S. (2003). *Applied multiple regression/correlation analysis for the behavioral sciences* (3rd ed.). Mahwah, NJ: Erlbaum.

Cook, R. D. (1977). Detection of influential observation in linear regression. *Technometrics, 19*, 15–18.

Cook, R. D. (1979). Influential observations in linear regression. *Journal of the American Statistical Association, 74*, 169–174.

Cook, R. D., & Weisberg, S. (1982). *Residuals and influence in regression.* New York, NY: Chapman and Hall.

Cortina, J. M. (2002). Big things have small beginnings: An assortment of "minor" methodological misunderstandings. *Journal of Management, 28*, 339–362.

Goerzen, A. (2007). Alliance networks and firm performance: The impact of repeated partnerships. *Strategic Management Journal, 28*, 487–509.

Grant, A. M. (2008). Does intrinsic motivation fuel the prosocial fire? Motivational synergy in predicting persistence, performance, and productivity. *Journal of Applied Psychology, 93*, 48–58.

Henkel, J. (2009). The risk–return paradox for strategic management: Disentangling true and spurious effects. *Strategic Management Journal, 30*, 287–303.

Hildebrand, D. (1986). *Statistical thinking for behavioral scientists.* Boston, MA: Duxbury Press.

Hitt, M. A., Harrison, J. S., Ireland, R. D., & Best, A. (1998). Attributes of successful and unsuccessful acquisitions of US firms. *British Journal of Management, 9*, 91–114.

Hollenbeck, J. R., DeRue, D. S., & Mannor, M. (2006). Statistical power and parameter stability when subjects are few and tests are many: Comment on Peterson, Smith, Martorana, and Owens (2003). *Journal of Applied Psychology, 91*, 1–5.

Huffcutt, A. I., & Arthur, W., Jr. (1995). Development of a new outlier statistic for meta-analytic data. *Journal of Applied Psychology, 80*, 327–334.

Hyvärinen, A., & Oja, E. (2000). Independent component analysis: Algorithms and applications. *Neural Networks, 13*, 411–430.

Iglewicz, B., & Hoaglin, D. C. (1993). *How to detect and handle outliers.* Milwaukee, WI: American Society for Quality Control.

Martin, M. A., & Roberts, S. (2010). Jackknife-after-bootstrap regression influence diagnostics. *Journal of Nonparametric Statistics, 22*, 257–269.

McCann, B. T., & Vroom, G. (2010). Pricing response to entry and agglomeration effects. *Strategic Management Journal, 31*, 284–305.

Meade, A. W., & Craig, S. B. (2012). Identifying careless responses in survey data. *Psychological Methods, 17*, 437–455.

Montes, S. D., & Zweig, D. (2009). Do promises matter? An exploration of the role of promises in psychological contract breach. *Journal of Applied Psychology, 94*, 1243–1260.

O'Boyle, E., & Aguinis, H. (2012). The best and the rest: Revisiting the norm of normality of individual performance. *Personnel Psychology, 65*, 79–119.

Orr, J. M., Sackett, P. R., & DuBois, C.L.Z. (1991). Outlier detection and treatment in I/O psychology: A survey of researcher beliefs and an empirical illustration. *Personnel Psychology, 44*, 473–486.

Pek, J., & MacCallum, R. C. (2011). Sensitivity analysis in structural equation models: Cases and their influence. *Multivariate Behavioral Research, 46*, 202–228.

Peterson, R. S., Smith, D. B., Martorana, P. V., & Owens, P. D. (2003). The impact of chief executive officer personality on top management team dynamics: One mechanism by which leadership affects organizational performance. *Journal of Applied Psychology, 88*, 795–808.

Stajkovic, A. D., & Luthans, F. (1997). A meta-analysis of the effects of organizational behavior modification on task performance, 1975–95. *Academy of Management Journal, 40,* 1122–1149.

Tabachnick, B. G., & Fidell, L. S. (2007). *Using multivariate statistics* (5th ed.). Boston, MA: Pearson.

Taylor, P. J., Russ-Eft, D. F., & Taylor, H. (2009). Transfer of management training from alternative perspectives. *Journal of Applied Psychology, 94,* 104–121.

Tukey, J. W. (1977). *Exploratory data analysis.* Reading, MA: Pearson.

Wright, P., Kroll, M., Krug, J. A., & Pettus, M. (2007). Influences of top management team incentives on firm risk taking. *Strategic Management Journal, 28,* 81–89.

Ziegert, J. C., & Hanges, P. L. (2009) Strong rebuttal to weak criticisms: Reply to Blanton et al. (2009). *Journal of Applied Psychology, 94,* 590–597.

11

PULLING THE SOBEL TEST
UP BY ITS BOOTSTRAPS

Joel Koopman, Michael Howe and John R. Hollenbeck

In the domain of building and testing theory, mediation relationships are among the most important that can be proposed. Mediation helps to explicate our theoretical models (Leavitt, Mitchell, & Peterson, 2010) and addresses the fundamental question of *why* two constructs are related (Whetten, 1989). One of the better-known methods for testing mediation is commonly referred to as the "Sobel test," named for the researcher who derived a standard error (Sobel, 1982) to test the significance of the indirect effect. Recently, a number of different research teams (e.g., Preacher & Hayes, 2004; Shrout & Bolger, 2002) have criticized the Sobel test because this standard error requires an assumption of normality for the indirect effect sampling distribution. This distribution tends to be positively skewed (i.e., not normal), particularly in small samples, and so this assumption can be problematic (Preacher & Hayes, 2004; Stone & Sobel, 1990). As a result, the statistical power of the Sobel test may be lessened in these contexts (Preacher & Hayes, 2004; Shrout & Bolger, 2002).

In light of this concern, some scholars have advocated instead for the use of bootstrapping to test the significance of the indirect effect (e.g., Shrout & Bolger, 2002). Bootstrapping requires no *a priori* assumption about the shape of the sampling distribution because this distribution is empirically estimated using a resampling procedure (Efron & Tibshirani, 1993). As a result, departures from normality are less troublesome when creating a confidence interval for the indirect effect. For this reason, bootstrapping is now widely believed to be inherently superior to the Sobel test when testing the significance of the indirect effect in organizational research. Our position is that this belief constitutes an urban legend.

Statistical and methodological myths and urban legends represent aspects of research that we "just know to be true" (Lance, Butts, & Michels, 2006, p. 206) but are, in reality, not quite so true after all. Instead, such beliefs originate from some underlying kernel of truth that has, over time, been altered in some way (Vandenberg, 2006). As with all statistical urban legends, there is an underlying kernel of truth to the belief that bootstrapping is superior to the Sobel test. However, as we discuss in this chapter, there are several reasons to be concerned with a broad belief in the superiority of bootstrapping. We begin with a brief overview of mediation testing focusing on the Sobel test and bootstrapping and then explain the underlying kernel of truth that has propelled bootstrapping to the forefront of mediation testing in organizational research. Subsequently, we discuss four areas of concern that cast doubt on the belief of the inherent superiority of bootstrapping. Finally, we conclude with recommendations concerning the future of mediation testing in organizational research.

Origin of the Urban Legend

Introduction of the Sobel Test

Figure 11.1 presents a simple mediated model. The indirect effect represents the path between the independent and dependent variables through the mediator, and the product of the path coefficients α and β (see Figure 11.1) quantifies the magnitude of the mediation relationship. The development of Sobel's standard error allowed for testing the significance of this effect using commonly accepted statistical approaches, improving upon the limited utility (LeBreton, Wu, & Bing, 2009) of the "causal-steps" method (Baron & Kenny, 1986) previously utilized by organizational researchers. However, even though the indirect effect is composed of the product of two normally distributed regression coefficients, its sampling distribution is not necessarily normal (for a detailed explanation, see Biesanz, Falk, & Savalei, 2010, pp. 668–671). Rather, in some instances, the sampling distribution tends to be positively skewed, reducing the statistical power of the Sobel test to detect a mediated effect (Bollen & Stine, 1990; Preacher & Hayes, 2004). In recognition of this shortcoming, psychological and organizational scholars began advocating for an alternative technique—bootstrapping.

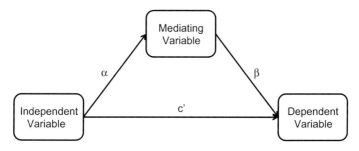

FIGURE 11.1 A partially mediated model

226 Joel Koopman et al.

The Rise of Bootstrapping

Bootstrapping does not rely on an assumption about the shape of the sampling distribution. Instead, the sampling distribution is estimated directly through an empirical resampling procedure. Resampling refers to a process of random sampling with replacement from the original sample to build a new "sample" of size N, corresponding to the original sample size. This process is repeated some large number of times (e.g., 1,000 or more) to generate a large number of "bootstrap samples." The indirect effect is estimated for each of these samples, and those values are sorted to "create" the sampling distribution (Efron & Tibshirani, 1993; Preacher & Hayes, 2004). Confidence interval endpoints are identified by selecting lower- and upper-bound values along this sampling distribution corresponding to the desired level of confidence (Shrout & Bolger, 2002). There are several different techniques for choosing the specific endpoint values (e.g., percentile, bias-corrected, and bias-corrected and accelerated; Efron & Tibshirani, 1993); however, these differences are not germane to our arguments and the reader is referred to Cheung and Lau (2008) for a discussion of these methods. For the remainder of this manuscript we will use the term "bootstrapping" to refer generally to this class of methods for estimating a confidence interval for the indirect effect.

Because bootstrapping permits confidence interval endpoints to be selected directly from the sampling distribution, several methodologists have advocated for its widespread use to test the significance of indirect effects. Preacher and Hayes (2004, p. 720) describe the Sobel test as an "underpowered test of mediation" and further state that bootstrapping may be a way of "circumventing the power problem introduced by asymmetries and other forms of nonnormality" in the indirect effect sampling distribution (Preacher & Hayes, 2004, p. 722). These comments are echoed by Shrout and Bolger (2002, p. 429), as these authors argue that bootstrapping tends to be "more powerful" than the Sobel test. These assertions have had a powerful effect on mediation testing in organizational research, as bootstrapping has come to be broadly seen as the superior method for testing mediation.

As evidence for this, we examined every article published in the journals *Academy of Management Journal, Journal of Applied Psychology, Journal of Management, Personnel Psychology*, and *Organizational Behavior and Human Decision Processes* for the 2 years 2009 and 2011. We coded each article that tested mediation for whether the Sobel test, bootstrapping, or an alternative method was used (focusing only on primary, single-level studies). In this short time span, we see a drastic switch in the dominant methods for testing mediation. In 2009, 49% of tests for mediation used the Sobel test compared to 19% using bootstrapping. However, by 2011, 31% of tests for mediation used the Sobel test compared to 58% using bootstrapping. In keeping with the tradition of statistical and methodological myths and urban legends scholarship, we now discuss the kernel of truth underlying advocacy for bootstrapping instead of the Sobel test.

Kernel of Truth about Bootstrapping

Advocacy for bootstrapping generally hinges on an assertion that the confidence intervals are "more powerful" than those created by the Sobel test (MacKinnon, Lockwood, & Williams, 2004; Shrout & Bolger, 2002). However, since its inception, bootstrapping was never explicitly intended to improve the *statistical power* of confidence intervals but rather to improve their *accuracy* (e.g., Efron, 1987). Accurate confidence intervals should be symmetric regarding the proportion of values in the sampling distribution that fall below the lower bound and above the upper bound (e.g., Cheung & Lau, 2008). Statistical power, on the other hand, reflects the long-run probability of rejecting a false null hypothesis in the population. Though distinct, these two characteristics overlap in the case of the positively skewed indirect effect sampling distribution.

A positively skewed sampling distribution results when more than 50% of the values in that distribution fall below the mean combined with an elongated tail encompassing values lying far above the mean (see Figure 11.2). Normal theory approaches like the Sobel test estimate confidence intervals by locating endpoints symmetrically, based on the standard error, above and below the distribution mean (Cohen, Cohen, West, & Aiken, 2003). Inaccuracies associated with either the point estimate of the mean or the standard error can therefore affect the selection of these interval endpoints, and so positive skew is likely to reduce statistical power of such confidence intervals for two reasons.

First, because more than half of the values for the positively skewed distribution lie below the mean, on average, the estimated indirect effect for a given sample has an increased likelihood of falling closer to zero. This is problematic because the point estimate locates the center of the confidence interval and, all things being

FIGURE 11.2 A positively skewed distribution

Notes: Figure is a stylistic representation of a positively skewed distribution. The dashed line represents the average value.

228 Joel Koopman et al.

equal, the closer this center is to zero, the more likely it is that the confidence interval will include zero. Second, the elongated tail of the distribution can inflate estimates of the standard error. This will lead to wider confidence intervals because the standard error directly influences the distance between confidence interval endpoints and the point estimate. This confluence of events increases the likelihood that Sobel test confidence intervals will include zero and thus be underpowered. Bootstrapping generally overcomes these issues because neither the point estimate nor the standard error is directly used in the creation of the confidence intervals and are thus not systematically shifted toward zero.

A Critical Examination of Bootstrapping

Bootstrapping's primary value comes from increased confidence interval accuracy. However, it is increasingly viewed as broadly superior to the Sobel test for reasons that go beyond accurate confidence intervals. We identified four areas of concern that cast doubt on this widely held belief. Following the tradition of previous manuscripts identifying statistical and methodological urban legends (e.g., Aguinis & Harden, 2009; Lance et al., 2006; Spector & Brannick, 2011), in the sections to follow, we identify specific published manuscripts using quotes to highlight the problems we discuss. We strongly assert that our commentary should not be interpreted either as demeaning these authors or as an indictment of their research. *We do not target these authors for criticism.* The very premise of this manuscript is that bootstrapping is widely believed to be a superior method for testing mediation, and as such, these authors were clearly conducting their research in accordance with commonly accepted practice (c.f., Vandenberg, 2006). Indeed, it is possible and even likely that these authors may have simply been responding to the demands of reviewers and editors (i.e., Spector & Brannick, 2011; Vandenberg, 2006). Our purpose is to simply use these quotes as exemplars of the state of the science to anchor our core argument that bootstrapping is perceived as the superior method for testing mediation.

Necessary Assumptions Cannot Be Ignored

> One particularly useful approach is the bootstrap framework, which can be applied even when sample sizes are moderate or small, that is, in the range of 20–80 cases (Efron & Tibshirani, 1993).
>
> *(Shrout & Bolger, 2002, p. 424)*

Shrout and Bolger (2002) specifically advocated for the use of bootstrapping in relatively small samples where the normal theory assumptions of the Sobel test are particularly apt to be violated. However, all statistical techniques have underlying assumptions that must be met if they are to be considered appropriate for a particular context, and bootstrapping is no exception. Indeed, using bootstrapping in small samples violates a different but equally important assumption: that the sample to be bootstrapped is sufficiently representative of the population. Bootstrapping is analogous to a large number of unique research teams (i.e., 1,000) each investigating the same research question with the same size sample drawn from the same overall population. In this analogy, the bootstrap resamples represent the unique samples from each research team and the sample being bootstrapped represents the population. This leads to a critical realization—when bootstrapping, the original sample must be assumed to be representative of the underlying population (Rubin, 1981; Schenker, 1985). This assumption is well known by statisticians; Mooney and Duval (1993, p. 10) directly state, "in bootstrapping, we treat the sample as the population" and go further in saying "we must believe that a representative sample of all the possible distinct values of the population is found in our data" (Mooney & Duval, 1993, p. 61). When considering the use of bootstrapping in small samples, we are left with three foundational statements that cannot all coexist.

1. Bootstrapping has been advocated as being particularly useful in small samples (e.g., Shrout & Bolger, 2002).
2. Bootstrapping necessarily assumes that a sample is representative of the population (Mooney & Duval, 1993).
3. Sampling error is particularly troublesome in small samples, rendering an assumption that a sample is representative of the population in this context tenuous at best (Schmidt, Hunter, & Pearlman, 1981).

It is well known that sampling error causes random distributional inaccuracies that affect the representativeness of a sample vis-à-vis the population (Schmidt et al., 1981; Tversky & Kahneman, 1971). While sampling always results in chance deviations affecting representativeness to some extent, these deviations tend to be minor in large samples, whereas they can be extreme in small samples (e.g., Kahneman & Tversky, 1972). Interestingly, when introducing bootstrapping methods for confidence interval creation, Efron actually warned against using bootstrapping for hypothesis testing in small samples. Specifically, Efron (1990, p. 4) commented that bootstrap confidence intervals were likely to be inaccurate in small samples and that this inaccuracy would be especially problematic for hypothesis testing as "small errors in the end-points can change the verdict of the test" (see also: Efron, 1992). Additionally, Efron and Tibshirani (1993, p. 178) remarked that bootstrap confidence intervals "can still be erratic for small sample sizes," and Efron (2000, p. 1295) states that bootstrapping "may still not give very accurate coverage in a small-sample non-parametric situation."

Thus, not only does bootstrapping clearly violate a necessary assumption concerning the representativeness of the sample, but its applicability for hypothesis testing in small samples was also questioned by its creator (Bradley Efron) himself. As sample size increases, concerns over representativeness owing to sampling error

230 Joel Koopman et al.

decrease (Schmidt et al., 1981); however, it is important to note that the positive skew of the indirect effect sampling distribution also fades with increasing sample size, likewise increasing the tenability of the Sobel test's normal theory assumptions (Cheung & Lau, 2008; Stone & Sobel, 1990).

More Powerful May Not Be Powerful Enough

> In addition, powerful bootstrapping methodologies have been proposed to test the statistical significance of indirect effects in mediation models (Shrout & Bolger, 2002) and moderated mediation models (Edwards & Lambert, 2007).
>
> *(Ozer, 2011, p. 1331)*

Statistical power is vitally important to hypothesis testing because it directly affects the long-term likelihood of rejecting a false null hypothesis. Underpowered research is detrimental to advancing knowledge and theory because conflicting results can occur that are solely explained by random error (Cohen, 1992; Schmidt et al., 1981). In the above quote, Ozer (2011) conveys the primary argument of bootstrapping proponents (e.g., Preacher & Hayes, 2004; Shrout & Bolger, 2002)—that bootstrapping is a "powerful" statistical tool. However, it is important to distinguish between "relative statistical power" (i.e., *more* powerful than the Sobel test) and "sufficient statistical power" (i.e., powerful).

Relative statistical power involves a comparison; two statistical methods may be compared and one may be found to be more powerful than the other. In contrast, sufficient statistical power reflects whether some standard (i.e., the generally accepted threshold of 80%; Cohen, 1992) has been met or exceeded. Thus, even if bootstrapping is relatively more powerful than the Sobel test in some contexts (Shrout & Bolger, 2002), this does not guarantee that bootstrapping is powerful *enough* in that context. For example, consider two individuals applying for a Ph.D. program. If one student's GMAT score is in the 40th percentile and the other student scores in the 60th percentile, then the second student performed better in a relative sense. However, if the department cutoff requires performance equal to or exceeding the 80th percentile, then neither student's performance was sufficient in an absolute sense.

This example illuminates an important issue: Relative comparisons are relatively meaningless indicators of sufficient performance. The criterion for selecting a suitable statistical test should not be simply whether one of those tests is relatively more powerful but instead whether one test is sufficiently powerful in a particular context *when the other is not*. When neither test achieves a sufficient level of power, our ability to draw meaningful conclusions is still hindered because as a field we fall victim to the well-known pitfalls (i.e., wide confidence intervals and contradictory findings) of underpowered research (Schmidt et al., 1981) regardless of the method employed.

To examine this alternative perspective on the comparative statistical power of bootstrapping and the Sobel test, we conducted a simulation study to examine the population parameter and sample size combinations under which bootstrapping provides a statistical test with sufficient power to reject a false null hypothesis while the Sobel test does not. We investigated a series of commonly encountered sample sizes ranging from $N = 20$ to $N = 200$, increasing in increments of 20 cases. In each condition, we simulated a simple mediated relationship (i.e., Figure 11.1) where some independent variable, X, has an effect on a dependent variable, Y, equal to $\alpha \star \beta$, that is fully mediated through a third variable, M (i.e., the total effect of X on Y is equivalent to the indirect effect and $c' = 0$; MacKinnon et al., 2004).

Following Cohen (1992), we modeled small, medium, and large effect sizes as standardized population values of 0.10, 0.30, and 0.50, respectively (e.g., Biesanz et al., 2010; Cheung & Lau, 2008; MacKinnon et al., 2004). Using these parameters to index the magnitude of the relationships in the population, we examined three different conditions—small/small, medium/medium, and large/large—representing the relationship between X and M and M and Y, respectively. Using R (R Core Team, 2012), we generated 1,000 random samples for each effect size/sample size combination from a standard multivariate normal population (using the "MASS" package; Venables & Ripley, 2002). The combination of the three effect size conditions and 10 sample sizes resulted in 30,000 unique data sets for analysis. For each, the indirect effect in each sample was evaluated with a Sobel (1982) test and then bootstrapped 1,000 times using the R package "boot" (Canty & Ripley, 2013). Following Efron and Tibshirani (1993), we created 95% bootstrap confidence intervals using "percentile (PCNT)," "bias-corrected (BC)," and "bias-corrected and accelerated (BCa)" procedures.

Table 11.1 provides the results of our power analysis. Consistent with previous assertions, in every condition where power is less than 100%, bootstrapping is indeed relatively more powerful than the Sobel test. However, our intended purpose was to examine the conditions under which bootstrapping demonstrates sufficient power (i.e., 80%) while the Sobel test does not. This analysis reveals that at least one method of bootstrap confidence interval construction has 80% or higher statistical power in 15 out of 30 conditions (specifically, nearly every condition with large effect sizes as well as moderate effect sizes when $N > 100$). However, the Sobel test also has at least 80% power in 13 of those 15 conditions.

We feel the more appropriate takeaway is that, when considering both methods in terms of sufficient power (i.e., achieving 80% power), neither test performs all that well in many instances. For example, when effect sizes are small, neither test ever exceeds 13% power. When effect sizes are medium, sample sizes of at least 100 are required for bootstrapping's power to be sufficient, and both methods exceed 80% power beyond 140 cases. When effect sizes are large, there is little difference in terms of statistical power between the two methods. In summary, when considering whether a mediation test has *sufficient power* to reject a false null hypothesis, the advantages of bootstrapping over the Sobel test are quite miniscule.

TABLE 11.1 Power Analysis of the Sobel Test and Bootstrapping for Detecting Indirect Effects

		N = 20	N = 40	N = 60	N = 80	N = 100	N = 120	N = 140	N = 160	N = 180	N = 200
	Sobel	.001	.000	.002	.006	.004	.004	.009	.010	.016	.014
$\alpha = .10$	PCNT	.006	.003	.009	.016	.036	.024	.042	.045	.066	.064
$\beta = .10$	BC	.017	.016	.031	.039	.066	.063	.086	.087	.123	.127
	BCa	.017	.016	.035	.041	.064	.064	.083	.090	.120	.127
	Sobel	.022	.074	.196	.373	.533	.656	**.800**	**.874**	**.933**	**.954**
$\alpha = .30$	PCNT	.067	.193	.375	.559	.715	.795	**.882**	**.933**	**.964**	**.976**
$\beta = .30$	BC	.109	.265	.482	.656	.797	**.861**	**.926**	**.956**	**.976**	**.982**
	BCa	.101	.265	.480	.649	.797	**.861**	**.929**	**.956**	**.977**	**.979**
	Sobel	.186	.642	**.919**	**.982**	**.995**	**.998**	**1.00**	**1.00**	**1.00**	**1.00**
$\alpha = .50$	PCNT	.323	.762	**.946**	**.987**	**.998**	**.998**	**1.00**	**1.00**	**1.00**	**1.00**
$\beta = .50$	BC	.446	**.830**	**.965**	**.993**	**.998**	**.999**	**1.00**	**1.00**	**1.00**	**1.00**
	BCa	.431	**.821**	**.960**	**.993**	**.997**	**.999**	**1.00**	**1.00**	**1.00**	**1.00**

Notes: Values represent the proportion of correct rejections of the population null hypothesis over 1,000 replications. α and β refer to the population effect sizes for the paths of the indirect effect in a mediation model. Bolded values represent power > 0.80, which is the typically accepted standard for organizational research. Sobel refers to confidence intervals calculated using Sobel's (1982) standard error; PCNT refers to "percentile" method bootstrap confidence intervals; BC refers to "bias-corrected" method bootstrap confidence intervals; BCa refers to "bias-corrected and accelerated" method bootstrap confidence intervals.

Type I Error Is Not Fixed at 5%

> [T]here is a smaller chance of making a Type I error because [bootstrapping] does not require normal distribution for the standard errors of the product term (Edwards & Lambert, 2007).
>
> *(Takeuchi, Yun, & Wong, 2011, p. 234)*

Type I error refers to the long-term probability of rejecting a true null hypothesis in the population (Cohen et al., 2003) and, while not yoked directly, is intimately related to statistical power. While statistical power in organizational research varies, the Type I error rate is generally treated as a fixed policy corresponding to the accepted level of risk for mistakenly rejecting a true population null hypothesis and is set *a priori* (nominally at 5%; Cortina & Landis, 2011). In the above quote, Takeuchi and colleagues (2011) articulate another reason that bootstrapping has come to be seen as a superior test of mediation compared to the Sobel test. However, recent evidence would seem to suggest that, in reality, it is bootstrapping and not the Sobel test that suffers from a high Type I error rate (Biesanz et al., 2010; Fritz, Taylor, & MacKinnon, 2012).

Realized Type I error rates can actually fluctuate in certain contexts, including in the case of the indirect effect (Biesanz et al., 2010). As a result, specification of a 95% confidence interval, generally taken to imply a 5% Type I error risk, may not actually reflect this policy in the long term. If the Type I error rate for bootstrapping regularly exceeds the expected criterion of 5%, this is a major concern that should be factored into discussions about how to test for mediation, especially in light of the results in the previous section suggesting that bootstrapping has little advantage over the Sobel test in terms of sufficient statistical power.

We conducted a second simulation study to probe this issue by following the same procedures described earlier with the only difference being that we fixed the "α" path in each effect size combination at zero (to model a null population indirect effect), again creating 30,000 unique data sets for analysis. Table 11.2 provides the results of this analysis. As is clear from this table, bootstrapping has an alarming tendency to exceed 5% Type I error, as at least one method of constructing 95% bootstrap confidence intervals exceeded the nominal 5% Type I error rate in 18 out of 30 conditions (specifically, every condition with a large effect size and nearly all with a moderate effect size as well). By comparison, the Sobel test never exceeded 5% Type I error rate in any condition. Furthermore, unlike in the previous section on statistical power, this problem is not mitigated by increasing sample size.

The same logic previously presented to explain why Sobel confidence intervals are relatively less powerful than bootstrap confidence intervals (i.e., that due to positive skew, these confidence intervals will on average tend to be too close to zero and have larger standard errors) applies here as well and explains why these

TABLE 11.2 Type I Error Analysis of the Sobel Test and Bootstrapping for Detecting Indirect Effects

		N = 20	N = 40	N = 60	N = 80	N = 100	N = 120	N = 140	N = 160	N = 180	N = 200
$\alpha = .00$ $\beta = .10$	Sobel	.000	.000	.000	.000	.001	.001	.001	.001	.002	.001
	PCNT	.004	.003	.006	.006	.009	.006	.006	.010	.013	.010
	BC	.010	.013	.019	.014	.022	.022	.028	.024	.027	.022
	BCa	.011	.012	.020	.015	.022	.021	.027	.025	.026	.023
$\alpha = .00$ $\beta = .30$	Sobel	.002	.004	.011	.011	.005	.015	.032	.013	.028	.030
	PCNT	.017	.018	.039	.039	.037	**.060**	**.056**	.045	**.054**	**.058**
	BC	.039	.042	**.072**	**.063**	**.077**	**.092**	**.080**	**.069**	**.080**	**.082**
	BCa	.030	.045	**.068**	**.063**	**.075**	**.091**	**.082**	**.068**	**.079**	**.080**
$\alpha = .00$ $\beta = .50$	Sobel	.008	.026	.034	.040	.038	.048	.039	.032	.044	.042
	PCNT	.035	**.058**	**.067**	**.062**	**.056**	**.066**	**.051**	.042	**.058**	**.053**
	BC	**.061**	**.096**	**.098**	**.083**	**.071**	**.074**	**.064**	**.054**	**.059**	**.059**
	BCa	**.066**	**.088**	**.101**	**.088**	**.071**	**.075**	**.065**	**.053**	**.060**	**.060**

Notes: Values represent the proportion of incorrect rejections of the population null hypothesis over 1,000 replications. α and β refer to the population effect sizes for the paths of the indirect effect in a mediation model (to model a null population indirect effect, the α was fixed at zero for these analyses). Bolded values are where Type I error > 0.05, which is the typically accepted standard for organizational research. Sobel refers to confidence intervals calculated using Sobel's (1982) standard error; PCNT refers to "percentile" method bootstrap confidence intervals; BC refers to "bias-corrected" method bootstrap confidence intervals; BCa refers to "bias-corrected and accelerated" method bootstrap confidence intervals.

intervals consistently exhibit a Type I error rate below 5%. These issues go hand in hand; because Sobel confidence intervals can be biased toward zero, when a Type I error policy of 5% is specified, the Sobel test actually presents an overly conservative test of statistical significance. In contrast, bootstrapping represents a more liberal hypothesis test. Although more statistically powerful at the margin, this comes at a cost, as bootstrapping frequently exceeds the expected 5% Type I error rate, including in several conditions where the Sobel test is sufficiently powerful and does not exceed a 5% Type I error rate.

Change Your Seed, Change Your Confidence Interval

> Because bootstrapping is based on random resampling of the data, bootstrap confidence intervals will differ slightly each time the macro is run as a result of the random sampling process.
>
> *(Hayes, 2013, p. 4)*

In contrast to the three previous sections, the topic of this section is not relevant to the Sobel test. Unlike the Sobel test, which generates only one confidence interval, when bootstrapping, it is possible for the confidence interval to change each time the analysis is executed. The quotation above comes from the technical documentation accompanying a macro for implementing bootstrapping (Hayes, 2013) and illustrates a worrisome but largely overlooked concern with bootstrapping—that the calculated confidence interval for a given set of data may sometimes change. This is not a minor issue; on the contrary, it suggests that bootstrapping violates the "first law of applied statistics, that two individuals using the same statistical method on the same data should arrive at the same conclusion" (Gleser, 1996, p. 220).

Bootstrapping is a Monte Carlo simulation method. Such methods utilize "pseudo-random" draws from some distribution in the course of statistical modeling (Rubinstein, 1981). The "pseudo" aspect of pseudo-randomness is important. While the process can generally be considered random in a practical sense, it actually unfolds in a completely deterministic pattern based on the algorithm driving the pseudo-random number generator in the statistical package. For the algorithm to function, it needs a starting value, sometimes referred to as a seed. In the context of bootstrapping, the content of each resample is determined by this starting seed value.

If a sample is bootstrapped using a particular seed value (i.e., zero) and then bootstrapped again using the identical seed value, the results will be identical because the bootstrapping samples would be constructed in an identical manner. However, if this seed changes between analyses, then the bootstrapping process necessarily unfolds in a slightly different fashion. The bootstrap samples will be different (even if only slightly), and the end points of the confidence intervals may

236 Joel Koopman et al.

be different as a consequence. As a hypothetical example, researchers are unlikely to quibble greatly over two generated confidence intervals with endpoints of (−.03, .15) and (−.05, .14), as both intervals will generally lead to the same conclusion in terms of hypothesis testing. However, what if instead those two confidence intervals had endpoints of (.01, .15) and (−.01, .14)? From the standpoint of null hypothesis significance testing, this might be the difference between supporting and failing to support a critical hypothesis.

To examine whether such differences could, in practice, affect the conclusion drawn from a hypothesis test, we conducted additional simulation studies for both statistical power and Type I error following the procedures previously described. Bootstrapping analyses still used 1,000 resamples, and the first analysis was conducted using the random seed "0" as in the initial simulations. However, we then repeated the entire analysis 24 more times for each condition, changing the starting seed each time, as could be expected to happen by default when using many popular bootstrapping routines (we return to this in the discussion).

Tables 11.3 and 11.4 summarize the results of our "reseeding" analysis. Each of the cells reflects either the statistical power (Table 11.3) or Type I error rate (Table 11.4) of bootstrapping, with and without reseeding. We present these results using two numbers in the form "A/B." The "A" value represents the outcome without reseeding (and corresponds to the value from our previous analyses). The "B" value (shown in italics) represents either the statistical power or Type I error when reseeding is taken into account. Statistical power and Type I error results were coded according to whether the null hypothesis was rejected at least once (i.e., whether at least one of the confidence intervals generated by reseeding for each sample excluded zero).

Table 11.3 displays the results of the reseeding analysis for statistical power. The effective power (i.e., the number of times bootstrapping correctly rejected the false null hypothesis) increased in every condition, but in only one condition ($N = 100$ with moderate effect sizes) does bootstrapping now achieve sufficient (i.e., 80%) statistical power where it did not previously. Therefore, although statistical power can be increased through reseeding, the increase is relatively miniscule. Our conclusions based on Type I error, however, are quite different.

Table 11.4 displays the results of the reseeding analysis for Type I error, and it shows that the number of times bootstrapping incorrectly rejected the true null hypothesis increased in every condition. We find these results extremely troubling, as bootstrapping now exceeds 5% Type I error rate in 20 out of 30 conditions tested (every condition with either a moderate or large effect size), and the effective Type I error rate exceeds 10% for at least one bootstrapping method in 12 out of those 20 conditions. Of note is that the Sobel test values did not change in either table; researchers are stuck with their data and confidence interval when using this method.

TABLE 11.3 Power Analysis of the Sobel Test and Bootstrapping for Detecting Indirect Effects with Reseeding

		N = 20	N = 40	N = 60	N = 80	N = 100	N = 120	N = 140	N = 160	N = 180	N = 200
	Sobel	.001	.000	.002	.006	.004	.004	.009	.010	.016	.014
$\alpha = .10$	PCNT	.006/.010	.003/.006	.009/.014	.016/.023	.036/.046	.024/.042	.042/.063	.045/.064	.066/.089	.064/.094
$\beta = .10$	BC	.017/.026	.016/.038	.031/.047	.039/.064	.066/.090	.063/.102	.086/.118	.087/.132	.123/.164	.127/.179
	BCa	.017/.026	.016/.034	.035/.051	.041/.062	.064/.088	.064/.103	.083/.120	.090/.134	.120/.162	.127/.177
	Sobel	.022	.074	.196	.373	.533	.656	**.800**	**.874**	**.933**	**.954**
$\alpha = .30$	PCNT	.067/.090	.193/.240	.375/.442	.559/.632	.715/.771	.795/**.855**	**.882/.920**	**.933/.950**	**.964/.976**	**.976/.984**
$\beta = .30$	BC	.109/.156	.265/.338	.482/.570	.656/.735	.797/**.859**	**.861/.906**	**.926/.949**	**.956/.969**	**.976/.986**	**.982/.993**
	BCa	.101/.156	.265/.338	.480/.568	.649/.729	.797/**.856**	**.861/.901**	**.929/.951**	**.956/.969**	**.977/.986**	**.979/.993**
	Sobel	.186	.642	**.919**	**.982**	**.995**	**.998**	**1.00**	**1.00**	**1.00**	**1.00**
$\alpha = .50$	PCNT	.323/.407	.762/**.809**	**.946/.961**	**.987/.992**	**.998/.999**	**.998/.999**	**1.00/1.00**	**1.00/1.00**	**1.00/1.00**	**1.00/1.00**
$\beta = .50$	BC	.446/.560	**.830/.878**	**.965/.978**	**.993/.995**	**.998/.999**	**.999/.999**	**1.00/1.00**	**1.00/1.00**	**1.00/1.00**	**1.00/1.00**
	BCa	.431/.539	**.821/.876**	**.960/.995**	**.993/.995**	**.997/.999**	**.999/.999**	**1.00/1.00**	**1.00/1.00**	**1.00/1.00**	**1.00/1.00**

Notes: Values represent the proportion of correct rejections of the population null hypothesis over 1,000 replications. α and β refer to the population effect sizes for the paths of the indirect effect in a mediation model. Bolded values represent power > 0.80, which is the typically accepted standard for organizational research. Sobel refers to confidence intervals calculated using Sobel's (1982) standard error; PCNT refers to "percentile" method bootstrap confidence intervals; BC refers to "bias-corrected" method bootstrap confidence intervals; BCa refers to "bias-corrected and accelerated" method bootstrap confidence intervals. Italicized values to the right of the "/" represent the new proportion of correct rejections of the null hypothesis after conducting the reseeding analysis.

TABLE 11.4 Type I Error Analysis of the Sobel Test and Bootstrapping for Detecting Indirect Effects with Reseeding

		N = 20	N = 40	N = 60	N = 80	N = 100	N = 120	N = 140	N = 160	N = 180	N = 200
	Sobel	.000	.000	.000	.000	.001	.001	.001	.001	.002	.001
$\alpha = .00$	PCNT	.004/*.007*	.003/*.004*	.006/*.009*	.006/*.011*	.009/*.015*	.006/*.008*	.006/*.015*	.010/*.015*	.013/*.016*	.010/*.017*
$\beta = .10$	BC	.010/*.017*	.013/*.027*	.019/*.032*	.014/*.024*	.022/*.036*	.022/*.035*	.028/*.044*	.024/*.045*	.027/*.048*	.022/*.048*
	BCa	.011/*.018*	.012/*.029*	.020/*.032*	.015/*.024*	.022/*.033*	.021/*.034*	.027/*.046*	.025/*.044*	.026/*.048*	.023/*.047*
	Sobel	.002	.004	.011	.011	.005	.015	.032	.013	.028	.030
$\alpha = .00$	PCNT	.017/*.031*	.018/*.033*	.039/***.054***	.039/*.050*	.037/***.062***	***.060/.084***	***.056/.076***	.045/***.063***	***.054/.070***	***.058/.078***
$\beta = .30$	BC	.039/***.057***	.042/***.077***	***.072/.095***	.063/***.096***	***.077/.107***	***.092/.129***	***.080/.118***	***.069/.109***	***.080/.110***	***.082/.119***
	BCa	.030/***.052***	.045/***.075***	***.068/.101***	.063/***.094***	***.075/.106***	***.091/.130***	***.082/.118***	***.068/.106***	***.079/.110***	***.080/.117***
	Sobel	.008	.026	.034	.040	.038	.048	.039	.032	.044	.042
$\alpha = .00$	PCNT	.035/*.047*	***.058/.084***	***.067/.090***	***.062/.082***	***.056/.079***	***.066/.083***	***.051/.075***	***.042/.067***	***.058/.068***	***.053/.071***
$\beta = .50$	BC	***.061/.099***	***.096/.121***	***.098/.124***	***.083/.112***	***.071/.102***	***.074/.102***	***.064/.097***	***.054/.091***	***.059/.081***	***.059/.093***
	BCa	***.066/.097***	***.088/.114***	***.101/.124***	***.088/.117***	***.071/.098***	***.075/.102***	***.065/.099***	***.053/.090***	***.060/.080***	***.060/.085***

Notes: Values represent the proportion of incorrect rejections of the population null hypothesis over 1,000 replications. α and β refer to the population effect sizes for the paths of the indirect effect in a mediation model (to model a null population indirect effect, the α was fixed at zero for these analyses). Bolded values are where Type I error > 0.05, which is the typically accepted standard for organizational research. Sobel refers to confidence intervals calculated using Sobel's (1982) standard error; PCNT refers to "percentile" method bootstrap confidence intervals; BC refers to "bias-corrected" method bootstrap confidence intervals; BCa refers to "bias-corrected and accelerated" method bootstrap confidence intervals. Italicized values to the right of the "/" represent the new proportion of incorrect rejections of the null hypothesis after conducting the reseeding analysis.

Discussion

Our goal for this manuscript was to argue that, in spite of the increasing advocacy and consensus for testing mediation with bootstrapping as opposed to the Sobel test, there are reasons to be skeptical of this movement. It is widely believed that bootstrapping constitutes a superior test of mediation compared to the Sobel test. This belief is evident from both the prevalence with which bootstrapping tends to be used in the course of mediation hypothesis testing and the content of arguments presented in favor of bootstrapping. We feel that this belief is an urban legend, something that researchers believe to be true that is actually not (Lance et al., 2006). A number of researchers have compared bootstrapping and the Sobel test and concluded that bootstrapping is superior (c.f., MacKinnon et al., 2004). We also compared bootstrapping and the Sobel test in our simulations; however, our results lead us to the opposite conclusion.

While much has been made of the problem that plagues the Sobel test in small samples—the unmet normality assumption for the indirect effect sampling distribution—in reality, bootstrapping suffers from an unsatisfied assumption in small samples as well. Thus, in small samples, we see little conceptual advantage to either approach. Likewise, when comparing the conditions under which the two methods exhibit sufficient (i.e., 80%) statistical power, there seems to be little difference between them. Indeed, the bigger issue for ensuring sufficient statistical power would seem to be adequate sample size. This is an important issue, and one that we feel gets overlooked when the discussion focuses only on relative power advantages.

When Type I error is simultaneously considered, we feel that the comparison between the two methods ceases to be a contest at all. Clearly, it is not the Sobel test that we should be concerned about regarding Type I error, but rather it is bootstrapping with its unsettling tendency to exceed the expected 5% Type I error rate in many commonly encountered conditions. Because Type I error is considered to be a fixed policy, our simulation results in this area are both provocative and disturbing. Given the small statistical power differences between bootstrapping and the Sobel test and the drastic differences from a Type I error standpoint, we express substantial misgivings regarding the use of bootstrapping instead of the Sobel test.

The issue of reseeding further complicates advocacy for bootstrapping. While it is impossible to know in practice whether analyses are frequently run using different seeds in search of significant results, the existence of this issue is disconcerting. There is nothing necessarily insidious at play here; this can actually happen innocently. Some statistical programs automatically change the random seed for each analysis; the SPSS macro provided by Preacher and Hayes (2004) sets the seed to a random number each time it is executed, and the same occurs in the boot package in R. Simply adding a new control variable (that itself has no effect on the mediation hypothesis) could lead to different results completely attributable to randomness from the starting seed. Importantly, the seed does not change in all programs; the seed defaults to a constant value in Mplus as well as with the syntax from Edwards and Lambert (2007).

Based on the evidence considered, we disagree with the current consensus that bootstrapping is preferable to the Sobel test for evaluating mediation hypotheses. In our opinion, not only does bootstrapping fail to demonstrate clear superiority relative to the Sobel test in any set of analyses, it is seemingly deficient when considering Type I error and reseeding. We therefore conclude that the belief that bootstrapping reflects a superior alternative to the Sobel test with regard to mediation testing is an urban legend and make the following recommendations.

Recommendations

1. Researchers should consider curtailing their advocacy for bootstrapping over the Sobel test based on the criterion that it is more powerful than the Sobel test. Instead, researchers (and reviewers) should be concerned with whether the method employed demonstrates sufficient (i.e., 80%) statistical power. From this perspective, sample size is a key factor, as bootstrapping and the Sobel test are largely comparable for a given condition.
2. Researchers should be wary of using bootstrapping in contexts involving indirect effects with medium or large effect sizes, as elevated Type I error rate concerns loom large here, even with relatively modest sample sizes. Reviewers and editors should similarly be cautious with such analyses and consider refraining from requesting them.
3. If researchers do utilize bootstrapping, they should include the name of the statistical program and the seed value used to ensure that results are replicable.
4. Researchers should consider reevaluating the utility of the Sobel test. When sample sizes exceed 140 cases with moderate effects, this test appears to satisfy necessary assumptions, avoids exceeding acceptable Type I error rates, and provides a sufficient level of statistical power for testing mediation hypotheses.
5. For instances in which sample size is small and obtaining additional cases is infeasible, researchers should explore alternatives to bootstrapping that may exhibit comparable statistical power while avoiding excessive Type I error (e.g., Taylor & MacKinnon, 2012; Yuan & MacKinnon, 2009).

Conclusion

Testing mediation is vitally important to building and testing theory; however, such importance should not outstrip our efforts to ensure that testing is both rigorous and replicable. Despite considerable advocacy and common beliefs to the contrary, bootstrapping does not necessarily provide a more rigorous method of hypothesis testing for the indirect effect than the Sobel test; in fact, based on our analyses, we find much to recommend the Sobel test (in the contexts for which it has sufficient power) over bootstrapping. Until such time as a new method for testing mediation arises that corrects deficiencies in the Sobel test without itself being comparatively deficient in other ways, we feel that in many contexts, organizational research relying on single-level mediation testing for theory building and testing can proceed apace with Sobel (1982) as a guide.

References

Aguinis, H., & Harden, E. E. (2009). Sample size rules of thumb: Evaluating three common practices. In C. E. Lance & R. J. Vandenberg (Eds.), *Statistical and methodological myths and urban legends: Doctrine, verity and fable in the organizational and social sciences* (pp. 267–286). New York, NY: Routledge/Psychology Press.

Baron, R. M., & Kenny, D. A. (1986). The moderator mediator variable distinction in social psychological research: Conceptual, strategic, and statistical considerations. *Journal of Personality and Social Psychology, 51*, 1173–1182.

Biesanz, J. C., Falk, C. F., & Savalei, V. (2010). Assessing mediational models: Testing and interval estimation for indirect effects. *Multivariate Behavioral Research, 45*, 661–701.

Bollen, K. A., & Stine, R. (1990). Direct and indirect effects: Classical and bootstrap estimates of variability. *Sociological Methodology, 20*, 115–140.

Canty, A., & Ripley, B. (2013). Boot: Bootstrap R (S-plus) functions. (Version 1.3-9).

Cheung, G. W., & Lau, R. S. (2008). Testing mediation and suppression effects of latent variables: Bootstrapping with structural equation models. *Organizational Research Methods, 11*, 296–325.

Cohen, J. (1992). A power primer. *Psychological Bulletin, 112*, 155–159.

Cohen, J., Cohen, P., West, S. G., & Aiken, L. S. (2003). *Applied multiple regression/correlation analysis for the behavioral sciences* (3rd ed.). Mahwah, NJ: Lawrence Erlbaum.

Cortina, J. M., & Landis, R. S. (2011). The earth is not round (p = .00). *Organizational Research Methods, 14*, 332–349.

Edwards, J. R., & Lambert, L. S. (2007). Methods for integrating moderation and mediation: A general analytical framework using moderated path analysis. *Psychological Methods, 12*, 1–22.

Efron, B. (1987). Better bootstrap confidence intervals. *Journal of the American Statistical Association, 82*, 171–185.

Efron, B. (1990). *Six questions raised by the bootstrap (technical report no. 139)*. Stanford, CA: Division of Biostatistics, Stanford University.

Efron, B. (1992). Six questions raised by the bootstrap. In R. Lepage & L. Billard (Eds.), *Exploring the limits of bootstrap* (pp. 99–126). New York, NY: Wiley.

Efron, B. (2000). The bootstrap and modern statistics. *Journal of the American Statistical Association, 95*, 1293–1296.

Efron, B., & Tibshirani, R. (1993). *An introduction to the bootstrap.* New York, NY: Chapman & Hall/CRC.

Fritz, M. S., Taylor, A. B., & MacKinnon, D. P. (2012). Explanation of two anomalous results in statistical mediation analysis. *Multivariate Behavioral Research, 47*, 61–87.

Gleser, L. J. (1996). Comment on "Bootstrap Confidence Intervals" by T. J. Diciccio and B. Efron. *Statistical Science, 11*, 219–221.

242 Joel Koopman et al.

Hayes, A. F. (2013, February 19). SPSS indirect macro syntax reference. Retrieved June 2, 2013, from www.afhayes.com/spss-sas-and-mplus-macros-and-code.html

Kahneman, D., & Tversky, A. (1972). Subjective probability: A judgment of representativeness. *Cognitive Psychology, 3*, 430–454.

Lance, C. E., Butts, M. M., & Michels, L. C. (2006). The sources of four commonly reported cutoff criteria: What did they really say? *Organizational Research Methods, 9*, 202–220.

Leavitt, K., Mitchell, T. R., & Peterson, J. (2010). Theory pruning: Strategies to reduce our dense theoretical landscape. *Organizational Research Methods, 13*, 644–667.

LeBreton, J. M., Wu, J., & Bing, M. N. (2009). The truth(s) on testing for mediation in the social and organizational sciences. In C. E. Lance & R. J. Vandenberg (Eds.), *Statistical and methodological myths and urban legends: Doctrine, verity and fable in the organizational and social sciences* (pp. 107–141). New York, NY: Routledge/Psychology Press.

MacKinnon, D. P., Lockwood, C. M., & Williams, J. (2004). Confidence limits for the indirect effect: Distribution of the product and resampling methods. *Multivariate Behavioral Research, 39*, 99–128.

Mooney, C. Z., & Duval, R. D. (1993). *Bootstrapping: A nonparametric approach to statistical inference*. Newbury Park, CA: Sage.

Ozer, M. (2011). A moderated mediation model of the relationship between organizational citizenship behaviors and job performance. *Journal of Applied Psychology, 96*, 1328–1336.

Preacher, K. J., & Hayes, A. F. (2004). SPSS and SAS procedures for estimating indirect effects in simple mediation models. *Behavior Research Methods, Instruments, & Computers, 36*, 717–731.

R Core Team. (2012). R: A language and environment for statistical computing (Version 2.15.1). Vienna, Austria: R Foundation for Statistical Computing. Retrieved from www.R-project. org/

Rubin, D. B. (1981). The Bayesian bootstrap. *The Annals of Statistics, 9*, 130–134.

Rubinstein, R. (1981). *Simulation and the Monte Carlo method*. New York, NY: Wiley.

Schenker, N. (1985). Qualms about bootstrap confidence intervals. *Journal of the American Statistical Association, 80*, 360–361.

Schmidt, F. L., Hunter, J. E., & Pearlman, K. (1981). Task differences as moderators of aptitude-test validity in selection: A red herring. *Journal of Applied Psychology, 66*, 166–185.

Shrout, P. E., & Bolger, N. (2002). Mediation in experimental and nonexperimental studies: New procedures and recommendations. *Psychological Methods, 7*, 422–445.

Sobel, M. E. (1982). Asymptotic confidence intervals for indirect effects in structural equation models. *Sociological Methodology, 13*, 290–312.

Spector, P. E., & Brannick, M. T. (2011). Methodological urban legends: The misuse of statistical control variables. *Organizational Research Methods, 14*, 287–305.

Stone, C. A., & Sobel, M. E. (1990). The robustness of estimates of total indirect effects in covariance structure models estimated by maximum likelihood. *Psychometrika, 55*, 337–352.

Takeuchi, R., Yun, S., & Wong, K.F.E. (2011). Social influence of a coworker: A test of the effect of employee and coworker exchange ideologies on employees' exchange qualities. *Organizational Behavior and Human Decision Processes, 115*, 226–237.

Taylor, A. B., & MacKinnon, D. P. (2012). Four applications of permutation methods to testing a single-mediator model. *Behavior Research Methods, 44*, 806–844.

Tversky, A., & Kahneman, D. (1971). Belief in the law of small numbers. *Psychological Bulletin,* *76*, 105–110.

Vandenberg, R. J. (2006). Statistical and methodological myths and urban legends: Where, pray tell, did they get this idea? *Organizational Research Methods, 9*, 194–201.

Venables, W. N., & Ripley, B. D. (2002). *Modern statistics with S.* (4 ed.). New York, NY: Springer.

Whetten, D. A. (1989). What constitutes a theoretical contribution? *Academy of Management Review, 14*, 490–495.

Yuan, Y., & MacKinnon, D. P. (2009). Bayesian mediation analysis. *Psychological Methods, 14*, 301–322.

PART IV

Inferential Issues

12

"THE" RELIABILITY OF JOB PERFORMANCE RATINGS EQUALS 0.52

Dan J. Putka and Brian J. Hoffman

Assessing individuals' job performance is a common practice in modern organizations, inextricably linked to a cross-section of talent management functions. Whether the focus of a talent management program is selecting a more effective workforce, training the existing workforce, or initiatives aimed at enhancing employee engagement, supervisor ratings of employee performance are a common criterion by which talent management processes are evaluated. Management research is also heavily dependent on performance ratings, and supervisor ratings of employee job performance are among the most commonly studied criteria. In short, the quality of supervisor ratings of performance is of central importance to management research and practice.

Despite the centrality of performance ratings to a cross-section of talent functions, management scholars and practitioners have had an uneasy relationship with performance ratings over the years. Indeed, Deming (1986) listed performance appraisal as one of the seven deadly sins of organizations. Less dramatically but no less damning, Murphy (2008) questioned the value of performance ratings, arguing that performance ratings do not reflect true performance. These criticisms are not new; concerns over the quality of humans' evaluations of others have persisted for as long as subjective ratings have been used to measure human attributes (Murphy, 2008; Thorndike, 1920).

In light of ongoing concerns about the accuracy of performance ratings, perhaps it is not surprising that researchers have paid a good deal of attention to methods for evaluating their quality. As a foundational property on which psychological measures are judged, it should come as no surprise that reliability remains a focal index of the quality of performance ratings (Murphy, Cleveland, & Mohler, 2001; Viswesvaran, Ones, & Schmidt, 1996). Reinforcing this focus has been continued reliance on reliability estimates to correct observed validity estimates for unreliability in criterion

248 Dan J. Putka and Brian J. Hoffman

measures—particularly in the context of meta-analyses and criterion-related validity studies (Schmidt & Hunter, 1996). The reasoning goes that observed correlations are attenuated by methodological shortcomings, such as measurement error. To account for these shortcomings, researchers estimate the reliability of the criterion measure they are using and then disattenuate observed correlations to estimate what the correlations would be if the criterion measure were free from error (Hunter & Schmidt, 2004). Correctly implementing such corrections requires an accurate and appropriate estimator of the reliability of performance ratings. Indeed, as the use of meta-analysis has increased, "researchers have become increasingly concerned with accurate estimates of criterion reliabilities" (Rothstein, 1990, p. 322).

Although intrarater, interrater, and stability-based estimates of reliability have each been used to index error in performance ratings, over the past three decades, interrater correlations have emerged as the most clearly recommended and most commonly used estimator of the reliability of performance ratings (Murphy, 2008; Rothstein, 1990). Indeed, Schmidt, Viswesvaran, and Ones (2000) have clearly stated interrater reliability, as estimated by an interrater correlation, is what should be used when correcting for error in job performance ratings: "In fact, it is the *only* appropriate reliability estimate for this correction" (p. 909; original emphasis). Consistent with this recommendation, Sackett, Laczo, and Arvey (2002) noted, "the type of reliability estimates used to correct validity estimates for measurement error are predominantly interrater reliability estimates" (p. 809)—and those in turn predominantly reflect interrater correlations. A cursory review of past meta-analyses involving job performance clearly substantiates this observation. For example, meta-analyses involving the relationship between job performance and stress (Gilboa, Shirom, Fried, & Cooper, 2008), job attitudes (Harrison, Newman, & Roth, 2006; Judge, Thoresen, Bono, & Patton, 2001; Riketta, 2005), managerial assessment centers (Hermelin, Lievens, & Robertson, 2007), intelligence tests (Bertua, Anderson, & Salgado, 2005; Schmidt & Hunter, 1998), and interviews (Huffcutt, Conway, Roth, & Stone, 2001; Taylor & Small, 2002), to name a few, have used interrater correlations when disattenuating observed correlations with performance ratings for measurement error.

The urban legend we will examine in this chapter is the notion an interrater correlation is *the* most appropriate estimator of the reliability of job performance ratings and, more generally, the notion that any single type of reliability estimator will universally be the most appropriate for a given type of measure (e.g., job performance ratings).

When Are Interrater Correlations Appropriate Estimators of Reliability?

The 2000 special issue of *Personnel Psychology* featured a spirited debate regarding interrater correlations and reliability (Murphy & DeShon, 2000a, 2000b; Schmidt et al., 2000). The focus of that debate was on whether interrater correlations are appropriate estimators of the reliability of job performance ratings. The debate largely hinged on disagreements regarding (a) assumptions underlying classical test theory–based estimators of reliability, (b) the substantive meaning and basis of sources of true score and error variance, and (c) distinctions between concepts of validity and reliability. Though fair points were made on both sides, in many respects, the debate arguably had little impact on actual research in industrial-organizational (I-O) psychology. As our introduction revealed, interrater correlations persist as the default "stamp" of choice by researchers seeking to document and evaluate the reliability of job performance ratings. Our intent here is neither to relive, moderate, nor reconcile the views raised. Rather, this chapter takes a step back from that debate and addresses more fundamental issues that render pronouncements over *the* most appropriate estimator of the reliability of job performance ratings moot.

The fundamental issue we focus on here, which is only tangentially raised in the 2000 *Personnel Psychology* special issue, is the myth that a single type of reliability estimate (e.g., interrater reliability as estimated by interrater correlations) as being the most appropriate estimate for a given type of measure (e.g., job performance ratings) is inconsistent with modern psychometric thought (American Educational Research Association, American Psychological Association, & National Council on Measurement in Education, 2014; Brennan, 2001; Haertel, 2006; Putka & Sackett, 2010). A careful examination of modern psychometric perspectives on reliability reveals that what sources of variance constitute true score and error variance, and therefore what functional form an appropriate reliability estimate should have, will depend on (a) the generalizations one wishes to make regarding scores produced by the measure, (b) whether one is interested in making relative comparisons among individuals' scores or absolute comparison to some standard (e.g., a cut-off score or performance threshold), and (c) characteristics of the measurement procedure (i.e., measurement design). These features can and do vary from situation to situation in research and practice involving job performance ratings.

To illustrate how these concepts relate to one another with regard to the reliability of job performance ratings and the implications they have for the appropriateness of interrater correlations in any given situation, we will consider a working example. Imagine the following scenario:

> A software company develops a new ratings-based measure of job performance for its software engineers. Ratings are gathered on the job performance measure, which is designed to assess six different dimensions of software engineer performance. Raters are asked to provide an assessment of those engineers with whom they have had sufficient opportunity to observe their performance. Two raters provide ratings for each incumbent. Raters make their ratings on a set of 7-point rating scales for each of five behavioral indicators per dimension that reflect important performance behaviors for that dimension.

To keep things simple, let's say that the researcher evaluating this measure wants to estimate the reliability of each dimension separately—for sake of illustration, let's say one dimension of interest is Problem Solving.

Based on prevailing research in I-O psychology, conventional wisdom would suggest that the appropriate reliability estimate for a situation such as this would be interrater reliability as estimated by an interrater correlation (e.g., Rothstein, 1990; Schmidt & Hunter, 1996; Schmidt et al., 2000; Viswesvaran et al., 1996). Specifically, one would average together the Problem Solving items of each of the two raters for each ratee and then correlate the resulting set of average ratings to arrive at the estimated reliability for ratings made by a single rater. If the researcher was interested in the reliability of the mean rating across both raters, conventional wisdom would dictate that the researcher use the Spearman-Brown prophesy to "step up" the interrater correlation so that it reflects the expected reliability for an average rating based on two raters. While this may reflect common organizational research and practice, simple adoption of an interrater correlation or the Spearman-Brown extension ignores the three aforementioned critical considerations to identifying appropriate reliability estimates in light of modern psychometric thought. We begin with desired generalizations.

Implications of Desired Generalizations for Reliability Estimation

Imagine we asked the researcher in the example to provide more information on the performance measure, and the researcher offered one of the following three descriptions noted in Figure 12.1.

Estimators of interrater reliability, such as a Pearson correlation or its Spearman-Brown extension, would only *potentially* be warranted for Condition A. In this condition, it is clear the researcher is not viewing item-specific variance as error and that interest only lies in generalizing the measure across raters. When items are averaged across raters and those average ratings are then correlated (across ratees), one will have an estimator of interrater reliability that allocates rater-specific variance to error variance and item-specific variance to true score variance. As we note in later sections, whether this correlation is an appropriate estimator of the reliability of job performance ratings will depend on the intended use of ratings and the measurement design underlying their data collection.

Under Condition B, an interrater correlation would not be an appropriate estimator of reliability regardless of intended use or measurement design, because the researcher does not desire to generalize ratings across raters. As noted in the example, this might be the case if the researcher believes that at least part of the specific variance associated with raters reflects legitimate job performance–related variance that would have meaningful relations with external variables (e.g., correlates or predictors of job performance; Murphy & DeShon, 2000a). This notion of performance-relevant rater-specific variance is consistent with early theoretical

Condition A: Generalizing across raters only	Condition B: Generalizing across items only	Condition C: Generalizing across raters and items
The researcher who developed the performance measure views each rater and item as providing measures of Problem Solving, but views ratings from each rater as an imperfect measure that reflects idiosyncrasies specific to the given rater and irrelevant to the Problem Solving measure. In contrast, the researcher views each item as reflecting a substantively different element of the Problem Solving criterion space that represents different contexts in which Problem Solving manifests itself on the job (e.g., collaboration problems, system integration problems, coding problems), and fully expects ratees to meaningfully vary in their Problem Solving performance across items.	The researcher who developed the performance measure views each rater and item as providing measures of Problem Solving, but views each item as an imperfect measure that reflects idiosyncrasies specific to the item and irrelevant to the Problem Solving measure. In contrast, the researcher views each rater as providing substantively different and meaningful perspectives on the Problem Solving criterion space given differences in the contexts under which each rater views the ratee engage in Problem Solving on the job.	The researcher who developed the performance measure views each rater and item as providing measures of Problem Solving, but views each rater and item as an imperfect measure that reflects idiosyncrasies specific to the rater and/or item and irrelevant to the Problem Solving measure.
Implication for Reliability Estimation: The researcher desires to generalize the measure across raters only. That is, s/he views rater-specific variation as error, and requires a coefficient that allocates rater-specific sources of variance to error variance, and item-specific variance to true score variance.	*Implication for Reliability Estimation*: The researcher desires to generalize the measure across items only. That is s/he views item-specific variation as error, and requires a coefficient that allocates item-specific sources of variance to error, and rater-specific variance to true score variance.	*Implication for Reliability Estimation*: The researcher desires to generalize the measure across raters and items. That is s/he views rater-specific and item-specific variation as sources of error, and requires a reliability coefficient that allocates rater-specific sources and item-specific sources of variance to error variance.

FIGURE 12.1 Implications of differences in desired generalizations for reliability estimation

perspectives on performance framed as "satisfactoriness" from the perspective of an individual observer or stakeholder (e.g., Dawis & Lofquist, 1984, i.e., performance to some extent is legitimately in the eye of the beholder) to more recent research on covariates of rater effects that have found nontrivial levels of "rater-specific variance" being meaningfully related to rater source and other substantively meaningful rater-level variables (e.g., Hoffman & Woehr, 2009; LaHuis & Avis, 2007; O'Neill, Goffin, & Gellatly, 2012; Putka, Ingerick, & McCloy, 2008). Similarly, raters situated in similar positions can also differ in substantively meaningful ways on the basis of the nature of the dyadic exchange relationship and

252 Dan J. Putka and Brian J. Hoffman

experience working together. Additionally, since raters are rating a common set of items for each individual, the covariance between average ratings (effectively the true score variance component in an interrater reliability estimate) will in part reflect shared item-specific variance—and under Condition B, the desire is for such variance to contribute to error, not true score.

Like Condition B, an interrater correlation would not be an appropriate estimator of reliability of job performance ratings under Condition C regardless of intended use or measurement design, because it only allocates rater-specific variance to error as opposed to rater- *and* item-specific variance.

The purpose of this demonstration was to begin to illustrate how universal use of interrater correlations as estimators of the reliability of job performance ratings can be problematic, as it ignores differences in hypotheses researchers may have regarding how raters and items function and the intended generalizations researchers want to make regarding their measures. Though researchers' desired generalizations will certainly be informed by prevailing science and theory regarding the measurement of job performance (e.g., MacKenzie, Podsakoff, & Jarvis, 2005), ultimately part of it will also depend on the local situation and precisely how the local researcher designed their measure—from identification of raters for inclusion to development of items in relation to how they were meant to represent or sample from the job performance criterion space. Blind adoption of interrater correlations as *the* de facto reliability estimator for job performance ratings ignores this reality.

Implications of Intended Use of Ratings for Reliability Estimation

In the previous illustration, we were careful to caveat Condition A by noting that interrater correlations may only be *potentially* warranted as appropriate estimators of reliability because that determination will also depend on the two other factors yet to be discussed, namely, intended use of ratings and measurement design underlying the collection of ratings. To illustrate how intended use of ratings can influence decisions regarding an appropriate estimator of the reliability of job performance ratings, consider Figure 12.2.

When job performance ratings are used as criteria in validity studies or interest is primarily in examining their correlation with other variables, it implies using the ratings to make relative comparisons of ratees based on their job performance (i.e., correlations reflect similarity in the relative ordering of individuals on job performance and another measure). In situations in which the primary interest is in the relative ordering of ratees, then an estimator of reliability as traditionally defined—that is, the proportion of observed, between-ratee variance that is attributable to true score variance—is warranted. As reflected in the previous section and reinforced in Figure 12.2, the exact composition of true score and error variance may differ depending on the generalizations one wishes to make regarding

	Condition A: Generalizing across raters only	Condition B: Generalizing across items only	Condition C: Generalizing across raters and items
Use 1: Relative comparison of ratees based on their performance ratings	Example Use: The organization will be using individuals' job performance ratings as a criterion measure in a criterion-related validation study for a new selection test.		
	Implication for Reliability Estimation: The researcher requires a coefficient that only allocates rater-specific components of *observed between-ratee variance* to error variance. These components reflect sources of inconsistency in the rank-ordering of ratees across raters.	*Implication for Reliability Estimation:* The researcher a coefficient that only allocates item-specific components of *observed between-ratee variance* to error variance. These components reflect sources of inconsistency in the rank-ordering of ratees across items.	*Implication for Reliability Estimation:* The researcher a coefficient that only allocates rater- and item-specific components of *observed between-ratee variance* to error variance. These components reflect sources of inconsistency in the rank-ordering of ratees across raters and items.
Use 2: Absolute comparisons between ratees' performance ratings and an established benchmark or cut-off value	Example Use: The organization will be comparing each individual's job performance ratings to a performance standard to identify incumbents in need of training.		
	Implication for Reliability Estimation: The researcher requires a coefficient that allocates rater-specific components of *total rating variance* to error variance. The denominator of this coefficient will not reflect an estimate of *observed between-ratee variance*, so technically, it is not a reliability coefficient, but rather a coefficient of absolute agreement.	*Implication for Reliability Estimation:* The researcher requires a coefficient that allocates item-specific components of *total rating variance* to error variance. The denominator of this coefficient will not reflect an estimate of *observed between-ratee variance*, so technically, it is not a reliability coefficient, but rather a coefficient of absolute agreement.	*Implication for Reliability Estimation:* The researcher requires a coefficient that allocates rater- and item-specific components of *total rating variance* to error variance. The denominator of this coefficient will not reflect an estimate of *observed between-ratee variance*, so technically, it is not a reliability coefficient, but rather a coefficient of absolute agreement.

FIGURE 12.2 Implications of differences in use of ratings for reliability estimation

the ratings, but the overarching interpretation as proportion of observed score variance attributable to true score does not.

In contrast, if one intends to use the ratings to compare individuals' ratings to an established standard or cutoff, then a reliability coefficient, as defined earlier, is not justified for indexing the level of error present in ratings. Technically, in this situation what is needed is an estimator of absolute agreement that is appropriate for the measurement design and type of generalization at hand (e.g., a G-theory based D-coefficient; see Brennan, 2001; McGraw & Wong's 1996 ICC[A,k]). Such coefficients differ from reliability coefficients in that their denominators are not estimates of *observed, between-ratee variance* but rather *total variance* across elements of the measurement design underlying the ratings. To illustrate the distinction between *observed, between-ratee variance* and *total rating variance*, let's revisit our working example.

Recall from our working example that each rater who rates a ratee provided ratings on all five Problem Solving items. Under such a design, one source of variance that contributes to total rating variance but not observed, between-ratee variance is item main effect variance (e.g., variance attributable to differences in item "difficulty"). Under Condition A, regardless of use, variance attributable to item main effects would not contribute to error variance, because there is no intention of the researcher to generalize the ratings across items. Under Conditions B and C, its contribution to error variance would depend on use. Under Use 1, even though item main effects represent a type of "item-specific effect," item main effect variance would not contribute to error. The reason is that such differences in item difficulty have no impact on *observed, between-ratee variance* whatsoever; or, framed differently, they do not reflect sources of consistency nor inconsistency in the relative ordering of ratees across items. The effects are in essence a set of constants across individuals that equally affect the ratings different individuals have on each item. In contrast, under Use 2, any item-specific effects that introduce deviations between an individual's true score and the established standard or cut-off score would be a source of error—item main effect variance included. That is, although such effects do not contribute to variance *between persons*, they do reflect discrepancies between individuals' true scores and the performance standard *within persons* and as such are a considered a source of error when the use of job performance ratings involves comparing them to some fixed standard. Depending on the sampling of items used in the study, these effects will "move" all ratees' scores up or down relative to the standard, which could reflect the accuracy of comparison of ratings to the standard. In that case, one would want an index of error in ratings that takes that into account and, in this example, an index that accounts for agreement among items (rather than consistency only).

Now it is possible that within any given study, a researcher may desire to use ratings to make relative comparisons among ratees, as well as to compare ratings to some fixed standard. In that case, separate coefficients for indexing reliability and agreement should be reported that are sensitive to the generalizations one desires to make and to measurement design considerations (which we discuss next).

Thus, between Figures 12.1 and 12.2, one can see that working from a common general example, one can derive six different scenarios that vary according to desired generalizations and intended use of ratings and that have implications for an appropriate estimator of the reliability of job performance ratings. In only one of these six variations is use of an interrater correlation as an estimator of reliability of ratings potentially most appropriate (Condition A, Use 1).

Implications of Measurement Design for Reliability Estimation

The previous sections present six different variants on our working example that clearly illustrate the folly in attributing a specific type of reliability coefficient for the job performance ratings. Indeed, in some cases, a "reliability" estimator, as traditionally defined, would not be an accurate index of the amount of error in ratings. The final piece missing from the discussion thus far involves measurement design underlying the ratings. Psychometricians have long recognized that measurement design has fundamental implications for reliability estimation, and ratings data are no exception (e.g., Cronbach, Rajaratnam, & Gleser, 1963; Ebel, 1951; Hoyt, 1941). To complete our illustration, Figures 12.3a and 12.3b present three potential measurement designs that, when crossed with the six cells reflecting different generalizations and intended use of ratings, result in 18 potential formulations for reliability based on our working example. Design I reflects a fully crossed design in which all raters rate all ratees on all items. Design II reflects a nested design in which each ratee is rated by a different set of raters on all items. Design III reflects a design in which raters are neither full crossed nor nested in relation to ratees—a design common in organizational research and labeled as ill structured (Putka, Lance, Le, & McCloy, 2011; Putka, Le, McCloy, & Diaz, 2008).[1]

The cells in Figures 12.3a and 12.3b present the functional form of reliability coefficients (or, in the case of Figure 12.3b, agreement coefficients) most appropriate for the situation, taking into consideration (a) the generalizations the researcher desires to make, (b) the intended use of the ratings, and (c) measurement design. All of these forms are derived from established Generalizability theory rules for formulating reliability and agreement coefficients as a function of these considerations (e.g., Brennan, 2001; Cronbach, Gleser, Nanda, & Rajaratnam, 1972), as well as recent treatments of reliability estimation for ill-structured measurement designs (Putka et al., 2008). Note also, all coefficients in these figures take on the same general form—the numerator reflects components of true score variance and the denominator reflects the sum of true score and error variance components; what differentiates them is the components that contribute to true score and error variance.

To aid in the interpretation of Figures 12.3a and 12.3b, it is important to understand the basic statistical model underlying the coefficients presented—namely, a simple linear random effects model common in the G-theory literature (Brennan,

	Condition A: Generalizing across raters only	Condition B: Generalizing across items only	Condition C: Generalizing across raters and items
Design I: **Fully** **Crossed** *p x r x i*	$$\rho^2 = \frac{\sigma^2_p + \dfrac{\sigma^2_{pi}}{n_i}}{\sigma^2_p + \dfrac{\sigma^2_{pi}}{n_i} + \left[\dfrac{\sigma^2_{pr}}{n_r} + \dfrac{\sigma^2_{pri,e}}{n_r n_i}\right]}$$	$$\rho^2 = \frac{\sigma^2_p + \dfrac{\sigma^2_{pr}}{n_r}}{\sigma^2_p + \dfrac{\sigma^2_{pr}}{n_r} + \left[\dfrac{\sigma^2_{pi}}{n_i} + \dfrac{\sigma^2_{pri,e}}{n_r n_i}\right]}$$	$$\rho^2 = \frac{\sigma^2_p}{\sigma^2_p + \left[\dfrac{\sigma^2_{pr}}{n_r} + \dfrac{\sigma^2_{pi}}{n_i} + \dfrac{\sigma^2_{pri,e}}{n_r n_i}\right]}$$
Design II: **Partially** **Nested** *r:p x i*	$$\rho^2 = \frac{\sigma^2_p + \dfrac{\sigma^2_{pi}}{n_i}}{\sigma^2_p + \dfrac{\sigma^2_{pi}}{n_i} + \left[\dfrac{\sigma^2_{r,pr}}{n_{r:p}} + \dfrac{\sigma^2_{ri,pri,e}}{n_{r:p} n_i}\right]}$$	$$\rho^2 = \frac{\sigma^2_p + \dfrac{\sigma^2_{r,pr}}{n_{r:p}}}{\sigma^2_p + \dfrac{\sigma^2_{r,pr}}{n_{r:p}} + \left[\dfrac{\sigma^2_{pi}}{n_i} + \dfrac{\sigma^2_{ri,pri,e}}{n_{r:p} n_i}\right]}$$	$$\rho^2 = \frac{\sigma^2_p}{\sigma^2_p + \left[\dfrac{\sigma^2_{r,pr}}{n_{r:p}} + \dfrac{\sigma^2_{pi}}{n_i} + \dfrac{\sigma^2_{ri,pri,e}}{n_{r:p} n_i}\right]}$$
Design III: **Ill-** **Structured** *pr* x i*	$$\rho^2 = \frac{\sigma^2_p + \dfrac{\sigma^2_{pi}}{n_i}}{\sigma^2_p + \dfrac{\sigma^2_{pi}}{n_i} + \left[q\sigma^2_r + q\dfrac{\sigma^2_n}{n_i} + \dfrac{\sigma^2_{pr}}{n_{r:p}} + \dfrac{\sigma^2_{pri,e}}{n_{r:p} n_i}\right]}$$	$$\rho^2 = \frac{\sigma^2_p + q\sigma^2_r + \dfrac{\sigma^2_{pr}}{n_{r:p}}}{\sigma^2_p + q\sigma^2_r + \dfrac{\sigma^2_{pr}}{n_{r:p}} + \left[q\dfrac{\sigma^2_{ri}}{n_i} + \dfrac{\sigma^2_{pi}}{n_i} + \dfrac{\sigma^2_{pri,e}}{n_{r:p} n_i}\right]}$$	$$\rho^2 = \frac{\sigma^2_p}{\sigma^2_p + \left[q\sigma^2_r + q\dfrac{\sigma^2_{ri}}{n_i} + \dfrac{\sigma^2_{pr}}{n_{r:p}} + \dfrac{\sigma^2_{pi}}{n_i} + \dfrac{\sigma^2_{pri,e}}{n_{r:p} n_i}\right]}$$

FIGURE 12.3A Estimators of reliability as a function of measurement design and desired generalizations: Use 1: Relative comparisons

Note. σ^2_x = Estimated variance component for effect x. p = person main effect. r = rater main effect. pi = person × item interaction effect. ri = rater × item interaction n_i = number of items averaged together to calculate the overall score. n_r = total number of raters. $n_{r:p}$ = number of raters per ratee (harmonic mean if number is unequal across ratees). q = q multiplier − indexes the degree to which raters for each ratee do not fully overlap (see Putka, Le et al., 2008). The numerator of each equation reflects estimated true score variance, whereas the term in brackets in the denominator reflects estimated error variance. Thus, all of these coefficients take on the classic reliability form of $\sigma^2_{True}/(\sigma^2_{True} + \sigma^2_{Error})$. Each of the estimated components above can be directly estimated using commonly available software packages (e.g., SPSS, SAS, R; see Putka & McCloy, 2008).

	Condition A: Generalizing across raters only	Condition B: Generalizing across items only	Condition C: Generalizing across raters and items
Design I: Fully Crossed $(p \times r \times i)$	$\rho^2 = \dfrac{\sigma^2_p + \dfrac{\sigma^2_{pi}}{n_i}}{\sigma^2_p + \dfrac{\sigma^2_{pi}}{n_i} + \left[\dfrac{\sigma^2_{pr}}{n_r} + \dfrac{\sigma^2_r}{n_r} + \dfrac{\sigma^2_{ri}}{n_r n_i} + \dfrac{\sigma^2_{pri,e}}{n_r n_i} \right]}$	$\rho^2 = \dfrac{\sigma^2_p + \dfrac{\sigma^2_{pr}}{n_r}}{\sigma^2_p + \dfrac{\sigma^2_{pr}}{n_r} + \left[\dfrac{\sigma^2_{pi}}{n_i} + \dfrac{\sigma^2_i}{n_i} + \dfrac{\sigma^2_{ri}}{n_r n_i} + \dfrac{\sigma^2_{pri,e}}{n_r n_i} \right]}$	$\rho^2 = \dfrac{\sigma^2_p}{\sigma^2_p + \left[\dfrac{\sigma^2_{pr}}{n_r} + \dfrac{\sigma^2_r}{n_r} + \dfrac{\sigma^2_{pi}}{n_i} + \dfrac{\sigma^2_i}{n_i} + \dfrac{\sigma^2_{ri}}{n_r n_i} + \dfrac{\sigma^2_{pri,e}}{n_r n_i} \right]}$
Design II: Partially Nested $r : p \times i$	$\rho^2 = \dfrac{\sigma^2_p + \dfrac{\sigma^2_{pi}}{n_i}}{\sigma^2_p + \dfrac{\sigma^2_{pi}}{n_i} + \left[\dfrac{\sigma^2_{r,pr}}{n_{r \cdot p}} + \dfrac{\sigma^2_{ri,pri,e}}{n_{r \cdot p} n_i} \right]}$	$\rho^2 = \dfrac{\sigma^2_p + \dfrac{\sigma^2_{r,pr}}{n_{r \cdot p}}}{\sigma^2_p + \dfrac{\sigma^2_{r,pr}}{n_{r \cdot p}} + \left[\dfrac{\sigma^2_{pi}}{n_i} + \dfrac{\sigma^2_i}{n_i} + \dfrac{\sigma^2_{ri,pri,e}}{n_{r \cdot p} n_i} \right]}$	$\rho^2 = \dfrac{\sigma^2_p}{\sigma^2_p + \left[\dfrac{\sigma^2_{r,pr}}{n_{r \cdot p}} + \dfrac{\sigma^2_{pi}}{n_i} + \dfrac{\sigma^2_i}{n_i} + \dfrac{\sigma^2_{ri,pri,e}}{n_{r \cdot p} n_i} \right]}$
Design III: Ill-Structured $pr^* \times i$	$\rho^2 = \dfrac{\sigma^2_p + \dfrac{\sigma^2_{pi}}{n_i}}{\sigma^2_p + \dfrac{\sigma^2_{pi}}{n_i} + \left[q\sigma^2_r + q \dfrac{\sigma^2_{ri}}{n_i} + \dfrac{\sigma^2_{pr}}{n_{r \cdot p}} + \dfrac{\sigma^2_{pri,e}}{n_{r \cdot p} n_i} \right]}$	$\rho^2 = \dfrac{\sigma^2_p + q\sigma^2_r + \dfrac{\sigma^2_{pr}}{n_{r \cdot p}} + \dfrac{\sigma^2_{pr}}{n_{r \cdot p}}}{\sigma^2_p + q\sigma^2_r + \dfrac{\sigma^2_{pr}}{n_{r \cdot p}} + q \dfrac{\sigma^2_{ri}}{n_i} + \dfrac{\sigma^2_{pi}}{n_i} + \dfrac{\sigma^2_i}{n_i} + \dfrac{\sigma^2_{pri,e}}{n_{r \cdot p} n_i}}$	$\rho^2 = \dfrac{\sigma^2_p}{\sigma^2_p + \left[q\sigma^2_r + q \dfrac{\sigma^2_{ri}}{n_i} + \dfrac{\sigma^2_{pr}}{n_{r \cdot p}} + \dfrac{\sigma^2_{pi}}{n_i} + \dfrac{\sigma^2_i}{n_i} + \dfrac{\sigma^2_{pri,e}}{n_{r \cdot p} n_i} \right]}$

FIGURE 12.3B Estimators of agreement as a function of measurement design and desired generalizations: Use 2: Absolute comparisons

Note. σ^2_x = Estimated variance component for effect x. p = person main effect. r = rater main effect. i = item main effect. pi = person × item effect. ri = rater × item interaction. n_i = number of items averaged together to calculate the overall score. n_r = total number of raters. n_{rp} = number of raters per ratee (harmonic mean if number is unequal across ratees). q = q multiplier — indexes the degree to which raters for each ratee do not fully overlap (see Putka, Le et al., 2008). The numerator of each equation reflects estimated true score variance, whereas the term in brackets in the denominator reflects estimated error variance. Thus, all of these coefficients take on the classic reliability form of $\sigma^2_{True}/(\sigma^2_{True} + \sigma^2_{Error})$. Each of the estimated components above can be directly estimated using commonly available software packages (e.g., SPSS, SAS, R; see Putka & McCloy, 2008).

258 Dan J. Putka and Brian J. Hoffman

2001; Cronbach et al., 1972; Jackson & Brashers, 1994). Based on this model, each person's (ratee's) observed rating (Y_{pri}) from a given rater on a given performance item is viewed as a simple additive function:

$$Y_{pri} = \mu + \nu_p + \nu_r + \nu_i + \nu_{pr} + \nu_{pi} + \nu_{ri} + \nu_{pri,e} \tag{1}$$

where μ is the grand mean score across all persons (ratees), raters, and items; ν_p is the person (ratee) main effect and conceptually reflects the expected value of a person's score (expressed as a deviation from the grand mean) across the population of raters and items; ν_r is the rater main effect and conceptually reflects the expected value of a rater's effect (again, expressed as a deviation from the grand mean) across the population persons and items; ν_i is the item main effect and conceptually reflects the expected value of an item's effect (again, expressed as a deviation from the grand mean) across the population of persons and raters; ν_{pr} is the person × rater interaction effect and conceptually reflects differences in the ordering of persons' expected rating (averaged over items) scores across raters; ν_{pi} is the person × item interaction effect and conceptually reflects differences in the ordering of persons' expected ratings (averaged over raters) across items; ν_{ri} is the rater × item interaction effect and conceptually reflects differences in the ordering of raters' expected ratings (averaged over persons) across items; and finally, $\nu_{pri,e}$ is the remaining residual after accounting for all other effects in the model.[2]

The assumptions underlying this model reflect common random-effects ANOVA assumptions. Namely, all effects in the model are assumed to be independently and identically distributed with means of zero and variances of σ^2_p, σ^2_r, σ^2_i, σ^2_{pr}, σ^2_{pi}, σ^2_{ri}, and $\sigma^2_{pri,e}$, respectively (Jackson & Brashers, 1994; Searle, Casella, & McCulloch, 1992). It is these *variance components* that provide the building blocks of reliability coefficients.

Though the connection between variance components is made most explicit through G-theory, previous researchers have illustrated how traditional "types" of reliability estimators such as coefficient alpha and intraclass correlations can also be expressed in terms of simple functions of variance components and considered as specific estimators within a G-theory framework (e.g., Cronbach & Shavelson, 2004; Feldt & Brennan, 1989; McGraw & Wong, 1996; Putka & Sackett, 2010). Thus, the coefficients in Figures 12.3a and 12.3b should not be viewed as any more complex than traditional reliability estimators; they are just being expressed within a conceptual framework that makes it much easier to see the implications that a researcher's desired generalizations, intended use of ratings, and prevailing measurement design have for sources of variance considered to be true score and error variance and, in turn, reliability estimation.

Given that each of the effects in the model depicted in Equation 1 is assumed to be independent (and therefore uncorrelated with one another), *the expected total variance* in ratings across all person × rater × item combinations in the population

Reliability of Job Performance Ratings **259**

(in sample data, these reflect cells in the person × rater × item data matrix) may be expressed as a simple sum of these variance components:

$$\sigma^2_{expected\ total} = \sigma^2_p + \sigma^2_r + \sigma^2_i + \sigma^2_{pr} + \sigma^2_{pi} + \sigma^2_{ri} + \sigma^2_{pri,e.} \tag{2}$$

Typically, in the context of reliability estimation, researchers are not interested in *expected total variance* in ratings but rather in *expected observed between-ratee variance*. The observed variance in ratings *across* ratees (persons) is the sum of only a subset of the variance components depicted in Equation 2. Beyond the ratee (person) main effect, which components can contribute to observed between-ratee variance follow a simple rule: only terms (a) that include an interaction between ratees (persons) and another factor, (b) in which ratees are nested within another factor (e.g., raters, items), or (c) that reflect a factor that is not fully crossed with persons contribute to observed between-person variance in ratings. Thus, the measurement design one uses to gather ratings becomes a critical determinant of which of the components from the general model shown in Equation 2 contribute to observed between-ratee variance and which ones do not—this is evident in Figure 12.3a and 12.3b. Specifically, note that the coefficients under Condition C in Figure 12.3a only reflect components that contribute to observed between-person variance, whereas coefficients under Condition C in Figure 12.3b reflect all components.

Measurement design also has implications for which components in the general model noted in Equation 2 can be uniquely estimated based on one's rating data and which are confounded (e.g., due to nesting). All of the components in the general model outlined can only be uniquely estimated when no nesting is present (i.e., when all factors are fully or partially crossed). As soon as nesting is introduced, it becomes impossible to uniquely estimate one or more of the effects (e.g., see Brennan, 2001; Shavelson & Webb, 1991). This is evident in Figures 12.3a and 12.3b. For example, the coefficients under Condition C in Figure 12.3b include all components of the general model outlined in Equation 2, but as indicated by the presence of commas between subscripts for some of the variance components in the designs that are not fully crossed (i.e., second and third rows of the last column in Figure 12.3b), not all variance components from the general model can be uniquely estimated (i.e., some estimates for the variance components in Equation 2 are confounded).

While measurement design determines what variance components can be uniquely estimated, the generalizations the researcher desires to make regarding the ratings determine which components are allocated to true score variance and error variance for purposes of estimating reliability. Conceptually, we made this point in Figure 12.1. Figures 12.3a and 12.3b make this point more concretely with actual formulae. For example, one can readily compare the composition of true score variance (i.e., the numerator) and error variance (i.e., the bracketed term in the denominator) in formulae across columns within a given row in Figures 12.3a and 12.3b to see how their composition changes as a function of desired generalizations holding measurement design constant and intended use constant.

With this background, we now return to Figures 12.3a and 12.3b with the goal of seeing what implications measurement design, coupled with generalization and use considerations, has for determining the most appropriate reliability estimator given one's situation and when interrater correlations—the current de facto choice for estimating *the* reliability of ratings—would be most appropriate.

Only in the situation in which the researcher (a) desires to make generalizations across raters only, (b) uses ratings for relative comparisons only, and (c) deals with a fully crossed design (i.e., the upper left cell in Figure 12.3a) are interrater correlations and their Spearman-Brown extension the most appropriate estimator of the reliability of job performance ratings.

To illustrate why this is the case, let's begin with the first factor—desired generalizations. Given the components of error variance reflected in interrater correlations noted earlier, they do not allow researchers to estimate the degree to which ratings generalize across items only or raters and items. This eliminates 12 of the 18 variants in which interrater correlations could potentially provide the most appropriate estimator. That leaves the six variants under Condition A.

Next, four of the variants under Condition A are ruled out given measurement design considerations. As detailed by Putka, Le, and colleagues (2008), application of interrater correlations to measurement designs that are nested or ill structured does not make sense on conceptual or mathematical grounds. First, doing so would require arbitrarily assigning one rater for each ratee to be "rater 1" and the other rater for each "rater 2" even though raters 1 and 2 may be different persons across ratees. Thus, there are myriad ways that researchers could assign raters to columns for each ratee that would introduce artificial variation into the correlation estimate and allow one to generate numerous estimates *based on the exact same data*. The hazards of this practice not only introduce arbitrariness into interrater correlations but also create situations in which one introduces arbitrariness and the potential for manipulation of CFA results of rating data (Putka et al., 2011).

The continued practice of using interrater correlations when raters are not fully crossed harkens to Cronbach's lament regarding the folly of applying coefficient alpha to nested data: "The alpha literature and most other literature prior to 1951 assumed that the sample matrix and the population matrix were crossed. Mathematically, it is easy enough to substitute scores from a nested sample matrix by simply taking the score listed first for each as belonging in column 1, but this is not the appropriate analysis" (Cronbach & Shavelson, 2004, p. 400). As Cronbach and Shavelson (2004) noted earlier in their presentation: "The obvious example is where person p is evaluated on some personality trait by acquaintances, and the set of acquaintances varies from person to person, possibly with no overlap. Then there is no rational basis for assigning scores on the two persons to the same column" (p. 399). Of course, in the case of case of interrater reliability estimation, one deals with raters rather than items or acquaintances per se, but if we would never adopt such practice with items, why does the practice of arbitrarily assigning potentially different raters to the same columns (as if they were actually the same person) and then calculating interrater correlations persist within organizational research and practice?

Fortunately, as Cronbach and Shavelson (2004) alluded to in their commentary, since at least the 1960s, methods *have* existed for estimating interrater reliability in nested designs, using intraclass correlations or their G-theory analogues. For example, coefficients such as ICC(1,k)—where k is set to 1 for estimating the reliability of a single rater per ratee or k is set to the average number of raters per ratee to reflect the reliability of the average ratings across k raters, are available to researchers (see Condition A, Use 1, Design II in Figure 12.3a; see also McGraw & Wong, 1996). For designs in which raters are not fully crossed or nested, Putka, Le, and colleagues (2008) provide a general solution for interrater reliability that can be applied to crossed, nested, or ill-structured designs and illustrates the hazards of applying coefficients that were designed for use with crossed designs (e.g., Pearson correlations, ICC[C,k]) or nested designs (e.g., ICC[1,k]) to designs that are ill structured in nature. In addition to the "off-the-shelf" coefficients mentioned, of course there is also an endless array of coefficients that can be derived based on G-theory rules that appropriately reflect the generalizations one desires to make regarding their ratings, their intended use, and measurement design (e.g., see Figure 12.3a and 12.3b, and also Brennan, 2001).

Thus, taking desired generalization and measurement design into account, we are now down to 2 of 18 variants across Figures 12.3a and 12.3b—both of which involve Condition A (generalize across raters only) and a fully crossed design—in which use of interrater correlations would potentially be most appropriate.

Finally, we note that interrater correlations are not appropriate for use when researchers wish to generalize ratings across raters only, have a fully crossed design, *and* intend to only use the ratings to make absolute comparisons of ratings to some standard (i.e., the upper left cell of Figure 12.3b) because they do not explicitly allow rater main effects (e.g., differences in leniency/severity) to contribute to error—which, as alluded to earlier, can lead to differences between observed ratings and the performance standard of interest.

In sum, Figures 12.3a and 12.3b help illustrate the core point of this chapter—strong claims that interrater correlations are the most appropriate estimators of the reliability of job performance ratings and their widespread use is unwarranted based on modern psychometric concepts. The kernel of truth in their use is that they can be appropriate estimators in a very narrowly defined and very rare situation. Figures 12.3a and 12.3b indicate that interrater correlations are appropriate in 1 of the 18 cells that depict various ways job performance ratings may manifest themselves in applied research and practice. When one takes stock of the fact that the likelihood of conditions characterizing that "cell" prevailing in applied research or practice is arguably nil for any reasonably sized performance rating collection, it helps clarify why we chose not to focus on moderating or directly following up on the 2000 *Personnel Psychology* debate. Arguing about the merits or demerits of interrater correlations seems like a secondary issue given the rarity with which

262 Dan J. Putka and Brian J. Hoffman

they can even possibly be most appropriate estimators given modern psychometric theory and conditions prevailing in practice. In our view, there are simply bigger issues regarding reliability estimation for performance ratings that have yet to be given adequate attention in our field—such as the issues raised herein—the importance of considering desired generalization, intended use, and measurement design for choice of reliability and agreement estimators for ratings, and the implications they have for substantive conclusions drawn in research and practice.

The other key point we hope readers take away from Figures 12.3a and 12.3b is the importance of writing Methods sections for articles involving performance ratings that are clear when it comes to (a) the generalizations researchers wish to make about those ratings, (b) the intended use of those ratings, and (c) the measurement design underlying their collection. Without that information, it is impossible to determine whether the reliability of ratings was appropriately estimated and weakens the ability of future researchers to learn from and capitalize on that work. Put a different way, it is impossible to have a theoretically meaningful discussion of the reliability of job performance ratings without addressing the issues of what generalizations one intends to make regarding those ratings, how those ratings will be used, and what measurement design will be used to gather the ratings. Once these key elements are considered, only then can the discussion of an appropriate estimator meaningfully follow. Unfortunately, as noted by past researchers, gleaning such information from published studies is often impossible (e.g., Putka, Le et al., 2008; Scullen, Mount, & Goff, 2000). However, this is something our field can start to immediately rectify—reviewers and journal editors must start demanding such information from manuscript authors (e.g., see discussion in Putka, Le et al., 2008).

So What?

Though there are clear, theoretically meaningful differences among the many coefficients depicted in Figures 12.3a and 12.3b, these figures do little to reveal how much choice of reliability coefficient can matter when estimating reliability in practice. As such, we looked to past literature to derive estimates for the general variance components model depicted in Equation 2 and then used these components to estimate each coefficient in Figures 12.3a and 12.3b. Doing so provides a concrete illustration of how much reliability estimates can vary depending on choices one makes regarding measurement design, desired generalizations, and intended use *given the same starting set of variance components.*

As noted earlier, to uniquely estimate each of the variance components underlying Equation 2, one would need a design in which ratees, raters, and items were fully crossed—something never really seen in applied research or practice. In light of the unavailability of such a study, we relied on findings from Greguras and Robie (1998) and Hoyt and Kerns (1998) to derive estimates that we felt were reasonable, at least for purposes of this illustration. The Greguras and Robie (1998) study involved a measurement design in which raters (supervisors) were nested

Reliability of Job Performance Ratings **263**

within ratees and evaluated ratees on the same set of items. This design is equivalent to the partially nested measurement design introduced in Figures 12.3a and 12.3b. As alluded to earlier, under such a design, variance attributable to rater main effects (σ^2_r) cannot be distinguished from variance due to ratee (person) × rater interaction effects (σ^2_{pr}) due to nesting. Furthermore, variance attributable to rater × item interaction effects (σ^2_{ri}), could not be distinguished from the combination of variance attributable to person × rater × item interaction effects and residual variance $(\sigma^2_{pri,e})$ due to nesting. Thus, we looked to other literature to help tease these confounded effects apart. In this case, we turned to Hoyt and Kerns's (1999) meta-analysis of rater main effect and person × rater interaction effect variance components. They estimated rater main effect variance to be .08 (i.e., 42.1% of $\sigma^2_{r,pr}$), and person × rater interaction effect variance to be .11 (i.e., 57.9% of $\sigma^2_{r,pr}$). We used these percentages to split Greguras and Robie's (1998) estimate for $\sigma^2_{r,pr}$ into two parts. With regard to the confounding of σ^2_{ri} and $\sigma^2_{pri,e}$, we arbitrarily chose a 50/50 split for purposes of illustration because no known estimates are available from the literature. Table 12.1 provides the final variance component estimates we used.

Table 12.2 shows the results of taking the estimated variance components from Table 12.1 and plugging them into the 18 reliability and agreement coefficient formulae presented in Figures 12.3a and 12.3b. For purposes of calculating these estimates, we assumed estimating reliability/agreement for a single rater per ratee, rating each ratee on a single item (e.g., a single behaviorally anchored rating

TABLE 12.1 Variance Component Estimates for Reliability Estimation Example

Variance Component	*Estimate*
σ^2_p	0.1787[a]
σ^2_i	0.0365[a]
σ^2_{pi}	0.0305[a]
$\sigma^2_{r,pr}$	0.2099[a]
σ^2_r	0.0884[b]
σ^2_{pr}	0.1215[b]
$\sigma^2_{ri,pri,e}$	0.3245[a]
σ^2_{ri}	0.1623[c]
$\sigma^2_{pri,e}$	0.1623[c]

Note. [a]Estimate drawn from Greguras and Robie (1998; Table 2, Supervisors). [b]Estimated split between σ^2_r and σ^2_{pr} based on Hoyt and Kerns (1999) meta-analysis of rater main effect and ratee × rater interaction variance components. They estimated to be σ^2_r to be .08 (i.e., 42.1% of $\sigma^2_{r,pr}$), and σ^2_{pr} to be .11 (i.e., 57.9% of $\sigma^2_{r,pr}$). We used these percentages to split Greguras and Robie's (1998) estimate for $\sigma^2_{r,pr}$ into two parts. [c]Estimated split between σ^2_{ri} and $\sigma^2_{pri,e}$ arbitrarily chosen to be 50/50 because no known estimates are available from the literature.

TABLE 12.2 Reliability and Agreement Estimates for the 18 Measurement Design × Desired Generalization × Intended Use Combinations from Figures 12.3a and 12.3b

Design	Desired Generalization	Use of Ratings	Coefficient	Estimated σ^2_{True}	Estimated σ^2_{Error}
		Reliability Coefficients (Figure 3a)			
I: Fully crossed	A: Across raters only	Relative comparisons	0.42	0.2092	0.2838
I: Fully crossed	B: Across items only	Relative comparisons	0.61	0.3002	0.1928
I: Fully crossed	C: Across raters & items	Relative comparisons	0.36	0.1787	0.3203
II: Partially nested	A: Across raters only	Relative comparisons	0.28	0.2092	0.5344
II: Partially nested	B: Across items only	Relative comparisons	0.52	0.3886	0.3550
II: Partially nested	C: Across raters & items	Relative comparisons	0.24	0.1787	0.5649
III: Ill-structured	A: Across raters only	Relative comparisons	0.34	0.2092	0.4091
III: Ill-structured	B: Across items only	Relative comparisons	0.56	0.3444	0.2739
III Ill-structured	C: Across raters & items	Relative comparisons	0.29	0.1787	0.4396
		Agreement Coefficients (Figure 3b)			
I: Fully crossed	A: Across raters only	Absolute comparisons	0.28	0.2092	0.5344
I: Fully crossed	B: Across items only	Absolute comparisons	0.43	0.3002	0.3915
I: Fully crossed	C: Across raters & items	Absolute comparisons	0.23	0.1787	0.6014
II: Partially nested	A: Across raters only	Absolute comparisons	0.28	0.2092	0.5344
II: Partially nested	B: Across items only	Absolute comparisons	0.50	0.3886	0.3915
II: Partially nested	C: Across raters & items	Absolute comparisons	0.23	0.1787	0.6014
III: Ill-structured	A: Across raters only	Absolute comparisons	0.34	0.2092	0.4091
III: Ill-structured	B: Across items only	Absolute comparisons	0.53	0.3444	0.3104
III Ill-structured	C: Across raters & items	Absolute comparisons	0.27	0.1787	0.4761

Note: Coefficient = Estimated reliability and agreement coefficients resulting from plugging variance component estimates from Table 12.1 into formulae in Figures 12.3a and 12.3b. Note that of all of these coefficients take on the classic reliability form of $\sigma^2_{True}/(\sigma^2_{True} + \sigma^2_{Error})$.

scale [BARS] for a given performance dimension).[3] As one can see, even starting with a common set of variance components, the appropriate reliability/agreement estimate for performance ratings could vary widely depending on the coefficient chosen—in this example, from a low of .23 to a high of .61. Thus, simply defaulting to a single type of reliability estimator as most appropriate or preferred, whether it be an interrater correlation or some other specific type of estimator (e.g., alpha, a particular intraclass correlation), fails to reflect sensitivity to the key issues of desired generalization, intended use, and measurement design.

The variation in estimates one can get from appropriately considering issues of desired generalization, intended use, and measurement design also has implications for using such estimates to correcting correlations for error in job performance ratings. For example, let's say we observe a correlation of .15 between a given predictor variable and job performance ratings. Furthermore, let's say we wish to correct that correlation for measurement error in job performance rating using a reliability coefficient from the previous example. Depending on measurement design and desired generalization considerations, one can come to vastly different conclusions regarding the magnitude of the corrected correlation. Table 12.3 shows what happens if those reliability estimates are used to correct an observed correlation of .15 for measurement error.[4] Depending on which reliability estimate is used, one obtains a corrected correlation that ranges from .19 to .31, representing between a 28.1% and 104% gain in validity over the observed estimate (Table 12.3). Clearly, this is a wide range of corrected correlations that would presumably have practical and scientific implications for conclusions drawn regarding

TABLE 12.3 Example of Variation in Corrected Validity Estimates across 9 Measurement Design × Desired Generalization Combination from Figure 12.3a

Design	Desired Generalization	Reliability Coefficient	Raw r_{xy}	Corrected r_{xy}	% Increase
I: Fully crossed	A: Across raters only	0.42	0.15	0.23	53.5
I: Fully crossed	B: Across items only	0.61	0.15	0.19	28.1
I: Fully crossed	C: Across raters & items	0.36	0.15	0.25	67.1
II: Partially nested	A: Across raters only	0.28	0.15	0.28	88.5
II: Partially nested	B: Across items only	0.52	0.15	0.21	38.3
II: Partially nested	C: Across raters & items	0.24	0.15	0.31	104.0
III: Ill-structured	A: Across raters only	0.34	0.15	0.26	71.9
III: Ill-structured	B: Across items only	0.56	0.15	0.20	34.0
III Ill-structured	C: Across raters & items	0.29	0.15	0.28	86.0

Note: Reliability Coefficient = Estimated reliability resulting from plugging variance component estimates from Table 12.1 into formulae in Figure 12.3a. Raw r_{xy} = Correlation between predictor and the job performance rating criterion (this value was arbitrarily chosen for purposes of illustration). Corrected r_{xy} = Raw correlation corrected for unreliability in the criterion (i.e., Raw r_{xy}/square root of the reliability coefficient). % Increase = Percentage increase in the corrected validity estimate relative to the raw estimate.

266 Dan J. Putka and Brian J. Hoffman

the expected utility of the predictor for selecting individuals and the magnitude of its relation with the job performance criterion. Simply defaulting to the use of interrater correlations as *the* most appropriate estimator for job performance ratings ignores the fact that one can come to very different conclusions about corrected validity estimates depending on the generalizations one desires to make regarding ratings and the measurement design underlying the ratings.

Meta-Analysis and Interrater Correlations

These illustrations were premised on the notion that the researcher actually had all of the data needed to generate a local estimate of the reliability of performance ratings for their given measurement situation. However, in reality, researchers may lack the data needed to locally estimate reliability and may desire to turn to past research or past meta-analytic summaries for a proxy estimate (e.g., Viswesvaran et al., 1996). For example, a fairly common occurrence in gathering of job performance ratings is the availability of only one rater per ratee—a situation that prevents local estimation of *interrater* reliability. This might happen if a researcher is collecting supervisor ratings for a sample of incumbents, where each group of incumbents is rated only by their supervisor. As alluded to earlier, in this case, it is not possible to separate a key type of rater-specific variance, namely person × rater interaction effects, from a core component of true score variance, namely person main effects. This is problematic in that researchers often do have an interest in generalizing their ratings across raters, but this design will not allow for local estimation of an appropriate coefficient. This doesn't mean that rater-specific error isn't affecting ratings—it is contributing to observed variance in ratings—the researcher is just unable to isolate it.

Now assume that the researcher in the previous example decides to conduct a validation study that uses the above ratings as a criterion and wishes to correct the resulting criterion-related validity estimate for unreliability in the criterion. What options does the researcher have? One option would be to "pretend" not to be interested in generalizing across raters and simply use a coefficient that treats item-specific variance as error (assuming the researcher's measure consists of multiple items that allow for estimation of item-specific variance) and allows rater-specific variance to contribute to true score (e.g., coefficient alpha). However, clearly this would be problematic in that it is not consistent with the generalization the researcher wishes to make (i.e., generalizing across raters) and would likely lead to an underestimate of validity (see also Schmidt & Hunter, 1996).

Another option, which brings us to the point of this illustration, would be to use a meta-analytic estimate of interrater reliability of supervisor ratings (e.g., .52 from Viswesvaran et al., 1996) as a proxy for interrater reliability of ratings in the local study. However, this would be problematic on several grounds. First, the primary studies that have fed into Viswesvaran and colleagues (1996) are unclear with regard to their measurement design, though they are surely not fully crossed

Reliability of Job Performance Ratings **267**

(Putka, Le et al., 2008; Scullen et al., 2000; Viswesvaran, Schmidt, & Ones, 2005). As such, we are unclear on what meaning there is to averaging together interrater correlations from different studies in which the substantive composition of true score variance and error variance they are attempting to summarize may differ across studies. That is, due to differences in measurement design across studies, interrater correlations become differentially accurate *estimators* of interrater reliability—not due to sampling error (which affects *estimates*) but due to differences in measurement design and the differential composition of true score and error variance (see Figure 12.3a).[5] As illustrated by Putka, Le, and colleagues (2008), measurement design can influence the accuracy of traditional reliability estimators such as Pearson correlations and intraclass correlations.

In essence, the issue here is a variance component–based analogue of the apples–oranges and garbage in–garbage out critiques that have been leveled at meta-analysis (e.g., Eysenck, 1978; Oswald & McCloy, 2003); only instead of the critique being based on substantive differences in the measures involved or quality of the studies involved, it has to do with substantive differences in measurement design underlying the gathering of ratings and the implications this has for the appropriateness and accuracy of use of interrater correlations as estimators of interrater reliability. Essentially it amounts to averaging together coefficients that are not comparable *estimators* of the quantities they are attempting to estimate (e.g., Figure 12.3a or 12.3b). This last point is particularly critical in that a common response to the apples–oranges criticism is that such differences can be "coded" as moderators because one is analyzing "results" in a meta-analysis not study differences (Hunter & Schmidt, 2004). However, if the differences involve the appropriateness of the *estimator* (i.e., an interrater correlation) used to estimate the quantity of interest (i.e., interrater reliability), then the logic behind coding this as a moderator seems weakened. One would essentially be coding whether the study estimator actually provides an appropriate estimate of reliability or not. This begs the question of what meaning an average of appropriate and inappropriate estimators taken across studies really has—particularly in light of differences in the functional composition of coefficients presented in Figures 12.3a and 12.3b.

For the sake of argument, pretend for a moment that all of the studies underlying a meta-analysis of interrater correlations were fully crossed, but the local study was not. Even in this case, the meta-analytic estimate would not be an appropriate proxy for interrater reliability in the local study in that it does not mimic the measurement design used in the local study. Given that different sources of variance are contributing to error variance and true score variance in ratings as a function of the measurement design *used locally*, the meta-analytic estimator and the reliability estimator appropriate for use in the local study are two different things.

Given these problems associated with blind adoption of a meta-analytic intercorrelations as proxies for interrater reliability in a local study, a third option would be to (a) estimate what variance components can be estimated locally based on the prevailing measurement design, (b) subtract out a preexisting estimate of

268 Dan J. Putka and Brian J. Hoffman

Step 1: Assuming the design is persons nested within raters (i.e., p:r) the following components can be estimated locally using SPSS, SAS, or R (or any other software that estimates variance components) and expressed as proportions of observed variance: $\sigma^2_{p,pr}$ and σ^2_r

Step 2: Obtain a pre-existing estimate of σ^2_{pr} expressed as a proportion of observed variance. For example, such an estimate could be drawn from a meta-analysis of variance components Hoyt & Kerns (1999) considering the moderator conditions that most closely resemble the local situation (e.g., Hoyt & Kerns, 1999) or previous research studies that resemble the current study, but allowed for unique estimation of σ^2_{pr}.

Step 3: Generate estimates of true score variance (σ^2_{True}) and error variance (σ^2_{Error}) by blending local and pre-existing variance component estimates as follows:

Est. σ^2_{True} = Local Est. $\sigma^2_{p,pr}$ – Pre-Existing Est. σ^2_{pr} = Est. σ^2_p

Est. σ^2_{Error} = Local Est. σ^2_r + Pre-Existing Est. σ^2_{pr} = Est. $\sigma^2_{r,pr}$

Step 4: Estimate interrater reliability as Est. σ^2_{True}/(Est. σ^2_{True} + Est. σ^2_{Error})

FIGURE 12.4 Estimating Interrater Reliability for a Design in Which Ratees Are Nested within Raters

person × rater interaction variance (σ^2_{pr}) from the locally available but cofounded, true score variance estimate, and then (c) formulate an interrater reliability estimator that reflects an appropriate combination of local and preexisting variance component data. An example of exactly how this could work is presented in Figure 12.4.

To illustrate precisely how this would work, we return to the example of the researcher who is collecting supervisor ratings for a sample of incumbents, where each group of incumbents is rated only by their supervisor. Following the steps outlined in Figure 12.4, the researcher first fits a simple nested random effects model to the local ratings data (i.e., a simple null or intercept-only hierarchical linear model; Bryk & Raudenbush, 1992) and happens to find the relative contribution of the rater main effect variance component (σ^2_r) to observed variance in ratings is .33 and the relative contribution of the combination of person main effects and the person × rater interaction variance ($\sigma^2_{p,pr}$) to observed rating variance is .67. In this case, the researcher cannot use these components alone to estimate the interrater reliability of the performance ratings because the source of true score variance (σ^2_p) is confounded with a key source of error variance (i.e., σ^2_{pr}). To deal with this issue, the researcher identifies an estimate of the relative contribution of person × rater interaction variance component to observed rating variance from past research (e.g., .11 from Hoyt & Kerns's 1999 meta-analysis) and uses it to adjust the locally estimated variance components.[6] Specifically, the researcher subtracts .11 from .67 to arrive at an estimate of .56 for σ^2_p (i.e., the true score variance estimate of interest) and adds .11 to .33 to arrive at an estimate of .44 for $\sigma^2_{r,pr}$ (i.e., the error variance estimate of interest). With these newly estimated variance components, the researcher estimates the interrater reliability of the ratings in to be .56 (i.e., true score variance over true score plus error variance).

Though clearly the approach outlined in Figure 12.4 is possible, to our knowledge this has not been done or evaluated in past research. Its accuracy will in part be contingent on the quality of the preexisting estimate of person × rater interaction variance (i.e., σ^2_{pr}). To illustrate just how much difference the choice of an estimate for σ^2_{pr} can make, consider the following. The ".11" estimate used in the previous illustration is based on Hoyt and Kerns's (1999) overall estimate for σ^2_{pr}, but many moderators of the magnitude of σ^2_{pr} were found in that study. For example, Hoyt and Kerns (1999) found that the estimate of σ^2_{pr} was .48 when raters were acquainted with the ratees they were rating—which is routine in the context of job performance ratings. If one used .48 to make the calculations as opposed to .11, very different conclusions would be reached about reliability, namely the estimate for interrater reliability would be .19 as opposed to .56. This clearly illustrates that the strategy would be heavily influenced by the quality of one's estimate of σ^2_{pr}. Thus, though we see promise in this approach, we urge caution in adopting it. Specifically, one should carefully consider whether the preexisting estimate of σ^2_{pr} is based on a past study or set of past studies and is similar enough to the local situation (e.g., comparable rating format, comparable rater training, comparable performance dimensions) to warrant use of the estimate locally. Given the promise and novelty of this approach, we suggest it be further evaluated in future research concerned with estimating interrater reliability.

Employing Interrater Correlations for Corrections within Meta-Analytic Studies

Beyond the use of meta-analytic estimates of interrater correlations within local studies, there are other applications of interrater correlations within the context of meta-analysis that warrant attention and suffer from similar logical limitations: (a) correction of individual studies within meta-analysis based on interrater correlations and (b) use of artifact distributions of interrater correlations to make corrections. Though not the focus of this work, we comment briefly on these practices given their prevalence.

In the former case, many of the same problems exist that were raised earlier, only this time, an additional issue is added—each study is corrected by what may be a more or less appropriate estimator of interrater reliability. Indeed, one may argue that if we follow current psychometric thought, then what is the appropriate estimator will be locally determined, so it also begs the question of what meaning it has to take a set of studies and correct them all for interrater reliability when within the context of some studies, raters may not be viewed as a source of error, or broader generalizations may have been desired by the authors. These are

270 Dan J. Putka and Brian J. Hoffman

conceptual and statistical issues that the meta-analysis literature and our field in general have yet to address, and we encourage future discussion of these topics.

Second, with regard to artifact distributions, given the perspective offered earlier, it appears somewhat dubious to employ a single distribution of coefficients that are differentially accurate estimators of the quantity of interest (again, not due to sampling error but rather due to design), particularly when one considers that the sampling distributions for the quantities of interest even have different functional forms. For example, contrast formulae for confidence intervals of various types of intraclass correlations (ICCs), based on one-way, two-way, and three-way designs—they are clearly very different (McGraw & Wong, 1996; Wong & McGraw 1999; Zhou, Muellerleile, Ingram, & Wong, 2011). Though they are all intraclass correlations, what meaning would it have to form a single distribution composed of different variants of these coefficients when (a) they all have a different functional form and (b) the standard error calculations are all quite different? A similar phenomenon occurs when Pearson correlations are applied to ratings data gathered using different measurement designs. As revealed in Figure 12.3a, the appropriate estimator may differ widely as a function of design, but one applies the same mathematical formulae (i.e., a Pearson correlation) regardless, when in fact different estimators are needed (e.g., Putka, Le et al., 2008; McGraw & Wong, 1996; Wong & McGraw, 1999). Again, this is a subtlety that has largely escaped the attention of organizational researchers in discussions of artifact corrections based on interrater correlations but is something that warrants future discussion.

In sum, using meta-analytic estimates of interrater correlations as proxies for the reliability of ratings in a local study (or meta-analyses for that matter) is fraught with serious hazards that are rarely discussed in the published literature. Namely, their use reflects no acknowledgement of the dependency of the composition, meaning, and magnitude of reliability estimates on the generalizations one wishes to make regarding the ratings in the local study, the measurement design underlying ratings gathered in the local study, or the intended use of ratings in the local study. All of these factors can and do legitimately differ from study to study.

Moving Forward—Key Takeaways

At its core, this chapter calls into question established practices for estimating the reliability of job performance ratings in the I-O psychology literature, which have grown inconsistent with modern perspectives on reliability estimation and psychometrics. These issues manifest themselves not only in the context of local studies but also in the context of meta-analyses that aggregate them. In this section, we close with a treatment of the primary observations made in this chapter and key takeaways for future researchers and practitioners to consider.

At the risk of being viewed as offering a nihilistic conclusion on where we stand with regard to reliability estimation for job performance ratings, we hope the preceding discussion illustrates there *are* more appropriate, readily available alternatives to use of interrater correlations. As noted in previous work, the calculation of the coefficients in Figures 12.3a and 12.3b has become more straightforward with the emergence of procedures within commonly available statistics packages (e.g., SPSS, SAS, and R), which allow for direct estimation of the variance components shown in Equation 2 and Figures 12.3a and 12.3b. Rather than having to rely on rather esoteric, ANOVA–based mean square formulae characteristic of common pedagogical treatment of Generalizability theory, there are now more direct ways to estimate coefficients (see DeShon, 2002; Putka & McCloy, 2008).

Though our focus here was on critiquing the widespread reliance on interrater correlations, it is important to note that the critique leveled here is not isolated to interrater correlations but rather applies to blind adoption of all "types" of reliability estimators, whether classical test theory, ICC, or G-theory based, if the considerations discussed—generalization, use, and measurement design—are ignored. Within any single study, there is no such thing as *the* reliability of performance ratings (just as there is no such thing as *the* validity of ratings); it is possible for many estimates to be calculated that are more or less appropriate depending on the generalization, use, and design considerations *in that particular study*. Just as we qualify statements of validity with statements of "validity for purpose X" or "evidence of validity for supporting inference X," so to must we take care when discussing reliability with statements such as "reliable for supporting generalization X." Different estimates tell us different things about the properties of our ratings and the degree to which various generalizations are warranted.

From our perspective, the only way to start remedying the disconnect is for our field to cease viewing reliability estimation as a "check in the box" that is done post hoc, particularly for measures that have been as error prone, as performance ratings have been from both reliability and validity perspectives for the past century. Key questions that should be asked *before* measure development and data collection occur are:

- What generalizations do I desire to make regarding my ratings?
- How will the ratings be used?
- What type of measurement design will *allow me* to evaluate the generalizations I want to make given my intended use of the ratings?
- If I can't obtain the measurement deign I need to support local estimation of reliability, do I have viable options or data from past work that will allow me to estimate the reliability coefficient I need?

These are critical questions that are, in our view, essential for our field to start asking if we are serious about accurately calibrating error in ratings. Moreover, making clear the answers to these questions in Methods sections of articles in which reliability information is reported is also critical to ensure alignment

Dan J. Putka and Brian J. Hoffman

between the study's reliability estimation strategy and the key considerations of desired generalizations, use, and measurement design.

The importance of giving these questions consideration up front is that they force one to think about what one wants to conclude regarding the quality of their ratings and the data that will be needed to evaluate those conclusions. This is in stark contrast to more of a post-hoc rationalization that may occur if one does not give forethought to these questions, such as "here's the type of data structure we have, so we're going to report coefficient X and call it *the* reliability of our ratings." That logic simply flies in the face of modern perspectives on reliability, which have been increasingly apparent in multiple fields (e.g., Haertel, 2006; Putka & Sackett, 2010) and in emerging professional standards (e.g., AERA, APA, NCME, 2014).

By aligning our research and practice with more recent psychometric perspectives, we can arguably move our field to a deeper understanding of error in ratings than is possible by simply cumulating and blindly averaging a garbled array of coefficients that are based on studies that may have differed in their desired generalization, use of ratings, and measurement designs—all of which we lack clarity on because primary studies have not historically documented such details when describing rating data.

In closing, we should note that the observations above do not apply simply to job performance ratings but also to other types of ratings studied by organizational researchers, such as assessment center ratings, multisource feedback ratings, employment interview ratings, and so forth. As such, caution and forethought are needed when considering use of interrater correlations as estimates of reliability in multiple domains of organizational research.

Notes

1 For the sake of parsimony, we have omitted a design in which ratees are nested within raters. Though common in situations in which a set of job incumbents is rated only by their supervisor (and each supervisor has a different set of subordinates), such a design does not allow for separation of rater-related effects from true score variance, nor does it allow for the calculation of interrater correlations based on locally collected data alone since there is only one rater per ratee. Thus, we omit it from discussion here but revisit it later given the frequency with which it arises in research and practice.

2 The notation "pri,e" is used to reflect the fact that the three-way person × rater × item interaction ("pri") is confounded with residual error ("e") in this particular model.

3 For the ill-structured measurement designs, we assumed a q-multiplier of .50, which corresponds to a level of crossing between ratees and raters that is about halfway between a design in which raters are fully crossed with ratees (in which case $q = 0$) and a design in which raters are fully nested within ratees (in which case $q = 1$, assuming one rater per ratee). See Putka et al. (2008) for more details on the q-multiplier in ill-structured measurement designs.

4 Note, since the coefficients in Figure 12.3b are agreement coefficients and not reliability coefficients, they should not be used to correct validity estimates for measurement error. Thus, only the reliability coefficients from Figure 12.3a are presented in Table 12.3.

5 Note we are careful here to draw the distinction between an *estimator* (i.e., a formula for calculating an estimate of a population parameter in a given sample) and an *estimate* (i.e., the number that results from applying that formula in a given sample).
6 Note, the .11 estimate here is obtained from Hoyt and Kerns's (1999) omnibus estimate of the relative contribution of person × rater interaction effects to observed between-ratee variance.

References

American Educational Research Association, American Psychological Association, & National Council on Measurement in Education. (2014). *Standards for educational and psychological testing* (4th ed.). Washington, DC: American Educational Research Association.

Bertua, C., Anderson, N., & Salgado, J. F. (2005). The predictive validity of cognitive ability tests: A UK meta-analysis. *Journal of Occupational and Organizational Psychology, 78,* 387–409.

Brennan, R. L. (2001). *Generalizability theory.* New York, NY: Springer-Verlag.

Bryk, A. S., & Raudenbush, S. W. (1992). *Hierarchical linear models.* Newbury Park, CA: Sage.

Cronbach, L. J., Gleser, G. C., Nanda, H., & Rajaratnam, N. (1972). *The dependability of behavioral measurements: Theory of generalizability for scores and profiles.* New York, NY: John Wiley.

Cronbach, L. J., Rajaratnam, N., & Gleser, G. (1963). Theory of generalizability: A liberalization of reliability theory. *British Journal of Statistical Psychology, 16, Part 2,* 137–163.

Cronbach, L. J., & Shavelson, R. J. (2004). My current thoughts on coefficient alpha and its successor procedures. *Educational and Psychological Measurement, 64,* 391–418.

Dawis, R. V., & Lofquist, L. H. (1984). *A psychological theory of work adjustment: An individual-differences model and its applications.* Minneapolis, MN: University of Minnesota Press.

Deming, W. E. (1986). *Out of the crisis.* Cambridge: MIT Institute for Advanced Engineering Study.

DeShon, R. P. (2002). Generalizability theory. In F. Drasgow & N. Schmitt (Eds.), *Measuring and analyzing behavior in organizations: Advances in measurement and data analysis* (pp. 189–220). San Francisco, CA: Jossey-Bass.

Ebel, R. L. (1951). Estimation of the reliability of ratings. *Psychometrika, 16,* 407–424.

Eysenck, H. J. (1978). An exercise in megasilliness. *American Psychologist, 33,* 517.

Feldt, L. S., & Brennan, R. L. (1989). Reliability. In R. L. Linn (Ed.), *Educational measurement* (3rd ed.; pp. 105–146). Washington, DC: American Council on Education/Macmillan.

Gilboa, S., Shirom, A., Fried, Y., & Cooper, C. (2008). A meta-analysis of work demand stressors and job performance: Examining main and moderating effects. *Personnel Psychology, 61,* 227–271.

Greguras, G. J., & Robie, C. (1998). A new look at within-source interrater reliability of 360 degree feedback ratings. *Journal of Applied Psychology, 83,* 960–968.

Haertel, E. H. (2006). Reliability. In R. L. Brennan (Ed.), *Educational measurement* (4th ed.; pp. 65–110). Westport, CT: American Council on Education and Praeger Publishers.

Harrison, D. A., Newman, D. A., & Roth, P. L. (2006). How important are job attitudes? Meta-analytic comparisons of integrative behavioral outcomes and time sequences. *The Academy of Management Journal, 49,* 305–325.

Hermelin, E., Lievens, F., & Robertson, I. T. (2007). The validity of assessment centres for the prediction of supervisory performance ratings: A meta-analysis. *International Journal of Selection and Assessment, 15,* 405–411.

Hoffman, B. J. & Woehr, D. J. (2009). Disentangling the meaning of multisource feedback: An examination of the nomological network surrounding source and dimension factors. *Personnel Psychology, 62*, 735–765.

Hoyt, C. (1941). Test reliability obtained by analysis of variance. *Psychometrika, 6*, 153–160.

Hoyt, W. T., & Kerns, M. (1999). Magnitude and moderators of bias in observer ratings: A meta-analysis. *Psychological Methods, 4*, 403–424.

Huffcutt, A. I., Conway, J. M., Roth, P. L., & Stone, N. J. (2001). Identification and meta-analytic assessment of psychological constructs measured in employment interviews. *Journal of Applied Psychology, 86*, 897.

Hunter, J. E., & Schmidt, F. L. (2004). *Methods of meta-analysis: Correcting error and bias in research findings* (2nd ed.). Thousand Oaks, CA: Sage Publications.

Jackson, S., & Brashers, D. E. (1994). *Random factors in ANOVA.* Thousand Oaks, CA: Sage Publications.

Judge, T. A., Thoresen, C. J., Bono, J. E., & Patton, G. K. (2001). The job satisfaction–job performance relationship: A qualitative and quantitative review. *Psychological Bulletin, 127*, 376.

LaHuis, D. M., & Avis, J. M. (2007). Using multilevel random coefficient modeling to investigate rater effects in performance ratings. *Organizational Research Methods, 10*, 97–107.

MacKenzie, S. B., Podsakoff, P. M., & Jarvis, C. B. (2005). The problem of measurement model misspecification in behavioral and organizational research and some recommended solutions. *Journal of Applied Psychology, 90*, 710–730.

McGraw, K. O., & Wong, S. P. (1996). Forming inferences about some intraclass correlation coefficients. *Psychological Methods, 1*, 30–46.

Murphy, K. R. (2008). Explaining the weak relationship between job performance and ratings of job performance. *Industrial and Organizational Psychology: Perspectives on Research and Practice, 1*, 148–160.

Murphy, K. R., Cleveland, J. N., & Mohler, C. J. (2001). Reliability, validity, and meaningfulness of multisource ratings. In D. W. Bracken, C. W. Timmreck, & A. H. Church (Eds.), *Handbook of multisource feedback* (pp. 130–148). San Francisco, CA: Jossey-Bass.

Murphy, K. R., & DeShon, R. (2000a). Interrater correlations do not estimate the reliability of job performance ratings. *Personnel Psychology, 53*, 873–900.

Murphy, K. R., & DeShon, R. (2000b). Progress in psychometrics: Can industrial and organizational psychology catch up? *Personnel Psychology, 53*, 873–900.

O'Neill, T. A., Goffin, R. D., & Gellatly, I. R. (2012). The use of random coefficient modeling for understanding and predicting job performance ratings: An application with field data. *Organizational Research Methods, 15*, 436–462.

Oswald, F., & McCloy, R. A. (2003). Meta-analysis and the art of the average. In K. R. Murphy (Ed.), *Validity generalization: A critical review* (pp. 311–338). Mahwah, NJ: Lawrence Erlbaum Associates.

Putka, D. J., Ingerick, M., & McCloy, R. A. (2008, April). Integrating reliability- and validity-based perspectives on error in performance ratings. In J. M. Cortina (Chair), *Write, for these words are true: Uncovering complexity in I-O.* Symposium conducted at the 23rd Annual Society for Industrial and Organizational Psychology Conference, San Francisco, CA.

Putka, D. J., Lance, C. L., Le, H., & McCloy, R. A. (2011). A cautionary note on modeling multitrait-multirater data arising from ill-structured measurement designs. *Organizational Research Methods, 14*, 503–529.

Putka, D. J., Le, H., McCloy, R. A., & Diaz, T. (2008). Ill-structured measurement designs in organizational research: Implications for estimating interrater reliability. *Journal of Applied Psychology, 93*, 959–981.

Putka, D. J., & McCloy, R. A. (2008). *Estimating variance components in SPSS and SAS: An annotated reference guide.* Alexandria, VA: Human Resources Research Organization. Available online at: www.humrro.org/corpsite/sites/default/files/dputkaFiles/Estimating%20Variance%20Components%20in%20SPSS%20and%20SAS.pdf

Putka, D. J., & Sackett, P. R. (2010). Reliability and validity. In J. L. Farr & N. T. Tippins (Eds.), *Handbook of employee selection* (pp. 9–49). New York: Routledge.

Riketta, M. (2005). Organizational identification: A meta-analysis. *Journal of Vocational Behavior, 66*, 358–384.

Rothstein, H. R. (1990). Interrater reliability of job performance ratings: Growth to asymptote level with increasing opportunity to observe. *Journal of Applied Psychology, 75*, 322–327.

Sackett, P. R., Laczo, R. M., & Arvey, R. D. (2002). The effects of range restriction on estimates of criterion interrater reliability: Implications for validation research. *Personnel Psychology, 55*, 807–825.

Schmidt, F. L., & Hunter, J. E. (1996). Measurement error in psychological research: Lessons from 26 research scenarios. *Psychological Methods, 1*, 199–223.

Schmidt, F. L., & Hunter, J. E. (1998). The validity and utility of selection methods in personnel psychology: Practical and theoretical implications of 85 years of research findings. *Psychological Bulletin, 124*, 262–274.

Schmidt, F. L., Viswesvaran, C., & Ones, D. S. (2000). Reliability is not validity and validity is not reliability. *Personnel Psychology, 53*, 901–912.

Scullen, S. E., Mount, M. K., & Goff, M. (2000). Understanding the latent structure of job performance ratings. *Journal of Applied Psychology, 85*, 956–970.

Searle, S. R., Casella, G., & McCulloch, C. E. (1992). *Variance components.* New York, NY: Wiley.

Shavelson, R. J., & Webb, N. M. (1991). *Generalizability theory: A primer.* Newbury Park, CA: Sage.

Taylor, P. J., & Small, B. (2002). Asking applicants what they would do versus what they did do: A meta-analytic comparison of situational and past behaviour employment interview questions. *Journal of Occupational and Organizational Psychology, 75*, 277–294.

Thorndike, E. L. (1920). A constant error in psychological ratings. *Journal of Applied Psychology, 4*, 25–29.

Viswesvaran, C., Ones, D. S., & Schmidt, F. L. (1996). Comparative analysis of the reliability of job performance ratings. *Journal of Applied Psychology, 81*, 557–574.

Viswesvaran, C., Schmidt, F. L., & Ones, D. S. (2005). Is there a general factor in ratings of job performance? A meta-analytic framework for disentangling substantive and error influences. *Journal of Applied Psychology, 90*, 108–131.

Wong, S. P., & McGraw, K. O. (1999). Confidence intervals and F-tests for intraclass correlations based on three-way random effects models. *Educational and Psychological Measurement, 59*, 270–288.

Zhou, H., Muellerleile, P., Ingram, D., & Wong, S. P. (2011). Confidence intervals and F-tests for intraclass correlations based on three-way mixed effects models. *Journal of Educational and Behavioral Statistics, 36*, 638–671.

13

USE OF "INDEPENDENT" MEASURES DOES NOT SOLVE THE SHARED METHOD BIAS PROBLEM

Charles E. Lance and Allison B. Siminovsky

Many researchers in applied psychology and the organizational sciences believe that common method bias represents a widespread and pervasive threat to the quality of research findings. For example, according to Spector (2006), "[i]t is widely believed that relationships between variables measured with the same method will be inflated due to the action of common method variance" (p. 221).

As a second example, Organ and Ryan (1995) wrote, "studies that use self-ratings of OCB along with self-reports of dispositional and attitudinal variables invite spuriously high correlations confounded by common method variance" (p. 779). As a final example, Podsakoff, MacKenzie, Lee, and Podsakoff (2003) argued that "[m]ost researchers agree that common method variance . . . is a potential problem in behavioral research" (p. 879).

As a result, it is not surprising that there is a lot of interest in discussing the sources, influences, and effects of common method variance and in documenting the extent of its pervasiveness (e.g., Buckley, Cote, & Comstock, 1990; Cote & Buckley, 1987; Crampton & Wagner, 1994; Doty & Glick, 1998; Kline, Sulsky, & Rever-Moriyama, 2000; Lance, Dawson, Birkelbach, & Hoffman, 2010; Lindell & Whitney, 2001; Spector, 1987; Williams & Brown, 1994; Williams, Cote, & Buckley, 1989). There has also been discussion surrounding various research design and statistical techniques for reducing, controlling for, or eliminating common methods variance (see Podsakoff et al., 2003, and Podsakoff, MacKenzie, & Podsakoff, 2012, for extensive reviews and Richardson, Simmering, & Sturman, 2009, for an empirical comparison of three different post-hoc statistical control techniques).

One design technique that alleges to control for common methods bias is the use of different methods to measure the predictor and criterion. As Podsakoff and colleagues (2003) wrote, "Because one of the major causes of common method variance is obtaining the measures of both predictor and criterion variables from the same rater or source, one way of controlling for it is to collect the measures of these variables from different sources" (p. 887). As a second example of this idea, Kammemeyer-Mueller, Steel, and Rubenstein (2010) wrote that "researchers . . . try to eliminate method effects by using one source to measure independent variables and another source to measure dependent variables" (p. 2). As just one example of this strategy in use, Wang and Verma (2009) wrote that ". . . because the independent, mediating and dependent data were collected from different sources, the paper avoided the common method variance that results from collecting data from a single source" (para. 18). This idea ranges beyond the organizational sciences. In an example from pediatric psychology, Holmbeck, Li, Schurman, Friedman, and Coakley (2002) recommended that researchers "consider using multiple sources and multiple methods to assess each construct" because doing so "allows one to examine associations between predictors and outcomes that do not share common method or source variance" (p. 14).

Thus, there appears to be a fairly widespread belief that if variables are measured using different methods, then the common method variance problem is circumvented. As such, the belief that use of measures obtained using different, allegedly independent methods solves the shared method bias problem is the urban legend that we address in this chapter. As we show in the remainder of this chapter, there is some truth to this belief—inflationary bias due to shared method effects is avoided by using different methods *as long as the methods are uncorrelated*. However, we then show that the situation is routinely more complex because (a) methods *are* fairly routinely correlated, not orthogonal, (b) attenuation due to measurement error must also be taken into account when comparing observed correlations to their true score counterparts, and (c) use of uncorrelated methods will actually have an additional attenuating effect on observed correlations above and beyond that of measurement error. We then review evidence presented by Lance and colleagues (2010) to illustrate these points empirically and also show that, perhaps paradoxically, monomethod correlations might be much more faithful to their true score counterparts than many have previously thought. Finally, we discuss and illustrate some recently proposed post-hoc statistical control procedures for common methods bias.

Effects of Common Method Variance (CMV) on Observed Correlations

Figure 13.1 illustrates the effects of CMV on observed correlations. Here, X_{ijk} is the kth realization of the ith person's standing on Trait_i (T_i) as measured by the jth measurement method (M_j), the E_{ijk}s represent nonsystematic measurement error associated with the kth measurement occasion, $\phi_{T_i T_{i'}}$ represents the correlation between two different traits, and the λs represent the causal effects of traits and methods on the respective measures (Borsboom, Mellenbergh, & van Heerden, 2004). It is assumed that $E(T_i,M_j) = E(T_i,E_{ijk}) = E(M_j,E_{ijk}) = E(E_{ijk},E_{ijk}) = 0$; for

278   Charles E. Lance and Allison B. Siminovsky

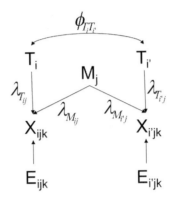

FIGURE 13.1 Effects of CMV on Observed Correlations

convenience, it is assumed that $E(T_i) = E(M_j) = E(E_{ik}) = 0$, and that X_{ijk}, T_i, and M_j have unit variances so that the λs are equivalent to standardized regression coefficients (or factor loadings; see what follows). Under these assumptions, the variances of the Xs are expressed as:

$$\sigma^2_{X_{ij}} = \lambda^2_{T_{ij}} + \lambda^2_{M_j} + \sigma^2_{E_{ij}}. \tag{1}$$

Equation 1 is a simple extension of classical test theory that shows that variance in any observed measure reflects true score and error score variance as well as variance attributable to the method employed to measure it. Also, to the extent that $\lambda^2_{M_{ij}}$ is large relative to $\lambda^2_{T_{ij}}$, the construct validity of X_{ij} is compromised (Lance et al., 2010). Given the assumptions listed, the correlation between X_{ij} and $X_{i'j}$ can be written as:

$$r_{X_{ij}X_{i'j}} = \lambda_{T_{ij}}\lambda_{T_{i'j}}\phi_{T_iT_{i'}} + \lambda_{M_{ij}}\lambda_{M_{i'j}} \tag{2}$$

Here it can be seen that the correlation between X_{ij} and $X_{i'j}$ ($r_{X_{ij}X_{i'j}}$) is indeed distorted (usually inflated) by a factor of $\lambda_{M_{ij}}\lambda_{M_{i'j}}$ – the common causal effect of the measurement method M_j. To the extent that the effects of M_j are large, covariance distortion (typically, inflation) will also be large. Accordingly, in a typical case where two variables are measured using the same method, the correlation between the measures ($r_{X_{ij}X_{i'j}}$) will be inflated by a factor equal to $\lambda_{M_{ij}}\lambda_{M_{i'j}}$. Consider the hypothetical example of an organization interested in the relationship between openness and organizational commitment, for which the true correlation is $\phi_{T_iT_{i'}} = .4$. These two constructs are each being measured by pen-and-paper survey. The connections between the constructs and their corresponding measurement method are reasonably strong ($\lambda_{T_{ij}} = \lambda_{T_{i'j}} = .80$) and effects of the common measurement method are "moderate" ($\lambda_{M_{ij}} = \lambda_{M_{i'j}} = .50$) In this case, the observed correlation ($r_{X_{ij}X_{i'j}} = .506$) is inflated as compared to the correlation among the constructs themselves ($\phi_{T_iT_{i'}} = .4$) due to the inflationary effect of common method variance. In fact, the observed correlation is about half construct-related variance ($\lambda_{T_{ij}}\lambda_{T_{i'j}}\phi_{T_iT_{i'}} = .256$) and half common method variance ($\lambda_{M_{ij}}\lambda_{M_{i'j}} = .25$). In other words, the use of surveys to measure both openness and organizational commitment is inflating the correlation between the two constructs—the .25 common method variance accounts for mechanisms of surveys as a method rather than the actual relationship between the two dimensions. This example helps illustrate the kernel of truth underlying the urban legend examined here—use of a single measurement method can and may routinely cause covariance distortion in relationships among observed measures and points to a possible solution—the use of different methods to measure X_{ij} and $X_{i'j}$.

However, this is not the full story. $\phi_{T_iT_{i'}}$ is also *attenuated* by a factor equal to $\lambda_{T_{ij}}\lambda_{T_{i'j}}$. The $\lambda_{T_{ij}}$s may be regarded as the Xs' reliability indexes (square roots of the variables' reliability coefficients), and it is this relationship that motivates the familiar correction for attenuation due to unreliability $\hat{\phi}_{T_iT_{i'}} = \frac{r_{X_iX_{i'}}}{\sqrt{r_{X_iX_i}}\sqrt{r_{X_{i'}X_{i'}}}}$ that is applied appropriately in the absence of CMV. Equation 2 also raises two important questions: (a) To what extent do the attenuating effects of variables' unreliability offset the inflationary effects of CMV in monomethod correlations? and (b) How can the familiar correction for attenuation formula be applied when CMV is known or suspected to be present? We will return to these questions later, but we will first explore the veracity of the claim that using different and allegedly independent methods solves the CMV problem.

Does Using Different Methods Solve the CMV Problem?

To answer this question, we turn to a broader multitrait-multimethod (MTMM) framework (Campbell & Fiske, 1959) that is shown in Figure 13.2, of which Figure 13.1 is a special case. Let us again consider the example of an organization

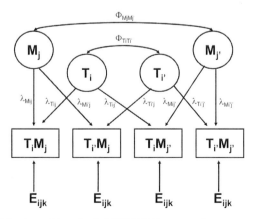

FIGURE 13.2 Multitrait-multimethod (MTMM) Framework

280 Charles E. Lance and Allison B. Siminovsky

attempting to study the role of openness on employee organizational commitment. Instead of only using surveys, the organization is now measuring each construct with both surveys and structured interviews. In Figure 13.2, each measured variable is denoted as T_iM_j or the ith trait as measured by the jth method (hence each variable is referred to as a trait-method unit), the alternate methods are denoted as $M_{j'}$ and $M_{j'}$. $\phi_{M_jM_{j'}}$ refers to the possible correlation between the methods, and other terms are defined as before. In MTMM vernacular, the heterotrait-monomethod (HTMM) correlation can be written as:

$$HTMM = \lambda_{T_{ij}}\lambda_{T_{i'j}}\phi_{T_iT_{i'}} + \lambda_{M_{ij}}\lambda_{M_{i'j}}$$ (3)

Note that this equation is the same as Equation 2. From Figure 13.2, the heterotrait-heteromethod (HTHM) and monotrait-heteromethod (MTHM) correlations can also be written as:

$$HTHM = \lambda_{T_{ij}}\lambda_{T_{i'j'}}\phi_{T_iT_{i'}} + \lambda_{M_{ij}}\lambda_{M_{i'j'}}\phi_{M_jM_{j'}}$$ (4)

and

$$MTHM = \lambda_{T_{ij}}\lambda_{T_{ij'}} + \lambda_{M_{ij}}\lambda_{M_{ij'}}\phi_{M_jM_{j'}}$$ (5)

respectively.[1] A comparison between Equations 3 and 4 addresses the question of whether use of different methods solves the shared methods problem. Obviously both equations contain the term $\lambda_{T_{ij}}\lambda_{T_{i'j'}}\phi_{T_iT_{i'}}$, so it follows that in both cases, the observed correlation is attenuated by measurement error ($\lambda_{T_{ij}}\lambda_{T_{i'j'}}$), as compared to the correlation between the traits themselves ($\phi_{T_iT_{i'}}$). Comparing the method components, Equation 3 includes $\lambda_{M_{ij}}\lambda_{M_{i'j}}$, while Equation 4 includes $\lambda_{M_{ij}}\lambda_{M_{i'j'}}\phi_{M_jM_{j'}}$. Importantly, *both* equations include a covariance distortion component attributable to measurement methods. In other words, regardless of whether structured interviews or surveys are being used, covariance between openness and organizational commitment will still be distorted due to method effects. In Equation 3, the covariance distortion component is the common causal effect of a single method ($\lambda_{M_{ij}}\lambda_{M_{i'j}}$). In Equation 4, the covariance distortion component is the combined effect of different but correlated methods ($\lambda_{M_{ij}}\lambda_{M_{i'j'}}\phi_{M_jM_{j'}}$). In this example, the covariance distortion component present in the correlations between openness and organizational commitment as measured by both methods could only be removed if one or both of the methods had zero effect on the measurement of the traits, or if the correlation between surveys and interviews was zero. Thus, this covariance distortion component will be eliminated for HTHM correlations *only* if (a) the effect of one or both of the methods on the observed measure is exactly zero or (b) the correlation between the methods ($\phi_{M_jM_{j'}}$) is zero. We consider that the former is very unlikely (Heisenberg, 1927; Messiah, 1961–1962; Spector, 2006). There is also evidence that we review in the following section that shows that the second possibility is similarly rare. Assuming for the moment, however, that $\phi_{M_j M_{j'}} = 0$, what would the net effect on the HTHM correlation be relative to the actual correlation between the constructs ($\phi_{T_x T_{x'}}$)? First, one can see from Equation 4 that the HTHM correlation will be attenuated by measurement error ($\lambda_{T_x} \lambda_{T_{x'}}$) relative to $\phi_{T_x T_{x'}}$. That is, even if methods are uncorrelated such that no covariance distortion is introduced into the HTHM correlations, they will still be biased downward by the attenuating effect of measurement error. The HTHM correlation will be attenuated even further *because* the methods are uncorrelated. The equation for the correlation coefficient, expressed in terms of variances and covariances, when no method variance is present, is:

$$ r_{xx'} = \frac{COV(T_x, T_{x'})}{\sqrt{VAR(T_x) + VAR(E_x)}\sqrt{VAR(T_{x'}) + VAR(E_{x'})}} \tag{6} $$

Now consider the same correlation when the two variables both contain method variance but the methods are uncorrelated:

$$ r_{xx'} = \frac{COV(T_x, T_{x'})}{\sqrt{VAR(T_x) + VAR(M_j) + VAR(E_x)}\sqrt{VAR(T_{x'}) + VAR(M_{j'}) + VAR(E_{x'})}} \tag{7} $$

Obviously, $r_{xx'}$ will be lower in Equation 7 than in Equation 6 because of the larger denominator in Equation 7. So to repeat the question stated earlier—does the use of different methods solve the CMV problem? The answer appears to be yes—the covariance distortion component introduced by CMV will be removed, but only if the different methods are truly independent (uncorrelated), a state of affairs that is very rare. Even so, compared to the actual correlation between the constructs, the observed correlation will be *attenuated* due to (a) measurement error and (b) method variance that is unique to each measure. For example, the correlation between openness and organizational commitment attenuated only by measurement error (from Eq. 6, each measure is assumed to have variance = 1.25 and reliability = .8) would be $.4/\sqrt{1+.25}\sqrt{1+.25} = .32$. If both measures contain even modest amounts of method variance, this correlation would be attenuated even further (from Eq. 7): $.4/\sqrt{1+.25+.25}\sqrt{1+.25+.25} = .27$. This illustration raises the additional important question of the extent and pervasiveness of method variance and whether methods in use are actually correlated.

Evidence on (Common) Method Variance

As mentioned previously, there have been a number of reviews on the causes, effects, and prevalence of CMV (e.g., Buckley et al., 1990; Cote & Buckley, 1987; Crampton & Wagner, 1994; Doty & Glick, 1998; Spector, 1987; Williams & Brown, 1994; Williams et al., 1989), most recently by Lance and colleagues (2010). Lance and colleagues (2010) meta-analyzed results from confirmatory factor analyses (CFAs)

282 Charles E. Lance and Allison B. Siminovsky

of 18 MTMM matrices using the correlated trait-correlated method (CTCM) parameterization. They purposely excluded MTMM matrices that used raters, rater sources, assessment center exercises, and rating occasions as "methods," as these measurement facets are now more properly conceptualized as representing aspects of their respective nomological networks that are meaningful in their own right (Lance, 2008; Lance, Baranik, Lau, & Scharlau, 2009; Lance, Hoffman, Gentry, & Baranik, 2008). The methods used in studies whose data were reanalyzed by Lance and colleagues (2010) included different scales to measure the same constructs, different rating scale anchors, different data collection approaches, and so on.

Some of Lance and colleagues' (2010) main findings were as follows:

- Mean trait factor loadings within studies analyzed ranged between .34 and .80 with an overall average across all studies equal to .635; thus, traits accounted for approximately 40% ($.635^2$) of the variance in measures overall.
- Mean method factor loadings within studies ranged between .24 and .62 with an overall average of .427; thus, approximately 18% of measures' variance was method variance.
- Mean trait correlations ranged between $-.103$ and .97 with an overall average of .37.
- Mean method correlations ranged between $-.20$ and .93 with an overall average of .52.
- Overall, the mean MTHM, HTMM, and HTHM correlations were .528, .340, and .248, respectively.

These results help to answer some of the questions posed previously. First, does use of different methods solve the shared method bias problem? The answer to this question lies in a comparison of the mean estimated correlation among the traits (estimated true score correlation) of .371 to the mean HTHM correlation of .248. In fact, the mean HTHM correlation is 33% *lower* than the mean trait correlation, and it is instructive to decompose the mean HTHM correlation using Equation 4 to see why. Doing so:

$$\text{HTHM} = .635^2 \times .371 + .427^2 \star .520 = .150 + .095 = .245 \tag{8}$$

shows that (a) the reproduced HTHM correlation (.245) is almost identical to the mean HTHM correlation estimated directly from the data (.248), (b) 61% of the reproduced HTHM correlation is due to trait (co)variance, and (c) 39% is due to covariance distortion. That is, using different methods leads to an *underestimate* of the true score correlation *even with the inflationary bias interjected by using correlated methods*. In fact, and as is described in Equations 6 and 7, had methods been *uncorrelated*, the attenuation would have been even more severe so that the reproduced HTHM correlation would have dropped to .15 (i.e., $.635^2 \times .371 + .427^2 \times 0 = .150$), a 60%

Another question posed earlier was whether the attenuating effects of measurement error offset the inflationary effects of CMV in HTMM correlations. The answer to this question lies in a comparison of the mean estimated correlation among the traits (estimated true score correlation) of .371 to the mean HTMM correlation of .340. In fact, the mean HTMM is 8% *lower* than the mean trait correlation. Once again, a decomposition of the HTMM from Equation 3 is instrumental in explaining why:

underestimate of the true score correlation. So the answer to the question of whether using different methods solves the CMV problem is "no," because using different (uncorrelated) methods may routinely cause more problems of attenuation in estimating the actual relationships among the constructs than the alleged solution solves. That is, using maximally different (uncorrelated) methods may routinely lead to additional attenuation in observed relationships, above and beyond measurement error, that would result in reduced statistical power and increased Type II errors because of problems inherent with using uncorrelated methods.

$$\text{HTMM} = .635^2 \times .371 + .427^2 = .150 + .182 = .322 \tag{9}$$

which is nearly identical to that estimated directly from the data (.34). On the average, the mean true score correlation is attenuated considerably by unreliability, but this attenuation is almost exactly offset by the inflationary effects of CMV. These findings suggest that the idea that CMV poses widespread covariance distortion threats is itself an urban legend, and that monomethod correlations may be much more trustworthy than many have believed.

Two other results from this analysis that are not directly related to this chapter's purpose are also noteworthy. First, MTHM correlations are often referred to as "convergent validities" (e.g., Woehr & Arthur, 2003, p. 242). However, as can be seen from Equation 5, MTHM correlations reflect the influence not only of the common trait ($\lambda_{T_{ij}} \lambda_{T_{ij'}}$, the "convergent validity" component) but also potentially of correlated methods ($\lambda_{M_{ij}} \lambda_{M_{ij'}} \phi_{M_j M_{j'}}$). In fact, it is possible that the MTHM correlations can reflect very little on convergent validity when trait factor loadings ($\lambda_{T_{ij}} \lambda_{T_{ij'}}$) are relatively low (i.e., convergent validity is actually low) and method factor loadings and correlations ($\lambda_{M_{ij}} \lambda_{M_{ij'}} \phi_{M_j M_{j'}}$) are relatively high (i.e., CMV effects are strong). From Lance and colleagues' (2010) data, the mean MTHM correlation of .528 is decomposed from Equation 5 as:

$$\text{MTHM} = .635^2 + .427^2 \times .520 = .499 \tag{10}$$

which was only slightly lower than that estimated directly from the data. These results illustrate the point made earlier that nearly 20% of the mean so-called "convergent validity" correlation (Woehr & Arthur, 2003) comes not from convergent validity ($\lambda_{T_{ij}} \lambda_{T_{ij'}}$) but from correlated method effects ($\lambda_{M_{ij}} \lambda_{M_{ij'}} \phi_{M_j M_{j'}}$).

284 Charles E. Lance and Allison B. Siminovsky

This relates to the second point. Some (e.g., Crampton & Wagner, 1994; Spector, 1987; Woehr & Arthur, 2003) have compared mean HTMM to mean HTHM correlations to assess the prevalence of method variance. This practice is incorrect and potentially very misleading. Returning to Equations 3 and 4, it can be seen that both the HTMM and HTHM reflect not only trait effects ($\lambda_{T_{ij}} \lambda_{T_{i'j}}, \phi_{T_i T_{i'}}$) but also method effects ($\lambda_{M_{ij}} \lambda_{M_{i'j}}$ and $\lambda_{M_{ij}} \lambda_{M_{ij'}} \phi_{M_j M_{j'}}$, respectively). This is true even of the HTHM correlations, which logically have nothing in common (these correlations reflect correlations between *different* traits as measured by *different* methods). Thus, to the extent that methods' effects on observed measures are nonnegligible and homogeneously signed (e.g., all positive) and method factors correlate positively, covariance distortion will incur even for heteromethod correlations. Of course, if the methods are uncorrelated, no covariance distortion will incur, even in the presence of substantial method variance. This analysis points to the single case in which comparisons between monomethod and heteromethod correlations provide an appropriate indication of covariance distortion: methods must be uncorrelated. Of course, in Lance and colleagues' (2010) analyses, the mean method correlation was .52. What effect did this have on the estimation of CMV bias? As was shown in Equation 9, the common method effect estimated from Lance and colleagues' results was $\lambda_{M_{ij}} \lambda_{M_{i'j}} = .427^2 = .182$ on the average, whereas the difference between the mean HTMM and HTHM correlations is $.342 - .248 = .094$, 48% lower than estimated from CFA results. This is because 39% of the .248 mean HTHM correlation is itself due to correlated method variance, or $\lambda_{M_{ij}} \lambda_{M_{i'j}} \phi_{M_j M_{j'}} = .427^2 \times .520 = .095$ from Equation 8. Thus, to the extent that methods are correlated, differences between HTMM and HTHM correlations will return inaccurate underestimates of CMV.

Summary

The urban legend that using different methods solves the CMV problem contains, like most statistical and methodological myths and urban legends, a kernel of truth. The use of *uncorrelated* methods removes the covariance distortion (usually inflation) component from heteromethod correlations. However, without some correction for the attenuating effects of measurement error and uncorrelated method variance, heteromethod correlations using uncorrelated methods will tend to yield serious underestimates of their true score counterparts. Three collateral but still important findings from the present analysis were that (a) monomethod correlations may often be surprisingly accurate estimates of their true score counterparts due to the offsetting contributions of attenuation by measurement error and inflation due to CMV, (b) so-called convergent validities reflect actual convergent validity as well as the effects of correlated method effects and so reference to MTHM as "convergent validities" should be made with caution, if at all, and (c) comparisons between HTMM and HTHM correlations to assess the extent of CMV should only be made when methods are uncorrelated;

Use of "Independent" Measures **285**

otherwise these comparisons can result in potentially serious underestimates of the extent of CMV.

So, What to Do about CMV?

Podsakoff and colleagues (2003) discussed several research design and post-hoc statistical control procedures for eliminating or reducing CMV. Of course, as we argue in this chapter, obtaining measures using different methods has several drawbacks that limit its promise as a design strategy. Separation of the different measures either temporally, proximally, or otherwise methodologically is a second possibility, but (a) there is little or no research on this strategy and (b) although we do not consider it here explicitly, we suspect that this strategy would suffer from some of the same limitations as the use of separate measurement sources or methods. Protecting respondent anonymity and reducing evaluation apprehension are reasonable suggestions, and indeed there is some indirect evidence from the literature on stereotype threat (Davis & Simmons, 2009; Roberson & Kulik, 2010) that suggests that these efforts may well be worthwhile in reducing CMV.

Podsakoff and colleagues (2003) also discussed a number of post-hoc statistical control techniques designed to eliminate or reduce CMV. One of these is Lindell and Whitney's (2001) partial correlation approach in which the minimum correlation between some "marker variable" and a study's focal variables is subtracted from the correlations among the focal variables to adjust for common method bias. According to Richardson and colleagues (2009), this approach has been frequently adopted (48 times as of June 2008), but usually to demonstrate that method bias was not a problem in the first place.

A second approach involves loading all study measures onto an unmeasured "method" factor and then analyzing relationships among the residualized variables. According to Richardson and colleagues (2009), at least 49 studies through June 2008 have used the unmeasured method factor approach. We see this approach as logically indefensible, as it may easily remove trait variance when multiple traits are correlated, as when they have a common cause (e.g., generalized psychological climate; James & James, 1989).

Both the partial correlation and unmeasured method techniques were evaluated in a simulation by Richardson and colleagues (2009), and both produced disappointing results. In fact, they produced less accurate estimates of correlations than did *no correction at all* when (a) method variance was present and (b) true correlations were greater than zero—conditions that are typical of organizational research. We therefore discourage use of either of these commonly used remedies for common method bias.

A third approach is Williams and Anderson's (1994) technique in which all focal latent variables' manifest indicators are loaded onto one or more substantive method latent variables (e.g., acquiescence, social desirability, positive/negative affectivity) on which also load the method factor's manifest indicators. One

286 Charles E. Lance and Allison B. Siminovsky

limitation of this technique is that it presumes that a researcher knows the source of method variance. The approach also appears to have been seldom applied and to have little effect on estimates among the focal constructs (Richardson et al., 2009).

Use of a multitrait-multimethod (MTMM) matrix to estimate relationships can be very effective for controlling common method bias (if methods are chosen carefully; see Lance et al., 2009). But the substantial demands of carrying out an MTMM study may make it difficult or impossible in many research situations, as each construct must be measured by multiple methods. Another complicating factor is the particular factor model that is applied to the MTMM matrix. Although the CTCM model is the most faithful theoretically to the original presentation of the MTMM matrix (Campbell & Fiske, 1959), it is known to have convergence and admissibility problems due to empirical underidentification (Brannick & Spector, 1990; Kenny & Kashy, 1992). Marsh's (1989) correlated uniqueness (CU) model largely avoids the convergence and admissibility problems endemic to the CTCM model, but it has its own set of limitations (Lance, Noble, & Scullen, 2002), including the required assumption that methods are orthogonal, which they obviously generally are not (Lance et al., 2010). Eid's (2000) CTC(M-1) also tends to overcome empirical underidentification problems of the CTCM model but at the expense of providing an incomplete specification of the methods' structure and consequent inability to unambiguously control for effects of all measurement methods included in the study.

Lance and colleagues (2010) proposed one final post-hoc statistical control procedure that builds on the familiar correction for attenuation formula but also includes a correction for CMV (see also Andrews, 1984). The correction for monomethod correlations is:

$$\hat{\rho}_{X_{ij}X_{i'j}} = \frac{r_{X_{ij}X_{i'j}} - \lambda_{M_{ij}}\lambda_{M_{i'j}}}{\lambda_{T_{ij}}\lambda_{T_{i'j}}} \tag{11}$$

and the correction for heteromethod correlations is:

$$\hat{\rho}_{X_{ij}X_{i'j'}} = \frac{r_{X_{ij}X_{i'j'}} - \lambda_{M_{ij}}\lambda_{M_{i'j'}}\Phi_{M_jM_{j'}}}{\lambda_{T_{ij}}\lambda_{T_{i'j'}}} \tag{12}$$

where $\hat{\rho}_{X_{ij}X_{i'j'}}$ is the estimated correlation corrected for attenuation due to measurement error and all other terms are defined as before. For example, and using the summary results presented by Lance and colleagues (2010) and above, the estimated true score correlation from the mean HTMM correlation is $(.340 - .427^2)/.635^2 = .39$ (from Equation 11) and the estimated true score correlation from the mean HTHM correlation is $(.248 - .427^2 \times .52)/.635^2 = .36$. Both of these estimates are very close to the actual estimated true score correlation of .37 presented earlier.

This is, of course, merely a demonstration that the estimated true correlation can be recovered approximately from additional independent information presented by Lance and colleagues (2010); more thorough evaluation of these proposed corrections should be effected in simulation studies. A separate question is how these corrections could be effected in practice. In particular, how could a researcher obtain the quantities needed to effect these corrections? As mentioned earlier, the λ_Ts are equivalent to variables' reliability indexes (square roots of the reliability coefficients), and reliability estimates for most measures are readily available or computable. λ_Ms can be estimated from a primary CFA of MTMM data, have been estimated previously in many primary studies, and are reported for a variety of different methods in Doty and Glick's (1988) Table 4, Williams and colleagues' (1989) Table 2, Buckley and colleagues' (1990) Table 1, and Lance and colleagues' (2010) Table 2. $\Phi_{M_jM_{j'}}$s can also be estimated from a primary CFA of MTMM data and estimates from previous studies and can be located in Buckley and colleagues' (1990) Table 1 and Lance and colleagues' (2010) Table 2. In both the case of monomethod and heteromethod correlations, prior estimates of similar methods' effects and correlations can be used to effect the corrections in Equations 11 and 12.

Note that Lance and colleagues (2010) also presented a multivariate version of the corrections in Equations 11 and 12:

$$C = D^{-1/2} (R - M)D^{-1/2} \tag{13}$$

where $\mathbf{C}$ is the matrix of corrected correlations, $\mathbf{D}$ is a diagonal matrix containing the variables' reliabilities, $\mathbf{R}$ is the original correlation matrix, and $\mathbf{M}$ is a square symmetric matrix containing corrections for method effects that are the subtrahends in the numerators of Equation 11 or 12, whichever is appropriate. The resulting matrix $\mathbf{C}$ can then be input to most any statistical software for analyses corrected for attenuation due to both unreliability and CMV.

Discussion and Conclusion

In the preceding pages, we have made a number of points with respect to CMV, how the use of different methods solves or does not solve the CMV problem, other roles that method variance can play in covariance distortion components in observed correlations, and procedures for reducing or controlling for CMV. These are summarized in Table 13.1 and discussed more generally in what follows.

CMV has been an important methodological concern for many, many years, and especially so since the publication of Campbell and Fiske's (1959) seminal article on the MTMM matrix. And today, nearly 55 years later, CMV is still a concern to authors. As an illustration, we performed a content analysis of all of the primary empirical studies published in the *Academy of Management Journal*, the *Journal of Applied Psychology*, and *Personnel Psychology* for 2010, and of the 137 articles

288 Charles E. Lance and Allison B. Siminovsky

TABLE 13.1 Summary of Main Takeaway Points

1. The use of different measurement methods results in no covariance distortion among observed measures only if (a) at least one of the methods interjects *no* method variance or (b) the methods are uncorrelated. Even so, the resulting observed correlation will routinely be (severely) attenuated due to measurement error and unique method variance.

2. Covariance distortion will still incur for measures obtained using different methods if the methods are correlated and research shows that methods *are* routinely correlated.

3. The attenuating effects of measurement error and the inflationary effects of CMV often offset one another so that monomethod correlations are often very close to the actual correlations among the traits.

4. MTHM correlations, often referred to as "convergent validities," routinely reflect covariance distortion due to method effects and thus provide inflated estimates of convergence of the measures in representing the underlying trait.

5. Comparisons between monomethod and heteromethod correlations to establish the presence of CMV are inappropriate, as both routinely contain covariance distortion components and thus underestimate the amount of CMV actually present.

6. Some research design procedures may help reduce CMV, but research on the effectiveness of available alternatives is sparse; the same may be said of post-hoc statistical control procedures.

identified, 13% (18) mentioned a potential limitation to the study relating to CMV. Of course, authors are concerned over the extent to which CMV poses a threat to the interpretation of their studies' findings, and these concerns are surely frequently amplified by reviewer and editorial concerns expressed during the peer-review process. Accordingly, many ways have been proposed to eliminate or at least minimize or reduce the effects of CMV. One seemingly widely acknowledged approach is to use separate sources or methods to measure different variables, and this is the urban legend we addressed in this chapter. As we showed earlier, there is a kernel of truth to the belief that using allegedly independent solved the CMV problem— in the event that the different methods are statistically independent (i.e., uncorrelated), heteromethod correlations will not be interjected with common or shared method bias and consequent covariance distortion. Even when different methods or sources are used to measure different variables, covariance distortion will still incur if the methods themselves are correlated. This raises the question—Are methods routinely correlated? Lance and colleagues' (2010) meta-analytic findings indicated that average methods' correlations across studies ranged between $-.10$ and $.97$, but overall, the mean method correlation across all studies reviewed was $.52$. Other reviews have reported similar findings. For example, Doty and Glick (1988) found that the mean estimated methods correlation ($\phi_{M_j M_{j'}}$) in the studies reviewed was $.34$, the studies reviewed by Buckley and colleagues (1990) had a mean estimated $\phi_{M_j M_{j'}}$ of $.37$, the studies reviewed by Cote and Buckley (1987) had a mean estimated $\phi_{M_j M_{j'}}$ of $.48$, and Williams and colleagues' (1989) studies' mean estimated $\phi_{M_j M_{j'}}$ was $.63$. Given the relative consistency of these findings, we must conclude that using different methods to measure multiple variables in a study does not solve the covariance distortion problem introduced by common or shared method bias. The problem is even more insidious when methods *are* uncorrelated because, as we showed earlier, two forms of attenuation of the correlation coefficient due to unreliability and to unique method variance will yield (perhaps drastic) underestimates of the actual correlation among the constructs under consideration.

So, what is one to do? Paradoxically, one reasonable recommendation might be *nothing*. Perhaps surprisingly, Lance and colleagues' (2010) meta-analytic results found that the mean HTMM correlation was nearly equal to that of the mean correlation among the traits themselves—covariance inflation on the part of CMV nearly exactly offset attenuation of the HTMM correlations due to unreliability. How common a finding this is and what research design factors might moderate this relationship are unknown, so obviously more work is need in this area. Another promising avenue for further research is the simultaneous corrections for variance distortion due to CMV and attenuation due to unreliability proposed by Lance and colleagues. The demonstrations in this chapter show that they approximately recovered the true correlation among constructs from independently estimated components, but these procedures are in need of additional independent verification.

There is an abundance of theory and research on CMV, and it is perhaps surprising how little the area has advanced in providing researchers with clear guidance as to the etiology, effects of, and ways to control for or otherwise manage CMV. Although it may ring as a cliché, these are areas where additional research is sorely needed.

Note

1 In simpler terms: HTHM = correlation between different traits as measured by different methods, such as the correlation between openness measured by structured interview and organizational commitment measured by survey; HTMM = correlation between different traits as measure by the same method, such as the correlation between openness and organizational commitment with both being measured by surveys; MTHM = correlation between one trait as measured by different methods, such as the correlation between openness as measured by survey and openness as measured by interview.

References

Andrews, F. M. (1984). Construct validity and error components of survey measures: A structural modeling approach. *Public Opinion Quarterly, 48*, 409–442.

Borsboom, D., Mellenbergh, G. J., & van Heerden, J. (2004). The concept of validity. *Psychological Review, 111*, 1061–1071.

Brannick, M. T., & Spector, P. E. (1990). Estimation problems in the block-diagonal model of the multitrait-multimethod matrix. *Applied Psychological Measurement, 14*, 325–339.

Buckley, M. R., Cote, J. A., & Comstock, S. M. (1990). Measurement errors in the behavioral sciences: The case of personality/attitude research. *Educational and Psychological Measurement, 50*, 447–474.

Campbell, D. T., & Fiske, D. W. (1959). Convergent and discriminant validation by the multitrait-multimethod matrix. *Psychological Bulletin, 56*, 81–105.

Cote, J. A., & Buckley, M. R. (1987). Estimating trait, method and error variance: Generalizing across 70 construct validation studies. *Journal of Marketing Research, 26*, 315–318.

Crampton, S. M., & Wagner, J. A. III. (1994). Percept-percept inflation in micro-organizational research: An investigation of prevalence and effect. *Journal of Applied Psychology, 79*, 67–76.

Davis, C. III, & Simmons, C. (2009). Stereotype threat: A review, critique, and implications. In H. A. Neville, B. M. Tynes, & S. O. Utsey (Eds.), *Handbook of African American psychology* (pp. 211–222). Thousand Oaks, CA: Sage.

Doty, D. H., & Glick, W. H. (1998). Common methods bias: Does common methods variance really bias results? *Organizational Research Methods, 1*, 374–406.

Eid, M. (2000). A multitrait-multimethod model with minimal assumptions. *Psychometrika, 65*, 241–261.

Heisenberg, W. (1927). Über den anschaulichen Inhalt der quantentheoretischen Kinematik und Mechanik [About the graphic content of quantum theoretic kinematics and mechanics]. *Zeitschrift für Physik, 43*, 172–198.

Holmbeck, G. N., Li, S. T., Schurman, J. V., Friedman, D., & Coakley, R. M. (2002). Collecting and managing multisource and multimethod data in studies of pediatric populations. *Journal of Pediatric Psychology, 27*, 5–18.

James, L. A., & James, L. R. (1989). Integrating work environment perceptions: Explorations into the measurement of meaning. *Journal of Applied Psychology, 74*, 739–751.

Kammemeyer-Mueller, J., Steel, P.D.G., & Rubenstein, A. (2010). The other side of method bias: The perils of distinct source research designs. *Multivariate Behavioral Research, 45*, 1–28.

Kenny, D. A., & Kashy, D. A. (1992). Analysis of the multitrait-multimethod matrix by confirmatory factor analysis. *Psychological Bulletin, 112*, 165–172.

Kline, T. J.B., Sulsky, L. M., & Rever-Moriyama, S. D. (2000). Common method variance and specification errors: A practical approach to detection. *The Journal of Psychology, 134*, 401–421.

Lance, C. E. (2008). Why assessment centers do not work the way they are supposed to. *Industrial and Organizational Psychology, 1*, 84–97.

Lance, C. E., Baranik, L. E., Lau, A. R., & Scharlau, E. A. (2009). If it ain't trait it must be method: (Mis)application of the multitrait-multimethod methodology in organizational research. In C. E. Lance & R. J. Vandenberg (Eds.), *Statistical and methodological myths and urban legends: Received doctrine, verity, and fable in organizational and social research* (pp. 339–362). New York, NY: Routledge.

Lance, C. E., Dawson, B., Birklebach, D., & Hoffman, B. J. (2010). Method effects, measurement error, and substantive conclusions. *Organizational Research Methods, 13*, 435–455.

Lance, C. E., Hoffman, B. J., Gentry, W. A., & Baranik, L. E. (2008). Rater source factors represent important subcomponents of the criterion construct space, not rater bias. *Human Resource Management Review, 18*, 223–232.

Lance, C. E., Noble, C. L., & Scullen, S. E. (2002). A critique of the correlated trait-correlated method (CTCM) and correlated uniqueness (CU) models for multitrait-multimethod (MTMM) data. *Psychological Methods, 7*, 228–244.

Lindell, M. K., & Whitney, D. J. (2001). Accounting for common method variance in cross-sectional research designs. *Journal of Applied Psychology, 86*, 114–121.

Marsh, H. W. (1989). Confirmatory factor analyses of multitrait–multimethod data: Many problems and a few solutions Applied Psychological Measurement, 13, 335–361.

Messiah, A. (1961–1962). *Quantum mechanics.* New York, NY: Interscience.

Organ, D. W., & Ryan, K. (1995). A meta-analytic review of attitudinal and dispositional predictors of organizational citizenship behavior. *Personnel Psychology, 48,* 775–802.

Podsakoff, P. M., MacKenzie, S. B., Lee, J.-Y., & Podsakoff, N. P. (2003). Common method biases in behavioral research: A critical review of the literature and recommended remedies. *Journal of Applied Psychology, 88,* 879–903.

Podsakoff, P. M., MacKenzie, S. B., & Podsakoff, N. P. (2012). Sources of method bias in social science research and recommendations on how to control it. *Annual Review of Psychology, 63,* 539–569.

Richardson, H., Simmering, M., & Sturman, M. (2009). A tale of three perspectives: Examining post hoc statistical techniques for detection and correction of common method variance. *Organizational Research Methods, 12,* 762–800.

Roberson, L., & Kulik, C. T. (2010). Stereotype threat at work. In J. A. Wagner III & J. R. Hollenbeck (Eds.), *Readings in organizational behavior* (pp. 27–47). New York, NY: Routledge.

Spector, P. E. (1987). Method variance as an artifact in self-reported affect and perceptions at work: Myth or significant problem? *Journal of Applied Psychology, 72,* 438–443.

Spector, P. E. (2006). Method variance in organizational research: Truth or urban legend? *Organizational Research Methods, 9,* 221–232.

Wang, J., & Verma, A. (2009, January). *Explaining organizational responsiveness to work-life balance issues: The role of business strategy and high performance work system.* Paper presented at the Labor and Employment Relations Association Annual Meeting, San Francisco, CA.

Williams, L. J., & Anderson, S. E. (1994). An alternative approach to method effects by using latent-variable models: Applications in organizational behavior research. *Journal of Applied Psychology, 79,* 323–331.

Williams, L. J., & Brown, B. K. (1994). Method variance in organizational behavior and human resources research: Effects on correlations, path coefficients, and hypothesis testing. *Organizational Behavior and Human Decision Processes, 57,* 185–209.

Williams, L. J., Cote, J. A., & Buckley, M. R. (1989). Lack of method variance in self-reported affect and perceptions at work: Reality or artifact? *Journal of Applied Psychology, 74,* 462–446.

Woehr, D. J., & Arthur, W., Jr. (2003). The construct-related validity of assessment center ratings: A review and meta-analysis of the role of methodological factors. *Journal of Management, 29,* 231–258.

14

THE NOT-SO-DIRECT CROSS-LEVEL DIRECT EFFECT

Alexander C. LoPilato and Robert J. Vandenberg

Summary of the Chapter's Goal

The legend: A cross-level direct effect/path from some higher-order situational attribute to some lower-order individual variable may be statistically estimated. The kernel of truth: Conceptually, yes, an effect from the higher-order attribute to some lower-order effect may be hypothesized. The myth: The observed parameter estimate taught to researchers as the one representing the cross-level direct effect is the direct conceptual effect from the situational higher-order attribute to the lower-order individual effect. The follow-up: If the within-group mean is truly representative of all individuals in a group, then extremely strong within-group agreement should be present. Only under those conditions will the "direct-effect" parameter estimate represent the theoretical cross-level direct effect.

The Theoretical Cross-Level Direct Effect

There are two broad theoretical contexts in which multilevel procedures and analyses are applied. One is in examining hypotheses pertaining to climate constructs (e.g., group-level safety climates) at the macro level but that were operationalized by aggregating individual-level perceptions within each group/team/cluster at the micro level (Bowen & Ostroff, 2004; James & Jones, 1974; Schneider, 1987). The second theoretical context is largely concerned with the interplay between micro- and macro-level phenomena or cross-level models (Griffin, 1997; Kozlowski & Klein, 2000). In fact, Kozlowski and Klein (2000) outlined a typology of multilevel models, and 6 out of the 11 models are theoretical representations of the different types of cross-level models found in organizational research. Cross-level models allow researchers to make cross-level inferences, which are inferences made from one level of analysis (e.g., macro level) to another level of analysis (e.g., micro level; Kozlowski & Klein, 2000; Pedhazur, 1982). Although it is theoretically plausible for micro-level phenomena to affect macro-level phenomena, the majority of multilevel research has concerned itself with the effects of macro-level constructs on micro-level constructs (Kozlowski & Klein, 2000). Specifically, organizational researchers have focused on two types of cross-level inferences: the cross-level direct effect and the cross-level interaction. *This chapter focuses solely on the cross-level direct effect.*

From a theoretical perspective, a cross-level direct effect is one in which a higher-level construct such as firm investment in employee training and development, for example, is hypothesized to directly impact a lower-level construct such as individual job satisfaction. James and Williams (2000) specifically defined the cross-level direct effect as "a hypothesis regarding how variations in a situational attribute are thought to be associated with variations in an individual attribute" (p. 385). However, the measurement of these higher-order constructs has proved to be quite difficult (Kozlowski & Klein, 2000; Kozlowski, Chao, Grand, Braun, & Kuljanin, 2013). Specifically, the measurement of the higher-level or situational attribute (aka the higher-order independent variable or IV) may stem from two sources. One source is measures collected only at the higher level as per the firm investment example. This source includes perceptual variables as well such as the teams' leaders' expectations of team members' capabilities (e.g., Richardson & Vandenberg, 2005).

The second measurement source for the higher-order IV is aggregation from some lower-order variable (Chan, 1998; James, 1982; Kozlowski & Klein, 2000). A concern underlying this source is how the higher-order IVs emerge from the lower-order variables. It has been argued that the emergence of the higher-order IV can be justified on the basis of either a composition model or a compilation model (Kozlowski & Klein, 2000). Under a composition model, the higher-order IV is considered isomorphic to its lower-order components—that is, the same conceptual structure/meaning at the lower-order level is thought to characterize the higher-order IV as well (Kozlowski & Klein, 2000; for example, see Zohar & Luria, 2005). In contrast, a compilation model does not assume that the constructs at both levels are isomorphic, and indeed, while the higher-order IV emerges from the lower-order variable, it is qualitatively different than its lower-order components (Bliese, 2000; Kozlowski & Klein, 2000; LeBreton & Senter, 2008; for example, see Stewart, Fulmer, & Barrick, 2005). Unlike a composition model in which high within-group agreement is required to justify isomorphism at both levels, compilation models place no such requirements on the variables (Chan, 1998; Kozlowski & Klein, 2000). That is, when the higher-order IV is based upon composition assumptions, researchers will typically provide estimates of within-group agreement (inter-rater agreement or IRA) and within-group reliability (interrater reliability or IRR) and argue that the estimate has passed a certain threshold, allowing them to aggregate the lower-level construct to a higher-level construct (Lance, Butts, & Michels, 2006; LeBreton & Senter, 2008).

In as much as the material in the forthcoming sections provides a detailed explanation for the following statements, only a cursory treatment of the dependent variable (DV) in the cross-level direct effect model is provided here. The doctrine accepted and followed by researchers (typically unquestioningly) is to conceptually treat the DV (the entity influenced by the higher-order IV) as something that varies across individuals—that is, as an individual-level variable. Of the 94 published studies reviewed by us in which cross-level direct effects were specified, this was true in 100% of those studies. Examples of such conceptual statements are:

- "Hypothesis 2 relates cross-level influences of group climate on individual outcomes. It specifies that group-level safety climate subscales should predict the likelihood of injury of individual group members, after controlling for the effects of individual-level overload and risk" (Zohar, 2000, p. 593).
- "Building on hypotheses 1 and 2, we propose that the direct effects of procedural and interactional justice climate on individual depression and anxiety will be moderated by organization structure" (Spell & Arnold, 2007, p. 729).
- "To summarize, we argue that cognitive team diversity is significantly related to individual team members' creativity because it is likely to be associated with creativity processes" (Shin, Kim, Lee, & Bian, 2012, p. 200).

As detailed shortly, *it is our belief that the unquestioning acceptance of treating the DV conceptually as an individual-level entity is inherently false when one examines the statistical treatment of that variable in estimating the path from the higher-order IV to it.* Thus, we question the validity of the inferences about such effects from the many published findings in which cross-level direct effects were hypothesized. Before proceeding, we would like our stance to be clearly understood. We agree that conceptually there are contextual factors (those at the higher-order or between level) influencing us as individuals. Statistically, however, it is not possible to operationalize such influences because the presumed lower-order DV is itself a higher-order variable. The issue is illustrated in Figure 14.1.

Figure 14.1 embodies the general cross-level direct-effect model characterizing many of the studies in our review of the published research literature (for example, see Figure 1, p. 43, Liao & Chuang, 2004; Figure 1, p. 11, Waldman, Carter, & Hom, 2012; Figure 1, p. 518; Walumbwa, Hartnell, & Oke, 2010). The dashed arrow from the higher-order or between-level IV (X_B) in Figure 14.1 to the lower-order or within-level DV (Y_W) is the conceptual hypothesis, that is, the one researchers believe is being statistically evaluated when following the doctrine and procedures guiding tests of cross-level direct effects. The earlier quotes illustrate such beliefs. The solid arrow, however, from X_B to the box signifying the between-level means on Y_W (e.g., the team means of Y, or the team intercepts of Y after accounting for some X_W) represents statistically what is actually being tested. Yet,

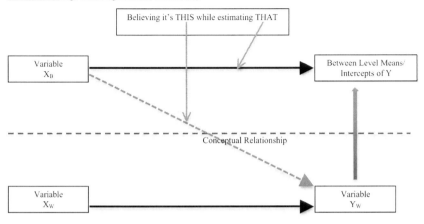

FIGURE 14.1 Illustration of basic direct-effect model

as illustrated by the following quotes, there is little, if any, recognition of this on the part of researchers as they frame their conceptual inferences from the statistical results:

- "We did find that procedural justice climate explained unique variance in helping behaviors. Counter to expectations, procedural justice climate was not positively associated with employees' reported levels of organizational commitment" (Naumann & Bennett, 2000, p. 887).
- "The direct relationship between empowerment climate and individual job performance failed to reach significance in our study, although there was evidence of an indirect link mediated by psychological empowerment" (Seibert, Silver, & Randolph, 2004, p. 344).
- "Our findings revealed that HPWS related to collective human capital and aggregated service orientation, which in turn related to individual-level service quality" (Aryee, Walumbwa, Seidu, & Otaye, 2013, p. 13).

It is the disconnection between what is being actually analyzed and the inferences from the results that is at the heart of the urban legend in this chapter. It is our belief that following the protocol for testing cross-level direct effects has been done unquestioningly, and what is statistically undertaken is not well understood by many researchers. Thus, they are inferring the outcome to be one thing when in fact that is not the case at all. A detailed explanation follows. We start with a review of the underlying equations and, through them, illustrate that the issue at hand has not been hidden but has been in plain sight the whole time.

The Statistical Cross-Level Direct Effect

To begin, we will explain and present the Level 1 and 2 equations. While there are several different notations in which the equations can be presented (see Appendix), we chose for present purposes to use the notation provided by Raudenbush and Bryk (2002):

$$Y_{ij} = \beta_{oj} + \beta_{1j} X_{ij} + r_{ij} \tag{1}$$

$$\beta_{oj} = \gamma_{0o} + \gamma_{01} W_j + u_{oj} \tag{2}$$

$$\beta_{1j} = \gamma_{1o} + \gamma_{11} W_j + u_{1j} \tag{3}$$

The Level 1 equation (Equation 1) models the relationship between the Level 1 DV (Y_{ij}) and any Level 1 covariates (X_{ij}). Equation 1 is conceptually similar to the ordinary least squares (OLS) regression equation such that the variance in the DV that is accounted for by the covariates is modeled by the regression coefficients (β_{oj}; β_{1j}), and any unexplained variance is modeled in the residual term (r_{ij}). However, unlike OLS regression, in multilevel modeling, the regression coefficients can vary by Level 2 groups (e.g., team or organization) and the resultant variance is modeled by the Level 2 equations (Equations 2 and 3). In the case of a model that has only one micro-level covariate, a researcher can specify both the Level 1 regression intercept (β_{0j}) and Level 1 slope (β_{1j}) to vary by Level 2 group. Level 2 covariates (W_j) can then be included in the Level 2 equations (Equations 2 and 3) to account for variance in the Level 1 intercepts and slopes. Specifically, Equation 2 models the relationship between the Level 1 regression intercepts and a Level 2 covariate (W_j) and Equation 3 models the relationship between the Level 1 slopes and the Level 2 covariate. Furthermore, the effect of the Level 2 covariate on the Level 1 intercepts is estimated by γ_{01}, which is commonly referred to as the cross-level direct effect, and the effect of the Level 2 covariate on the Level 1 slopes is estimated by γ_{11}, which is referred to as the cross-level interaction. Finally, variance in the Level 1 intercepts and slopes that cannot be accounted for by the macro-level independent variables is modeled by the Level 2 residuals u_{0j} and u_{1j}, respectively.

To create a descriptive reference, we mapped the equation components onto Figure 14.2. Focusing on Figure 14.2, it depicts both the cross-level direct effect and the cross-level interaction effects. However, as noted at the start of this chapter, the cross-level interaction is not the target of concern here, and thus, it is included for illustration only. Additionally, Figure 14.2 includes a Level 1 (micro) covariate of the Level 1 DV. From our review of the published research literature, sometimes the covariate is a theoretically justified predictor (e.g., Chuang, Jackson, Jiang, 2013; Gruys, Stewart, Goodstein, Bing, & Wicks, 2008; Liu, Zhang, Wang, & Lee, 2011), and at other times, it is a control variable (Eisenberger et al., 2010; Gong, Kim, Zhu, & Lee, 2013; Mero, Guidice, & Werner, 2012). When a covariate is present, Raudenbush and Bryk (2002) refer to the cross-level direct-effect model as an

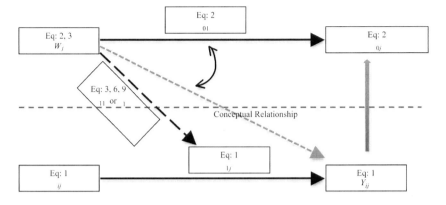

FIGURE 14.2 Direct-effect model illustrating components from the equations

intercepts-as-outcome model (p. 80). Although the vast majority of cross-level direct-effect studies in our review had at least one Level 1 covariate (97% of the 94 studies), a covariate is not necessary (for example, see Model 1, p. 693, Shanock & Eisenberger, 2006). In those cases, Raudenbush and Bryk (2002) refer to the cross-level direct-effect model as a means-as-outcome model (p. 72).

The key points from the previous review are as follows. The first point is that although the cross-level direct effects are often interpreted as involving an individual-level dependent variable (see earlier quotes), this is not the case at all. Rather, the dependent variable is the intercept/mean of the dependent variable between each of the Level 2 units (e.g., teams, organizations, etc.). Thus, the idiosyncratic (individual) nature of the dependent variable is not considered.

A second point is that the equations have not hidden this fact. Therefore, the disconnection between the conceptual inference and statistical result is not due to any form of mathematical or computational inaccuracy. From our perspective, what happened (as has been the case with other statistical and methodological myths and urban legends) is that a manuscript was published at some point in which the results were interpreted as reflecting a direct effect from the Level 2 covariate to the within DV. This publication was subsequently used as justification by others to engage in the same form of analyses to evaluate their direct-effect hypotheses, but the researchers did so without truly understanding the analyses themselves. After some time point, though, the analyses are applied unquestioningly, because "How could so many published studies be wrong?" It is traditional in many of the SMMUL chapters and articles to find the original source(s) in which the urban legend (UL) first appeared. We could have perhaps gone further back in time, but because the sixth issue of the 1997 *Journal of*

298 Alexander C. LoPilato and Robert J. Vandenberg

Management was one of the first comprehensive reviews of multilevel modeling in the organizational sciences, we opted instead to use it as our starting point. Our reason is that the articles in this review have been highly impactful, as evidenced by how frequently the articles are cited to this day (for example, Hofmann, 1997, has been cited 839 times; Kidwell, Mossholder, & Bennett, 1997, has been cited 260 times). Indeed, we found an example of the urban legend (UL) in the Griffin (1997) article. While the author recognizes the cross-level analysis (from the upper level to lower) as being conducted using the group-mean as the DV (see p. 763), he clearly interprets the effect as occurring at the individual level: "The model in Figure 1 indicates that group-level cohesion influences the experience of individual affect within the group" (p. 760). Hence, from our perspective, the UL goes back at least 17 years.

A third point is that even if it was understood that the DV was a between-level outcome, the operating premise in either case is that the between intercept/mean is equally representative of all entities nested within the between or grouping factor, that is, Y_{ij} must have zero variance within each group.

Demonstrating It Is a Between-Level Intercept/Mean

In order to establish, mathematically, that the dependent variable of a cross-level direct effect is a between-level intercept/mean—not an individual-level outcome—we will build upon the listed equations. However, to make our conclusions more concrete, we will employ the terms found in Equations 1 through 3 in a hypothetical research scenario. In this scenario, an organizational researcher is interested in the effects that an organization's justice climate has upon individual employee job satisfaction. That is, the researcher is interested in the cross-level direct effect of organizational justice climate (W_j) on employee job satisfaction ratings, Y_{ij}. Further, the researcher also wants to examine the effect that an employee's rated role ambiguity, X_{ij}, has upon their job satisfaction. To test this hypothesis, the researcher has collected data from J different organizations with n_j employees nested within each organization for a total sample size of $N = \sum_{j=1}^{J} n_j$. Through the following sets of equations, we will show that the cross-level hypothesis the researcher wishes to test can be neither confirmed nor disconfirmed by the statistical cross-level direct effect.

First, consider the one-way ANOVA model with random effects (Raudenbush & Bryk, 2002), which is a multilevel model that allows the intercept to vary across the j different organizations but does not include any Level 1 or Level 2 covariates to explain either the between- or within-group variance. The Level 1 and Level 2 equations are:

$$Y_{ij} = \beta_{0j} + r_{ij} \tag{4}$$
$$\beta_{0j} = \gamma_{00} + u_{0j} \tag{5}$$

In our research scenario, Equation 4 shows that an employee's job satisfaction is a function of their organization's intercept (β_{0j}) and a Level 1 random effect, r_{ij}, that is unique to each employee across all of the organizations. Further, from Equation 5 we can see that an organization's intercept is a function of the grand mean of job satisfaction (γ_{00}, the average job satisfaction taken across both employees and organizations) as well as a Level 2 random effect, u_{0j}, which is unique to each organization. Similar to the Level 1 random effect, the Level 2 random effect is an estimate of how an organization's average job satisfaction deviates from the grand mean of job satisfaction (i.e., the mean of job satisfaction taken over every organization).

Further, we derived the following equations by taking the within-organization average of Equation 4 and then we rearranged the terms:

$$\beta_{0j} = \overline{Y}_j \tag{6}$$

Equation 6 shows that, without any Level 1 or 2 covariates, an organization's intercept is equal to the average job satisfaction within an organization, $\overline{Y}_j$ (Enders & Tofighi, 2007). Then we replaced β_{0j} in Equation 5 with $\overline{Y}_j$, which created Equation 7:

$$\overline{Y}_j = \gamma_{00} + u_{0j} \tag{7}$$

Equation 7 demonstrates that the within-organization mean of job satisfaction is a function of the grand mean of job satisfaction and the Level 2 random effect, or the deviation of the jth mean from the grand mean.

Next, to test the cross-level hypothesis, the Level 2 covariate, organizational justice climate or W_j, was added to Equation 7. The addition of a Level 2 covariate changes Equation 7 to a means-as-outcomes model (Raudenbush & Bryk, 2002):

$$\overline{Y}_j = \gamma_{00} + \gamma_{01} W_j + u_{0j} \tag{8}$$

From Equation 8 we can see that the cross-level direct effect, γ_{01}, is the estimated effect of organizational-level justice climate on an organization j's mean job satisfaction and not the estimated effect of organizational justice climate on the job satisfaction ratings of individual employees within organization j.

Following this, the Level 1 covariate, employees' rated levels of role ambiguity or X_{ij}, was added to Equation 4, which changes Equation 4 to Equation 9:

$$Y_{ij} = \beta_{0j} + \beta_1 X_{ij} + r_{ij} \tag{9}$$

Equation 9 is conceptually similar to Equation 4, only it includes a measure of an employee's role ambiguity to explain the within-group variance in employee job satisfaction. β_1 is the estimated effect of an individual employee's role ambiguity on their job satisfaction. Additionally, as can be seen in Equation 10, the

300 Alexander C. LoPilato and Robert J. Vandenberg

addition of X_{ij} has altered the interpretation of β_{0j} so that it is now understood to be an adjusted group mean (i.e., the intercept; Enders & Tofighi, 2007; Raudenbush & Bryk, 2002):

$$\beta_{oj} = \bar{Y}_j - \beta_1 \bar{X}_j \tag{10}$$

What this entails is that β_{0j} is no longer equivalent to the within-organization mean of job satisfaction; it's now equal to the within-organization mean minus the effect of organization j's mean levels of role ambiguity. That is, it is equivalent to the expected job satisfaction score for an employee i belonging to organization j after controlling each organization on their average role ambiguity.

Finally, similar to what was done with Equations 6 and 7, Equation 11 was formed by replacing β_{0j} with its equivalent interpretation as an adjusted group mean, $\bar{Y}_j - \beta_1 \bar{X}_j$.

$$\bar{Y}_j - \beta_1 \bar{X}_j = \gamma_{0o} + \gamma_{01} W_j + u_{0j} \tag{11}$$

$$\bar{Y}_j = \gamma_{0o} + \gamma_{01} W_j + \beta_1 \bar{X}_j + u_{0j} \tag{12}$$

Equation 11 is conceptually similar to Equation 8 except that the cross-level direct effect is now an estimate of the effect of organizational justice climate on an adjusted organization mean of job satisfaction. Finally, Equation 12 moved the term $\beta_1 \bar{X}_j$ to the right of the equal sign to further show that we're only modeling the organization mean of job satisfaction, which could be interpreted as the effect of justice climate on mean job satisfaction controlling for an organization's mean role ambiguity.

Thus, with or without a Level 1 covariate, the researcher is never testing the effect of organizational justice climate on an employee's job satisfaction, but rather they are testing the effect of organizational justice climate on an organization j's mean job satisfaction.

The Importance of Within-Group Agreement

As we just demonstrated, the estimated cross-level direct effect is the effect of a Level 2 covariate on the group means of the DV. That is, the DV is being averaged by group and then the group average is being used as the DV in the Level 2 equations. Given that the hypothesized cross-level direct effect concerns the relationship between a Level 2 covariate and a Level 1 DV (James & Williams, 2000), in order for researchers to statistically test such a relationship using a multilevel model, it must be assumed that the individual scores and the groups' means are equal to one another; that is, the researcher must first be able to demonstrate that there is little to no within-group variation on the DV. This is because within-group variation occurs when individuals within a given group disagree on the DV. For example, imagine a scenario in which employees A and B respond to a five-point job satisfaction scale. Employee A is "Very Satisfied" with their job and records a 5, whereas Employee B is "Very Dissatisfied" with their job and records a 1. Now in this hypothetical situation, if we were to use a multilevel model to examine how organizational culture affects an employee's job satisfaction (a cross-level direct-effect hypothesis), both employees would receive a 3, which corresponds to them being "Neither Satisfied Nor Dissatisfied." Given what we know about the job satisfaction of both these employees, assigning both of them the average of their scores makes little to no sense. Now let us change the scenario so that Employee A records a 4, meaning they are "Moderately Satisfied" with their job, and Employee B records a 5. Now each employee will be assigned an average score 4.5, which is more representative of their individual scores.

Moreover, when within-group variance is high, such as in our first scenario, it is inappropriate to use a multilevel model to make inferences regarding the effect that organizational culture has on an individual employee's job satisfaction. Rather, it can only be inferred as to how organizational culture affects the group average of employee job satisfaction. And, thus, to the extent that the group average of the DV is a poor proxy for an individual's actual standing on the DV, any inferences made to the individual level will necessarily be biased.

Guidelines for Future Research

It is important that we recognize the multilevel nature of organizations, whether it is subordinates nested within a leader or departments nested within an organization—the nested nature of organizations does influence one's data (Bliese, 2000; Mathieu & Chen, 2011). Further, we have strong theoretical reasons to believe that lower-level constructs are affected by higher-level constructs (James & Jones, 1974; Mathieu & Chen, 2011; Meyer, Dalal, & Hermida, 2010). Individuals do not work in a vacuum, and theories need to acknowledge and explain how situational characteristics of work interact with characteristics of the worker (Meyer et al., 2010; Tett & Burnett, 2003). So it is imperative that researchers continue to employ multilevel analytic techniques. However, it is also important that researchers understand the limitations of these techniques and what they are able to infer from them.

As we have previously shown, the theoretical cross-level direct effect is different from the statistical direct effect, and researchers need to be aware of this. In instances of large within-group disagreement, the estimated cross-level direct effect may not be theoretically interpretable and could possibly result in an ecological fallacy if the researcher tries to make inferences with it (Robinson, 1950). Therefore, we outline the following theoretical and statistical guidelines for researchers to follow.

302 Alexander C. LoPilato and Robert J. Vandenberg

Acknowledging Within-Group Variance

Theoretically, a researcher needs to understand if and how their individual-level DV can be conceptualized at a higher level. We recommend reviewing Kozlowski and Klein's (2000) differentiation between composition and compilation processes. If the process linking the DV measured at the individual level to the group level is a compilation process, then a researcher cannot theoretically justify making inferences from the higher-level construct to the lower-level construct. This is because a compilation process results in a higher-level construct that is qualitatively different then the individual-level construct that it emerged from and may exhibit different relationships with other constructs than if those same relationships were examined using its lower-level construct (Kozlowski & Klein, 2000). Therefore, a researcher should consider looking into alternative statistical techniques other than hierarchical linear modeling (HLM) and multilevel structural equation modeling if they are interested in estimating and interpreting a cross-level direct effect as a higher-level variable affecting a lower-level variable (Kozlowski et al., 2013).

Next, if the process linking the lower-level construct to its higher-level construct is a composition process, then theoretically a researcher can generalize relationships across different levels. However, if a researcher wants to begin making cross-level inferences using the estimated cross-level direct effect, they must first demonstrate that the DV has extremely high within-group agreement using an IRA index such as r_{wg} (James, Demaree, & Wolf, 1993; Lindell, 2001; LeBreton & Senter, 2008). The within-group variance gives the researcher an estimate of the average within-group variance for each group, but the researcher needs to establish that each group has high within-group agreement by calculating an IRA for each group on the DV (see Woehr et al., Chapter 15 in this volume). Concerning within-group agreement, there are two cases that could possibly prevent researchers from interpreting the cross-level direct effect as an effect of a higher-level variable on a lower-level variable:

(a) Small within-group variance estimate but low within-group agreement for a small number of groups
(b) Large within-group variance estimate, indicating low within-group agreement for most, if not all, groups

Focusing on the first case, this is the reason researchers need to estimate an IRA for each group and not rely solely on the average within-group variance estimate. It is not enough to show that the estimated within-group variance is small; if the researcher is going to generalize the results of the cross-level direct effect across every group, then every group needs to meet some required level of within-group agreement. This is typically done when researchers aggregate IVs to a higher level (Chen, Sharma, Edinger, Shapiro, & Farh, 2011; Erdogan & Bauer, 2010; Wu & Chaturvedi, 2009), and failing to do so could lead to false inferences. The few

Not-So-Direct Cross-Level Direct Effect **303**

groups that lack within-group agreement can be thought of as outliers, and their treatment should follow along with the current best practices on dealing with outliers (Aguinis, Gottfredson, & Joo, 2013). However, some treatment of outliers may require that entire groups be deleted, which may not be feasible in cases in which the number of groups is low and removing them could drastically lower the statistical power of the HLM (Mathieu, Aguinis, Culpepper, & Chen, 2012).

As for our second recommendation, it can be used to address both cases of low within-group agreement. Namely, if there is a theoretical reason to believe that the within-group agreement for the DV will be low, then a researcher should include theoretically grounded Level 1 covariates to help explain the within-group variability. Once all of the relevant lower-level covariates have been specified, then the conditional variance of the DV can be used to calculate conditional IRAs for each group. We refer to these as conditional IRAs because the IRA is calculated using the conditional variance of the DV (which is essentially the variance of the residuals) rather than the observed variance of the DV. If the within-group agreement meets some required level (LeBreton & Senter, 2008), then the researcher can specify and interpret a cross-level direct effect. However, the interpretation of the cross-level direct effect must now reflect that the DV has been conditioned upon Level 1 covariates.

As for our two recommendations, we would like to caution researchers against abusing such recommendations by (a) artificially reducing within-group variability by identifying and only selecting individuals who are high in agreement and (b) including Level 1 covariates without theoretical reason. Regarding our first caution, although within-group variability renders the cross-level direct effect uninterruptable, within-group variation should be substantively interesting to the researcher. That is, the researcher should attempt to understand and explain why there is within-group variability. To adopt the language of Aguinis and colleagues (2013), such variation may be due to interesting outliers, which are "accurate (i.e., nonerror) data points that lie at a distance from other data points and may contain valuable or unexpected knowledge" (p. 275). The identification of interesting outliers can lead to new, exciting research and is something researchers should always be on the lookout for. Concerning our second caution, researchers should not include Level 1 covariates just to reduce the within-group variance. Doing so is atheoretical, and it is possible that a researcher's statistically significant findings will in part be due to chance. There are some excellent treatments on the uses and abuses of control variables, and we recommend consulting those before using control variables (Becker, 2005; Spector & Brannick, 2011).

Recommended Steps for Testing a Cross-Level Direct Effect

Despite the challenges that arise from testing the cross-level direct effect, we by no means wish to discourage researchers from pursuing multilevel research. However, it is necessary that researchers recognize the statistical limitations and potential

304 Alexander C. LoPilato and Robert J. Vandenberg

inferential errors that are inherent in the statistical modeling of the cross-level direct effect. Thus, to help encourage further multilevel research, we will provide steps that researchers can follow when they want to test a hypothesized cross-level direct effect. These steps are by no means definitive, but they should provide a useful starting point.

Step 1: Determining if between-group variance exists. Before any multilevel analyses can be conducted, it must first be determined that a significant amount of variation occurs among the Level 2 groups. That is, if the group mean of the Level 1 DV does not differ by group, then there is no statistical requirement that a researcher use a multilevel statistical model. Yet it is worth noting that as the between-group variance approaches zero, the parameter estimates obtained from a multilevel regression model will converge to those obtained from an OLS regression model (Gelman & Hill, 2007).

Researchers can statistically test the between-group variance by using a maximum likelihood algorithm to fit Equation 1 first without a random intercept and then with a random intercept (Bliese & Ployhart, 2002; Snijders & Bosker, 2011). A likelihood ratio test can then be used to determine the better-fitting model.

Step 2: Specifying the Level 1 model. If the model with the random intercept is found to be the better fitting of the two models, then the researcher can begin to include their theoretically relevant Level 1 covariates. It is during this time that researchers can begin to test the significance of the Level 1 covariates and, if relevant, the random slopes associated with some or all of the Level 1 covariates (Snijders & Bosker, 2011). An example of a model with a random intercept and one Level 1 covariate with a random slope is given in Equation 1.

Step 3: Calculating conditional IRAs. Once the Level 1 model is specified, conditional IRAs using the conditional variance of the DV can be calculated for each Level 2 group. The purpose of using the conditional variance and not the total variance of the DV is that the conditional variance models the DV variance that remains after the inclusion of the Level 1 covariates for each group. Similar to how IRAs are reported for independent variables (Bono, Foldes, Vinson, & Muros, 2007; Hon, Bloom, & Crant, 2011), researchers should also report the conditional IRAs for the DV. It is important to note that a researcher can continue to Step 4 even if the conditional IRAs do not meet an appropriate cut-off. However, the interpretation of the final model will be different.

Step 4: Specifying the Level 2 model. Similar to Step 2, Step 4 entails specifying and testing all of the theoretically relevant Level 2 covariates (Snijders & Bosker, 2011). These covariates can be used to explain both intercept and slope variance (Raudenbush & Bryk, 2002; Snijders & Bosker, 2011).

Step 5: Interpreting the cross-level direct effect. Once the full model has been specified (e.g., all statistically and theoretically significant Level 1 and Level 2 covariates have been included), it is now possible to interpret the Level 2 effects. Specifically, if the conditional IRAs for each group were found to be acceptable, then testing (e.g., the regression coefficient that models the effect of a Level 2 covariate on the Level 1 intercepts) can be interpreted as a test of the hypothetical cross-level direct effect. However, if the conditional IRAs are low, then testing cannot be interpreted as a test of the hypothetical cross-level direct effect. Because within-group variance is still high, it is incorrect for a researcher to assume that predicting the group mean of a DV is equivalent to predicting a group member's actual standing on that DV.

Summary

Multilevel models offer a powerful statistical framework under which one can empirically investigate theoretical claims made by meso theories (House, Rousseau, & Thomas-Hunt, 1995; Mathieu & Chen, 2011; Raudenbush & Byrk, 2002). However, much like any other statistical framework, there are limitations to what can be inferred from the parameter estimates. Specifically, the statistical cross-level direct effect is analogous to the theoretical cross-level direct effect only in cases in which the DV has high within-group agreement. High within-group agreement on the DV needs to be established because when a cross-level direct effect is estimated, it really represents the effect of a higher-level construct on the group average of the DV (Hofmann, 1997; Raudenbush & Byrk, 2002; Snijders & Bosker, 2011). So if the group mean is a poor representation of the individuals within the group, the statistical cross-level direct effect cannot be interpreted as the theoretical cross-level direct effect.

References

Aguinis, H., Gottfredson, R. K., & Joo, H. (2013). Best-practice recommendations for defining, identifying, and handling outliers. *Organizational Research Methods, 16*, 270–301.

Aryee, S., Walumbwa, F. O., Seidu, E. Y.M., & Otaye, L. E. (2013). Developing and leveraging human capital resource to promote service quality: Testing a theory of performance. *Journal of Management*. doi: 10.1177/0149206312471394

Becker, T. E. (2005). Potential problems in the statistical control of variables in organizational research: A qualitative analysis with recommendations. *Organizational Research Methods, 8*, 274–289.

Bliese, P. D. (2000). Within-group agreement, non-independence, and reliability: Implications for data aggregation and analysis. In K. J. Klein & S. W. J. Kozlowski (Eds.), *Multilevel theory, research, and methods in organizations* (pp. 349–381). San Francisco, CA: Jossey-Bass.

Bliese, P. D., & Ployhart, R. E. (2002). Growth modeling using random coefficient models: Model building, testing, and illustrations. *Organizational Research Methods, 5*, 362–387.

Bono, J. E., Foldes, H. J., Vinson, G., & Muros, P. (2007). Workplace emotions: The role of supervision and leadership. *Journal of Applied Psychology, 92*, 1357–1367.

Bowen, D. E. & Ostroff, C. (2004). Understanding HRM-firm performance linkages: The role of the "strength" of the HRM system. *Academy of Management Review, 29*, 203–221.

Chan, D. (1998). Functional relations among constructs in the same content domain at different levels of analysis: A typology of composition models. *Journal of Applied Psychology, 83*, 234–246.

Chen, G., Sharma, P. N., Edinger, S. K., Shapiro, D. L., & Farh, J.-L. (2011). Motivating and demotivating forces in teams: Cross-level influences of empowering leadership and relationship conflict. *Journal of Applied Psychology, 96*, 541–557.

Chuang, C. H., Jackson, S. E., & Jiang, Y. (2013). Can knowledge-intensive teamwork be managed? Examining the roles of HRM systems, leadership, and tacit knowledge. *Journal of Management*. doi: 10.1177/0149206313478189

Eisenberger, R., Karagonlar, G., Stinglhamber, F., Neves, P., Becker, T. E., Gonzalez-Morales, M. G., & Steiger-Mueller, M. (2010). Leader–member exchange and affective organizational commitment: The contribution of supervisor's organizational embodiment. *Journal of Applied Psychology, 95*, 1085–1103.

Enders, C. K., & Tofighi, D. (2007). Centering predictor variables in cross-sectional multilevel models: A new look at an old issue. *Psychological methods, 12*, 121–138.

Erdogan, B., & Bauer, T. N. (2010). Differentiated leader–member exchanges: The buffering role of justice climate. *Journal of Applied Psychology, 95*, 1104–1120.

Gelman, A., & Hill, J. (2007). *Data analysis using regression and multilevel/hierarchical models.* Cambridge, UK: Cambridge University Press.

Gong, Y., Kim, T. Y., Zhu, J., & Lee, D. R. (2013). A multilevel model of team goal orientation, information exchange, and creativity. *Academy of Management Journal, 56*, 827–851.

Griffin, M. A. (1997). Interaction between individuals and situations: Using HLM procedures to estimate reciprocal relationships. *Journal of Management, 23*, 759–773.

Gruys, M. L., Stewart, S. M., Goodstein, J., Bing, M. N., & Wicks, A. C. (2008). Values enactment in organizations: A multi-level examination. *Journal of Management, 34*, 806–843.

Hofmann, D. A. (1997). An overview of the logic and rationale of hierarchical linear models. *Journal of Management, 23*, 723–744.

Hon, A. H., Bloom, M., & Crant, J. M. (2014). Overcoming resistance to change and enhancing creative performance. *Journal of Management, 40*, 919–941.

House, R., Rousseau, D. M., & Thomas-Hunt, M. (1995). The meso paradigm: A framework for the integration of micro and macro organizational behavior. In B. M. Staw & L. L. Cummings (Eds.), *Research in organizational behavior* (Vol. 17; pp. 71–114). Greenwich, CT: JAI Press.

James, L. R. (1982). Aggregation bias in estimates of perceptual agreement. *Journal of Applied Psychology, 67*, 219–229.

James, L. R., Demaree, R. G., & Wolf, G. (1993). Estimating within-group interrater reliability with and without response bias. *Journal of Applied Psychology, 69*, 85–98.

James, L. R., & Jones, A. P. (1974). Organizational climate: A review of theory and research. *Psychological Bulletin, 81*, 1096–1112.

James, L. R., & Williams, L. J. (2000). The cross-level operator in regression, ANCOVA, and contextual analysis. In K. J. Klein & S. W. J. Kozlowski (Eds.), *Multilevel theory, research, and methods in organizations* (pp. 382–424). San Francisco, CA: Jossey-Bass.

Kidwell, R. E. J., Mossholder, K. W., & Bennett, N. (1997). Cohesiveness and organizational citizenship behavior: A multilevel analysis using work groups and individuals. *Journal of Management, 23*, 775–793.

Kozlowski, S. W., Chao, G. T., Grand, J. A., Braun, M. T., & Kuljanin, G. (2013). Advancing multilevel research design: Capturing the dynamics of emergence. *Organizational Research Methods, 16*, 581–615.

Kozlowsi, S. W. J., & Klein, K. J. (2000). A multi-level approach to theory and research in organizations: Contextual, temporal, and emergent processes. In K. J. Klein &

S. W. J. Kozlowski (Eds.), *Multilevel theory, research, and methods in organizations* (pp. 3–90). San Francisco: Jossey-Bass.

Lance, C. E., Butts, M. M., & Michels, L. C. (2006). The sources of four commonly reported cutoff criteria: What did they really say? *Organizational Research Methods, 9*, 202–220.

LeBreton, J. M., & Senter, J. L. (2008). Answers to 20 questions about interrater reliability and interrater agreement. *Organizational Research Methods, 11*, 815–852.

Liao, H., & Chuang, A. (2004). A multilevel investigation of factors influencing employee service performance and customer outcomes. *Academy of Management Journal, 47*, 41–58.

Lindell, M. K. (2001). Assessing and testing interrater agreement on a single target using multi-item rating scales. *Applied Psychological Measurement, 25*, 89–99.

Liu, D., Zhang, S., Wang, L., & Lee, T. W. (2011). The effects of autonomy and empowerment on employee turnover: Test of a multilevel model in teams. *Journal of Applied Psychology, 96*, 1305–1316.

Mathieu, J. E., Aguinis, H., Culpepper, S. A, & Chen, G. (2012). Understanding and estimating the power to detect cross-level interaction effects in multilevel modeling. *Journal of Applied Psychology, 97*, 951–966.

Mathieu, J. E., & Chen, G. (2011). The etiology of the multilevel paradigm in management research. *Journal of Management, 37*, 610–641.

Mero, N. P., Guidice, R. M., & Werner, S. (2012). A field study of the antecedents and performance consequences of perceived accountability. *Journal of Management*. doi: 10.1177/0149206312441208

Meyer, R. D., Dalal, R. S., & Hermida, R. (2010). A review and synthesis of situational strength in the organizational sciences. *Journal of Management, 36*, 121–140.

Naumann, S. E., & Bennett, N. (2000). A case for procedural justice climate: Development and test of a multilevel model. *Academy of Management Journal, 43*, 881–889.

Pedhazur, E. J. (1982). *Multiple regression in behavioral research* (2nd ed.). Fort Worth, TX: Holt, Rinehart and Winston, Inc.

Raudenbush, S. W., & Bryk, A. S. (2002). *Hierarchical linear models: Applications and data analysis methods* (2nd ed.). Thousand Oaks, CA: Sage Publications.

Richardson, H. A., & Vandenberg, R. J. (2005). Integrating managerial perceptions and transformational leadership into a work-unit level model of employee involvement. *Journal of Organizational Behavior, 26*, 561–589.

Robinson, W. S. (1950). Ecological correlations and the behavior of individuals. *American Sociological Review, 15*, 351–357.

Schneider, B. (1987). The people make the place. *Personnel Psychology, 40*, 437–453.

Seibert, S. E., Silver, S. R., & Randolph, W. A. (2004). Taking empowerment to the next level: A multiple-level model of empowerment, performance, and satisfaction. *Academy of Management Journal, 47*, 332–349.

Shanock, L. R., & Eisenberger, R. (2006). When supervisors feel supported: Relationships with subordinates' perceived supervisor support, perceived organizational support, and performance. *Journal of Applied Psychology, 91*, 689–695.

Shin, S. J., Kim, T. Y., Lee, J. Y., & Bian, L. (2012). Cognitive team diversity and individual team member creativity: A cross-level interaction. *Academy of Management Journal, 55*, 197–212.

Snijders, T. A. B., & Bosker, R. J. (2011). *Multilevel analysis: An introduction to basic and advanced multilevel modeling* (2nd ed.). London: Sage Publications.

Spector, P. E., & Brannick, M. T. (2011). Methodological urban legends: The misuse of statistical control variables. *Organizational Research Methods, 14*, 287–305.

Spell, C. S., & Arnold, T. J. (2007). A multi-level analysis of organizational justice climate, structure, and employee mental health. *Journal of Management, 33,* 724–751.

Stewart, G. L., Fulmer, I. S., & Barrick, M. R. (2005). An exploration of member roles as a multilevel linking mechanism for individual traits and team outcomes. *Personnel Psychology, 58,* 343–365.

Tett, R. P., & Burnett, D. D. (2003). A personality trait-based interactionist model of job performance. *Journal of Applied Psychology, 88,* 500–517.

Waldman, D. A., Carter, M. Z., & Hom, P. W. (2012). A multilevel investigation of leadership and turnover behavior. *Journal of Management.* doi: 10.1177/0149206312460679

Walumbwa, F. O., Hartnell, C. A., & Oke, A. (2010). Servant leadership, procedural justice climate, service climate, employee attitudes, and organizational citizenship behavior: A cross-level investigation. *Journal of Applied Psychology, 95,* 517–529.

Wu, P., & Chaturvedi, S. (2009). The role of procedural justice and power distance in the relationship between high performance work systems and employee attitudes: A multilevel perspective. *Journal of Management, 35,* 1228–1247.

Zohar, D. (2000). A group-level model of safety climate: Testing the effect of group climate on microaccidents in manufacturing jobs. *Journal of Applied Psychology, 85,* 587–596.

Zohar, D., & Luria, G. (2005). A multilevel model of safety climate: Cross-level relationships between organization and group-level climates. *Journal of Applied Psychology, 90,* 616–628.

APPENDIX

The appendix presents several different notations that have been used in the multi-level model literature. The purpose of presenting them all together is to show that despite notational differences, the equations are all mathematically equivalent. That is, equations 1, 4, and 7 are identical, equations 2, 5, and 8 are identical, and equations 3, 6, and 9 are identical.

- Raudenbush, S. W., & Bryk, A. S. (2002). *Hierarchical linear models: Applications and data analysis methods.* Thousand Oaks, CA: Sage Publications. Equations on p. 65.

$$Y_{ij} = \beta_{0j} + \beta_{1j}X_{ij} + r_{ij} \tag{1}$$

$$\beta_{0j} = \gamma_{00} + \gamma_{01}W_j + u_{0j} \tag{2}$$

$$\beta_{1j} = \gamma_{10} + \gamma_{11}W_j + u_{1j} \tag{3}$$

- Snijders, T.A.B., & Bosker, R. J. (2011). *Multilevel analysis: An introduction to basic and advanced multilevel modeling.* London: Sage Publications. Equations on pp. 80–81.

$$Y_{ij} = \beta_{0j} + \beta_{1j}x_{ij} + R_{ij} \tag{4}$$

$$\beta_{0j} = \gamma_{00} + \gamma_{01}z_j + U_{0j} \tag{5}$$

$$\beta_{1j} = \gamma_{10} + \gamma_{11}z_j + U_{1j} \tag{6}$$

310 Alexander C. LoPilato and Robert J. Vandenberg

- Gelman, A. & Hill, J. (2007). *Data analysis using regression and multilevel/ hierarchical models.* Cambridge, UK: Cambridge University Press. Equations on p. 282.

$$y_i = \alpha_{o j[i]} + \beta_{1 j[i]} x_i + \varepsilon_i \tag{7}$$

$$\alpha_{o j} = \gamma_o^\alpha + \gamma_1^\alpha u_j + \eta_j^\alpha \tag{8}$$

$$\beta_{1 j} = \gamma_o^\beta + \gamma_1^\beta u_j + \eta_j^\beta \tag{9}$$

15

AGGREGATION AGGRAVATION

The Fallacy of the Wrong Level Revisited

David J. Woehr, Andrew C. Loignon and Paul Schmidt

Multiple levels of analysis have become increasingly important in the study of organizational phenomena. This is evidenced by the expanding use of multilevel modeling techniques. Much of this research relies on data gathered at the individual level and then aggregated to a higher-level *unit* (e.g., team, work group, organization).[1] The aggregated response is then interpreted as an assessment of a unit-level characteristic. It has long been recognized that the construct validity of many of these unit-level constructs is dependent on the extent to which one can demonstrate a sufficient level of within-unit agreement (Bliese, 2000; Klein & Kozlowski, 2000b).

Within this context, we argue that a statistical myth of sorts has emerged via common practice. More specifically, it is typical practice to justify aggregation by demonstrating an adequate level of agreement *across* units. However, when using this approach, potential aggregation bias emerges because individual units may not demonstrate adequate levels of interrater agreement for the construct of interest. Moreover, including individual units that fail to demonstrate adequate within-unit homogeneity may inadvertently limit the construct validity of the higher-level construct. With that in mind, the primary goals of this chapter are to (a) describe the rationale for aggregation within a multilevel framework, (b) provide a review of the existing literature demonstrating that researchers typically rely on aggregate indices of agreement to justify their compositional models, (c) describe how this approach could lead to the inclusion of data that may reflect aggregation bias and limit construct validity, and (d) provide recommendations to help researchers avoid falling victim to this myth.

Background

Multilevel research (broadly defined) has become increasingly prevalent over the past decade. A cursory search of the management and applied psychology literatures using the Web of Science database indicates that well over 1,000 articles have

312 David J. Woehr et al.

addressed "multilevel models" over the past 10 to 15 years. Beginning with early writings on multilevel theory (e.g., Kozlowski & Klein, 2000; Rousseau, 1985), researchers have acknowledged that organizations are inherently multilevel with lower-level units nested within higher-level units (e.g., employees working within work teams or business units; Klein, Dansereau, & Hall, 1994; Klein, Tosi, & Canella, 1999). Furthermore, although organizational researchers often focus on micro topics at the individual level or macro topics at the organization or industry level, many scholars are also interested in research questions that span levels or focus on the intermediary levels within an organization (i.e., meso research; Hackman, 2003; Rousseau, 1985). Multilevel research has proliferated as a result of the potential to better explain organizational phenomena, as well as more readily accessible resources on how to formulate multilevel theories (e.g., Klein & Kozlowski, 2000b) and conduct multilevel analyses (e.g., Preacher, Zyphur, & Zhang, 2010).

Composition Models

The theoretical basis for the majority of unit-level constructs used in multilevel research follows from the typology of composition models described by Chan (1998). Specifically, the conceptual basis for most of these constructs relies on the logic of either a *direct consensus* or a *referent-shift consensus* model. Direct consensus models use aggregated individual data to operationalize group-level constructs. Team satisfaction, for example, may be operationalized as the mean team-member score on a measure of individual satisfaction (i.e., the referent of the measure is each individual's level of satisfaction with the team; e.g., De Dreu & Van Vianen, 2001). Alternatively, referent-shift consensus models require individuals to provide individual input with respect to group-level phenomena. For example, team conflict may be operationalized as the mean team-member description of the team's interactions (i.e., the referent of the measure is the team as opposed to the individual; e.g., Behfar, Mannix, Peterson, & Trochim, 2011).

Common to both of these *consensus* models, however, is a requirement that there is a substantial level of within-unit homogeneity or agreement such that the unit-level construct is only meaningful to the extent that it represents *shared* characteristics of the unit (Chan, 1998). In other words, "in the absence of substantial with-in unit agreement," the aggregated measure "has no construct validity" (Klein, Conn, Smith, & Sorra, 2001, p. 4).

To be clear, while the need to justify aggregation is inherent with the consensus models described, there are other types of composition models that do not require this justification. Chan's (1998) typology also includes additive, dispersion, and process models. With additive models, lower-level responses are aggregated regardless of the variance across these responses. Alternatively, in dispersion models, the meaning of the unit-level response is derived from the variance or dispersion across lower-level responses. Finally, process models focus on the assessment of unit-level change and development. There is no doubt that it is important to consider these models in multilevel research. To date, however, consensus models serve as the theoretical basis for the majority of the constructs examined at the unit-level and are thus far more prevalent in the literature.

Justifying Aggregation

As noted, constructs with consensus-based models as their conceptual basis are valid only to the extent that they represent the shared characteristics of the unit. Consequently, the operationalization of a construct in terms of either direct or referent-shift consensus composition models typically involves a two-step process. The first step involves assessing the level of homogeneity or agreement across individuals. To the extent that the results of this step reflect an adequate level of agreement, the second step involves computing an aggregate index to represent the higher-level construct (e.g., a mean of individual ratings). Again, the key point here is that the validity of the higher-level construct is dependent on a sufficient degree of within-unit agreement.

The importance of assessing within-unit agreement has long been recognized in the organizational literature (e.g., James, 1982; Roberts, Hulin, & Rousseau, 1978). Much of the literature addressing the importance of agreement across individual perceptions has focused on psychological and organizational climate. Within this context, James (1982) defines aggregation bias in estimates of perceptual agreement as "interpreting estimates of agreement based on functions of means as if they applied to agreement among individuals . . ." (p. 223). James states that this aggregation bias is a form of the "fallacy of the wrong level," which is defined as "a direct translation of properties or relations from one level to another" (Roberts et al., 1978, p. 103). Within the climate literature, then, using aggregated individual perceptions in the absence of substantial agreement across individuals to represent an organizational-level phenomenon would constitute aggregation bias such that disparate individual perceptions are fallaciously assumed to indicate organizational constructs. Like the man with one foot in the oven and the other in the freezer who, when asked the temperature replies, that it is just right, aggregating disparate responses does not present an accurate picture of the situation.

While initially emerging from the climate literature, aggregation issues are relevant in a wide variety of organizational phenomena, especially in the context of multilevel models and teams research. There are three primary issues that emerge in the literature. These issues are (a) the appropriate metric for assessing agreement, (b) the appropriate level of agreement to justify aggregation, and (c) the appropriate way to deal with units that do not demonstrate adequate agreement. Specifically, a great deal of literature has emerged focusing on which indices best assess agreement. While traditional measures such as intraclass correlations are widely used, other direct measures of agreement have also been proposed.

In addition, the literature also addresses how to interpret estimates of within-unit agreement with the primary question focusing on what levels of agreement

314 David J. Woehr et al.

are sufficient to justify aggregation. Although researchers have typically used general rules of thumb for interpreting these indices (e.g., values > .70; Lance, Butts, & Michels, 2006), more recent recommendations encourage considering a range of values (Lebreton & Senter, 2008) or benchmarking one's findings to the specific area of literature (Biemann, Cole, & Voelpel, 2012).

Finally, the issue of how to deal with units in which lower-level responses do not demonstrate adequate consensus also emerges in the literature (e.g., Lebreton & Senter, 2008), The primary concern here is whether units that do not demonstrate an adequate level of consensus should be included in subsequent analyses or discarded on the basis of a lack of validity. As we demonstrate, however, this issue has not been very widely reflected in the literature.

Statistical Myths Surrounding Aggregation Indices

Our primary focus, however, is on another issue—one that has received much less attention in the literature. That is, once an index or indices of agreement have been computed and a cutoff score established (issues 1 and 2 above), how are these metrics typically applied in establishing the construct validity of the higher-level construct? Here it is important to note that there are two types of indices typically used to assess agreement. The first are based on a partitioning of within- and between-unit variance (Lebreton & Senter, 2008). Most common are various forms of intraclass correlations (Bliese, 1998, 2000). ICC(1) describes the amount of variance in a variable that can be attributed to belonging to the higher-level unit (e.g., team or division; Biemann et al., 2012). ICC(1) also indicates the degree to which the value for any member of the unit can serve as a reliable estimate of the aggregated variable (Bliese, 1998). James (1982) states that ICC(1) may also be interpreted as an indicator of agreement in that higher values are associated with less within-unit variance. ICC(2), on the other hand, provides an estimate of the reliability of the higher-level unit's group means within a sample. It adjusts ICC(1) for group size; therefore, values of ICC(2) are higher when there are more lower-level observations per higher-level unit (e.g., more team members per group; Klein & Kozlowski, 2000a). Both forms of the ICC are calculated using an ANOVA framework in which the higher-level grouping variable is the independent variable (e.g., team identification code) and the construct of interest is the dependent variable (e.g., team cohesion). Of particular note is that these intraclass correlations are not available at the individual unit level but rather provide an index of the average level of agreement across units. In other words, ICC(1) and ICC(2) estimates are calculated for the entire sample rather than each unit.[2] For example, when aggregating individual employees' conflict ratings to the work group, a researcher would estimate a single ICC(1) and ICC(2) value to represent the level of agreement across teams (e.g., Simons & Peterson, 2000). This approach focuses on the construct and assumes that an adequate mean level of within-group agreement across groups is sufficient to justify aggregation.

Alternatively, direct measures of interrater agreement (i.e., measures assessing agreement for each unit) are available. The most common approach to directly assessing interrater agreement is through the r_{wg} index (Bliese, 2000; James, 1982; James, Demaree, & Wolf, 1984). This measure and its corollary for multiple-item assessments (i.e. $r_{wg(j)}$) compare the amount of observed variance among lower-level units to the amount of variance one would expect due to random responding (Cohen, Doveh, & Eick, 2001; James et al., 1984). Higher r_{wg} values suggest higher levels of within-group agreement. Unlike the intraclass correlation coefficients, the r_{wg} index is calculated for each individual unit. In other words, rather than providing a single estimate for the entire sample, the r_{wg} index provides a range of values across units. For example, when aggregating employees' perceptions of their business-units' cohesiveness, a researcher would examine estimates of r_{wg} for each unit (e.g., Hausknecht, Trevor, & Howard, 2009). Because estimates are provided for each unit, aggregation can be justified on a unit-by-unit basis and those that do not demonstrate sufficient within-group agreement can be identified (Klein & Kozlowski, 2000b). However, while the r_{wg} index may be the most widely used index of within-unit agreement, many researchers have noted a number of drawbacks with this measure (e.g., alternative theoretical null distributions, inadmissible values; Lebreton, James, & Lindell, 2005). Thus, a variety of alternative measures have been proposed, including the α_{wg} (Brown & Haunstein, 2005), r*$_{wg}$ (Lindell, Brandt, & Whitney, 1999), AD_M (Burke, Finkelstein, & Dusig, 1999), and α_d indices (Kreuzpointner, Simon, & Theis, 2010).

Regardless of the specific agreement indices used, we contend that a statistical myth has emerged via typical practice. Specifically, when justifying aggregation, researchers usually focus on the level of agreement across units such that if the mean or median value exceeds some threshold, then aggregation is warranted for all units. This occurs either through the use of agreement metrics that are not available at the unit level (e.g., ICCs) or through the use of aggregated direct measures of agreement (e.g., mean r_{wg} across units). The following excerpts are typical of this approach:

> Here it is important to note that the use of these aggregated variables as indicators of team level processes requires sufficient agreement across team members to warrant aggregation (James 1982; James et al. 1984). Thus, before aggregating, we examined the level of agreement across team members. To assess interrater reliability, we calculated intraclass correlations coefficients (ICCs) where ICC = (MSbetween—MSwithin)/MSbetween (Shrout & Fleiss, 1979). The ICC estimates across all teammates were .62 for team efficacy, .77 for team cohesion, .78 for role conflict, and .85 for task conflict. Landis and Koch (1977) suggest that interrater reliabilities above .61 should be considered substantial levels of agreement. Nonetheless, recent research indicates that ICCs tend to underestimate levels of agreement

(Lebreton, Burgess, Kaiser, Atchley, & James, 2003). Thus, we also calculated $r_{wg(j)}$ for each of these variables for each team. Results (included in Table 15.1) indicate adequate agreement to justify aggregation, (i.e., overall mean $r_{wg(j)}$ was approximately .85).

(Woehr, Arciniega, & Poling, 2013, p. 115)

And:

The average ICCs for HPWS were ICC1 = 0.19 and ICC2 = .93. The inter-rater agreement (r_{wg}) was equal to .94, assuming that the data were uniformly distributed (James et al., 1993). For power distance, the ICC1, ICC2, and rwg scores were .24, .95, and .81, respectively. The high ICC1 scores showed sufficient between-group variance in the construct to explain the variance in the dependent variables. The ICC2 and rwg scores, indicating whether the construct could be aggregated to a higher level, were above .80, which was much more than the accepted threshold of .70 (James, 1982). The aggregated statistics showed that it is reasonable and meaningful to aggregate HPWS and power distance to the firm level.

(Wu & Chatuvedi, 2009, p. 1238)

To be sure, there is a kernel of truth here. Specifically, for unit-level constructs (e.g., group, team, organization) that are predicated on either direct consensus or referent-shift consensus models, aggregate measures demonstrating a sufficient level of within-unit agreement (e.g., η^2, ICC, mean r_{wg}) are *necessary* to justify aggregation for a given data set. Yet it is not *sufficient*. At issue here is the fact that it is quite likely that any given data set will contain units with both high and low levels of agreement, suggesting that aggregation may be warranted in some units but not in others. Thus, even if the overall measure of agreement (either overall variance-based indices or aggregated direct agreement indices) exceeds one's cut-off, there is still a possibility that a substantial number of units may not demonstrate sufficient within-unit homogeneity. By including units that demonstrate low agreement when relying on either a direct consensus or referent-shift consensus composition model, one may limit the construct validity of their higher-level construct. Yet, while the challenges associated with estimating agreement across groups have long been recognized (e.g., Klein & Kozlowski, 2000b), the prevalence of this issue within the literature is not well known. Thus, to get a better overall picture of the literature and to ascertain the extent to which aggregation justification is based on aggregated measures of agreement (as we contend), we systematically review the extant literature. This review targets five research questions: Specifically:

- What proportion of studies in the literature recognizes and reports the need to justify aggregation?

- What are the most frequently used indices of agreement and how they are applied?
- To what extent do studies include information on the level of homogeneity across individual units?
- What proportion of units typically do not demonstrate adequate within-unit agreement?
- How do researchers typically treat specific units that do not demonstrate adequate within-unit agreement?

Literature Review

Our review consisted of studies published over the 15-year period from 1998 to 2012. This timeframe helped ensure we had a relatively large and diverse sample of studies that included aggregation indices. Using PsycINFO and Business Source Complete, we first identified articles that cited either Chan's (1998) seminal article on composition models or Lebreton and Senter's (2008) guidelines for using interrater agreement and interrater reliability in multilevel research. Both of these articles are important resources for conducting multilevel research that may appeal to different audiences. Chan's article provides a useful typology for formulating and developing aggregation models, while Lebreton and Senter's (2008) article may be more accessible for researchers who are beginning to explore multilevel theory and analyses. Thus, these articles are logical sources from which to identify a representative sample of articles using aggregation criteria.

Additionally, to complement this initial search, we also identified articles from 1998 to 2012, using PsycINFO and Business Source Complete, that included the term "aggregation" or its derivative in the title or abstract. Specifically, we searched for articles in the following top-tier journals from management and applied psychology: *Journal of Applied Psychology*, *Academy of Management Journal*, *Personnel Psychology*, and *Organizational Research Methods*. These two searches yielded a total of 754 articles that were reviewed using the inclusion criteria described below (see Table 15.1).

Exclusion criteria. After identifying these articles, we first excluded studies that were literature reviews, were conceptual papers, or did not include any empirical

TABLE 15.1 Summary of Search Results

Type of Article	Frequency (Percentage)
Removed article for exclusion criteria	209 (27.7%)
Failed to report aggregation criteria	327 (43.4%)
Reported aggregation criteria	218 (28.9%)

Note: $N = 754$

318 David J. Woehr et al.

data. Next, we excluded studies that only reported aggregation criteria for coding processes. For instance, one study reported r_{wg} and ICC values for three coders who retrospectively evaluated the personality of CEOs (Peterson, Smith, Martorana, & Owens, 2003). Although this process represents one form of aggregation, it diverges from the typical conceptualization of direct consensus or referent-shift compositional models in which the existence of a higher-level unit is justified based on data collected from a lower-level unit (Chan, 1998). After applying these exclusion criteria, 209 studies were removed from further analysis. Thus, we identified a total of 545 articles that reported data on variables based on consensus composition models. This set of studies served as the basis for our review.

What proportion of studies in the literature recognizes and reports the need to justify aggregation?

Of the 545 articles, a substantial proportion ($n = 327$) failed to recognize the need to justify aggregation. More specifically, 61% of the studies did not report aggregation indices. Apparently, authors of these studies tended to assume that multilevel analyses, such as random coefficient modeling, would allow them to consider individual-level ratings at a higher level. In these circumstances, the authors simply did not mention that their constructs relied on composition models and proceeded to the substantive tests of their hypotheses (e.g., Li, Frenkel, & Sanders, 2011; Molleman, Nauta, & Jehn, 2004). Alternatively, when the authors did feel the need to justify aggregation, they either included a brief sentence that preceded the description of the indices (e.g., "To test the appropriateness of conducting our analyses at the team level of analysis . . . ," Greer, Homan, De Hoogh, & Den Hartog, 2012, p. 207) or an extended description of their composition model. For example, Ehrhart, Bliese, and Thomas (2006, pp. 159–173) prefaced their aggregation results by stating:

> As mentioned earlier, the referent-shift consensus model implies that unit members generally agree on the level of the construct of interest in their units (Chan, 1998). In this case, five variables (unit-level helping behavior, cohesion, conflict, leader effectiveness, and the outcome variable of combat readiness) were rated by unit members and then aggregated, thus requiring an evaluation of within-group agreement (the other variables were already measured at the unit level and were only available in that form, rendering such evaluation unnecessary).

The tendency of authors to elaborate on their composition model prior to reporting aggregation indices may reflect the time period (i.e., authors of more recent articles assuming that readers understand the rationale behind these statistics) or the novelty of the construct (e.g., collective efficacy versus unit-level organizational citizenship behaviors).

What are the most frequently used indices of agreement and how they are applied?

Conversely, of the 545 articles, 218 (39%) reported estimates of within-unit agreement as a means of justifying the aggregation of individual-level data to a unit-level construct. These unit levels ranged from dyads and work groups all the way up to organizations and occupations. In total, these studies reported 1,677 estimates of agreement. That is, many studies reported multiple estimates for the same variables as well as reporting estimates for multiple variables ($M = 7.69$ estimates per article, $SD = 7.31$).

Oftentimes these articles would describe the shared nature of the construct being aggregated and make reference to Chan's typology or multilevel theory (e.g., Klein & Kozlowski, 2000b). For example, Chen, Thomas, and Wallace (2005) stated, "Collective efficacy . . . is based on a referent-shift composition model (Chan, 1998) in that it involves a shared belief among team members regarding their ability to perform team, not individual, tasks" (p. 830). On the other hand, some articles simply mention the need to justify aggregation while reviewing the validity of their measures. For instance, Erhart, Witt, Schneider, and Perry (2011, p. 426) "[assessed] the appropriateness of aggregating scores to the branch level" for their measures by presenting r_{wg} and ICC indices. The latter approach tends to be more common for constructs that have been established at the unit level (e.g., climate).

As shown in Figure 15.1, the most widely used indices by far were the r_{wg} (38%), ICC(1) (28%), and ICC(2) (24%), indices—accounting for more than 90% of the agreement indices provided. Additionally and in accordance with recent recommendations from multilevel researchers (Bliese, 2000; Lebreton & Senter, 2008), many studies reported both direct and aggregate assessments of within-unit homogeneity. Specifically, of the 218 studies we reviewed, 56% ($n = 123$) included ICC indices as well as one of the direct measures of agreement. However, while direct measures were used in a large number of studies, the vast majority (i.e., 72%) presented only aggregated versions of these indices (e.g., the mean r_{wg} across units).

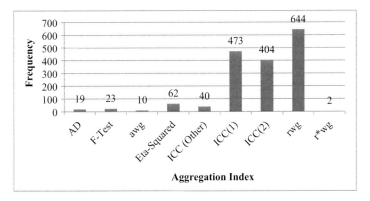

FIGURE 15.1 Frequency of aggregation indices

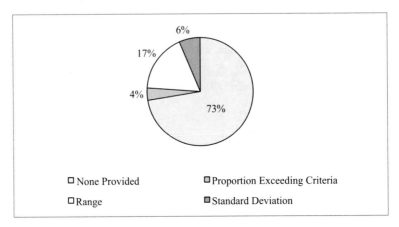

FIGURE 15.2 Proportion of studies reporting distribution information for aggregation indices

To what extent do studies include information on the level of homogeneity across individual units?

Of the 218 studies that reported aggregation indices, distributional information was reported in less than 28% ($n = 60$; see Figure 15.2). Researchers tended to report the range ($n = 38$) more often than they reported the standard deviation ($n = 14$). In addition, it is interesting to note the degree of variability of agreement indices within these studies. For example, when only considering the r_{wg} estimates, the average standard deviation was .19 (.02 to .38). Likewise, the average difference between the minimum and maximum r_{wg} estimates in a single study (i.e., the range) was .39 (.03 to .99).

What proportion of units typically does not demonstrate adequate within-unit agreement?

Here it is important to note that only slightly less than 4% of the studies that reported aggregation indices ($n = 8$) indicated the proportion of units for which the estimate of agreement exceeded the cutoff used to justify aggregation. Of those reporting these data, the percentage of units that failed to reach the cutoff value ranged from 0 to 28%.

How do researchers typically address specific units that do not demonstrate adequate within-unit agreement?

Again, it is important to note that an extremely small percentage of the agreement indices presented included information as to the proportion of units for which the estimate of agreement exceeded the cutoff used to justify aggregation. However, in all cases, these units were simply included in subsequent analyses. Furthermore, only six of the eight studies explicitly described how they dealt with the specific units that failed to exceed the stated cutoff score. For instance, Zohar and Luria (2004, p. 328) stated that "although some of the groups did not meet [the cutoff of .70], they were included in the analyses because $r_{wg(j)}$ exceeded .56 in all cases." Likewise, after stating that the r_{wg} value for one of their predictors was less than .70 for 28% of the workgroups in their sample, Wagner, Parker, and Christiansen (2003, p. 860) indicated that "aggregating responses of individuals into group-level composites was justified because of the strength of the within-group correlations and our belief that we had a reasonable theoretical rationale for aggregating variables." Finally, Bratton, Dodd, and Brown (2011, p. 135) claimed that having 83% of their supervisory units exceed the cutoff value of .70 "easily clear[ed] the threshold for aggregation" and these results, in conjunction with the ICC estimates "strongly support the contention that aggregation is appropriate."

Summary and Conclusions

Summary of Findings

We began our chapter with the contention that the issue of justifying aggregation with respect to consensus-based compositional variables was not being well handled in the extant literature. Our initial concern focused on the practice of aggregation by that demonstrating an adequate level of agreement *across* units. Our review certainly highlights this concern. Nearly 72% of the estimates we observed either relied solely on indices that examine within-unit agreement across units or failed to provide information on the distribution of direct measures of within-group agreement. This pattern of findings may be even more problematic given the range of values that can be observed across units within the same study.

Even more surprising, however, is the overall picture revealed with respect to how the need to justify aggregation is dealt with in the literature. Specifically, out of a total of 545 studies using variables based on consensus composition models, less than half (39%) recognize the need to justify aggregation and thus report any agreement indices. Moreover, less than 12% report anything other than aggregated agreement indices (i.e., provide no unit-level information). Also, less than 8% report data on the number of units that do not demonstrate adequate agreement and even fewer provide any indication of what was done with units that did not demonstrate adequate agreement. Taken as a whole, our review suggests that there is considerable potential for aggregation bias within the multilevel literature, because some individual units may not demonstrate sufficient levels of interrater agreement, which could subsequently reduce the construct validity of these higher-level constructs (see Table 15.2 for a summary).

Few would argue with the contention that consensus across individuals within higher-level units is a necessary, albeit not sufficient, condition for validity. Or, more specifically, constructs that rely on either direct consensus or referent-shift composition models must demonstrate adequate levels of within-unit homogeneity (Chan, 1998). Yet while this issue is not particularly novel, it has not been handled well in

322 David J. Woehr et al.

TABLE 15.2 Summary of Findings for Research Questions

Research Question	Findings
What proportion of studies in the literature recognizes and reports the need to justify aggregation?	Sixty-one percent of the studies failed to report aggregation criteria.
What are the most frequently used indices of agreement and how they are applied?	The most widely used indices by far were the r_{wg} (38%), ICC(1) (28%), and ICC(2) (24%), indices—accounting for more than 90% of the agreement indices provided.
To what extent do studies include information on the level of homogeneity across individual units?	Of the 218 studies that reported aggregation indices, distributional information was reported in less than 28% ($n = 60$).
What proportion of units typically does not demonstrate adequate within-unit agreement?	Of those reporting these data, the percentage of units that failed to reach the cutoff value ranged from 0 to 28%.
How do researchers typically address specific units that do not demonstrate adequate within-unit agreement?	In all cases, these units were simply included in subsequent analyses.

practice. It should be. As our review demonstrates, many researchers appear to assume (albeit perhaps implicitly) that providing evidence of adequate levels of homogeneity for *most* units justifies retaining *all* units.

Recommendations

With that in mind, we propose four recommendations to help researchers avoid falling victim to this statistical myth. First, researchers should clearly identify the conceptual basis for aggregating individual responses to higher-level units. Without clarifying the underlying composition model, researchers are limited in their ability to operationalize their higher-level construct and link it to other phenomena (Chan, 1998). Such clarification should also help limit the likelihood of blindly aggregating individual response to represent higher-level units when other forms of measurement may be more appropriate (e.g., expert judges, archival data; Kozlowski & Klein, 2000).

Second, within-group homogeneity should be considered at the unit level rather than simply an aggregation across units. It is important to be able to assess the level of within-unit agreement for each individual unit.

Third, researchers should report distributional information pertaining to direct agreement indices (e.g., r_{wg}). This information could be a standard deviation, minimum or maximum value, frequency distribution, or the percentage below a specified cutoff value. Reporting this information will ensure that researchers have considered the extent to which all of their groups exceed the specified cutoff values. Furthermore, such information will allow reviewers and readers to determine the appropriateness of aggregating individual responses to a higher level. A useful example for presenting aggregation indices and the recommended distributional information can be seen in Shaw and colleagues (2011, p. 394), who state:

> ICC(1) values for task conflict and relationship conflict were .27 and .33, respectively. ICC(2) values for the two measures were .55 and .62. We found high levels of mean $r_{wg(j)}$ for both task conflict (.87; range = .00 –1.00) and relationship conflict (.90; range = .47–.99); 86% of teams on task conflict and 96% of teams on relationship conflict had $r_{wg(j)}$s = .70. Although several teams had $r_{wg(j)}$ values less than the recommended .70 threshold, we followed Chen, Mathieu, and Bliese (2004) and retained all available cases for analysis. Tests of hypotheses after deleting teams with low $r_{wg(j)}$ values on a case-by-case basis yielded substantively identical results.

Fourth, it may be helpful to consider the potential impact of retaining units with low levels of within-unit homogeneity on subsequent analyses (e.g., tests of hypotheses). Although some researchers have questioned the appropriateness of excluding data based on aggregation indices (e.g., Lebreton & Senter, 2008), others have highlighted how retaining such units calls into question the construct validity of the higher-level construct (Klein et al., 2001). By including these units and overlooking instances of heterogeneity, a researcher could ignore potentially interesting phenomena. For example, low levels of within-unit homogeneity for certain units may suggest that under certain circumstances, the higher-level variable may be better represented by a dispersion model (Chan, 1998). In such models, variability in patterns of individual characteristics drives compilation processes that lead to higher-level variables that are similar in function but distinctly different in meaning or form (Kozlowski & Klein, 2000; Roberson, Sturman, & Simons, 2007). Furthermore, some simulation studies have suggested that removing higher-level units with low levels of interrater agreement has minimal effects on statistical power for detecting aggregate relationships (Biemann & Heidemeier, 2012). Given these considerations, researchers should conduct their analyses with and without units that demonstrate adequate levels of within-unit homogeneity. This, at the very least, will ensure that retaining these units does not adversely affect any subsequent analyses.

Notes

1 In the remainder of the chapter, we use the term "unit" to refer the level of analysis at which the construct of interest is targeted. Thus, a unit is composed of individuals and may be a team, work group, department, organization, etc.

2 Similar approaches for justifying aggregation include eta-squared coefficients and within-and-between-analysis (WABA). These approaches, which are far less common in the multilevel literature, also provide information across groups.

324 David J. Woehr et al.

References

Behfar, K. J., Mannix, E. A., Peterson, R. S., & Trochim, W. M. (2011). Conflict in small groups: The meaning and consequences of process conflict. *Small Group Research, 42*, 127–176.

Biemann, T., Cole, M. S., & Voelpel, S. (2012). Within-group agreement: On the use (and misuse) of r_{wg} and $r_{wg(j)}$ in leadership research and some best practice guidelines. *The Leadership Quarterly, 23*, 66–80.

Biemann, T., & Heidemeier, H. (2012). Does excluding some groups from research designs improve statistical power? *Small Group Research, 43*, 387–409.

Bliese, P. D. (1998). Group size, ICC values, and group-level correlations: A simulation. *Organizational Research Methods, 1*, 355–373.

Bliese, P. D. (2000). Within group agreement, non-independence and reliability: Implications for data and analysis. In K. J. Klein & S. W. J. Kozlowski (Eds.), *Multilevel theory, research, and methods in organizations: Foundations, extensions, and new directions* (pp. 349–381). San Francisco, CA: Jossey-Bass.

Bratton, V. K., Dodd, N. G., & Brown, F. W. (2011). The impact of emotional intelligence on accuracy of self-awareness and leadership performance. *Leadership and Organization Development Journal, 32*, 127–149.

Brown, R. D., & Haunstein, N.M.A. (2005). Interrater agreement reconsidered: An alternative to the r_{wg} indices. *Organizational Research Methods, 5*, 159–172.

Burke, M. J., Finkelstein, L. M., & Dusig, M. S. (1999). On average deviation indices for estimating interrater agreement. *Organizational Research Methods, 2*, 49–68.

Chan, D. (1998). Functional relations among constructs in the same content domain at different levels of analysis: A typology of composition models. *Journal of Applied Psychology, 83*, 234–246.

Chen, G., Mathieu, J., & Bliese, P. D. (2004). A framework for conducting multilevel construct validation. In F. Dansereau & F. J. Yammarino (Eds.), *Research in multi-level issues: The many faces of multi-level issues* (Vol. 3, pp. 273–303). Oxford, UK: Elsevier Science.

Chen, G., Thomas, B., & Wallace, J. C. (2005). A multilevel examination of the relationships among training outcomes, mediating regulatory processes, and adaptive performance. *Journal of Applied Psychology, 90*, 827–841.

Cohen, A., Doveh, E., & Eick, U. (2001). Statistical properties of the $r_{wg(j)}$ index of agreement. *Psychological Methods, 6*, 297–310.

De Dreu, C., & Van Vianen, A.E.M. (2001). Managing relationship conflict and the effectiveness of organizational teams. *Journal of Organizational Behavior, 22*, 309–328.

Ehrhart, M. G., Bliese, P. D., & Thomas, J. L. (2006). Unit-level OCB and unit effectiveness: Examining the incremental effect of helping behavior. *Human Performance, 19*, 159–173.

Erhart, K., Witt, L. A., Schneider, B., & Perry, S. J. (2011). Service employees give as they get: Internal service as a moderator of the service climate–service outcomes link. *Journal of Applied Psychology, 96*, 423–431.

Greer, L. L., Homan, A. C., De Hoogh, A.H.B., & Den Hartog, D. N. (2012). Tainted visions: The effects of visionary leader behaviors and leader categorization tendencies on the financial performance of ethnically diverse teams. *Journal of Applied Psychology, 97*, 203–213.

Hackman, J. R. (2003). Learning more by crossing levels: Evidence from airplanes, hospitals, and orchestras. *Journal of Organizational Behavior, 24*, 905–922.

Hausknecht, J. P., Trevor, C. O., & Howard, M. J. (2009). Unit-level voluntary turnover rates and customer service quality: Implications of group cohesiveness, newcomer concentration, and size. *Journal of Applied Psychology, 94*, 1068–1075.

James, L. R. (1982). Aggregation bias in estimates of perceptual agreement. *Journal of Applied Psychology, 67*, 219–229.

James, L. R., Demaree, R. G., & Wolf, G. (1984). Estimating within-group interrater reliability with and without response bias. *Journal of Applied Psychology, 69*, 85–98.

James, L. R., Demaree, R. G., & Wolf, G. (1993). Rwg: An assessment of within-group interrater agreement. *Journal of Applied Psychology, 78*, 306–309.

Klein, K. J., Conn, A. B., Smith, D. B., & Sorra, J. S. (2001). Is everyone in agreement? An exploration of within-group agreement in employee perceptions of the work environment. *Journal of Applied Psychology, 86*, 3–16.

Klein, K. J., Dansereau, F., & Hall, R. J. (1994). Level issues in theory development, data collection, and analysis. *Academy of Management Review, 19*, 195–229.

Klein, K. J., & Kozlowski, S.W.J. (2000a). From micro to meso: Steps in conceptualizing and conducting multilevel research. *Organizational Research Methods, 3*, 211–236.

Klein, K. J., & Kozlowski, S.W.J. (2000b). *Multilevel theory, research, and methods in organizations: Foundations, extensions, and new directions.* San Francisco, CA: Jossey-Bass.

Klein, K. J., Tosi, H., & Canella, A. A. (1999). Multilevel theory building: Benefits, barriers, and new developments. *Academy of Management Review, 24*, 243–249.

Kozlowski, S.W.J., & Klein, K. J. (2000). A multilevel approach to theory and research in organizations: Contextual, temporal, and emergent processes. In K. J. Klein & S.W.J. Kozlowski (Eds.), *Multilevel theory, research, and methods in organizations* (pp. 3–90). San Francisco, CA: Jossey-Bass.

Kreuzpointner, L., Simon, P., & Theis, F. J. (2010). The a_d coefficient as a descriptive measure of the within-group agreement of ratings. *British Journal of Mathematical and Statistical Psychology, 63*, 341–360.

Lance, C. E., Butts, M. M., & Michels, L. C. (2006). The sources of four commonly reported cutoff criteria: What did they really say? *Organizational Research Methods, 9*, 202–220.

Landis, J. R., & Koch, G. C. (1977). The measurement of observer agreement for categorical data. *Biometrics, 33*, 159–174.

Lebreton, J. M., Burgess, J.R.D., Kaiser, R. B., Atchley, E. K., & James, L. R. (2003). The restriction of variance hypothesis and interrater reliability and agreement: Are ratings from multiple sources really dissimilar? *Organizational Research Methods, 6*, 80–128.

Lebreton, J. M., James, L. R., & Lindell, M. K. (2005). Recent issues regarding rwg, $rwg(j)$, and $r\star wg(j)$. *Organizational Research Methods, 8*, 128–138.

Lebreton, J. M., & Senter, J. L. (2008). Answers to 20 questions about interrater reliability and interrater agreement. *Organizational Research Methods, 11*, 815–852.

Li, X., Frenkel, S. J., & Sanders, K. (2011). Strategic HRM as process: How HR system and organizational climate strength influences Chinese employee attitudes. *International Journal of Human Resources Management, 22*, 1825–1842.

Lindell, M. K., Brandt, C. J., & Whitney, D. (1999). A revised index of interrater agreement for multi-item ratings of a single target. *Applied Psychological Measurement, 23*, 127–135.

Molleman, E., Nauta, A., & Jehn, K. A. (2004). Person–-job fit to teamwork: A multilevel approach. *Small Group Research, 35*, 515–539.

Peterson, R. S., Smith, D. B., Martorana, P. V., & Owens, P. D. (2003). The impact of chief executive officer personality on top management team dynamics: One mechanism by which leadership affects organizational performance. *Journal of Applied Psychology, 88*, 795–808.

Preacher, K. J., Zyphur, M. J., & Zhang, Z. (2010). A general multilevel SEM framework for assessing multilevel mediation. *Psychological Methods, 15*, 209–233.

Roberson, Q. M., Sturman, M. C., & Simons, T. L. (2007). Does the measure of dispersion matter in multilevel research? A comparison of the relative performance of dispersion indexes. *Organizational Research Methods, 10*, 564–588.

Roberts, K. H., Hulin, C. L., & Rousseau, D. M. (1978). *Developing an interdisciplinary science of organizations*. San Francisco, CA: Jossey-Bass.

Rousseau, D. M. (1985). Issues of level in organizational research: Multi-level and cross-level perspectives. *Research in Organizational Behavior, 7*, 1–37.

Shaw, J. D., Zhu, J., Duffy, M. K., Scott, K. S., Shih, H.-A., & Susanto, E. (2011). A contingency model of conflict and team effectiveness. *Journal of Applied Psychology, 96*, 391–400.

Shrout, P. E., & Fleiss, J. L. (1979). Intraclass correlations: Uses in assessing rater reliability. *Psychological Bulletin, 86*, 420–428.

Simons, T. L., & Peterson, R. S. (2000). Task conflict and relationship conflict in top management teams: The pivotal role of intragroup trust. *Journal of Applied Psychology, 85*, 102–111.

Wagner, S. H., Parker, C. P., & Christiansen, N. D. (2003). Employees that think and act like owners: Effects of ownership beliefs and behaviors on organizational effectiveness. *Personnel Psychology, 56*, 847–871.

Woehr, D. J., Arciniega, L. M., & Poling, T. L. (2013). Exploring the effects of value diversity on team effectiveness. *Journal of Business and Psychology, 28*, 107–121.

Wu, P.-C., & Chatuvedi, S. (2009). The role of procedural justice and power distance in the relationship between high performance work systems and employee attitudes: A multilevel perspective. *Journal of Management, 35*, 1228–1247.

Zohar, D., & Luria, G. (2004). Climate as a social-cognitive construction of supervisor safety practices: Scripts as proxy of behavior patterns. *Journal of Applied Psychology, 89*, 322–333.

16

THE PRACTICAL IMPORTANCE OF MEASUREMENT INVARIANCE

Neal Schmitt and Abdifatah A. Ali

Psychologists and organizational scientists and others interested in measurement have long been concerned about the reliability and validity of instruments that are used with different groups and in different situations. In the past several decades, the increased globalization of many business enterprises and other institutions has resulted in the need and desire to use research instruments with individuals in different cultures. Most major consulting firms with practices that include survey research and the assessment of human potential work in countries in multicultural and multilingual contexts. Researchers are also interested in extending their ideas and theories beyond the U.S. culture in which much of our psychological research has been conducted. The major assumption, often untested, is that individuals with the same observed score on some measuring device have the same standing on the construct that is the target of measurement. However, differences (e.g., in culture, in language) in the populations being measured necessitate examining the degree to which the instrument measures the same construct across these groups. Test equivalence (alternatively, measurement equivalence/invariance) is recognized as an important concern for different cultural or gender groups even when members of these groups use the same language, highlighting the fact that nonequivalence can occur along a wide variety of dimensions. More formally defined, measurement invariance means that individuals whose standing on some construct is equivalent receive the same observed scores on a measure regardless of group membership or status.

Assessment of the degree to which instruments are invariant across demographic groups and situations has been greatly facilitated by the development of item response theory (IRT) and confirmatory factor analysis (CFA) and combinations of the two techniques (Stark, Chernyshenko, & Drasgow, 2006). The CFA or MACS (mean and covariance structure) approach (e.g., Byrne, Shavelson, & Muthen, 1989; Meredith, 1993; Vandenberg & Lance, 2000) has become increasingly popular because it allows for the identification of different types of group differences (i.e., configural, metric, and scalar, defined later) at the item and scale level. This approach provides multiple measures of fit (e.g., RMSEA, CFI, NNFI) for the various models tested. In addition, models incorporating partial invariance (some indicators are invariant, others are not) can be defined and used to account for nonequivalence in specific indicators (or items) of a latent construct and to model those differences in subsequent tests of equivalence. Previous reviews of the literature on measurement equivalence (Chen, 2008; Schmitt & Kuljanin, 2008; Vandenberg & Lance, 2000) provide many examples of nonequivalence along gender, age, mode of measurement, test-retest conditions, race, time of testing, and other dimensions. Atienza, Balaguer, and Garcia-Merita (2003), for example, found nonequivalence across gender groups when measuring life satisfaction of men and women. Cheng and Watkins (2000) evaluated self-esteem and found measurement nonequivalence across both gender and age subgroups. Cole, Bedeian, and Field (2006) found nonequivalence in the measurement of leadership when modes of assessment (web-based versus paper measures) were compared. Nye and Drasgow (2012) reported 522 comparisons in which factor loadings differed across groups.

However, the literature on differential item functioning (DIF) using IRT analyses is replete with studies in which the incidence of DIF across the items in a measure is not much different from chance and the few incidents of DIF that are identified defy theoretical explanation (see Scheuneman, 1982). Moreover, when such items are removed from tests, the impact on overall test scores is usually minimal; hence, decisions based on tests with DIF items were usually no different from decisions based on test scores from which DIF items were removed. The latter finding led to the development of a measure of differential test functioning (DTF; Raju & Ellis, 2002), though the focus in that literature remains statistically significant results rather than practical significance. In research on measurement equivalence in the CFA tradition, there has been little attention to the practical significance of findings of a lack of measurement equivalence. The question this chapter addresses is the extent to which concern about measurement invariance and partial invariance is much ado about nothing. Does accounting for a lack of measurement invariance have an impact on latent factor intercorrelations, estimates of group differences in the latent means, and estimates of relations with other latent constructs? Lack of measurement equivalence may be theoretically or practically interesting in itself, but usually the most substantively important are considerations involving relationships with other constructs or mean comparisons across groups.

Recently, there has been some concern about the practical significance of findings of a lack of invariance or partial invariance. As an illustration, Schmitt, Golubovich, and Leong (2011) analyzed the extent to which accounting for partial invariance affected estimates of the relationship of the latent construct involved with other latent constructs. Millsap and Kwok (2004) evaluated the impact of partial invariance on selection decisions. Likewise, Stark, Chernyshenko, and Drasgow (2004) examined the effect of DIF and DTF on selection decisions. Nye and Drasgow (2011) have provided some effect size indices for measurement non-equivalence in the CFA context and have linked their effect size measure to empirical estimates of a lack of invariance. These various developments suggest that the statistical significance tests often employed in examinations of measurement equivalence may or may not indicate that caution is warranted when a measurement device is used with dissimilar groups. At the very least, they suggest that applied researchers should examine the practical importance of findings of nonequivalence of measures across groups before embarking on expensive efforts to resolve the differences or ignoring data comparing groups.

In this chapter, we first define what is meant by measurement invariance and then examine how it has been operationalized in the research literature. This is followed by a brief summary of the results of the research using these methods. We then use the arguments for a "customer-centric" science presented by Aguinis and colleagues (2010) to suggest that we really do not know the seriousness of the problem presented by measurement invariance and that it should be examined in light of the impact of a lack of invariance on key substantive issues being addressed by the researcher.

Even with some calls that researchers attend to the practical significance of statistical evidence of a lack of measurement equivalence, the legend remains. That is, researchers are cautioned that findings of statistical nonequivalence across groups of test respondents preclude meaningful comparisons of the groups on the measure being considered. Our position is that very often, the observed levels of nonequivalence make little or no practical difference in the attributions derived from the measures across the groups being considered.

Definition of Invariance

A measure is invariant when members of different populations who have the same standing on the construct being measured receive the same score on the test. Conversely, a measure lacks equivalence when two individuals from different populations who are identical on the construct score differently on the test.

Item Response Theory

Two methods have been used to identify invariance. The first, arising from IRT, posits that test items are equivalent when the curve representing the relationship between the underling trait and the probability of a correct response is identical across subgroups of individuals (Embretson & Reise, 2009). This relationship is assumed to be a nonlinear normal ogive. That is, persons with equal standing on

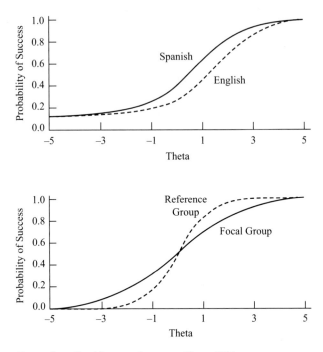

FIGURE 16.1 Examples of uniform and non-uniform DIF

the trait should have equal likelihood of a correct response on the item being studied. Two types of DIF are displayed in Figure 16.1. Uniform DIF in which the expected scores of the Spanish group are uniformly higher than those of the English group is displayed in the top half of the figure. Nonuniform DIF is pictured in the bottom half. In this case, whether scores are lower (or higher) than expected is a function of their ability level on the trait being measured. Tests of significance of DIF are available, as are effect sizes and, as stated, there is also a cumulative index of DIF called DTF (Raju & Ellis, 2002). Most of the research using IRT and DIF has focused on the degree to which items display a lack of equivalence when used with groups differing on some characteristic.

Confirmatory Factor Analysis

The second approach employs CFA or MACS to assess measurement equivalence. In factor analytic terms, each item or indicator of a latent construct is composed of variance related to the underlying factor (the factor loading represents this linear relationship), unique variance unrelated to the factor, and a constant or intercept. The most basic level of invariance, termed configural invariance, is represented by a situation in which items load on the same factor across multiple groups, but the degree of relationship represented by the factor loadings may vary across groups. This baseline model is compared with a metric invariance model in which the factor loadings for each group are constrained to equality. Factor loadings represent the strength of the relationships between items and factors—or, in a regression sense, the weights obtained by regressing the items on the factor they are thought to represent. When factor loadings are equal, the unit of measurement is equal across groups and cross-group predictive relationships (relationships with variables external to the factor model) are comparable. Scalar invariance requires that the intercepts, as well as the factor loadings, associated with item-factor relationships be equal across groups. With scalar invariance, the observed means of different groups can be compared meaningfully. The fourth form of measurement invariance is the invariance of the uniquenesses associated with each item. Invariance of uniquenesses indicates equivalence in the precision of measurement of each item. Some maintain that strict factorial invariance including metric, scalar, and uniqueness invariance is required for valid comparisons of observed group means. Equivalence in uniquenesses is not required for comparisons of latent means, as the measurement errors are partialed out in CFA analyses (Meredith, 1993).

As mentioned, when some items are invariant while others lack equivalence, we have a condition referred to as partial invariance. Partial invariance can be incorporated into CFA models. Statistical tests of invariance follow a sequence of steps outlined by Vandenberg and Lance (2000) as well as others; they are summarized as follows.

1. A test of *configural invariance* that specifies a similar pattern of loadings across groups but separately estimated parameters is conducted. All factor loadings, intercepts, uniquenesses, and the factor variance-covariance matrix are separately estimated for the two groups. Estimates of factor means are also included in the model. Adequate fit of this baseline model is followed by the evaluation of more constrained models.

2. A test of *metric invariance* specifying equal factor loadings across groups is next tested. If the metric invariance model fits the data less well than the configural model as indicated by a chi-square test of significance and other indices of fit, then partially invariant models are sometimes specified in which separately estimated factor loadings are allowed when those loadings were statistically significantly different. DIF as defined in IRT applications is similar to the test for metric invariance in CFA.

3. Next a test of *scalar invariance* that specifies equal subgroup differences in the intercepts is compared with the metric invariance model. As before, a test of significance and fit indices helps the researcher decide whether the measure being examined is scalar invariant. Again, partially invariant models separately estimating intercepts that differ greatly across subgroups may be evaluated.

4. Finally, a test of the *invariance of the uniquenesses*, again with provisions for partial invariance, is conducted. These four models and their comparative levels of fit comprise tests of measurement equivalence in the CFA model.
5. Tests of the equality of factor variances and covariances provide evidence of the equivalence of construct relationships. Test of the equality of latent means—which would be conducted next—may often be the central research question.

Figure 16.2 is a graphical depiction of a CFA model. If all parameters in this figure are freely estimated for two or more groups, we have a configural model. Constraining the *f* values across groups to equality produces a metric invariance model. Likewise, equality constraints on the c values produce a test of scalar equivalence, and equality constraints on the u values produce a model in which uniquenesses are also equivalent. If tests for measurement invariance indicate differences in factor loadings and intercepts, then comparisons of observed scores of different groups are not appropriate (e.g., French & Finch, 2006). In the case of a lack of scalar invariance, statistical conclusions and practical implications based on analyses of observed mean differences between groups will be distorted. However, the unanswered question of how severe this distortion may be under various levels of invariance has not been addressed. We next turn to brief summaries of the results of tests of invariance using IRT and CFA models.

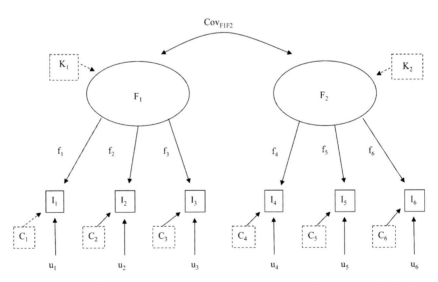

FIGURE 16.2 Confirmatory Factor Analytic Model. F refers to factor, K equals the factor means, I refers to indicators, f refers to factor loading, c equals indicator intercept, and u indicates uniqueness. Cov refers to covariance.

Results of DIF and DTF Analyses of Equivalence

To our knowledge, there have not been recent literature reviews synthesizing the results of DIF and DTF. After searching several major organizational science–related journals (e.g., *Journal of Applied Psychology, Personnel Psychology, Journal of Management, Organizational Research Methods, Applied Psychological Measurement*, and *Psychological Methods*) since year 2000, using key words such as "differential item/test functioning," "test bias," and "differential prediction," we located several articles that tested for DIF and DTF. These articles and some older but relevant articles are discussed next.

Drasgow (1987) states that "in IRT item bias studies there has been little concern with the distinction between *significant* differences and *practically important* differences; almost all emphasis has been on statistical significance" (p. 27). On testing the measurement equivalence for two standardized tests, Drasgow concluded that although a few items displayed DIF, their effects on total test score were nonexistent. In similar work, Roznowski (1987) tested whether purposefully including items that contained systematic, nontrait variance (which would manifest in DIF) had any effect on the psychometric properties of a measure of intelligence. Her findings suggested that items that do display group differences are not necessarily biased and also seem to not have an effect on the test as a whole. These findings are in line with a study by Roznowski and Reith (1999), which examined whether biased items lead to poor measurement and found that scores based on composites that included biased items were similar to scores on test composites that did not include biased items. The findings from these studies, to a certain degree, clarify some of the complexities dealt with when addressing issues of measurement equivalence. Simply identifying items that display DIF does not necessarily warrant making judgments about the adequacy of the measure as whole. These findings also refute the legend identified earlier in the chapter: namely, that findings of a lack of equivalence for parts of a test or a particular type of invariance preclude use of the test to make comparisons of individuals in different groups. Further steps that take into account the functioning of the overall test composite as well as its relation to other constructs of interest must be addressed before making a valid judgment of whether a test is biased. We now turn to more recent studies examining DIF/DFT and their implications.

More recently, Stark, Chernyshenko, Chan, Lee, and Drasgow (2001) investigated the extent to which measurement distortion occurred at both the item and scale levels as a function of faking on the 16 Personality Factor Questionnaire (PFQ). Using data collected from two independent samples (job applicants vs. non–job applicants) and employing various IRT–based analyses, they found that DIF was present in all scales and that a majority of the scales manifested DTF across testing situations, but the removal of items identified as containing DIF eliminated overall DTF. Furthermore, they also found substantial evidence of DIF/DTF for the impression management scale across both testing situations, which raises construct validity concerns. Although Stark and colleagues did not find strong statistical support for the measurement quality of the 16 PFQ and its functioning across testing situations, it does not inform us on how these findings translate over to impact key relationships of interest. Indeed, Stark and colleagues (2001) note, "it is entirely possible that statistically significant DIF/DTF can be present but may be of little practical significance" (p. 952).

Educational researchers have also found it difficult to interpret (Scheuneman, 1987) or replicate (Skaggs & Lissitz, 1992) DIF findings for standardized tests, though research does continue. One topic of debate in education research is findings from standardized tests that indicate DIF and item difficulty are correlated such that majority (i.e., White) examinees are more likely to get easy verbal questions correct than are minority (i.e., Black) examinees, whereas the opposite is true for difficult questions. A line of research by Freedle and his colleagues (Freedle, 2003; Freedle & Kostin, 1997) found support for the aforementioned relationship and attributed the findings to cultural differences between Black and White examinees. Freedle and Kostin (1997) argue that test questions with easy vocabulary words inherently vary in meaning as a function of cultural background, and since standardized tests are written with the dominant culture as a referent, those items tend to favor White examinees. This ambiguity in meaning based on cultural differences does not occur in difficult words because of the higher education needed to answer such questions—which creates a uniform understanding of the underlying meaning of the word. Freedle's finding and explanations have come under scrutiny by various researchers on the grounds of methodological and conceptual issues. Some of the main issues included the fact the SAT and GRE data used by Freedle were old and outdated, the significant effect is not of practical importance, the methods used to examine DIF were flawed, and the lack of ability to control for the effects of guessing. Although various criticisms have been raised on the subject matter, recent research attempting to address such concerns is described next.

Scherbaum and Goldstein (2008) tested the relationship between race-based DIF and item difficulty using archival data from the Civic Education of the International Association. They tested both the original analytical method used by Freedle and colleagues (i.e., the standardization method) as well as IRT–based methods. For the standardization method, they found a marginally significant relationship between race-based DIF and item difficulty ($r = -.557$, $p < .076$)—which is consistent with findings from Freedle and Kostin (1997). Using a 2 parameter logistic (PL) to fit the data, the results from the DFIT analysis supported the finding. Moreover, the results suggested evidence for DTF effects (DTF = .30, $p < .05$), but Scherbaum and Goldstein (2008) noted that each item's effect size was small. Results from simulated data were not consistent with findings from their real data such that they found no relationship between DFIT and item difficulty and a nonsignificant correlation when they used the standardization method ($r = .177$, $p < .61$). Beyond this inconsistency, their findings are limited in the sense that they only address a few of the original concerns that were raised by other researchers.

To answer the question of whether the original findings by Freedle and Kostin (1997) were nothing more than artifacts because of the methodology employed, Santelices and Wilson (2012) reexamined the same question using SAT data from 1994 and 1999 (with two different test forms for each year) including White, Black, and Hispanic participants. They compared findings from a 1PL model—which is similar to the standardization method—and the 3PL model, which would primarily address the effects of guessing on the relationship between DIF and item difficulty across race groups. In sum, findings from the 1PL model generally supported Freedle and Kostin's (1997) work across various SAT test forms and race groups. There was also support for Freedle and colleagues' findings using the 3PL model, although the results were not consistent across SAT test forms and race groups. Santelices and Wilson conclude that their results are more consistent with findings from Freedle's (Freedle, 2003; Freedle and Kostin, 1997) work and that even after addressing the concerns voiced by other researchers, the relationship between race-based DIF and item difficulty was replicable. Overall effects on test scores or the practical significance of the effect was not addressed.

Findings from these studies highlight the over-focus on the identification of items and tests that may be biased but rarely address the degree to which that bias impacts the decisions made on the basis of these tests and, as has been the case in the educational arena, what the bias may mean substantively. To what extent does measurement unequivalence affect the nature of the relationships we want to examine, and what are some of the ramifications if those differential effects are not dealt with? The seriousness of differential effects and the proper way to address them has to be connected to the decisions being made based on these measures, and only then can judgments on whether to revise a test or use some alternative means to make decisions be discussed in an informed manner.

Results of CFA Analyses of Measurement Equivalence

There have been at least three reviews of the literature on MEI using the CFA model. Vandenberg and Lance (2000) summarized the manner in which invariance had been tested in the empirical literature in organizational behavior. They reported that 67 investigators reported tests of invariance prior to tests of their major substantive hypotheses. Of these, 88% reported a consideration of configural invariance and all but one reported tests of metric invariance. However, tests for scalar invariance were relatively infrequent (12%) even though 21% reported testing latent mean differences. Slightly over half tested for invariance of uniquenesses, but there appeared to be little understanding of why such tests were conducted. Schmitt and Kuljanin (2008) replicated and extended the Vandenberg and Lance (2000) review to include papers published after the earlier review. The 75 empirical studies they reviewed differed in the manner and type of tests conducted from those reviewed by Vandenberg and Lance (2010). All studies in the second review addressed configural and metric invariance. However, the biggest change was that 54% of the Schmitt and Kuljanin (2008) studies tested for scalar invariance. This may be due to a

336 Neal Schmitt and Abdifatah A. Ali

difference in research objectives, but it is probably also a function of an increased understanding among empirical researchers of the manner in which group mean differences as well as relational differences can be handled with the CFA framework. A final major difference in practices across the time periods covered by these two reviews involved the use of models that included provision for partial invariance by researchers. Only 14 of the 67 studies reviewed by Vandenberg and Lance (2000) allowed for separate estimates of some parameters (factor loadings, intercepts, or uniquenesses) across groups, while more than half of the studies reviewed by Schmitt and Kuljanin allowed for some form of partial invariance.

The Vandenberg and Lance (2000) and Schmitt and Kuljanin (2008) studies described in this section involve the extent to which various types of invariance have been investigated. However, a more important question relates to the extent and magnitude of invariance found in published studies. This question was addressed by Chen (2008). In 74 of 97 studies that reported a lack of metric invariance, the average difference between the groups being compared was .13 in standardized terms. In 14 of these studies, all loadings were higher in one group than in the other; in 7 comparisons, exactly half of the loadings were higher in one group, while the other half of the loading differences favored the second group. Comparisons of the magnitude of other forms of invariance were not reported. As stated, Nye and Drasgow (2011) identified 16 studies involving 522 comparisons of factor loading differences and reported that nearly 60% of those studies reported a standardized factor loading difference of .10 or less. The 16 studies all reported factor loadings for both groups being compared, involved data collected in field settings, and were published in industrial-organizational peer-reviewed journals. Reading these reviews of the literature on measurement invariance would lead to the conclusion that we have major problems whenever we use many psychological measures with different groups of respondents. As we will discuss later in the chapter, we believe this conclusion is not warranted when we consider the practical importance of the observed differences.

Some researchers have also combined or compared the results of IRT and CFA approaches, and we turn next to those studies.

Combining/Comparing IRT and CFA Models

Reise, Widaman, and Pugh (1993) used the responses of Minnesota and Nanjing samples to a five-item Likert-type scale of mood to illustrate the commonalities and differences between CFA and IRT analyses of measurement invariance. There are two theoretical differences between the models. CFA analyses assume a linear relationship between the theoretical trait and individuals' responses, whereas the graded-response IRT model assumes this relationship is a normal ogive. In addition, the CFA model does not include the difficulty or threshold parameters included in the IRT model. Practically, the specification of the underlying model was much easier in CFA models using software extant in the early 1990s. Both modes of analysis produced a conclusion that full measurement invariance was not an adequate description of the data. Ignoring the difficulty parameters in CFA analyses meant that two items identified as lacking invariance in the IRT analyses were not detected in the CFA model. At the latent variable level, similar mean differences between groups were reported, suggesting that insofar as estimating the latent factor means is concerned, the inability to model item difficulty parameters is not very important. Reise and colleagues call for the development of practical fit indices for IRT models similar to those available in the assessment of CFA models. While these model fit indices do exist for CFA models, we will argue that they do not yield information on the actual impact of a lack of invariance on the inferences we usually hope to draw from our measurements.

Meade and Lautenschlager (2004) did a simulation to compare the results of CFA and IRT analyses when the degree of invariance was manipulated along with the sample size. Invariance was manipulated such that either two or four items in a six-item scale had items for which extreme responses were or were not likely among hypothetical respondents given the change in the difficultly parameters. The items were five-point Likert-type scales, and the graded response IRT model was used so there were four difficulty parameters for each item. The focus in their study was on the ability of these two analysis methods to detect the invariance. CFA analyses were largely unable to detect manipulations of the difficulty parameter, especially when sample sizes were low (i.e., 150 or 500), whereas the IRT approach was generally effective at identifying the invariance as well as the specific items that were the problem. It was also the case that CFA analyses were less effective in detecting invariance resulting from differing item discrimination parameters. Meade and Lautenschlager conclude that when the desire is to detect a lack of invariance in item parameters, it is best to use IRT. When scale-level or factor relationships are of interest, it may be best to use CFA. However, their preference is to use both methods of analysis. It should be pointed out that in comparing these analyses, the authors were primarily interested in the power to detect differences, not in whether those differences were practically important. Nor did they make any attempt to translate their manipulations of lack of invariance into practical outcomes for inferences based on the use of these measures.

Raju, Laffite, and Byrne (2002) used actual data on a work satisfaction measure to compare the results of IRT and CFA approaches to the assessment of measurement equivalence across Black and White respondents. They found greater evidence of nonequivalence using the CFA approach. They pointed to the difference in the assumption of item-latent factor relationships in the two models (i.e., nonlinear for IRT and linear for CFA) as the reason for the relatively slight difference in results across the two analyses. However, plots of item differences were made against a theta scale that went from -5 to $+5$ standard deviations. Only at the extremes were differences relatively large. Practically, then, the differences observed in either model would have had implications for a tiny proportion of respondents at the very extreme of the distribution of scores.

A final study comparing IRT and CFA approaches is reported by Stark and colleagues (2006). They proposed a common strategy to identify DIF items that was implemented in both CFA and IRT approaches. They found that IRT and CFA analyses produced very similar levels of power and Type I error rates (probability of erroneously identifying DIF) when both intercept and slope parameters were compared simultaneously. Most critically, they found that a free baseline strategy (one in which the referent loading in the analysis was DIF free) was critical. When the referent item was chosen randomly, the Type I error rate was very high. They also found that CFA analyses conducted to identify DIF were superior to IRT analyses when sample sizes were relatively low (i.e., less than 1,000) and when the items were polytomous as opposed to dichotomous (see also Meade & Lautenschlager, 2004). Equally important was the finding that true differences on the latent trait, referred to as impact, had little influence on the finding of DIF.

Many papers doing measurement equivalence analyses pay little attention to the identification of a bias-free referent. Hence, reported levels of a lack of measurement invariance are likely inflated (Meade & Wright, 2012). A nonequivalent referent item will confound comparisons and make the results meaningless. Johnson, Meade, and DuVernet (2009) found that a nonequivalent referent item can either hide or increase findings of nonequivalence in other items. This has the effect of producing low-power or high Type I error rates.

These comparisons of the two methods of analysis both yield results that are highly similar under comparable conditions. In the simulation studies, rather large amounts of DIF were introduced across conditions with predictable outcomes; in the two studies that used actual response data (Raju et al., 2002; Reise et al., 1993), the extent of DIF seems as though it would have minimal implications for test takers. Thus, there is more evidence disputing the legendary status of the conclusion that tests with even a relatively large number of items that show cross-group differences yield total test scores that are not comparable across groups.

Practical Significance

The research described would lead to the general conclusion that many of the measures organizational researchers use cannot be used to compare the responses of individuals or groups of individuals whose demographic status on a host of variables is different. However, all of these studies have focused on statistically significant differences, or, in some cases, standardized effect sizes related to the measurement properties of the instruments used. Most of the research on tests of measurement invariance has focused on the power and sensitivity of the tests used to identify measurement invariance (e.g., Cohen, Kim, & Wollack, 1996; Kim & Cohen, 1995; Meade, Johnson, & Braddy, 2008). These steps are important as we evaluate our measures and the manner in which they are used. However, Aguinis and colleagues (2010) have argued that researchers should also attend to the practical impact (what they call customer-centric impact) of our research findings. They argue that three interdependent and sequential steps be taken in evaluating research results. First, researchers should focus on the statistical significance of their findings and concerns of power and Type I and II errors must be considered. Second, effect sizes (e.g., correlations and standardized mean differences) should be reported and considered. Third, results of the study for different stakeholders should be considered. This may involve effect size estimates, since in some areas of research we know the practical impact of a given effect size, but it often goes beyond that to consider whether some person or group is likely to be treated differently (i.e., selected or not selected for some treatment) if a test is not invariant.

Recently, Nye and Drasgow (2011) developed an effect size index that allows for evaluation of CFA estimates of nonequivalence. This index is directly comparable to standardized metrics proposed by Cohen (1988) and allows for the comparison of estimates on nonequivalence across studies. However, Nye and Drasgow (2012) pointed out that this effect size, like Cohen's d, does not tell the researcher about the impact or practical importance of the lack of measurement invariance. They then proceeded to tie their effect size index to estimates of DIF from the extant literature. The magnitude of DIF based on 522 comparisons from 16 different studies of different groups' factor loadings was set at .10, .20, and .30 (in approximately 230 of the 522 comparisons, factor loading differences were less than .10) to reflect small, medium, and large effect sizes. Only one of these studies reported intercept differences; hence, they were set at .20, .30, and .40 to reflect previous simulation research. This simulation (Nye & Drasgow, 2012) then provided values of their index that reflect small, medium, and large degrees of lack of invariance. While certainly a useful new index tied to previous research results, the index is not tied to practical outcomes in terms of test scores or relationships with outcome variables or faulty decisions that might be based on test scores that originate from measures that do not exhibit invariance.

Research Using Customer-Centric Indices

As stated, the overwhelming attention in the research literature has been on the statistical significance of subgroup differences in both the IRT and CFA literature. The very few studies that have attended to the practical differences, or customer-centric nature of these findings, are summarized in this section.

IRT Analyses

Stark and colleagues (2004) examined the degree to which large numbers of items with significant DIF and overall DTF had practical effects on observed score differences and selection decisions for personality measures, professional licensure exams, and college admissions tests. In the case of personality tests, they found that item and test bias had little or no impact on the scores of applicants (presumed to be motivated to fake good) and nonapplicants. For licensure and admission exams, DIF and DTF had almost no effect on mean observed scores and

340 Neal Schmitt and Abdifatah A. Ali

the rates of examinees selected or admitted across different demographic groups. Subgroup differences in licensing and admission rates were likely due to real differences in the trait assessed rather than the influence of bias in the items or tests.

Recently, Meade (2010) has published a paper in which he presents a taxonomy of effect size measures for the differential functioning of items and scales. This paper, along with the software he provides on his website (www4.ncsu. edu/~awmeade), represents a major advance in providing researchers with the means to go beyond statistical significance (DIF) to address the practical significance and effect sizes related to findings of DIF. Meade provides several examples of the use of this program in the computation of various effect size indices along with graphs of expected score plots for the groups being compared. He also argues that several of these indices be reported routinely to enable future meta-analyses of DIF effects. For most of the graphed differences in his article, differences between groups appear very small even when statistically significant DIF is reported, particularly when total scale scores are being compared. He argues, as do we, that there are varying levels of DIF and the magnitude of the effect is more important than its statistical significance. In justifying his work, he notes that there is rarely an indication of "how much of an effect the DIF exerts on test scores for each group" and rarely are "implications for organizational measurement made explicit in quantitative terms" (Meade, 2010, p. 729). If future researchers do heed Meade's advice, we will, at some future date, be able to state definitively whether concerns about DIF are practically important.

CFA Indices

In a simulation, Millsap and Kwok (2004) examined the impact of partial invariance on the selection of members of differing groups. In their simulation, a single-factor model represented item responses, and the composite of these item responses was used to select individuals for some hypothetical treatment or intervention. In evaluating partial invariance, a complicating factor occurs when differences in subgroup parameters across items are contradictory (i.e., higher in one comparison for one group and lower in comparison for that group for a different indicator or item). Millsap and Kwok (2004) constructed conditions in which all subgroup parameters differed in the same direction across subgroups. This should have the effect of maximizing the effect of lack of invariance. The results reported by Millsap and Kwok (2004) in their Tables 5 through 7 show there were not large changes in selection errors (most often less than 5%) even when only half of the items were invariant and usually less than 10% when none of the items were invariant across groups. So, even in these instances in which there was a relatively great lack of invariance, the practical impact was minor.

Using a MIMIC (Finch, 2005) model to detect DIF in continuous responses to the IPIP measure of the Big Five, Ehrhart, Ehrhart, Ali, Roesch, and Palmer (2012) found 9 of 50 items displayed DIF. DIF was assessed by identifying significant direct effects of an acculturation latent variable on the item indicators of the latent personality traits. Correlations between the latent personality traits when DIF relationships were included in the model revealed an average difference of .037 across the 10 interfactor correlations. In all but one case, the correlations between factors were lower when DIF was included in the model. Latent correlations between the Big Five and the acculturation factor differed by .02 or less with the exception of the Emotional Stability factor (correlation with DIF was −.025 and with DIF adjustment, .026). In this case, the degree of DIF is probably more representative of real-world data than is the manipulation provided in the Millsap and Kwok (2004) simulations. Changes in the estimates of correlations between the latent factors were relatively trivial, though Ehrhart and colleagues did not attempt to relate these differences to decisions about examinees that might be made based on these tests.

In a similar study, Schmitt and colleagues (2011) estimated the impact of measurement invariance and the provision for partial invariance in CFA models on factor intercorrelations, latent mean differences, and estimates of relationships with external variables. The partially invariant model included separate estimates of factor loadings, intercepts, and uniquenesses that differed significantly across groups. The inclusion of separate subgroup parameters seemed to make little difference in the estimates of the relationships among 11 personality and interest constructs. Some estimates were modestly lower and others slightly higher. Average absolute differences were .017 for the African-American group and .026 for the Caucasian-American group. In comparing models that included provisions for partial invariance with models that did not, 1 of 11 standardized mean differences between the subgroups was relatively large (i.e., .30; all other comparisons were .06 or less). There were relatively small differences in relationships with several external variables; none of the regression coefficients relating the constructs to two external variables (high school and college GPA) were significant when incorporating provision for partial invariance in one group and nonsignificant when the lack of invariance was ignored in the model. Standardized regression coefficients did not differ by more than .04. Hence, differences in measurement properties would not have had any large impact on the use of tests or the decisions that came about as a function of their use in making college admissions decisions.

Chen (2008) conducted a simulation in which factor loading differences of .15 and .07 in different proportions (ranging from 25% to 87.5%) of items were investigated as determinants of regression slopes and factor means. With the loading imbalance at 75% or greater of the items loading on a measure, the bias in estimates of regression slopes was relatively large (20% or more), but with imbalances of 25 or 50%, the bias in slope estimates was smaller (17% or less). Differences were greatest when sample sizes in the two groups differed (240 vs. 60). The group that had higher loadings had regression slopes that were underestimated, while the reverse was true for the group in which factor loadings were lower. When some loadings were higher and lower in a first group than those of a second group, the

342 Neal Schmitt and Abdifatah A. Ali

bias in regression slopes was much less. The impact of a lack of invariance on factor means was quite small (less than .07 standard deviations units) when the proportion of items that lacked invariance was 50% or lower and loading differences were mixed across groups. With all differences favoring one of the two groups, the bias was greater (.16 to .77) when 25 or 50% of the items were biased. With a greater proportion of biased items (75 or 87.5%), the bias was quite large in most cases. It should be pointed out that the proportion of biased items, the magnitude of bias (.15), and the directionality of bias (all one way) were extreme relative to the empirical findings of invariance reported in the empirical literature. While Chen (2008) reports both statistically significant results and effect sizes based on her simulations, the impact on decision making is not addressed, though one could infer that impact in some of the situations considered would be substantial.

Nye and Drasgow (2011) reported results comparing Greek-, Chinese-, and English-speaking American respondents on measures of the Big Five personality measures. They showed the impact of DIF on observed and latent means across these groups and linked their effect size index described previously to these differences. They also calculated adverse impact ratios (the ratio of the percentages of each group selected using various test score cutoffs). DIF alone, removing the impact of latent mean differences, did not produce different adverse impact ratios except in the case of the extraversion measure, when relatively stringent cut scores were applied. This linkage of the magnitude of DIF to practical outcomes is the type of research required to discern whether a lack of measurement invariance is of concern to researchers using psychological measurements. In most cases in which this has been done in the IRT and MACS literature, the impact has been minimal or negligible.

Summary and Conclusions

In summary, both CFA and IRT approaches to the evaluation of measures can be used in an informative way to tell whether these measures can be used with different groups of people under differing circumstances. A lack of measurement invariance across groups and situations is frequently reported using existing tests of significance and effect size measures. However, post-hoc interpretations or explanations of these differences have been elusive. In addition, studies that attempt to relate a lack of invariance to differences in the decisions that would be made using tests demonstrating a lack of invariance usually report very small, and possibly inconsequential, differences unless there is a relatively extreme lack of invariance in the responses provided by different groups. This is also true when relationships between the constructs that are targeted and other theoretically related constructs are estimated. Hence, we call for more research on the implications of a lack of invariance that includes what Aguinis and colleagues (2012) term "customer-centric" measures. Our conclusions may not be warranted when investigators attempt to translate measures into new languages and then assess equivalence. Translations across

Importance of Measurement Invariance **343**

languages that produce demonstrably equivalent measures of the same construct are difficult and often prove elusive (Schmit, Kihm, & Robie, 2000).

Future research should include simulations in which the impact of various factors (e.g., number of nonequivalent indicators, magnitude of the nonequivalence, type of nonequivalence) on estimates of substantively interesting relationships or decisions is estimated. These simulations and the use of relevant effect size estimates tied to practical outcomes should reveal the degree to which analyses of measurement equivalence or invariance are mythical or represent serious problems that should be considered in multigroup comparisons. *Researchers should continue to analyze responses to their measures for a lack of invariance, but they should also focus on the degree to which findings of a lack of invariance are interpretable, have relevance for decisions that are made using the instrument, and the evaluation of substantive hypotheses regarding relationships among variables.*

These cautionary statements are summarized in Table 16.1. In our opinion, they represent relatively conservative practices in the presence of a finding of a

TABLE 16.1 Decision Guide for Measures Used in the Presence of a Lack of Invariance in CFA Results[a]

Situation	Suggested Course of Action
Comparing groups when a measure has been translated to a different language.	Do MEI analyses and expect practical and significant differences between groups and the necessity to adjust measures to achieve valid comparisons.
Comparing groups whose language is the same	
1. Finding a lack of equivalent covariance matrices	Proceed to do tests of increasingly restrictive covariance matrices models (Vandenberg & Lance, 2000) to ascertain the nature and magnitude of the lack of invariance.
2. Configural invariance lacking	Valid comparisons between groups using the measure are not possible using the measure and the hypothesized factor structure.
3. Metric invariance lacking	Valid comparisons may be possible if at least half the items are invariant. Use partial invariant models but do not expect large practical differences between fully and partially invariant models.
4. Scalar invariance	Valid comparisons of latent variables are possible using partially invariant models when less than half of the items lack invariance. However, beware of comparing observed score means.
5. Finding a lack of invariance at the level of item uniquenesses	Relevant only when comparing observed scores of different groups.

[a]With large sample sizes and high levels of power in testing invariance, one should also use a practical level of difference as a guide in deciding that invariance exists. For this purpose, the effect sizes reported by Chen (2008) and Nye and Drasgow (2012) should be helpful.

lack of invariance across measures used with different groups of people. In all cases, we think researchers should try to compare the practical decisions based on measures that include (and do not include) provisions for lack of invariance across groups before deciding that such adjustments are universally required or that the measures cannot be used to provide valid comparisons of individuals belonging to different groups.

References

Aguinis, H., Werner, S., Abbott, J. L., Angert, C., Park, J. H., & Kohlhausen, D. (2010). Customer-centric science: Reporting significant research results with rigor, relevance, and practical impact in mind. *Organizational Research Methods, 13,* 515–539.

Atienza, F. L., Balaguer, I., & Garcia-Merita, M. L. (2003). Satisfaction with life scale: Analysis of factorial invariance across sexes. *Personality and Individual Differences, 35,* 1255–1260.

Byrne, B. M., Shavelson, R. J., & Muthen, B. (1989). Testing for the equivalence of factor covariance and mean structures: The issue of partial invariance. *Psychological Bulletin, 105,* 456–466.

Chen, F. F. (2008). What happens if we compare chopsticks with forks? The impact of making inappropriate comparisons in cross-cultural research. *Journal of Personality and Social Psychology: Attitudes and Social Cognition, 95,* 1005–1018.

Cheng, C.H.K., & Watkins, D. (2000). Age and gender invariance of self-concept factor structure: An investigation of a newly developed Chinese self-concept instrument. *International Journal of Psychology, 35,* 186–193.

Cohen, A. S., Kim, S.-H., & Wollack, J. A. (1996). An investigation of the likelihood ratio test for detection of differential item functioning. *Applied Psychological Measurement, 20,* 15–26.

Cohen, J. (1988). *Statistical power analysis for the behavioral sciences* (2nd ed.). Hillsdale, NJ: Lawrence Erlbaum.

Cole, M. S., Bedeian, A. G., & Field, H. S. (2006). The measurement equivalence of web-based and paper-and-pencil measures of transformational leadership: A multinational test. *Organizational Research Methods, 9,* 339–368.

Drasgow, F. (1987). Study of the measurement bias of two standardized psychological tests. *Journal of Applied Psychology, 72,* 19–29.

Ehrhart, M. G., Ehrhart, K. M., Ali, A. A., Roesch, S. C., & Palmer, L. (2012). *A MIMIC model of acculturation and the International Personality Item Pool Five-Factor Model Measure.* Poster presented at the 27th Annual Conference of the Society for Industrial and Organizational Psychology, San Diego, CA.

Embretson, S. E., & Reise, S. P. (2009). *Item response theory for psychologists.* Mahwah, NJ: Lawrence Erlbaum Associates.

Finch, H. (2005). The MIMIC model as a method for detecting DIF: Comparison with Mantel- Haenszel, SIBTEST, and IRT Likelihood Ratio. *Applied Psychological Measurement, 29,* 278–295.

Freedle, R., & Kostin, I. (1997). Predicting Black and White differential item functioning in verbal analogy performance. *Intelligence, 24,* 417–444.

Freedle, R. O. (2003). Correcting the SAT's ethnic and social-class bias: A method for reestimating SAT scores. *Harvard Educational Review, 73,* 1–44.

French, B. F., & Finch, W. (2006). Confirmatory factor analytic procedures for the determination of measurement invariance. *Structural Equation Modeling, 13*, 378–402.

Johnson, E. C., Meade, A. W., & DuVernet, A. M. (2009). The role of referent indicators in tests of measurement invariance. *Structural Equation Modeling, 16*, 642–657.

Kim, S.-H., & Cohen, A. S. (1995). A comparison of Lord's chi-square, Raju's area measures, and the likelihood ratio test on detection of differential item functioning. *Applied Measurement in Education, 8*, 291–312.

Meade, A. W. (2010). A taxonomy of effect size measures for the differential functioning of items and scales. *Journal of Applied Psychology, 95*, 728–743.

Meade, A. W., Johnson, E. C., & Braddy, P. W. (2008). Power and sensitivity of alternative fit indices in tests of measurement invariance. *Journal of Applied Psychology, 93*, 569–592.

Meade, A. W., & Lautenschlager, G. J. (2004). A comparison of item response theory and confirmatory factor analytic methodologies for establishing measurement equivalence/invariance. *Organizational Research Methods, 7*, 361–388.

Meade, A. W., & Wright, N. A. (2012). Solving the measurement invariance anchor item problem in item response theory. *Journal of Applied Psychology, 97*, 1016–1031.

Meredith, W. (1993). Measurement invariance, factor analysis, and factorial invariance. *Psychometrika, 53*, 525–543.

Millsap, R. E., & Kwok, O. (2004). Evaluating the impact of partial factorial invariance on selection decisions in two populations. *Psychological Methods, 9*, 93–115.

Nye, C. D., & Dragsow, F. (2011). Effect size indices for analyses of measurement equivalence: Understanding the practical importance of differences between groups. *Journal of Applied Psychology, 96*, 966–979.

Nye, C. D., & Dragsow, F. (2012). *How big are my effects? Examining the magnitude of effect sizes in organizational studies of measurement equivalence.* Paper presented at the annual conference of the Academy of Management, Boston, MA.

Raju, N. S., & Ellis, B. B. (2002). Differential item and test functioning. In N. Schmitt & F. Dragsow (Eds.), *Measuring and analyzing behavior in organizations.* (pp. 156–188). San Francisco, CA: Jossey-Bass.

Raju, N. S., Laffite, L. J., & Byrne, B. M. (2002). Measurement invariance: A comparison of methods based on confirmatory factor analyses and item response theory. *Journal of Applied Psychology, 87*, 517–529.

Reise, S. P., Widaman, K. F., & Pugh, R. H. (1993). Confirmatory factor analysis and item response theory: Two approaches for exploring measurement invariance. *Psychological Bulletin, 114*, 552–566.

Roznowski, M. (1987). Use of tests manifesting sex differences as measures of intelligence: Implications for measurement bias. *Journal of Applied Psychology, 72*, 480–483.

Roznowski, M., & Reith, J. (1999). Examining the measurement quality of tests containing differential functioning items: Do biased items result in poor measurement? *Educational and Psychological Measurement, 59*, 248–269.

Santelices, M. V., & Wilson, M. (2012). On the relationship between differential items functioning and item difficulty: An issue of methods? Item response theory approach to differential item functioning. *Educational and Psychological Measurement, 72*, 5–36.

Scherbaum, C., & Goldstein, H. (2008). Examining the relationship between race-based differential item functioning and item difficulty. *Educational and Psychological Measurement, 68*, 537–553.

Scheuneman, J. D. (1982). A posteriori analyses of biased items. In R. A. Berk (Ed.), *Handbook of methods for detecting item bias* (pp. 180–198). Baltimore, MD: Johns Hopkins University Press.

Scheuneman, J. D. (1987). An experimental, exploratory study of causes of bias in test items. *Journal of Educational Measurement, 24*, 97–118.

Schmit, M. J., Kihm, J. A., & Robie, C. (2000). Development of a global measure or personality. *Personnel Psychology, 53*, 153–193.

Schmitt, N., Golubovich, J., & Leong, F.T.L. (2011). Measurement invariance and construct correlations, mean differences, and relationships with external correlates. *Assessment, 18*, 412–427.

Schmitt, N., & Kuljanin, G. (2008). Measurement invariance: Review of practice and implications. *Human Resource Management Review, 18*, 210–222.

Skaggs, G., & Lissitz, R. W. (1992). The consistency of detecting item bias across different test administrations: Implications of another failure. *Journal of Educational Measurement, 29*, 227–242.

Stark, S., Chernyshenko, O.S., Chan, K., Lee, W. C., & Drasgow, F. (2001). Effects of the testing situation on item responding: Cause for concern. *Journal of Applied Psychology, 86*, 943–953.

Stark, S., Chernyshenko, O. S., & Drasgow, F. (2004). Examining the effects of differential item functioning and differential test functioning on selection decisions: When are statistically significant effects practically important? *Journal of Applied Psychology, 89*, 497–508.

Stark, S., Chernyshenko, O. S., & Drasgow, F. (2006). Detecting differential item functioning with confirmatory factor analysis and item response theory: Toward a unified strategy. *Journal of Applied Psychology, 91*, 1292–1306.

Vandenberg, R. J., & Lance, C. E. (2000). A review and synthesis of the measurement invariance methods and procedures. *Organizational Research Methods, 5*, 139–158.

INDEX

Note: Page numbers with *f* indicate figures; those with *t* indicate tables.

Abdifatah, A. A. 327–44
absolute cutoffs, influential outliers and 214–16
Academy of Management Journal (AMJ) 20, 29, 54, 67, 68, 69, 70, 73, 74*t*, 75*t*, 77, 78, 79–80*t*, 80, 115*t*, 208, 226, 287, 317
Academy of Management Review (AMR) 21, 22, 23
acquiescence 114
Administrative Science Quarterly (ASQ) 67, 68, 70, 71, 73–4, 74*t*, 75*t*, 76, 77, 78, 79–80*t*, 208
aggregation bias within multilevel framework 311–23; background 311–12; composition models 312–13; defined 313; justifying 313–14; literature review 317–21, 317*t*, 319–20*f*; overview of 311; recommendations for researchers 322–3; statistical myths surrounding 314–17; summary and conclusions 321–2, 322*t*
aggregation indices, frequency of 319*f*
Aguinis, H. 206–21, 217*t*, 329, 338, 342
Aiken, L. S. 86
Ali, A. A. 340
American Freshman Survey (AFS) 107, 108
American Political Science Association 10
American Psychological Association 53, 69
Anderson, S. E. 285–6
ANOVA 95–6

APA Task Force on Statistical Inference 133
Arthur, W., Jr. 17
Arvey, R. D. 248
Ashforth, B. E. 92
Association of American Publishers 10
Atienza, F. L. 328
attitudinal ambivalence 122
attitudinal indifference 122

Baby Boomers 101, 102, 103, 106–7
Balaguer, I. 328
Baldridge, D. C. 218
B- and C-tier journals, incentives for publications in 55, 57*t*
Banks, G. C. 36–58
Bansal, T. 80
Barnette, J. J. 123–4
Barrett, L. F. 24
Becker, B. J. 44
Becker, W. J. 26
Bedeian, A. G. 115, 116, 328
Begg, C. B. 50
Bell, A. J. 220
Belsley, D. A. 214, 215
Bentler, P. M. 175, 176*t*, 177, 178
Berntson, G. G. 122
Berry, J. W. 21, 26
between-level intercept/mean, cross-level direct effect as 294, 295*f*, 298–300

348 Index

bias-corrected and accelerated (BCa) procedures 231, 232*t*
bias-corrected (BC) procedures 231, 232*t*
binary thinking 134
Blanton, H. 119, 213
Bliese, P. D. 20, 95, 318
Bogert, J. D. 213
Bolger, N. 226, 228
Bonett, D. G. 181
bootstrapping: confidence interval accuracy and 227; critical examination of 228–38; foundational statements concerning 229; kernel of truth about 227–8, 227*f*; recommendations for 240; rise of 226; seed values and confidence intervals with 235–6, 237–8*t*; small samples and 228–30; statistical power and 230–1, 232*t*; Type I error and 233–5, 234*t*; *see also* Sobel test
Bosco, F. A. 39
Bosker, R. J. 181, 309
box-and-arrow models 94
brain science 26–7
Brannick, M. T. 52
Bratton, V. K. 321
Brett, J. 2, 20
Brown, F. W. 321
Bryk, A. S. 296–7, 309
Buckley, M. R. 287, 288
Buehring, A. 69–70
Business Source Complete 317
Butts, M. M. 2, 134
Byrne, B. M. 337

Cacioppo, J. T. 122
Cambré, B. 170
Campbell, D. T. 287
Campbell, S. M. 103
Campbell, W. K. 100–9
Carter, N. T. 112–28, 124
Cassell, C. 69–70
Cennamo, L. 102, 103
Center for Creative Leadership 4
Center of Research Methods and Analysis (CARMA) 4, 30, 80, 96
Chan, D. 312, 317
Chan, K. 333
Charlton, K. 42
Chen, F. F. 336, 341–2
Chen, G. 20, 319
Cheng, C. H. K. 328
Chernyshenko, O. S. 333, 339
Cheung, G. W. 226

Chou, C. 175, 176*t*, 177, 178
Christiansen, N. D. 321
Coakley, R. M. 277
cognitive ability, measurement of 17
Cohen, J. 12, 86, 90, 162, 164, 165, 165*t*, 169–70, 211, 212, 214, 231
Cohen, P. 86, 162, 164, 165, 165*t*, 169–70
cohort effects 101, 101*t*
cohort-sequential design, time-lag design as 103
Cole, D. A. 91
Cole, M. S. 328
commonality analysis 198
common method variance (CMV) 276–89; effects of, on observed correlations 277–9, 278*f*; eliminating or reducing, procedures for 285–7; evidence on 281–5; heterotrait-monomethod (HTMM) correlation and 280–4, 289; overview of 276–7; problem solving methods used for 279–81, 279*f*; study findings 287–9, 288*t*
completely random missingness 138, 139*t*, 153*t*
complex casual analysis models 20
complexity 23–4, 24–5*f*
conceptualization 15–16
configural invariance 331
confirmatory factor analysis (CFA) 117; of customer-centric indices 340–2; decision guide for measures used in 343*t*; development of 327–8; IRT comparison to 336–8; of measurement equivalence, results of 335–6; measurement invariance and 330–2; model of 332*f*; partial invariance and 331–2
context tipping point 78
convergent validities 283
Cook, R. D. 214
Cooper, H. 42
Cooperative Institutional Research Program (CIRP) Freshman Survey 107
cooperativeness 14, 15
correlated uniqueness (CU) model 286
Cortina, J. M. 9–31, 119–20
Cottrell, J. M. 133–59
covariance matrix, weighted linear composites and 189–92, 189*t*, 190*t*, 191*t*
Coyle-Shapiro, J. A. 91
Craig, S. B. 124, 125
Cronbach, L. J. 92, 114, 260–1
Cropanzano, R. 26

cross-level direct effect 292–305; as between-level intercept/mean 298–300; defined 293; as intercepts-as-outcome model 296–7; as means-as-outcome model 297; overview of 292; research guidelines, future 301–5; statistical equation of 296–8, 297*f*; testing, steps for 303–5; theoretical contexts of 292–5, 295*f*; within-group agreement and, importance of 300–1; within-group variance and 302–3

cross-sectional designs 100–9; described 102–3, 104*t*; generations and 101; kernel of truth to 105; *versus* longitudinal research 86–7; overview of 100–1; *versus* time-lag designs 105–7; *see also* generational differences research

cross-temporal meta-analysis (CTMA) 108–9

CrowdFlower 109

crowdsourcing 109

C-tier journals, incentives for publications in 55, 57*t*

cumulative meta-analysis 48, 49*f*, 50

customer-centric indices research: CFA indices of 340–2; IRT analyses of 339–40; measurement invariance 339–42

Daft, R. L. 77

Dahling, J. J. 115, 116

Dalal, D. K. 112–28

Dalton, D. R. 37, 38, 40, 68, 80

data analysis 19–20; complex casual models 20; multilevel/nested models 20

data measurement, waves of 86, 87–90, 88*f*, 89*f*; *see also* longitudinal research

datasets, national 107–8

data sharing, publication bias prevention and 54, 57*t*

data treatment: mediation effects, testing for 224–41 (*see also* bootstrapping; Sobel test); outliers, identifying influential 206–21; weighted linear composites 187–202

Davis, D. D. 172

Davison, H. K. 17

definition of invariance 329

Demaree, R. G. 134

Deming, W. E. 247

DeNeve, K. 42

dense theoretical landscape 26

Denzin, N. 28

DeRue, D. S. 206

De Witte, H. 113

Diamond, J. 10, 14

Dickersin, K. 40

differential item functioning (DIF) 328; uniform and non-uniform examples of 330*f*

direct consensus logic 312

direct range restriction 138, 139*t*, 140–1*f*, 142–4, 143*f*, 144*f*, 153*t*

disciplined imagination 22

Dobson, P. 142

Dodd, N. G. 321

dominance analysis 198

Doty, D. H. 287, 288

Drasgow, F. 328, 329, 333, 336, 339, 342

Dublin City University 3

Dulac, T. 91

Duval, R. D. 229

DuVernet, A. M. 338

dynamic growth modeling 20

Eby, L. T. 68, 69, 72–3

editors, qualitative research tipping point and 77–8

Edwards, J. R. 20, 21, 26, 240

effective weights 193, 197

effect size: bootstrapping and 231, 232*t*; publication bias and 36; Sobel test and 231, 232*t*; suppression 45; trim and fill technique and 47–8

Efron, B. 229, 231

Ehrhart, K. M. 340

Ehrhart, M. G. 318, 340

Eid, M. 286

Eisenberger, R. 171

embedded null effect 26

Emerson, G. B. 41

employment interviews, structured 17

experience sampling 18–19

experience sampling modeling (ESM) 19

exploratory factor analyses (EFA) 117

failsafe N *see* myth 3, failsafe N and subgroup comparisons as detection techniques

falsifiability 15

Ferguson, C. J. 52

Ferguson, E. 177

Ferreter, J. M. 170, 171, 171*t*, 174

Ferris, G. R. 115

Fidell, L. S. 162, 164, 165*t*, 167–8, 211

Field, H. S. 328

Field, J. G. 39

350 Index

field experiments 19
50/20 rule 171, 171t, 173–4
Financial Times 70
Fiske, D. W. 287
Five Factor Model (FFM) 18
Fletcher, T. D. 172
Floyd, S. W. 218
Folger, R. G. 26
Freedle, R. O. 334
Friedman, D. 277
funnel plots 45, 46f, 47
Furby, L. 92

Garcia-Merita, M. L. 328
Gardner, D. 102, 103
Gardner, W. L. 122
Gellatly, I. R. 165–6
Gelman, A. 310
General Social Survey (GSS) 107, 108
generational differences research: best
    practices for 107–9; cross-sectional
    designs and 101t, 102–3, 104t;
    methodological approaches to 101–5,
    101t; time-lag designs and 101t, 103–5,
    104t, 107; in work attitudes 106; in
    work values 106–7
Generation Me 101
Generation X 101, 102, 103, 106–7
Gentile, B. 100–9
Gentry, W. A. 172
Gephart, R. 69
Gerber, A. S. 39
Germano, L. M. 172
Ghoshal, S. 80
Gilliland, S. W. 17
Gladwell, M. 77–8
Glick, P. 19
Glick, W. H. 287, 288
Goerzen, A. 219
Goffin, R. 113, 116
Goffin, R. D. 165–6
Golden-Biddle, K. 70, 71
Goldfarb, B. 24
Goldstein, H. 334
Goldstein, N. B. 17
Golubovich, J. 328–9, 341
Gonzalez-Mule, E. 39
Graduate Record Examination (GRE) 17
Grant, A. M. 218–19
Green, S. B. 164, 165, 165t, 166, 168
Greguras, G. J. 262–3
Griffin, M. A. 298
growth curve methodologies 93

growth mixture modeling 20
Guion, R. M. 119

Hale, D. Jr. 89
hard sciences: described 11; examples of 9;
    goal of 11
hard *versus* soft sciences: conceptualization
    and 15–16; distinction between 11–14;
    effect sizes and 13; in-groups/out-
    groups and 13; National Academy of
    Sciences case 10–11; operationalization
    and 14–15; overview of 9–10;
    psychology distinction and 11–13;
    roles of 14
Harris, R. J. 164, 165T, 167
Hayes, A. F. 226, 239
Hebl, M. R. 19, 27
Hedges, L. V. 16
Henderson, D. J. 91
Henkel, J. 211
heterogeneous variance 45
heterotrait-monomethod (HTMM)
    correlation 280–4, 289
Hildebrand, D. 211
Hill, J. 310
Hinkin, T. R. 127
Hoffman, B. J. 103, 247–72
Holcombe Erhart, K. 319
Holland, S. 20, 24, 29
Hollenbeck, J. R. 206, 224–41
Holmbeck, G. N. 277
honor codes 53–4, 57t
Howard, G. S. 33
Howe, M. 224–41
Hox, J. J. 170, 171, 171t, 172, 174
Hoyt, W. T. 262, 263, 269
Hu, C.-Y. 2, 3f
Huffcutt, A. 17
Hunter, J. E. 38, 142
Huntington, S. 10–11
Hyvärinen, A. 220

ideal-point response 127
identified published *vs.* unpublished
    samples 44
Ilies, R. 18
implicit measures, of personality 18
independent component analysis (ICA)
    220
indirect range restriction 139t, 148, 149f,
    150, 153t
influential outliers: defined 206; distance
    and 206–8, 207f

influential outliers, identifying 206–21; absolute cutoffs and 214–16; best-practice recommendations on 216–20, 217t; myths and urban legends about 208, 209–10t, 210–11; overview of 206–8, 207f; univariate cutoffs and 211–12; visual plots and 212–14
in-group 13
intercepts-as-outcome model, cross-level direct effect as 296–7
International Personality Item Pool (IPIP) 18
interrater agreement (IRA) 293
interrater correlations: data, interpreting 270–2; employing, for corrections 269–70; generalizations and 250–2, 251f; job performance ratings and 247–72; measurement design and 255–62, 256–7f; meta-analysis and 266–9, 268f; overview of 247–8; ratings use and 252–5, 253f; reliability of 248–50; variance components comparison 262–6, 263–4t, 265t
interrater reliability (IRR) 293
Interview Anxiety 113
intraclass correlation (ICC) 174
intraobservation change 93
invalid response data, identifying 123–6; methodological approaches to 123t; statistical approaches to 126t
invariance: configural 331; confirmatory factor analyses and 330–2, 332f; definition of 329; identifying 329–32; item response theory and 329–30, 330f; metric 331; scalar 331
invariance of the uniquenesses 332
item response theory (IRT) 329–30, 330f; CFA comparison to 336–8; of customer-centric indices 339–40; development of 327–8; differential item functioning (DIF) using 328; multilevel 20

Jackson, D. L. 175, 176t, 178
James, L. R. 2, 18, 20, 134, 293, 313, 314
Johnson, E. C. 338
Johnson, P. 69–70, 71
Jones, K. P. 19
Joo, H. 206–21
Journal Article Reporting Standards (JARS) 53
Journal of Applied Psychology (JAP) 20, 29, 68, 115t, 163, 208, 210, 226, 287, 317
Journal of Business Venturing 54

Journal of Management (JOM) 68, 70–1, 115, 115t, 208, 226, 297–8
Journal of Management Studies 54, 70
Journal of the American Medical Association 41
journal submissions/communications, release of 55, 58t
Judge, T. A. 18

Kacmar, K. 21
Kammemeyer-Mueller, J. 277
Kaplan, A. 22
Kay, V. S. 21
Kazama, S. 19
Kelley, K. 181
Kenny, D. 175
Kepes, S. 36–58
Kerns, M. 262, 263, 269
Kidd, S. A. 69
King, E. B. 19
Kirk, R. E. 92
Klein, K. J. 28–9, 292–3, 302
Kline, R. B. 175, 176–8, 176t
Knight, A. P. 28–9
Koczwara, A. 177
Koopman, J. 224–41
Kozlowski, S. W. J. 292–3, 302
Kreft, I. G. G. 170, 171t, 172, 173
Kroll, M. 215
Krug, J. A. 215
Kuh, E. 214
Kuljanin, G. 335, 336
Kwok, O. 329, 340, 341

Laczo, R. M. 248
Laffite, L. J. 337
Lai, K. 181
Lake, C. J. 124
Lambert, L. S. 20, 240
Lance, C. E. 1–5, 103, 122, 134, 276–89, 331, 335–6
Landis, R. S. 9–31
Lang, J. W. 95
Lang, S. 10–11
Langfred, C. W. 91
Lau, R. S. 226
Lautenschlager, G. J. 337
law of the few tipping point 77–8
Le, H. 260, 261, 267
Leavitt, K. 26
LeBreton, J. M. 162–81, 317
Lee, J.-Y. 276–7
Lee, T. 77
Lee, W. C. 333

352 Index

Lens, W. 113
Leong, F. T. L. 328–9, 341
Levy, P. E. 115
Lewin, A. Y. 77
Li, S. T. 277
Lichtenthaler, U. 54
Likert, R. 113
Likert scales 112; *see also* negatively worded
    items
Lilienfeld, S. O. 12
Lin, B. C. 124
Lincoln, Y. 28
Lindell, M. K. 285
Linderbaum, B. A. 115
linear composites, weighted 187–202;
    allocating points to variables and 194–6,
    196*t*; contribution of variables and
    196–201; covariance matrix and 189–92,
    189*t*, 190*t*, 191*t*; overview of 187; real-
    world examples of 187–8; research-based
    examples of 188–9; urban legend 1
    surrounding 189–92; urban legend 2
    surrounding 192–4; urban legend 3
    surrounding 194–6; urban legend 4
    surrounding 196–201; variable
    weighting and 192–4, 193*t*, 194*t*
Lipsey, M. W. 13, 44
listwise deletion 133, 135, 136*t*
Locke, K. 70, 71
Loignon, A. C. 311–23
longitudinal research 85–97; benefits of
    86–7; concerns over 96–7; defined 86;
    evidence and variations of myth 90–2;
    kernel of truth to 92–3; meta-analyses
    and 96; myth, two waves of
    measurement 87–90; overview of 85–6;
    recommendations for 93–6
LoPilato, A. C. 292–305
Luria, G. 320–1
Luthans, F. 211

Maas, C. J.M. 170, 171*t*, 172, 174
MacCallum, R. C. 176, 176*t*, 178–9
MacKenzie, S. B. 276–7
MacKenzie, W. I., Jr. 85–97
Madden, L. T. 67–81
Major, D. A. 172
Malhotra, N. 39
Mannheim, K. 101
Mannor, M. 206
Markóczy, L. 218
Marsh, H. W. 122, 286
Martorana, P. V. 206

Mathieu, J. E. 20
maximum likelihood (ML) 133, 137*t*, 151
Maxwell, S. E. 91, 164, 165*t*, 166,
    168–9, 181
Mazumdar, M. 50
McCann, B. T. 212
McCarthy, J. 113, 116
McDaniel, M. A. 36–58
McGill University 3
McGrath, J. 68
McKay, P. F. 44
Meade, A. W. 124, 125, 337, 338, 340
mean and covariance structure (MACS)
    approach 328; *see also* confirmatory
    factor analysis (CFA)
means-as-outcome model, cross-level
    direct effect as 297
measurement 16–18; of cognitive ability
    17; of cooperativeness 15; described
    16–17; employment interviews,
    structured 17; personality, self-report
    measures of 17–18; situational
    judgement tests 17
measurement error variance, effects of 199
measurement invariance: CFA analysis
    results 335–6; combining/comparing
    IRT and CFA models 336–8;
    confirmatory factor analysis approach
    to 330–2, 332*f*; customer-centric
    indices research 339–42; decision guide
    for 343*t*; defined 329; future research
    for 342–4; importance of 327–44; IRT
    analysis results 333–5; item response
    theory and 329–30, 330*f*; overview of
    327–9; practical impact of research
    findings 338–9
Mechanical Turk, Amazon 109
mediation 2; testing methods for
    224–6, 225*f* (*see also* bootstrapping;
    Sobel test)
Meehl, P. E. 12
meta-regression procedure 47
methodological urban legends:
    dichotomous decisions and 134; pairwise
    deletion and 134–5; source of 134
method variance 2, 20, 87, 118, 121,
    276–7; effects of, on observed
    correlations 277–9, 278*f*; eliminating or
    reducing 285–7; evidence on 281–4
metric invariance 331–2, 335, 343*t*
Michels, L. C. 2, 134
Millennials 101, 102, 103, 106–7
Millsap, R. E. 329, 340, 341

missing at random (MAR) 135, 136t, 138, 139t, 151–2

missing completely at random (MCAR) 135, 135t, 138, 139t

missing data bias 133–59; definition of 135t; explained 133–4; future research 156, 156–7t, 158–9; pairwise deletion urban legend and 134–5; problems and solutions overview 135, 135–7t; quantifying, under pairwise deletion 137–50 (see also missing data selection mechanisms)

missing data error 135t

missing data selection mechanisms 137–50; completely random missingness 138, 139t; direct range restriction 138, 139t, 140–1f, 142–4, 143f, 144f; indirect range restriction 139t, 148, 149f, 150; overview of 137–8; probabilistic direct range restriction 139t, 144–8, 147f; as special cases of indirect range restriction 150–5, 153t; stochastic direct range restriction 139t, 144–8, 147f

missing data techniques 133

missing not at random (MNAR) 135, 136t, 139t, 154–5

Mitchell, R. R. 26

Mixed-Model Item Response Theory (MM-IRT) 124–5

MLM see multilevel modeling (MLM) sample size

model fit indices 29

moderated mediation model 20

Molina-Azorin, J. F. 70

Monitoring the Future (MTF) 107, 108

Montes, S. D. 215

Mooney, C. Z. 229

Moradi, B. 176

Motowidlo, S. J. 18

Mplus 240

Mulaik, S. A. 2

multilevel item response theory (IRT) 20

multilevel modeling (MLM) sample size 170–5; kernels of truth to 173–5; myths 171–2; rules of thumb 170–1, 171t

multilevel/nested analysis models 20

multiple imputation (MI) 133, 136–7t, 151

multiple regression sample size 163–70; described 163–4; kernels of truth 167–70; myths 165–6; rules of thumb 164–5, 165t

multitrait-multimethod (MTMM): common method variance (CMV) and

279–80, 279f, 283; data 117; problems with using 286

Murphy, K. R. 247

myth 1, effect size availability, publication bias 37–40; kernel of truth to 38–9; overview of 37–8; recommendations for 57t; sorting truth from fiction 39–40

myth 2, editorial review as primary publication bias cause 40–2; kernel of truth to 41; overview of 40; recommendations for 57t; sorting truth from fiction 41–2

myth 3, failsafe N and subgroup comparisons as detection techniques 42–51; cumulative meta-analysis 48, 49f, 50; funnel plots and 45, 46f, 47; kernel of truth to 43–4; overview of 42–3; recommendations for 57t; selection models and 48; sorting truth from fiction 44–51; triangulation and 50–1; trim and fill technique 47–8

myth 4, prevention of publication bias 51–3; kernel of truth to 51–3; overview of 51; recommendations for 57t; sorting truth from fiction 53

myths to urban legend of mixed-items scales and invalid responding 116–22; myth 1, no impact to scale quality 117–20; myth 2, no change to validity conclusions 120–1; myth 3, negatively and positively worded items measure same construct 121–2

Nanyang Technological University 3

National Academy of Sciences (NAS) case, hard versus soft sciences 10–11

National Opinion Research Center (NORC) 107

National Taiwan University of Science and Technology 3

Need Satisfaction Scale 113

negated regular, as negatively worded example 112

negative attitudes construct 122

negatively worded items 112–28; assumptions of including 113; described 112; existing scale data and 126–7; identifying invalid response data 123–6, 123t, 126t; kernel of truth to legend 113–14; loading of, on separate factor 117–19; measurement error of mixed-item scales and 118–20; myths addressed 116–22; necessary instances of 127;

354 Index

overview of 112–13; reasons for including 114–15; recommendations for 123–7; urban legend addressed 113–16, 115*t*; *see also* myths to urban legend of mixed-items scales and invalid responding
NEO-PI-R 18
neuromanagement 26
Newman, D. A. 133–59
Nifadkar, S. 92
nominal weights 193
nonqualitative studies 71, 72, 72*f*, 73*t*, 74*t*
North Carolina Society for Industrial and Organizational Psychology 4
Nunnally, J. C. 164, 165*t*, 166, 167
Nye, C. D. 328, 329, 336, 339, 342

O'Boyle, E. H. 39, 52
observed correlations, common method variance and 277–9, 278*f*
Ock, J. 187–202
Oja, E. 220
operationalization 14–15
Organ, D. W. 276
Organizational Behavior and Human Decision Processes (OBHDP) 68, 115*t*, 226
organizational behavior and human resource management (OBHRM) 37
organizational neuroscience 26
Organizational Research Methods (symposium paper) 2, 115*t*, 317
organizational sciences, integrity of: brain research and 26–7; conceptualization and operationalization, problems of 14–16; data analysis and 19–20; design and analysis needs 27–30; hard *versus* soft science distinction 11–14; improvement recommendations for 30–1; measurement and 16–18; National Academy of Sciences case 10–11; research design and 18–19; selection models and 48; theories and 21–6
Organization Science (OS) 54, 67, 70, 73, 74, 74*t*, 75*t*, 77
Oswald, F. 187–202
outcome-level publication bias 36, 37, 39, 52; *see also* publication bias, preventing
out-group 13
outlet bias 41
outlier, defined 206; *see also* influential outliers
Owens, P. D. 206

pairwise deletion 133, 136*t*; listwise deletion and 156; missing data bias and 134–5; summary statements about 156–7*t*; urban legends about 134–5, 158–9
Palmer, L. 340
Parent, M. C. 176
Parker, C. P. 321
partial correlation approach 285
Patterson, F. 177
Payne, S. C. 17
Pearson, K. 145
Pelham, B. W. 119
percentile (PCNT) procedures 231, 232*t*
performance ratings, accuracy concerns of 247–8; *see also* interrater correlations
Perry, S. J. 319
personality, self-report measures of 17–18
Personnel Psychology 115*t*, 208, 226, 248, 249, 261, 287, 317
Peterson, J. 26
Peterson, R. S. 206
Pettus, M. 215
Pierce, C. A. 39
Pitariu, A. H. 86
Plowman, D. A. 67–81
Ployhart, R. E. 20, 85–97
Podsakoff, N. P. 276–7
Podsakoff, P. M. 68, 80, 114, 276–7, 285
polar opposite, as negatively worded example 112
power analysis use, sample size and 178–9; alternative to 179–81
practically important differences 333
Pratt, M. G. 69
Preacher, K. J. 226, 239
precise parameter estimation (PPE), sample size and 179–81
probabilistic direct range restriction 139*t*, 144–8, 147*f*
pseudo-random draws 235
PsycINFO 317
publication bias, organizational sciences 36–58; defined 37, 39; myth 1, effect size availability 37–40; myth 2, editorial review as primary cause 40–2; myth 3, failsafe N and subgroup comparisons as detection techniques 42–51; myth 4, prevention of 51–3; overview of 36–7; recommendations for preventing 53–6, 57–8*t*; term use of 36; *see also individual headings*

publication bias, preventing 53–6, 57–8*t*;
B- and C-tier journals, incentives for 55;
data sharing 54; honor codes 53–4;
journal submissions/communications,
release of 55; registration protocol, for
studies 56; replication studies, exact and
conceptual 55–6; supplemental
information on Internet 54; two-stage
review process 54–5
publication rates, of qualitative research *see*
qualitative research, in management
journals
Pugh, R. H. 336
Putka, D. J. 187–202, 247–72

qualitative advice 69–70
qualitative authorship 75*t, 76f*
qualitative publishing, growth trends in
73*t, 74t*
qualitative research, in management
journals 67–81; advice offered by
researchers 69–70; assessment of 70–1;
award winners 79–80*t*; discussion of
76–7; editors and 77–8; findings of
72–6, 72*f,* 73*t,* 74*t,* 75*t,* 76*f*;
methodology used in 71–2; overview
of 67–8; quantitative reviews of 68–9;
special issues and 78; winning
publications and 78–80, 79–80*t*
quantitative reviews, in management
literature 68–9
questionable research practices (QRPs) 53–4

Raju, N. S. 337
range restriction, variables and 199
rank correlation test 50
Rao, C. R. 93
Raudenbush, S. W. 296–7, 309
R code packages 198
Ree, M. 2
Reeve, C. L. 116
referent-shift consensus model 312
registration protocol, for studies 56, 58*t*
Reise, S. P. 336
Reith, J. 333
relaimpo 198
relative weight analysis 198
reliability of interrater correlations 248–50;
variance component estimates for
262–6, 263*t*
repeated measures 96
replication studies, exact and conceptual
55–6, 58*t*

research design 18–19; experience
sampling and 18–19; field experiments
and 19
response set 114
response styles 114
reverse oriented 112
reverse wording 112
Richardson, H. 285
Robie, C. 262–3
Roe, R. A. 86, 89, 94
Roesch, S. C. 340
Rogelberg, S. G. 145, 158
Rogosa, D. R. 92, 93
Rosenberg Self-Esteem Scale 122
Rosenthal, R. 43
Roth, P. L. 144
Rothstein, H. R. 37–8, 39, 42
Roznowski, M. 333
R. Simply 239–40
Rubenstein, A. 277
Rubin, D. B. 145
rules of thumb 162–3; for multilevel
modeling (MLM) sample size 170–1,
171*t*; for multiple regression sample size
164–5, 165*t*; ratio-type 175–6; sample
sizes produced by 165*t*; for structural
equation modeling (SEM) sample size
175–6, 176*t*
Russ-Eft, D. F. 220
Ryan, A. M. 90–1
Ryan, K. 276

Sackett, P. R. 248
sample-adjusted meta-analytic deviancy
(SAMD) 219–20
sample-level publication bias 36
sample size, statistical analyses 162–81;
multilevel modeling (MLM) 170–5;
multiple regression 163–70; overview of
162–3; power analysis use and 178–9;
precise parameter estimation (PPE) and
179–81; produced by rules of thumb
165*t*; structural equation modeling
(SEM) 175–9; *see also individual headings*
Sanders, L. D. 115
Santelices, M. V. 335
Saris, W. E. 176, 176*t, 178*
Satorra, A. 176, 176*t, 178*
Sauley, K. S. 115, 116
scalar invariance 331
Scandura, T. A. 68–9
Scherbaum, C. A. 170, 171, 171*t, 174, 334*
Schmidt, F. L. 38, 44, 142

356 Index

Schmidt, P. 311–23
Schmitt, N. 327–44
Schneider, B. 319
Schriesheim, C. A. 121
Schurman, J. V. 277
Scott, B. A. 18
seed values, confidence intervals and 235–6, 237–8t
Sejnowski, T. J. 220
selection models 48
SEM *see* structural equation modeling (SEM)
Senter, J. L. 317
Seo, M.-G. 24
Shapiro, J. L. 19
Shavelson, R. J. 260–1
Shaw, J. D. 323
Shore, D. 20
Shrout, P. E. 226, 228
significant differences 33
Silent Generation 101
Silvester, J. 177
Siminovsky, A. B. 276–89
Simonton, D. K. 12
single imputation 133, 136t
Singletary, S. L. 19
situational judgement tests (SJTs) 17
Smith, A. D. 67–81
Smith, C. S. 116
Smith, D. B. 206
Smola, K. W. 107
Snijders, T. A. 181, 309
Sobel test 224–41; *vs.* bootstrapping 228–38; introduction of 225, 225f; overview of 224–5; recommendations for 240; seed values and confidence intervals with 235–6, 237–8t; statistical power and 230–1, 232t; Type I error and 233–5, 234t; *see also* bootstrapping
Society for Industrial and Organizational Psychology (SIOP) 2
Soenens, B. 113
soft sciences: challenging perceptions of 16–20; described 11; examples of 9; psychology as 11–13; *see also* hard *versus* soft sciences
Sparks, T. E. 172
special issues, qualitative research tipping point and 74–5, 74t, 78
Spector, P. E. 2, 276
SPSS macro 239
Stajkovic, A. D. 211
Stark, S. 328, 329, 333–4, 339

statistical cutoff criteria 2
statistical power 200; bootstrapping and 230–1, 232t
Staw, B. M. 22–3
Steel, P. D. G. 277
stickiness factor, described 78
stochastic direct range restriction 139t, 144–8, 147f, 153t
Strategic Management Journal (SMJ) 54, 70, 208, 210
"Strategies of Qualitative Inquiry" (Denzin and Lincoln) 28
structural equation modeling (SEM) 20, 29
structural equation modeling (SEM) sample size 175–9; described 175; kernels of truth 177–9; myths 176–7; rules of thumb 175–6, 176t
study and protocol registration 56, 58t
Suddaby, R. 69
supplemental information on Internet, publication bias and 54, 57t
suppressor effects 199
Sutton, C. D. 107
Sutton, R. I. 22–3
Switzer, D. M. 144
Switzer, F. S. 144
Symon, G. 69–70

Tabachnick, B. G. 162, 164, 165t, 167–8, 211
Takeuchi, R. 233
Taormina, R. J. 166
Taylor, H. 220
Taylor, P. J. 220
temporal separation 96
test of the intercept, Egger's 50
theoretical development 21–2
theories, organizational sciences and 21–6; complexity and 23–4, 24–5f; specificity and 26; testing of 21–3
theory proliferation, publication bias and 36
30/30 rule 171, 171t, 173
Thomas, B. 319
Thomas, J. L. 318
Thurstone scales 127
Tibshirani, R. 229, 231
time-lag designs: to examine generational change 105–7; generational research and 101t, 103–5, 104t
tipping point: context 78; defined 77; editors and 77–8; law of the few 77–8; special issues and 74–5, 74t, 78; winning publications and 78–80, 79–80t

Tonidandel, S. 162–81
triangulation 50–1; defined 50
trim and fill technique 47–8
true-false items 114
Truhon, S. 2
Tsui, A. S. 92
Tucker, L. R. 93
Tukey, J. W. 211
Turner, S. 19
Twenge, J. M. 100–9
two-stage review process, publication bias prevention and 54–5, 57*t*
two waves of measurement myth 87–90; *see also* longitudinal research
Type I error: bootstrapping and 233–5, 234*t*; IRT/CFA models and 338; recommendations for 240; reseeding and 235–6, 238*t*; Sobel test and 233–5, 234*t*

uniqueness coefficients 198
uniquenesses, invariance of the 332
univariate cutoffs, influential outliers and 211–12
University of Alabama 3
University of Georgia 4
University of South Australia 3
unmeasured method factor approach 285
Urry, V. W. 142

validity-diversity dilemma 198
Vandenberg, R. J. 1–5, 86, 292–305, 331, 335–6
Van den Broeck, A. 113
Van Maanen, J. 23, 71, 77
Vansteenkiste, M. 113
variables: allocating points to 194–6, 196*t*; contribution of 196–201; weighting of 192–4, 193*t*, 194*t*
variable weighting 192–4, 193*t*, 194*t*
Verma, A. 277
Vevea, J. L. 48
visual plots, influential outliers and 212–14
Viswesvaran, C. 266–7
Vroom, G. 212

Wagner, S. H. 321
Wallace, J. C. 319
Wang, J. 277
Watkins, D. 328

waves of data measurement 86, 87–90, 88*f,* 89*f*; *see also* longitudinal research
Wayne, S. J. 91
Weick, K. E. 22
weighted linear composites 187–202; allocating points to variables and 194–6, 196*t*; contribution of variables and 196–201; covariance matrix and 189–92, 189*t*, 190*t*, 191*t*; overview of 187; real-world examples of 187–8; research-based examples of 188–9; urban legend 1 surrounding 189–92; urban legend 2 surrounding 192–4; urban legend 3 surrounding 194–6; urban legend 4 surrounding 196–201; variable weighting and 192–4, 193*t*, 194*t*
Weisberg, S. 214
Welsch, R. E. 214
West, S. G. 86
Whetzel, D. L. 42
Whitaker, B. G. 115
Whitfield, J. 21
Whitney, D. J. 285
Widaman, K. F. 336
Williams, E. A. 68–9
Williams, E. B. 162–81
Williams, L. J. 285–6, 287, 288, 293
Wilson, D. B. 13, 44
Wilson, M. 335
winning publications, qualitative research tipping point and 78–80, 79–80*t*
within-group agreement, cross-level direct effect and 300–1
within-group variance, cross-level direct effect and 302–3
Witt, L. A. 319
Woehr, D. J. 311–23
Wolf, G. 134
Wood, L. A. 100–9
Woods, C. M. 48
Wright, P. 215
Wright, T. A. 181

Xiao, Y. 28–9

yhat 198

Zickar, M. J. 124
Ziegert, J. C. 28–9
Zohar, D. 320–1
Zweig, D. 215